(4)

"Captain" John Pillsbury – Susan Wadleigh

John S. Pillsbury – Mahala Fisk
(1827 – 1901)   (1832 – 1910)

George A. Pillsbury – Margaret Sprague Carleton
(1816 – 1898)   (1817 – 1901)

See opposite page

Charles A. Pillsbury – Mary Ann Stinson
(1842 – 1899)   (1841 – 1902)

Frederick C. Pillsbury – Alice Thayer Cook
(1852 – 1892)   (1860 – 1943)

Charles Stinson Pillsbury – Helen Pendelton Winston
(1878 – 1939)   (1878 – 1957)

John Sargent Pillsbury – Eleanor Jerusha Lawler
(1878 – 1968)   (1887 – 1991)

Phillip Winston Pillsbury – Eleanor Bellows
(1903 – 1984)   (1913 – 1971)

Mary Stinson Pillsbury – Oswald Bates Lord
(1904 – 1978)   (1903 – 1986)

Katherine Stevens Pillsbury – Elliot Bates McKee
(1905 – 1978)   (1904 – 1990)

Helen Winston Pillsbury – John Austin Becker, Jr.
(1907 – 1963)   (1906 – 1975)

John Sargent Pillsbury, Jr. – Katharine Clark
(1912 – 2005)   (1916 – 2006)

Edmund Pennington Pillsbury – Priscilla Keator
(1913 – 1951)   (1915 –   )

Ella Sturgis Pillsbury – Thomas M. Crosby
(1915 –   )   (1914 – 1988)

Charles Alfred Pillsbury
(1917 – 1943)

Jane Lawler Pillsbury – Stanley R. Resor
(1920 – 1994)   (1917 –   )

George Sturgis Pillsbury – Sally Lucille Whitney
(1921 –   )   (1924 –   )

Abridged Family Tree for George Alfred Pillsbury

The Pillsburys of Minnesota

It only took Charles A. Pillsbury and his partners twelve years to establish a flour company that boasted the largest mill in the world. This poster, showing mills on both sides of the Mississippi, was used in store windows, ca. 1888. (Courtesy of the General Mills Archives)

The Pillsburys
of Minnesota

Lori Sturdevant

with

George S. Pillsbury

NODIN PRESS

ISBN 978-1-935666-22-6

Design: John Toren

A complete list of photo credits can be found on page 387.

Library of Congress Cataloging-in-Publication Data

Sturdevant, Lori, 1953-
The Pillsburys of Minnesota / by Lori Sturdevant with George Pillsbury.
p. cm.
ISBN 978-1-935666-22-6
1. Pillsbury family. 2. Minnesota--Biography. 3. Pillsbury Flour Mills Company--History. 4. Minnesota--Politics and government. 5. Minnesota--Genealogy. I. Pillsbury, George S. II. Title.
F605.S78 2011
929'.20973--dc22
                                        2011002760

Nodin Press, LLC
530 North Third Street
Suite 120
Minneapolis, MN
55401

to Martin and Sally

CONTENTS

Preface and Acknowledgments

At its sesquicentenary, Minnesota is a standout among the fifty United States. On many measures—economic diversity, household income, educational attainment, natural environment, cultural amenities—the North Star State shines.

Yet as Minnesota begins the second decade of the 21st century and its 16th decade as a state, unease about the sustainability of Minnesota's quality of life is palpable from my perch as a state Capitol journalist. Much is changing, not least this: Old-line businesses and the families that founded and ran them for many decades are disappearing. They've given way to businesses controlled elsewhere, led locally by people who aren't from Minnesota, don't plan to stay long, and don't have personal reasons to care about what they will leave behind.

Minnesotans have habitually looked to the families that established its biggest businesses for political and civic leadership. Increasingly, no one's there.

"Then look to yourselves," Gov. John S. Pillsbury would surely say, were he alive 109 years after his death to give Minnesotans counsel. He would reject any suggestion that he and his brother George came to Minnesota to found a local aristocracy, or that they had any special claim to leadership. They left the foothills of Kearsarge Mountain in New Hampshire in the mid-nineteenth century for two simple reasons: to make money and to live as honorable citizens. In fact, John Pillsbury may have seen those not as two reasons, but as one. Of course they would participate in the advancement of the common good in their new home. That's what American citizenship requires, John would say—and it's not bad for business either. Those sons of New England had been reared in a place and time that took seriously the obligation of every citizen, regardless of means, to play a role in local governance and civic betterment. For them, personal and community gain were always inextricably linked.

This book seeks to describe and probe that linkage. It aims not so much to praise one family's contributions to Minnesota's past as to lift that family up as a model for Minnesotans of the future. Minnesota is still a young state. Its opportunities still call to people of ambition and vision from around the world. The Pillsbury story should tell those latter-day pioneers that if they come with the intention to build both gainful businesses and wholesome communities, they can thrive here. It should tell Minnesota entrepreneurs that much can be gained from marrying their own enrichment to their community's. And it should tell the grandchildren and great-grandchildren of the pioneers who might have voted for Gov. Pillsbury that the project of state-building that their forebears began is not over.

★ ★ ★

This book's roots lie in the friendship that developed at the state Capitol in the early 1980s between a young journalist and a quotable state senator with a famous name. It sprouted twenty-five years later in the sad time after the deaths of two leading Minnesotans who had been dear to them both. When former Gov. Elmer L. Andersen and John S. Pillsbury Jr. died within four months of each other in 2004 and 2005, George Pillsbury and I talked about their contributions as twentieth-century business leaders who were also devoted to building a better Minnesota. We also shared our perception, based on a surge in the number of speaking invitations we both were receiving, that many Minnesotans are eager to know more about their state's history. Like us, they felt uncertainty about the state's course, and they sensed that in Minnesota's past lay wisdom for the future. By late 2007, we were committed to producing a book.

We went first for help where all history-minded Minnesotans go—to the Minnesota Historical Society. There, books curator and a member of another notable Minnesota family, Patrick Coleman, got our research started and imparted welcome advice and encouragement. But we soon discovered that the wonderful archives kept by the Pillsbury Co., now carefully housed at General Mills' corporate headquarters in Golden Valley, were our goldmine. Suzy Goodsell, the manager of internal communications and archives, was generous in arranging after-hours opportunities for me to dig into the materials there. Archivist Isabel Sanz became this project's best friend, adjusting her family's schedule to suit mine as we opened box after box of well-preserved and organized family and corporate records. (When I asked how the material came to be so beautifully archived, I learned that General Mills invited the Minnesota Historical Society staff to do the work when the Pillsbury records came to them. May other Minnesota corporations be as wise with their records.) Archivist Sue Lappi was helpful in Isabel's absence. I appreciated the warm welcome I always received at General Mills' reception desk from Ramona Kastenbauer, who greeted me by name and often had my visitor's badge waiting for me when I arrived.

George wisely insisted that our research include a trip to New Hampshire to see where the nineteenth-century Pillsbury brothers George and John lived and worked before coming to Minnesota, and what they gave back to their hometowns decades later. My daughter Emelia Carroll was my personal assistant as Warner/Sutton historians Jack Noon and Rebecca Courser gave us a tour of notable sites. Director Nancy Ladd of the Pillsbury Free Library in Warner made us feel right at home and showed us useful material. And the staff at Rauner Special Collections Library at Dartmouth College in Hanover, N.H. were waiting for us on a snowy day with pre-sorted materials that made light work of our search.

Plymouth Congregational Church archivist James Thompson could not have been nicer as he shared Pillsbury lore and dusty volumes of hand-written meeting records bearing Charles A. Pillsbury's signature. Barbara Bezat at the Performing Arts Archive at the University of Minnesota's Elmer L. Andersen Library made it easy for me to learn about John S. Pillsbury Jr.'s role in building Orchestra Hall. Barbara Benson of the Granite Falls Historical Society helped us learn more about the least well-known of the 19th century Minnesota Pillsburys, Benjamin. We had quick e-mail answers to our questions when we needed it from Gary Kubat at the Orono School District and David Pavelich at Regenstein Library at the University of Chicago.

Many people outside of the family generously shared their memories and knowledge as we pursued the Pillsbury story. At the risk of unintended omission, for which we apologize, our honor roll of gratitude includes Bruce Dayton, Mark Dayton, Arne Carlson, Wheelock Whitney, Winston Wallin, Al Quie, Barbara Flanagan, Tony Owens, John Turner, Russell Bennett, Carl Platou, Bill Frenzel, Paul Overgaard, Chuck Slocum, Luella Goldberg, Thomas Keller, Joann Nelson, Anne Hage, John Cummins, Kathleen Hemken, Lou Gelfand, Mark Ritchie Marlys Clutich, Edward Jay Phillips, and Ann Pflaum.

I owe a great deal to my employer of nearly thirty-five years, the Minneapolis *Star Tribune*—not least because of the access I have enjoyed to its well-kept library. I've become quite familiar with its basement archives, and was never disappointed by the wealth of material there. An even greater treasure lies in the newspaper's excellent photo archives, which were also generously opened to me. As the photo credits in this book indicate, the newspaper was our best source of the images reproduced in this book. I'm also appreciative of several brief leaves of absence from my day job for the sake of this project, and for the interest and support I consistently find from my coworkers and from editorial page editor Scott Gillespie.

We're grateful to Norton Stillman of Nodin Press for agreeing without hestitation to be our publisher, and to his lieutenant, John Toren, for enhancing our copy with his keen editing and crafting a pleasing design. This is the fourth time I've worked with Norton and John on a book. I'm gratified that they let me keep coming back with more. Also invaluable was the exceptional work done by Beverly Hermes, transcriber extraordinaire, who also worked with me on books about the lives of Elmer Andersen and W. Harry Davis.

George and I are both blessed with wonderful families who advanced this work in more ways than we can describe. Ella Pillsbury Crosby and several of her children were gracious and generous with their time, memories and photos. George's nephew Jock Pillsbury and cousins Phil Pillsbury Jr. and Charlie Lord provided very helpful information, as did more distant cousins Al and Edward Gale and

Helen Snyder Waldron. Phil was very kind to let us mine his family photo albums, which proved to be a rich source of material. George's children, Charlie, George Jr., Sarah, and Kathy, became my friends as we worked together, and my children, Ted, John, and Emelia Carroll, became huge Pillsbury fans. Emelia took a turn as my literary advisor and research companion. Sally Pillsbury was our best source of facts, encouragement, tea, homemade cookies and beautiful homegrown flowers, and Martin Vos demonstrated as he has before that an electrical engineer can also be a terrific copy editor. We love them all the more for their patient, indulgent support of this project. This book is one fruit of nearly three years of collaboration. Our abiding friendship is another.

– Lori Sturdevant, March 2011

The Pillsburys of Minnesota timeline

1855: John S. Pillsbury of Concord, N.H. arrives at St. Anthony and opens a hardware store. Wife Mahala joins him the next year.

1858: Minnesota is granted statehood.

1863: John Pillsbury is elected to the Minnesota Senate and to the University of Minnesota Board of Regents.

1869: Charles A. Pillsbury arrives in Minneapolis from Montreal and becomes the manager and co-owner of a flour mill purchased in part by his father George and uncle John. Alfred F. Pillsbury is born.

1870: Fred C. Pillsbury, Charles' younger brother, arrives in Minneapolis.

1871: The milling operation grows and takes the name C.A. Pillsbury & Co.

1873: The brand Pillsbury's Best XXXX is used for the first time.

1875: John S. Pillsbury elected governor of Minnesota; state endures grasshopper plague.

1877: Charles A. Pillsbury is elected to the Minnesota Senate; serves eight years.

1878: George A. and Margaret Pillsbury move to Minneapolis from Concord, N.H.; Benjamin F. and Susan Pillsbury move to Granite Falls, MN from Sutton, N.H.; twin sons John and Charles are born to Charles A. and Mary Ann Pillsbury.

1881: Pillsbury A Mill opens on the east bank of the Falls of St. Anthony.

1884: George A. Pillsbury is elected mayor of Minneapolis; serves one term.

1889: C.A. Pillsbury & Co. is sold to British interests who create Pillsbury-Washburn Co. Ltd. Charles becomes its manager. John and Mahala Pillsbury donate Pillsbury Hall to the University of Minnesota.

1890: Benjamin F. Pillsbury dies.

1892: Fred C. Pillsbury dies. Alfred F. Pillsbury concludes seven seasons as quarterback for the Minnesota Golden Gophers with a conference championship.

1898: George A. Pillsbury dies.

1899: Charles A. Pillsbury dies. Alfred F. Pillsbury marries Eleanor "Gretchen" Field.

1901: John S. Pillsbury and Margaret Carleton Pillsbury die. Charles S. Pillsbury marries Helen "Nelle" Winston.

1903: Philip (Phil) Winston Pillsbury, first of four children of Charles and Nelle Pillsbury, is born.

1905: Gift from John and Charles Pillsbury establishes Pillsbury Settlement House.

1908: Pillsbury–Washburn Co. falls into receivership.

1910: Mahala Fisk Pillsbury, last of the family's pioneers from New Hampshire, dies.

1911: Pillsbury Flour Mills Co. is born and takes over the Pillsbury–Washburn mills. John S. Pillsbury marries Eleanor "Juty" Lawler.

1912: John Pillsbury Snyder and his bride survive the sinking of the *Titanic*. John S. Pillsbury Jr. is born.

1921: George S. Pillsbury, last of John and Juty's six children, is born at Southways.

1923: Pillsbury Flour Mills Inc. is born, ending British involvement in Minneapolis milling. Corporate expansion begins in Buffalo, NY and Atchison KS.

1924: Philip. W. Pillsbury graduates from Yale and joins the family milling company.

1925: Alfred F. Pillsbury accepts a seat on the Minneapolis Parks and Recreation Board.

1935: Alf Pillsbury becomes chairman of the Society of Fine Arts, the governing body of the Minneapolis Institute of Arts.

1939: Charles S. Pillsbury dies.

1940: Philip W. Pillsbury becomes CEO of Pillsbury Flour Mills Inc. Richard Pillsbury Gale is elected to Congress.

1943: Four Pillsbury brothers and two sons-in-law are involved in World War II. Lt. Charles A. Pillsbury dies when his plane is shot down over Bougainville.

1944: Richard Pillsbury Gale loses bid for a third term in the U.S. House.

1947: George S. Pillsbury marries Sally Lucille Whitney; Charles Alfred, the first of their four children, is born.

1949: Pillsbury Co. stages its first Bake-Off, featuring celebrity judge Eleanor Roosevelt.

1950: Alfred F. Pillsbury dies; John S. Pillsbury Jr. succeeds him on the board of Northwestern National Life Insurance Co.

1951: Edmund P. Pillsbury dies in an airplane crash in Nebraska.

1952: Phil Pillsbury becomes chairman of the Pillsbury Co.; John S. Pillsbury Sr. takes the title "honorary chairman."

1956: John S. Pillsbury Jr. becomes president of Northwestern National Life Insurance as the board successfully combats a hostile takeover attempt.

1966: John S. Pillsbury Jr. runs unsuccessfully for governor.

1968: John S. Pillsbury Sr. dies.

1969: George S. Pillsbury leaves the Pillsbury Co.

1970: George S. Pillsbury is elected to the Minnesota State Senate. Serves 12 years.

1974: Minnesota Orchestra board chairman John S. Pillsbury Jr. oversees the building of Orchestra Hall.

1982-83: Sally Pillsbury chairs the University of Minnesota Hospital governing as it plans and builds a new hospital.

1984: Philip Pillsbury dies.

1991: Eleanor "Juty" Pillsbury dies.

1997-2000: George Pillsbury founds and leads Citizens Committee for a Single House Legislature.

2005: John S. Pillsbury Jr. dies.

Foreword

In many respects, America's remarkable story is the story of families. To be sure, unique individuals stand out. But often families, through multiple generations, worked to develop, improve and renew the places in which they lived. The Pillsburys of Minnesota are such people, and I'm pleased to introduce their story.

It is fascinating reading when a book contains both lessons in history and information about noted people. The word "history" may turn some people off. As I began my sophomore year in Northfield High School, Miss Magner, my history teacher, walked up to my desk in study hall, stopped, and said, "You don't like history do you, Albert?" My parents taught me to be honest, so I said, "No." She inquired, "Why not?" My retort was, "All we learn is a bunch of dates and what happened in the past." She took me aside and in about five minutes, she explained the importance of history. It changed my life. She helped me see that one needs to set goals and plan for the future both individually and corporately, but it is also necessary to look back to see if your path is straight. I had already learned that important lesson while building fences on the farm.

Studying history helped me see that individuals, families and communities are the most important components of a society. America is made up of people who moved here from other nations, kept moving within this country in response to opportunities, raised families and built communities as they went. In a large or small way, they made a name for themselves. Minnesota's good name arose when people like the Pillsburys brought ideas and innovation to the development of this state's natural resources, in a way that had significance for other people. The theme that connected the Pillsburys then and now has been, "Commitment to community for the common good."

Recently I mentioned this book to a friend. He said. "The Pillsburys—that's the family that made flour." Making flour is an important part of Minnesota's history. It had a great impact on both our metropolitan area and Minnesota's farm communities. That impact was felt in my family. As a child, I remember hearing stories about my grandfather who came to Minnesota from Wisconsin in 1856, along with other immigrants from the same Hallingdal valley in Norway, to farm between Northfield and Kenyon. The Minneapolis mills gave him a market for his wheat. His means of getting his wheat to Minneapolis was to bring it to the Mississippi River port at Hastings with horses and wagon. A round trip was at least fifty-five miles. My father showed me the grain sacks they used, which held 300 pounds of wheat. The tools for harvesting wheat were still on our farm. Dad showed me how to cut wheat with a scythe and cradle and make bundles (sheaves) for drying in shocks, using the wheat stems themselves rather than twine. That is an art. We still had a flail for threshing the wheat on the barn floor; the wood rake for lifting the wheat stems from the kernels; a means for blowing away the chaff from the kernels powered by a sheep buck on a tread mill and grinder with which they could grind a small amount of flour for their own use.

My family learned the name Pillsbury when they began bringing home the 100-pound sack of Pillsbury flour for their own baking. When I was in high school, I ground up some wheat in that little ancient mill in our granary and asked my mother to bake bread with that flour. The bread had a harsh taste. I realized then how important the innovations in flour milling were to American consumers' palates.

In the Pillsbury story, certain principles span generations. Among them:

• Everyone should build up a net worth, as a shield against the poverty that can scar future generations. Poverty is the biggest reason for the educational achievement gap.

• Joy comes from helping others. Character comes when you don't get credit for it.

- Don't hold grudges. If you do, you become the problem. You put up a wall that prevents you from learning something.
- The arts are important. They communicate in a universal language.
- Integrity is the most important attribute in making choices.
- If you are an employer, treat your employees right, and encourage innovation and collaboration among them.
- In your family, insist on quality education, and give children the freedom to leave as well as come back. Spend time together, engaging each other, especially intellectually.
- Pass on to the next generation the ability to engage in governance at all levels—first in the family, then community, business, and civil society.

I applaud this story's focus on a family. After all, it is in the family where respect for the dignity of all human beings and the ability to engage in congenial disputation begin. Parents truly are children's first teachers. In the family, children learn character. They learn to love by being loved, or they grow angry from rejection.

In sixty years, the United States has gone from 5 percent of its children born out of wedlock to 41 percent. We imprison more of our citizens than any other country. We need to learn again that families matter, that our choices about our family lives have lasting impact, and the most important outcomes from our choices should be love and justice that extend outside the family to a much wider circle. The Pillsbury story has much to teach us now.

– Al Quie, October 2010

The Pillsburys
of Minnesota

British explorer Jonathan Carver's 1778 travelogue *Travels Through the Interior Parts of North America in the Years 1766, 1767 and 1768* included this sketch of the Falls of St. Anthony.

Chapter One

The Falls Beckon

Saint Anthony Falls, wide and wild, the only waterfall on the mighty Mississippi, beckoned to young men of pluck and ambition in the middle of the nineteenth century. Its siren song was especially compelling to boys of New England. Those who came of age near the mills of New Hampshire, Maine, Massachusetts, and Vermont knew that the power of rushing water could be converted into fortunes. Word of a large and lovely cataract in the new territory, Minnesota, echoed off Kearsarge Mountain in Merrimack County, New Hampshire, and piqued interest in the hillside streets of Warner and the hollows of North and South Sutton.

John Sargent Pillsbury, a bright and curious son of Sutton, was twenty-six years old in 1853,[1] and restless. The third son of a respected family of middling means and the namesake of his father, John had consumed all the schooling locally available to him, but no more. He was reared in a household reputed to have checked out more books than any other from the local library, an institution his father

3

helped found. His eldest brother, Simon Wadleigh Pillsbury, sixteen years his senior, had been considered a genius at mathematics, and was regarded as a youth of great promise. The first temperance lecture ever given in the Sutton schoolhouse was delivered by young Simon. But when John was nine, Simon died of an illness attributed in those medically unlearned days to excessive study.[2]

Falling ill from too much schooling would not be John's fate. Much as he loved books, he itched to make money and know the security and respect that money brings. He must have been much aware of the quiet despair that had taken hold of many of his elders in the 1840s, after nearly two decades of unrelieved economic distress in rural New England. Central New Hampshire's population peaked in 1820, then declined steadily for more than a century. Farms on the rocky White Mountain foothills couldn't produce enough to compete with crops beginning to arrive from the flat, fertile west. Already during the years immediately following the Revolutionary War, John's grandfather Micajah—the first Pillsbury to come to Sutton—found that farming alone would not support a family, and began to supplement his farm income with blacksmithing. When he died suddenly in 1801 at age fifty, the estate he left to his widow, Sarah Sargent Pillsbury, proved to be insolvent.[3]

John's father was only twelve at the time, but he quickly learned a trade, becoming a joiner (a specialty carpenter), and he also signed up for the local militia. His rise to militia captain's ranks and his retention of the nickname "Captain John" for the rest of his life attest to innate leadership ability. So did his elections as a Sutton selectman (city council member), legislator, and justice of the peace. A land sale contract filed in 1821, when Captain John was a mere thirty-two years old, already refers to him as "gentleman." The title and the handsome house he built in Sutton at about that time suggest that he was by then a person of some financial substance. It was said of the family that they were noted for their "personal integrity and force of character."

To such a New England man in the nineteenth century, involvement in civic affairs and in government almost went without saying. It was what citizenship required and neighbors expected. It was also

The house Captain John Pillsbury built in Sutton in the early 1800s.

what members of the Pillsbury family had been doing almost since their arrival in North America in 1640. When the struggle for independence from Britain erupted into a shooting match on Lexington Green on April 19, 1775, four men named Pillsbury were among the colonial militiamen. Captain John's grandfather Caleb, of Amesbury, Massachusetts, and all of his five sons took their turn of service in the Continental Army. Caleb "held at one time or another almost every office within the gift of the people," a nineteenth-century family history says.[4] Then as now, New Hampshire towns governed themselves via highly participatory annual town meetings. No self-respecting adult male would stay away. Local governing responsibilities were shared widely among office-holders, selectmen, various commissioners, and board members, as well as state legislators. In those days little New Hampshire already had the nation's largest state legislature. It still does. Called the General Court, the legislature is comprised today of 400 representatives and 24 senators. Established men of Sutton in John S. Pillsbury's day expected to take their turn at local office. (Women's suffrage was still a dream of the radical fringe.) Discussion of the politics inevitably associated with local elections was a dominant pastime in the state's rural regions.

By the 1840s, Captain John's life wound down to homely pursuits, including much socializing with a large extended family. The captain had three brothers and four sisters, all of whom lived well into adulthood and spent their days in Sutton. Captain John's wife, Susan Wadleigh Pillsbury, was from a similarly large, established Sutton family whose livelihood centered on a hilltop farmstead and a large house still standing today. The Wadleighs were as involved in civic affairs as the Pillsburys. Whatever their household lacked financially as their third son came of age, it undoubtedly made up for in richness of familial and community connections.

After young John Sargent finished common school—about the equivalent of sixth grade today—he set out to learn a trade as a painter. But he abandoned that pursuit at age seventeen when his brother George Alfred, eleven

George's store in Warner, as it looked in 2008.

years his senior and the second son born to Captain John and Susan Pillsbury, asked John to work alongside him at his general store in Warner, eleven miles southeast of Sutton. George had a young family in 1844, including a precocious toddler, Charles. They lived across the street from the store in a house big enough to accommodate a teen-aged brother. (It houses a bookstore today.) George may have hinted at an eventual partnership. No record exists of any formal understanding between them. But in that little store in Warner, as John learned the mercantile trade and grew to full manhood under George's tutelage, the Pillsbury brothers developed the mutual trust and regard that successful family business ventures require.

George had much to teach his brother about business. He'd left Sutton ten years earlier to experience life in the big city. Boston was a strong magnet for ambitious New England lads. There, Job Davis of Sutton, certainly an acquaintance and likely a friend, had set up shop selling fruit and other groceries at Boylston Market. George went to work for Davis as a clerk.[5] What he learned there sparked his entrepreneurial imagination.

A little more than a year later, George returned to Sutton with the idea to manufacture stoves and sheet-iron ware. Such metal manufacture was in its infancy in New Hampshire, and he and a willing cousin, John C. Pillsbury, could get in on the ground floor. A larger immediate market might well have yielded success. But in tiny Sutton and pinched rural New Hampshire, the young men gave the venture a five-year run, then conceded defeat. Surviving records show that one of their customers was the Sutton Poor Farm, which bought a stove from the Pillsbury cousins for $30 soon after its founding in 1837.[6] George's other activities in those years included service in the same state militia in which his father had served; like his father, George rose to the rank of captain.[7]

It must have been humbling for George in 1840, at age twenty-six, to ask his friend John H. Pearson for a job as a clerk in his Warner general store. He was starting over after five years of struggling to build his own business and establish himself in the community. But this time, George was landing well. In Pearson, he was attaching himself to a businessman who was not much attached to his own enterprise. Pearson was looking for a financial partner as well as a clerk, and would prove willing to be bought out by that partner a few years hence.

In Warner, too, George found a treasure—Margaret Sprague Carleton. Born in 1817 in Bucksport, Maine, into another old and large New England family, Margaret and her seven siblings moved with their parents, Henry and Polly Greeley Carleton, back to Polly's native Warner, N.H., in 1823. Henry became the operator of a clothing mill situated on a steep hillside between Warner and Sutton.[8] There, Margaret "made her own way," attending school, being baptized and becoming a devout Baptist, then setting up shop as a "tailoress."[9] The story of her courtship with George Pillsbury was remembered at the end of her life this way: "Mr. Pillsbury at that time was engaged in the mercantile business . . . In those days he bought cut sections of garments from Boston, and the making of the suits was let out among the people of the neighborhood. Some of this work fell to Miss Carleton, and in this way an acquaintance and later an attachment sprang up between the two."[10] George and Margaret married on May 9, 1841.

Young wives in nineteenth-century America were confined by rigid social strictures. Margaret may have been making her own way before marriage, but she was obliged to behave as a properly subservient homemaker and mother thereafter—at least publicly. Yet her private role in Pillsbury business affairs throughout her marriage may have been substantial. A biographical sketch prepared in 1895, when attitudes about women's rightful roles were beginning to change, noted that Margaret had been "a judicious adviser to her husband in their mutual business affairs." And at her funeral in 1901, it was said, "Mrs. Pillsbury possessed a mind which, if it had belonged to a man, would have made him a great businessman—broad, capacious, discerning, incisive, decisive and cautious."[11]

While the role played by Margaret's influence remains conjectural, in any case the store in Warner was the Pillsbury store by 1844. Unremarkable in size and profitability, it was an unlikely launching pad for one of the nineteenth century's leading American business success stories. Nevertheless, the lessons John S. Pillsbury learned there about hard work, honest dealing, and customer service would serve him well.

Brothers George and John worked side by side for much of the next seven years, cementing their relationship. With John to help him, George had time to take on a New England businessman's civic responsibilities. He was postmaster in Warner for five years and served the town as a selectman and treasurer. In 1848, George likely left John (and Margaret) in charge in Warner, while he went to Boston to pursue an opportunity to expand their business to include wholesale dry goods. That venture was short-lived, and perhaps cut short by sorrow. George and Margaret's only daughter, Mary, died May 11, 1849. Sources vary in reporting her birth year; when she died, she was either a newborn of three weeks or an infant of one year.[12] George came home to Warner, to grieving Margaret and six-year-old son Charles, and he and John assessed their circumstances. The store would provide a modest livelihood for one family but a meager one for two. John was twenty-two and may have been itching for more independence. Both brothers began looking for other options.

George looked to Concord, the state capital, twenty-two miles east of Warner. He was elected to the state Legislature in 1849, and so came to know the city well during the 1850-51 session. His organizational ability must have made a quick and positive impression on his peers. In 1851, the county convention of representatives in the Legislature decided to build a new jail for Merrimack County. George was appointed to the site selection committee, then became the project's construction superintendent. The jail was completed on time and as ordered in the spring of 1852.[13]

Just then, a new mode of transportation, the railroad, was coming to Concord, luring men of business acumen to come to work with a promise that as the Concord Railroad Corporation prospered, so would they. Records are scant, but officers in the corporation likely acquired ownership stakes. Rather than run for reelection, George signed on with the railroad as its purchasing agent in November 1851, and sold the store in Warner the following spring. Forty years later, he would address his former Warner customers and recall of his eleven years in the little town: "I brought with me less than $500; and during the 11 years I carried on business here I worked day and night to secure some of this world's goods. How well I succeeded you can judge, when I say that I took away with me less than $3,000." [14]

At about the same time, John launched his own venture. A similarly ambitious and able friend, Walter Harriman, wanted to try his hand at retailing in Warner, his hometown. John had earned enough—or, perhaps, had received a share of the proceeds of the sale of George's store—to go into business with Harriman. Their association, and their friendship with a neighbor, Nehemiah Ordway, is notable for this coincidence: All three would go on to become governors of American states—Pillsbury of Minnesota, Harriman of New Hampshire, and Ordway of Dakota Territory. [15]

Little is known about the short-lived Harriman-Pillsbury partnership. It was over by 1853. But it must have produced some success. The sale of the business evidently yielded proceeds rich enough to underwrite a trip John decided to take that summer. New Englanders had been heading west for decades, finding rich land for farming, rushing water for milling, gold in California. The West had been beckoning John Pillsbury for some time. He decided to make a scouting mission.

The trip, begun a full fifteen years before the completion of the transcontinental railroad, was an arduous one. John went all the way to San Francisco, and concluded that the gold rush had largely ended. He had come too late to make his fortune there. He went on to Oregon, and reportedly bought options on "large tracts of lumber."[16] Though his full itinerary is not known, one stop is certain: Sometime in midsummer or fall 1853, John Pillsbury came to

Walter Harriman's New Hampshire gubernatorial portrait. He was governor from 1867 to 1869.

Minnesota Territory and for the first time laid eyes on St. Anthony Falls. On its east bank, a village called St. Anthony was springing up, rough-hewn, raw, but already familiar in design to New England eyes. The bulk of its inhabitants had their origins in New England or New York. On the west bank, a few mills and a smattering of dwellings had not yet taken the name Minneapolis. Decades later John recalled:

> When I first reached the Falls of St. Anthony, where now stands the commanding city of Minneapolis, I arrived in a stagecoach. The railroads were then only completed to Rock Island, Ill., some 700 miles distant. The distance from Rock Island to St. Paul was made by steamboat, and the remainder of the trip was made in a Concord stagecoach. There were then less than 1,000 people around the Falls of St. Anthony.

But that was to change rapidly. Between 1849 and 1858, Minnesota was the fastest-growing region in the United States. People were arriving as quickly as riverboats and stagecoaches could bring them. They were drawn by rich farmland, business opportunities, and, oddly, the climate. Minnesota's bracing cold winters were widely advertised as "exhilarating" and healthful, particularly for those who suffered lung diseases.[17] In the decade of the 1850s, the combined populations of St. Anthony and Minneapolis grew tenfold.

The Falls of St. Anthony had come to European awareness much earlier. A Belgian friar, Father Louis Hennepin, published an exaggerated eyewitness account of their grandeur in 1683. The cataract came into American hands in 1805 when Zebulon Pike, acting under authority granted by President Thomas Jefferson, negotiated a land cession with the Dakota tribe. Establishing a pattern that would provoke bloodshed a half-century later, the U.S. Senate did not ratify the deal until 1808, and the $2,000 negotiated payment was not transmitted to the Dakota until ten years later. U.S.-Dakota relations were off to a bad start.

A military post that would soon be known as Fort Snelling, after its second commander, Josiah Snelling, was established at the juncture of the Minnesota (then St. Peter) and Mississippi rivers in 1819. Almost immediately, the falls nine miles to the northwest captured the soldiers' attention. By 1823, a sawmill, a grist mill, and two barracks for soldiers had been erected on the west bank of the falls. Already in 1824, Snelling boasted that the flour produced at the little grist mill was "equal to any in the world."[18] It wasn't true, but it was prescient.

A treaty with the Dakota opened the east bank of the falls to U.S. settlement in 1838, while the west bank remained in Fort Snelling's "military reserve" until 1855. The reserve deserves the quotation marks, because hundreds of squatters, settlers, and speculators were by then defying government rules and occupying choice tracts of land west of the falls. Some wanted to farm, though many of the people John Pillsbury met on his first Minnesota visit were employed in the riverside mills that cut timber and wove textiles at what was already being called the "New England of the West."

John saw in the village of St. Anthony a few modest frame houses, many crude log huts, and constantly whining sawmills that produced lumber for both local use and commercial sale downriver. He also saw what was lacking: a local dispensary of tools and equipment for millers, timbermen, farmers, and builders. He could fill that void, he thought. John returned to Concord in late fall 1853 or early 1854 to the merchant tailoring business he had opened in the capital city after the Harriman venture ended. But his heart was no longer there. He laid plans—characteristically thorough ones—to make his move to Minnesota as a hardware merchant in the summer of 1855.

He would not go alone. In Warner, he had become quite friendly with schoolteacher Mahala Fisk and her brother Woodbury. Mahala, born in Springfield, Mass., was five years younger than John, and better educated. Her father, another "Captain John," and mother, Sarah Goodhue Fisk, were long-time residents of Warner who both traced their roots to Puritan settlers. The Fisk lineage went back to England

Mahala Fisk Pillsbury, circa 1856.

and to Simon Fisk, lord of the manor for King Henry VI. Mahala stood out among her six siblings as a proficient musician and a lively, fun-loving, industrious girl. She attended Hopkinton Academy and a finishing school for young women called Sanbornton Seminary. By the time she graduated at age seventeen, she had already been teaching for a year. Teaching assignments took her to several towns, Keene and Merrimack among them, but also allowed her frequent returns to Warner and contact with John S. Pillsbury.[19]

Mahala was remembered as a spirited and popular teacher. One of her students, Lucretia A. Davis, wrote as an octogenarian in the 1920s of her memories of "very popular and very successful" Miss Fisk. "The older boys were greatly pleased to have her slide with them down the long hill, sometimes on a sleigh bottom, and across the bridge. But this was not thought by some of the parents to be really ladylike!" Davis's memory suggests that John didn't wait for

Mahala's return visits to Warner to court her. "She boarded at my grandmother's and her fiancé, John Pillsbury of Warner, used to come there to see her, and my Uncle Charles would put his horse in the stable. One night (John) stayed unusually late, and the hostler had retired some time earlier, and when he went for his horse, he could not find the way to the stable. I think it was snowing, so Miss Fisk had to go out and show him the way."[20]

John S. Pillsbury, circa 1856.

Mahala's brother Woodbury was her elder by six years and the man of the Fisk house by 1850. Census records suggest that Sarah Fisk was a widow by the time she was forty-four years old. In 1850, her home also housed three boarders, presumably to help her make ends meet.[21] The Fisk house was situated not far from the Pillsbury store. Woodbury may have introduced John to his pretty schoolmarm sister.

John and Mahala evidently made plans in 1854 for marriage, migration to Minnesota, and life as merchants in St. Anthony. John, Woodbury, and George F. Cross, a younger friend who was then twenty-two, would go west first, in the late spring of 1855. Their company would also include two Pillsbury cousins, Thomas and George Andrews. (Their mother, Dolly Sargent Pillsbury Andrews, was Captain John's youngest sister. Thomas would eventually marry one, then, after her death, another of Mahala's younger sisters.[22]) Mahala would stay in New Hampshire to teach during the winter of 1855-56 while the men established their store. John would return the following summer or fall to be wed and fetch his bride to Minnesota.

Meanwhile, brother George, his wife Margaret, and sons Charles and Fred (born in 1852) were prospering in Concord, and plans were underfoot to build a stately house a few blocks from the state capitol. Later Pillsburys believe that George's profits from the railroad business boom were large enough for him to finance John's frontier venture. There's no record that George was a personal investor in the Minnesota hardware business, though he may well have been, given the brothers' association in many other ventures through the years. But George's familiarity with sources of venture capital was probably crucial in securing an adequate start-up stake for John and Woodbury. Loans from New England financiers helped launch J.S. Pillsbury & Co.

John chose a business site in St. Anthony rather than Minneapolis because at the time the older community had a Main Street and a more promising commercial district. (No street on the west bank ever took that name.) In 1855, six years after St. Anthony's platting, twenty-one people filed a plat for the "town of Minneapolis." They used a composite Dakota-Greek name that originated either with George D. Bowman, editor of the *St. Anthony Express*, or Charles Hoag, a teacher and man of letters who is believed to have written Bowman's article.[23] The Territorial Legislature didn't authorize the establishment of a city government on the west side of the river until the next year, however, and a city election did not take place until 1858.[24]

Pillsbury acquired a commercial parcel on Main Street between the riverbank and the street. (A quarter of a century later, the world's largest flour mill would be built on the site.) It was within view of an observation tower constructed eight years earlier on a high riverbank a half-mile downriver by farmer William A. Cheever, who platted the town of St. Anthony. The tower can be considered the area's first tourist trap. Over the door of his observatory Cheever hung a sign reading, "Pay your dime and climb." On that spot, one of the nation's great universities would rise. [25] A few blocks upriver from Pillsbury's store, a bridge had been installed in January 1855 that would contribute greatly to St. Anthony's eventual eclipse by its west-bank neighbor. The Hennepin Avenue Bridge was the first to span the Mississippi River anywhere in the country. That bridge would have been an impressive sight when Pillsbury, Fisk, and Cross got off the stagecoach from St. Paul in June.

John must have been amazed at other changes in St. Anthony in the short time since his first visit. Its population had tripled to

The 1855 Hennepin Avenue Bridge.

three thousand. Families had come to settle, and schools and churches had gone up. So had hotels and boarding houses, to accommodate the large number of single laborers who had come to work in the constantly humming mills. New England style was evident in the emerging village, but pigs roamed the streets at will. Housewives complained of walls and floors built of green wood that constantly oozed moisture. [26]

Pillsbury, Fisk, and Cross took up residence at a low-cost boarding house operated by Mrs. E. B. West, undoubtedly aiming to conserve cash for the purchase of inventory. How their store's ownership was divided among them is not known, but it is clear from the enterprise's founding name—J.S. Pillsbury & Co.—which partner took the financial and managerial lead. The success of that first year can only be guessed at—but the guess is that it was a very good year. One early account said John "bought large stores of hardware goods, which had to be brought up the river by steamboat, so he could be sure of having stock on hand."[27] A December 1855 newspaper report, recalled forty years later by attorney and historian

Isaac Atwater, described the hazards associated with merchandizing in the years before a railroad reached the falls:

> *A party of young men who were fellow boarders at Mrs. E. B. West's, consisting of Mr. Thomas Andrews, J. S. Pillsbury, Woodbury Fisk, George S. Rowell, John Bailey and a Mr. Merrill, started in December, 1855 with a team on their way east, for Dubuque, a distance of some five hundred miles. They encountered severe weather, and once thought they were lost in a storm on one of the trackless prairies. One night they stopped in a lone log house on the site of the present city of Rochester. On the night of their arrival at Dubuque the mercury fell to forty degrees below zero, covering the river with a coating of ice, too strong for boating, but too weak to bear their weight. Pushing their trunks before them, they followed, one at a time, on a footing of boards. Having safely gained the eastern bank, the party pursued their way East, except Messrs. Pillsbury and Fisk, who went to Guttenburg and packed pork, which they shipped to St. Anthony in the spring.[28]*

The boom at the falls continued in 1856. Sawmilling was a galloping industry, and the territory north of St. Anthony was amply covered with white pine. A bid for statehood was being prepared at the territorial capitol in St. Paul.

Insight into how quickly Pillsbury & Co. grew can be gleaned from the number of people working at the store when a census taker came by in October 1857. Pillsbury, Fisk, and Cross were all present that day, as were three clerks, John Dutton, William Peck, and J.K. Judkins, and three "tinners," or tin craftsmen, Fallon Castner, Charles P. Rowell, and J.D. Othert. Fisk, age thirty-one, and Pillsbury, thirty, were the oldest men in the shop; St. Anthony Falls' beckoning call was audible primarily to the young. (That census record is the last trace of George F. Cross in Minnesota. He turns up again in the 1880 census in Saginaw, Michigan, a married lumberman whose mother Caroline had moved from Merrimack County in New Hampshire to join his household. By comparison, Woodbury Fisk spent the rest of his days near his brother-in-law and sister in Minnesota, and prospered.)

John returned to New Hampshire in the fall of 1856 to fetch his bride-to-be Mahala, and may have arrived in time to be at his father's bedside when Captain John died on Oct. 11. The wedding took place in Warner on November 3, 1856, consummating the plans laid the year before and putting two powerhouses under a single yoke. John's drive, discipline, and business sense were complimented by Mahala's bright energy and determination to be of service to those around her. When they married, they were mature people—twenty-nine and twenty-four, respectively—accustomed to supporting themselves. With that experience came a practical sense of what financial success required. John was described later in life as "thoroughly temperate," possessed of a "modest disposition. He never parades his doings." [29]

On their journey west to Minnesota, the couple stopped in Dubuque, Iowa, where John lingered to purchase supplies for the store while Mahala bravely continued by steamboat up the Mississippi— a chilly journey the likes of which she had never made before. At Hastings, she left the boat (winter was coming, and that's as far as the boat would go) and went by stagecoach the final twenty miles north to St. Anthony. Her new husband arrived on horseback a few days later. They stayed at the St. Charles Hotel for a few weeks, then rented a furnished house from Dr. J. H. Murphy. After a few months, they moved to a small house with four rooms on Leonard Street. Not long after, they built their own house on Third Street. Some years later, they bought lots at the corner of Fifth Street and Tenth Avenue South, which was still in St. Anthony at the time. (After the cities merged in 1872, that address would take the designation Southeast Minneapolis.) That corner would be their home for the rest of their lives. [30]

Mahala found more freedom to choose her role in St. Anthony than George's wife Margaret had in Warner and Concord. Much later, a friend described Mahala's early life in St. Anthony: "Manners were plain, luxuries were few, and the ladies not only thought it no hardship to attend to their own household work, but they regarded themselves as the helpmeets and assistants of their husbands; the work of the husband and wife was one—each seeking to assist the other in building up a happy and prosperous home." [31]

St. Anthony in 1857, looking northwest from the Winslow House roof. The wooded tip of Nicollet Island is visible. Under construction in the foreground is the Universalist Church, dedicated September 27, 1857. It was purchased in 1877 by French-speaking Roman Catholics, who renamed it Our Lady of Lourdes Church—its name today.

The role Mahala played at the hardware store is not known, but her role in one community institution is well documented, and was significant from the start of her life in Minnesota. First Congregational Church was organized in 1851 to bring to St. Anthony the religious tradition of the Puritan and Congregational movements in New England. Mahala joined the church in 1858, when the congregation worshipped in a frame building on East Hennepin Avenue and Fourth Street South, its home until 1874. Her husband did not join the church as a lay member, but was a member of its "society," a financial leadership panel.

A distinction between ordinary lay members and society members, who functioned as trustees, was common among Congregational churches in the nineteenth century. In Minneapolis, one leading Congregational parish, Plymouth, maintained those parallel membership categories until after World War II.[32] Some historians who were unfamiliar with that Congregational parish structure took John Pillsbury's status at First Church as an indication that he had some objection to its theology or doctrine. His consistent attendance, generous gifts, and long service in the First Church's Society argue for the opposite conclusion. "You cannot read the minutes of those days

18

without seeing everywhere the impress of his leadership," said Guy Stanton Ford, president of the University of Minnesota and the parish's historian, in an address delivered as First Congregational observed its eightieth anniversary in 1931. "So long as Governor Pillsbury was on hand to lead and plan, nothing seemed too large a task for First Church to undertake."[33]

Mahala found an outlet for her leadership talent, musical ability, and love of children and teaching at First Congregational. She sang in the choir, was a Sunday school teacher, and functioned "unconsciously as a pastor's assistant" by welcoming new members. For twenty years, she was president of the congregation's Benevolent Society, organizing fundraisers and fellowship events. It was said of her late in life, "No item of church work has ever been too small to engross her time, or too hard or wearying for her. She has always possessed the happy faculty of harmonizing differences, and bringing together into pleasant relations and systematic work the different elements of the church and Sunday school, all the while keeping herself modestly in the background and never magnifying her own importance."[34]

The Pillsburys' faith in things both spiritual and temporal would be put to the test not long after the young couple set up housekeeping in St. Anthony. The year 1857 started with promise. The St. Anthony Falls Water Power Company and its west-bank counterpart, the Minneapolis Mill Company, had been chartered by the 1856 Legislature, and were at work building a V-shaped dam that would harness the Mississippi's power for the development of additional mills on both sides of the river. The project undoubtedly meant more business for Pillsbury & Co.

But on August 24, the New York City branch of the Ohio Life Insurance and Trust Co. failed. The immediate cause was embezzlement, but there was more. The end of the Crimean War had brought Russia back into world grain markets, depressing crop prices. The Dred Scott decision by the U.S. Supreme Court seemed (wrongly, as it turned out) to open the west to settlement by slave-owners, depressing Eastern land values and the value of railroad bonds. Speculators in both land and railroads lost their investments. A mid-September hurricane off North Carolina sank a ship containing thirty thousand pounds of gold, shaking public confidence in the value of paper currency. By fall, British investors were withdrawing funds from American banks, and the Panic of 1857 was on.[35]

Minnesota may have been geographically remote from failing banks in New York and New England, where a bank holiday in October was said to be "a vain effort to avert runs on those institutions."[36] But the territory's economy that fall was already firmly linked to that of the rest of the nation. The panic slowed immigration to Minnesota and halted the flow of capital from eastern banks. Construction all but stopped; land speculators went bust. Richard Chute, a principal in the St. Anthony Falls Water Power Co., said the effect was "a financial tornado that swept over the country" and "throwed Minnesota on its beam ends…We undertook…to bridge the crisis, but our timbers were too short."[37]

The panic would have been bad enough, but 1857 brought worse for Pillsbury & Co. and at least nine other Main Street businesses. A "terrible conflagration" on September 29, a windy night, wiped out two blocks of stores and several other buildings. The losses were collectively estimated at $40,000.[38] J.S. Pillsbury & Co. was not the worst affected. Its "large stone building . . was saved almost by a miracle," a local newspaper reported two days later. The report attributed the cause of the fire to "the work of an incendiary." The volunteers, who lacked even the rudimentary firefighting equipment of the nineteenth century, battled the fire with little success. ("When will our citizens take the hint from these disasters and organize and equip a Fire Company?" the newspaper wailed.)

Though Pillsbury's main building was spared, some of the firm's inventory was lost. So said later accounts, which described John and Mahala's need to cut personal expenses and seek additional financing from Eastern banks to replenish supplies and stay in business. "His fair dealing, business sagacity, great industry and promptness, which every one with whom he did business recognized, were all the capital he had" after the fire, a New Hampshire friend said years later about that moment in John's business career.[39] John and Mahala made a vow: They would buy no new clothing until the debt they owed the Eastern banks was repaid. Neither of them had a new thing to wear for nearly six years. Had the newlyweds been less devoted to their Minnesota adventure, they might have chosen at this juncture to return to the comparative security of Concord. Instead, they stayed on their Minnesota course. Their story, and the state's, would have been quite different had they chosen otherwise.

John's search for additional capital was complicated by the larger credit crisis unfolding in the fall of 1857. Financing for a two-year-old, fire-damaged hardware business in a rough Northwestern outpost was not easily arranged. Yet somehow John and Woodbury secured a combination of new loans and extensions on previous ones sufficient to carry on. (There is no documentary evidence to support the claim, but today's Pillsburys believe brother George, back in Concord, played a role.) While Eastern banks were clearly involved, one notable loan was local, as John's great-nephew would relate years later. "When the new Farmers and Mechanics Bank, in what had become Minneapolis, had only $8,000 in deposits in its beginning year, its founders made their first loan to [John,] $1,000 at 12 percent. Within a few years, well on the black side of the ledger, he was to be offered the presidency of the same bank."[40]

In the ensuing years, John Pillsbury dutifully sent to his creditors in the East what he could each month, at the start as little as $25. Pillsbury's friend William Watts Folwell, president of the University of Minnesota and fellow layman at First Congregational, wrote in his exhaustive history of the state that John's good relationship with a Boston bank was crucial after the fire. "The Boston firm to which he was chiefly indebted refused to allow him to assign, but urged him to continue in business and proposed to supply him with goods on his personal credit. It is related that the head of the firm told him he might hold his notes and whenever he had redeemed one by remittance, he might tear it up."[41] A more detailed account of that business connection is found in Pillsbury Co. archives:

> *Later when he went to Boston to visit his chief creditors, he was warmly greeted with the remark: "You are the man who pays $1,200 notes $25 at a time. I'm glad to see you." Turning to his*

*manager, the creditor said, "Whatever Mr. Pillsbury wants, let him
have it, and if you haven't got it, send out and buy it for him. If they
want to know anything about Mr. Pillsbury in New York, tell them
he's one of the best men on earth."* [42]

In that fashion, the debt on the store was retired in a little more
than five years. Notably, those five years, 1857 to 1862, were not the
boom times for Minnesota that the previous five had been. Statehood
came in 1858, but the era also saw the onset of both the Civil War in
1861 and the Dakota Conflict in the Minnesota River valley in 1862.
Yet Pillsbury & Co. prospered. "It is significant that from the first, Mr.
Pillsbury was successful," wrote a journalist who interviewed John
near the end of his life. "It is said of him that in these early days, he
held his trade because he never misrepresented the quality or value
of his goods, and because he was uniformly courteous to people of
every class and condition, and very early manifested those warm sympathies which so enriched his later years." [43]

Any businessman who had suffered the reversal John did in 1857
would have been justified in spurning civic activities that would take
time and resources from his business, at least for a few years. Thus it is
remarkable—but much in keeping with his New England heritage—
to observe the date on which the name John Pillsbury first appeared
on a ballot: April 2, 1860. At age thirty-three, just five years off the
stagecoach and riverboat from New Hampshire, John was elected
to the St. Anthony village council, representing the fourth ward. He
would serve three years. [44]

Telegraph lines reached Minneapolis and St. Anthony in the fall
of 1860. The link made immediate news of events in the East, just
as those events were taking an ominous turn. Minnesotans braced
for civil war in the winter of 1860-61. The Minnesota Legislature
pledged in January to send men and money to the extent of the
state's ability to check rebellion by southern states, should it erupt,
and keep navigation on the Mississippi unimpeded. [45] That pledge
was redeemed when hostilities commenced in April. Minnesota
Governor Alexander Ramsey was in Washington on Sunday, April
14, when news of the occupation of Fort Sumter, South Carolina, by

Confederate forces reached the nation's capital. Ramsey immediately offered a thousand troops. It was the first such offer to reach the secretary of war's hands.

At age thirty-four, and with a business deemed increasingly vital to Minnesota as the economy recovered, Pillsbury was not a candidate for military service. But he knew—and undoubtedly employed—others who were. He was credited with helping to organize the First, Second, and Third Regiments of Minnesota volunteers for the Army of the Republic. He played a similar role in the summer of 1862, when starving Dakota Indians mounted a series of violent attacks on white settlers in the Minnesota River valley. Again Governor Ramsey issued a call for volunteer soldiers, and Pillsbury responded by helping to recruit and equip a mounted company.[46]

Mahala, too, was touched by those conflicts. During the Civil War, she helped organize "a society for the relief of the sick and the care of the families of the soldiers," undoubtedly working through First Congregational Church. During the Dakota uprising, she went so far as to take lessons in the use of a rifle, an action indicating both how much fear was generated in St. Anthony by hostile Indians a hundred miles to the west, and how often she and John were apart. She evidently felt the need to be able to protect herself.

Maternal responsibilities likely added to her worry. Sometime between 1860 and 1862, John and Mahala adopted a daughter, Addie Eva. Addie was born in 1860, at a time when Minnesota lacked organized services for orphans or unwed mothers. She became a Pillsbury at such a tender age that it was soon widely assumed that she was their biological child. She was raised as their own, and John sought to ensure that she would always be treated as such. While he was governor, he arranged for a special act of the legislature to make her his legal heir. More children followed, at three-year intervals: Susan M., on June 23, 1863; Sarah Belle, on June 30, 1866; and Alfred Fisk, on October 20, 1869. [47]

John's civic activity, already keeping him frequently away from home in 1862, intensified in 1863. Minnesota legislators and governors were elected in odd-numbered years then. John was recruited to stand for the state Senate. He had just assented to his name

Old Main, the University of Minnesota's first building, as it appeared in about 1880. It had been enlarged in 1874.

going on the November ballot when an emissary from the newly inaugurated governor, Henry A. Swift, approached him about taking on one more duty. Would he become one of three regents of the University of Minnesota?

The University of Minnesota was established in 1851 as a preparatory school. It operated intermittently, and was elevated to collegiate status with construction of Old Main on the site of farmer Cheever's tourist-attracting tower in St. Anthony in 1858. But the school closed soon thereafter, a victim of the Panic of 1857. By 1863, Old Main stood vacant, with cattle pasturing around it (and wandering in it, some accounts say.)[48] The university was insolvent, unable even to pay Pillsbury & Co. for the locks and nails used to build the place. In tapping John to be a regent, Governor Swift may have believed that a creditor would have the incentive needed to get the university out of debt and functional once more. [49] He may also have believed that a St. Anthony businessman would have particular motivation to rescue a troubled public institution within that city's borders. Then again, Swift's attitude may have matched that of other war-stressed residents near the Falls: They thought the university a boondoggle, and believed it best that its assets be sold, creditors paid, and higher education left to the realm of church folk.

Pillsbury would say later in life that his initial impulse was to decline the governor's offer. But "after a forceful statement from this visitor, he yielded to the impulse to help, which was characteristic of his life," an admiring journalist wrote decades later. "'I thought for a moment, and then told him I would accept the appointment,' is his simple reference to this, a momentous moment in the history of a great institution." [50]

There was nothing great about the University of Minnesota in 1863, save for the size of its debt and its potential. The former ranged upward of $100,000. The latter sprang from the Morrill Act, or land-grant bill, approved by the Congress of the United States in 1862. The project of Justin Morrill, a congressman from Vermont, it donated large acreages of public lands as a permanent endowment for the support of colleges committed to teaching "such branches of learning as are related to agriculture and the mechanic arts." The University of Minnesota didn't qualify for the land grant in 1863 because it was not able to hire a single faculty member. Non-functional institutions were not eligible for land grants. But, John Pillsbury reasoned, cash might be raised against the promise of the land that would come to the university if and when it became functional. The original Morrill Act allotted each state 30,000 acres of land for each member of its delegation to Congress. Minnesota, with two senators and two representatives, would be entitled to receive 120,000 acres if its school could get up and running. John saddled his horse and set out to see if he could sell university land that the university didn't yet own.

In the ensuing four years, John Pillsbury's quest to retire enough of the university's debt to make it operational became a near-obsession. Beginning in 1863 and for the rest of his life, about a third of his active hours were spent in service of the university, a journalist reported decades later. "He was comparatively a poor man, with his future to prepare for; yet he gave his time. . . [When he was elected regent,] he at once began to labor for the college, taking much time away from his business."[51] It may have been an unlikely cause to be championed

25

by a man who himself had experienced no higher education. Perhaps by his mid-thirties, he had come to wish that he had received more formal learning. Perhaps being married to a woman better educated than he was affected his thinking about the value of college study. Perhaps the idea of a university springing up almost in his backyard appealed to the developer in him, and to his resolve that Minnesota, not New Hampshire, would be home for the rest of his days. The thought of offering to the children of Minnesota pioneers the same chance at higher learning that his nephews had in New Hampshire deeply appealed to John Pillsbury. He was enormously drawn to the idea that he could help make Minnesota a state of well-educated people.

John was elected to the state Senate, and in the 1864 session he sponsored a bill to give the university's three regents sweeping power to "adjust its obligations on such terms as they might deem best, and as if they were their own." Seldom does a legislature grant such unlimited authority to an unelected board—unless legislators doubt that anything will come of the move. That the freshman senator from St. Anthony could engineer the placing of so much power in his own and two other hands suggests that most of Pillsbury's fellow Minnesotans had given up on the University of Minnesota. He had not. He undertook to care for the university as if it were his own property, occasionally strolling the campus grounds at night to make sure they were secure.[52] John, it was later written, "rode thousands of miles through a new country, hunting up lands or showing them to creditors or buyers. He traveled to the East. He wrote letters innumerable. He brought into play all the resources of a skillful man of business."[53]

In the process, he got to know his adopted state and its leading citizens, and they got to know him. It might be said that in those fundraising trips, he was once again on a scouting mission, not so different from the one he made in 1853. With his store finally out of debt and flourishing, he was looking for prime parcels of northern timberland as investment property. He surveyed the land grant property and claimed choice acres in exchange for his own financial donation to the university cause, even as he sold others on the investment. Along the way, he forged relationships that a future candidate for statewide office would find beneficial. Whether he knew it at the time or not, John was scouting for votes.

In 1867, Pillsbury reported to a surprised Legislature that the regents had paid off the university's debts. With that fact confirmed by the state auditor, state Senator Pillsbury sponsored the University Reorganization Act of 1868. The bill set the university in operation, making it able to take title to the land promised under the Morrill Act. Then, in turn, it could trans-fer titles of the parcels purchased by investors under the terms of agreements Pillsbury and his fel-low regents had made. It was not the originally expected 120,000 acres, but 46,000, that came to the university, but of that amount, 32,000 acres of the land grant remained in university control when the transactions were com-plete. It was enough to assure the young institution financial sta-bility and the capacity to grow. Classes resumed in 1868, most of them in the preparatory (high

William Watts Folwell, circa 1870.

school) department. The first students included a young easterner John had personally recruited. It was also John, by then the father of three daughters, who insisted that women be enrolled alongside men.[54] John had literally willed the University of Minnesota to life, and was shaping its character.

He and his fellow regents did their fledgling school one more good turn the next fall, luring thirty-six-year-old William Watts Folwell from New York's Hobart College to be the university's first president. Folwell was a Civil War veteran and a scholar said to be "interested in every-thing from Plato to hog cholera."[55] Folwell became John and Mahala's neighbor and, for the rest of their lives, their dear friend. Folwell would give remarkable service to Minnesota over a long lifetime.

With his university thus launched, John looked for a new chal-lenge. He did not need to look far—only across the Mississippi.

Falls of St. Anthony, late 1860s.

Chapter Two

New Arrivals

In the winter of 1869, Charles Alfred Pillsbury was living in Montreal, Canada, but his thoughts were turned westward to the Falls of St. Anthony, just as his uncle John's had been sixteen years earlier. Though the falls was in the process of being tamed, it still beckoned to ambitious New England men, and the voice of Charles's energetic uncle, who had lived with his family in Warner and played with him when he was a boy, was stronger still. A letter from John set Charles's mind racing. It contained a plea and a proposal: Come to Minneapolis, and join your father and me in investing in a flourmill. You can be its salaried manager, as well as a co-owner.

It was time for this twenty-six-year-old to return to the United States and make a fresh start. The elder son of George and Margaret Pillsbury had chosen for Canada after graduating from Dartmouth College in July 1863, only days after a ferocious battle in Gettysburg, Pennsylvania, turned the tide of the brutal War Between the States in the Union's favor. Of the sixty-six students who enrolled with Charles at the wooded Hanover, N.H., campus in 1859, fifty-five either had already enlisted in the Army of the Republic, or would do so shortly after graduation. Nine classmates would lose their lives in the war.[1] Charles Pillsbury made sure he would not be among them. He opted to leave the country rather than take up arms.

That decision must have been agonizing, both for the young man and for his parents. The Hanover campus may have been far removed geographically from the hostilities that erupted off the coast of South

Carolina in the spring of 1861, but distances on the eastern seaboard of the United States had shrunk markedly with the arrival of the telegraph, and the latest war news typically reached Hanover within hours; the Boston newspapers were not far behind. War fever quickly infected the all-male student body. "Everybody talks of war," wrote a member of the Dartmouth class of 1862, Edward Tuck, days after war had been declared. He was addressing his father, President Abraham Lincoln's chief naval officer at the port of Boston. "Nine out of 10 [students] profess willingness to 'go down and fight,' and I've no doubt a majority of these talkers would really go if things came to the worst. Two or three really think of taking up their standing and joining some volunteer corps."[2] The

The young Charles A. Pillsbury.

college's handful of southern students, including three in Charles's class, left for home and war soon after hostilities commenced.

Subsequent letters from Tuck indicate that the zeal for war on campus abated only slightly as the months wore on and Union casualties mounted. Some of Dartmouth's best students left for military service before graduating. Tuck did not, continuing his studies evidently at the urging of his father. But he and many other students formed a drill club in the fall of 1861, under the instruction of President Jackman of Norwich University, just across the Vermont-New Hampshire state line. For those military lessons, the students paid the not-inconsequential price of $1 per week.[3] This was serious military activity. Norwich was the nation's first private military academy, the birthplace of the Reserve Officer Training Corps, and the training ground for hundreds of Civil War soldiers. They are "drilling an hour every afternoon," Tuck reported to his father.

Whether Charles ever joined them as they marched on the campus green is not known. What is known is that, like perhaps a majority of his fellow students, Charles had an "off-campus" job in the winter months—teaching. At the time, Dartmouth was the prime source of the teaching corps that served the tiny rural schoolhouses that dotted the hillsides of western New Hampshire and Vermont. Its undergraduates then "derived from the rural sections of New England," and had modest means. "In general, they brought with them little of the polish acquired from luxurious or even refined surroundings; they were somewhat uncouth and rough, with little regard for the amenities of life." [4]

That description does not match the circumstances of the Pillsburys of Concord in the late 1850s and early 1860s. George was not yet a wealthy man, but as a railroad purchasing agent and shareholder, he was able to afford a life much more comfortable for Margaret and his two sons than they had known a decade before as Warner storekeepers. After Charles finished common school in Concord at age sixteen, he was sent to preparatory school at New London Academy (now Colby College) for one year. It was, literally and figuratively, on the way to Dartmouth.

But if not poor, George Alfred Pillsbury was still a long way from easy street. As a schoolboy Charles had delivered newspapers in Concord "to help out his father," one family account says. [5] The Panic of 1857 coincided with Charles's last year in school at Concord, and likely reinforced George's bent toward frugality and his faith in the virtue of self-sufficiency. He wanted his elder son to continue his education. But as much as practicable, he also wanted the young man to make his own way.

Thus Charles joined nearly half of his fellow Dartmouth students in accepting a teaching assignment at a country school during the winter months, or longer. Dartmouth served as a talent brokerage for those one-room schools, its administration recognizing that teaching was the main financial resource of many needy undergraduates, and that unless students landed those jobs, enrollment would plummet. [7] A typical teaching assignment in 1860 would fetch $93.95, or nearly half the cost of a year at Dartmouth. Tuition then ranged from

$124.50 to $174.50 per year, depending on the course of study. Living costs would run up the tab to about $200 per year. [6]

Most teaching assignments lasted for about two months. But at least in Charles' freshman year, he may have had a longer stint. Class records show that he had 121 excused absences that year, far more than other students. A heavy teaching load may explain that record; so might illness. Later in life, Charles exhibited a Herculean appetite for work. His many absences from Dartmouth might be early evidence of that trait. In any event, he maintained grades that were at least average. [7] His course of study focused heavily on languages—three years of Greek and Latin, a year of French and German. A contemporary said of Charles, "He did not seek to attain high scholarship; he did a good deal of general reading; he was a good talker and kept the fact constantly in mind that he meant to be a successful 'business man,' and this fact he did not conceal from anyone." [8]

No letter between Charles and his parents has survived from his college days, though it's likely they discussed the war and how Charles should respond to it. Twentieth-century Pillsburys are confident that George, Margaret, and Charles saw eye-to-eye on the slavery question with their distant cousin Parker Pillsbury, a clergyman who was drummed out of the Congregational Church in 1840 for his anti-slavery activism. By the 1850s, Parker Pillsbury's views were becoming more widely accepted, and he lectured widely in opposition to slavery, including in England. Concord was his home base. George, Margaret, and their sons were almost certainly acquainted with him. [9]

Commencement week came in 1863 with an extensive range of ceremonies that were nevertheless judged "quiet in comparison with those of former years." Charles was among twenty students chosen by lot to present an assigned research paper. If his thoughts about war had turned pacifist, as appears likely, his paper's topic was an ironic one: "Iron-Clad Fleets." The choice illustrates the extent to which military matters had penetrated academic ones. Congress had only ordered the country's first venture in metal-clad shipbuilding in July 1861, and the first such Union ship, the *USS Monitor*, scored several successes in 1862 before running aground in a storm off Cape

George and Margaret Pillsbury, circa 1860.

Hatteras on New Year's Eve. Charles's paper warranted no extraordinary mention in a review that said the presenting students "showed that their subjects had been thoroughly investigated and studied."[10]

George and Margaret very likely were present for the four-day commencement festivities, to both applaud and advise their son. He had chosen to move to Montreal soon after graduation, out of the reach of Union conscription. No surviving correspondence illuminates what passed between parents and son during those crucial weeks, but one letter from not long afterward has been carefully passed down through decades of relocation and change.[11] It's a letter from father to son, dated Oct. 8, 1863. Its tone is conciliatory; its message of support for Charles—if not explicitly for his decision—is clear. It's a letter a son who had been in conflict with his parents might treasure. It's also the best window left to posterity on a relationship that was important not only to a family, but to an industry and a state.

The letter is a reply to one Charles had written to his parents, now lost, which likely announced that he had acquired a position in Montreal as a clerk in a produce commission house, Buck, Robertson and Co. His father replied that same week, though repeated references to "we" indicates that Margaret also contributed to its contents. George expresses appreciation for what Charles had written about his parents' efforts "to fit and prepare you for the duties of life upon which you have now entered...We are well paid for all of this care and anxiety from the fact you appreciate what has been done for you."

George wants for his son "a life of usefulness," not of riches or fame. He opines that Montreal "is as favorable a position for a young man to locate himself in as any place that I know of." Charles had just turned twenty-one, and apparently asserted in his letter that he was now "his own man." [12] George advises in response that while that was true in the eyes of the law, "you are our son yet. And so long as either of us live, [your mother and I] shall feel a deep interest in your welfare."

The Baptist faith that George acquired with marriage had become by 1863 a pillar of his own life, and a recurring theme in his words and deeds. George's letter expresses interest in Charles's "future and final happiness beyond the affairs of this life." He fretted, "I have perhaps come short of my duty in your spiritual welfare. That you have a good moral character, we do not doubt, and whether you succeed in pecuniary matters or not, I hope you will always endeavor to maintain a respectable standing in society." That had indeed been George's own aim, as it was his father's before him.

The only reference to the presumably tender topic of the war is the line, "The conscription is still going on, as you will see by the papers that we send you." It's a note dropped in almost casually, amid brief tidbits about family and friends. There's no mention of whether conscription affected anyone in their acquaintance.

"Let us hear from you at least as often as once in two weeks," George asks, and signs off not with "love," or "affectionately," but "yours truly, Geo. A. Pillsbury." It's a stiff closure, though the tenor of the letter itself had been warm. If there was strain in the relationship between father and son, perhaps it was eased by this missive.

And that strain, if it did exist, was probably due to young Charles's response to his nation's crisis. Evidence for such an assertion emerges only decades later, but it is worth getting ahead of our story to relate it here. When Pillsbury brothers George and John were wealthy elders, they made a series of gifts to their New Hampshire hometowns:

Sutton, Warner, and Concord. The first among them was a memorial statue, a tall granite pillar topped by a sculpture of a Union soldier, chosen by George as "a monument dedicated to the memory of the men of Sutton who served in the war of the rebellion for the preservation of the Union." At the dedication ceremony on Sept. 1, 1891, George spoke at eloquent and emotional length of his admiration for the sacrifices of Union soldiers and their families. "I have thought that I could bestow no more worthy testimonial of my love for my native place than to cause to be erected on this spot this soldiers' monument, in commemoration of the valor and courage of those men who, in the hour of their country's need, took their lives in their hands to uphold and preserve our national heritage," he said.[11] A huge crowd converged for an all-day party to honor the new statue, the region's aging veterans, and the local boys who had made good in Minnesota. One expected guest—Charles A. Pillsbury—found a last-minute reason to stay away.

Charles labored in Montreal with enough success to acquire an interest in Buck, Robertson in 1865, and to fetch a bride from New Hampshire the following year. Nothing is known about how Charles came to know, court, and wed Mary Ann Stinson, but we do know that they were married in Dunbarton, N.H., on Sept. 12, 1866.

Mary Ann, born in Dunbarton on Aug. 1, 1841, was a year older than Charles. She was the youngest in a blended family of sisters. Her father Charles Stinson and his first wife, Susan Cochran, had three daughters before she died in the winter of 1838, when her youngest was less than five months old. Charles chose a second wife fourteen months later—Mary Ann Poor Richards, a widow eleven years his junior with a six-year-old daughter, the same age as the eldest Stinson girl. Baby Mary Ann came two years later, the only child born to Charles and the second Mrs. Stinson.[14]

Mary Ann's father was a successful Merrimack County farmer, to judge from the 1850 census, which finds him farming with four hired hands. His recorded history includes none of the civic and political activities that often recur in the Pillsbury line, and Mary Ann's own social life was undoubtedly crimped by the long winters and

The Stinson farmstead in New Hampshire.

muddy springs of rural New Hampshire—not to mention her older parents protective attitude toward "their" only daughter. By the time Mary Ann was in her mid-teens, her half-sisters had all left home in marriage, the single exception being her mother's first daughter, Elizabeth, who died in 1856 at the age of twenty-three; the cause is unknown. Mary Ann's teen years may have been spent caring for a sickly older sister. One account written decades after Mary Ann died, likely provided by one of her children or grandchildren, said she was educated for a time in New York State.[15]

Hints and speculation are all we have. Of all the principal characters in the story of the Pillsburys in Minnesota, the least is known about Mary Ann Stinson Pillsbury. That may be merely the consequence of disinterest in women among record-keepers in the nineteenth century, but it also may be an indication of a particularly home-centered and reclusive life, one that took little advantage of even the one outlet for community involvement afforded women of her day—the church. Mary Ann's grandchildren, who did not know her, surmise that she and Charles were introduced to each other by mutual friends, perhaps a Dartmouth chum, during one of Charles's recurrent visits to New Hampshire in 1864, 1865, or early 1866. It may have been a case of opposites attracting. Charles was often described as a gregarious, venturesome, hard-driving fellow, while Mary Ann has left few traces of her activities or personality at all.[16]

When Uncle John's fateful business proposition arrived in Montreal in the winter or early spring of 1869, Charles and Mary Ann considered it together. If he was moving to the Falls of St. Anthony for a fling in the flour business, she would be by his side right from the start, they decided. Numerous letters were exchanged about the idea "in critical appraisal," Charles' grandson would write years later. "They were not plunging into the unknown."[17] He would sell his interest in his Montreal business, which was not flourishing. He netted $1,500—and valuable business experience—to take with him to Minneapolis.[18]

Two other parties to the young couple's decision were Charles's parents, George and Margaret. The 1860s had been good to them. Their family expanded in 1868 or soon thereafter, when they took four-year-old Minnie Chamberlin into their home. Minnie's mother was Margaret's first cousin Theresa Carleton Chamberlin, who died that year. What became

Mary Ann Stinson Pillsbury as a young bride.

of her father, John Chamberlin of Charlestown, Mass., is not known. Census records for 1870 do not appear to include him. Minnie was twelve years younger than Charles's brother Fred, and was raised as virtually an only child by doting older parents. She returned their devotion for the rest of their lives.[19]

Eastern railroads prospered during and after the Civil War, allowing George to make shrewd investments in two new business-promoting ventures in Concord and thereby expand his own career. In 1864, he helped organize the First National Bank of Concord. Two years later, he became its president, a post he would hold for the next twelve years. In 1867, he helped start the city's National Savings Bank. He was elected its first president that year, and kept that post until 1874.[20] Apparently, it was not seen as a conflict of interest for the same man to lead both institutions, while continuing to function as an officer of the Concord Railroad Corp. Both banks were well launched by the winter of 1869, and George was in a good position to help Charles start anew in a business venture in Minnesota alongside his younger brother John.

According to John, Minnesota was booming. Its population had nearly tripled in the 1860s, to 439,076. The big draw: free land, through the federal government's homestead program, and the prospect of selling crops produced on that land to a national or even world market, via rail and river transport. The acreage under production in the state quadrupled from 556,250 acres in 1860 to 2,322,102 acres in 1870. Sixty percent of those acres were devoted to hard spring wheat, and the yields were exceptional. Wheat output increased ninefold in Minnesota during the 1860s, aided by newly invented mechanical threshers and reapers. Railroads were coming fast to move those bumper crops to mills and market. The first railroad line from St. Paul to Minneapolis, the St. Paul and Pacific, was laid in 1862. By the end of 1869, 764 miles of rail were in operation in the state—and the rail building boom was only beginning.[21]

So was the surge in milling capacity at St. Anthony Falls. A sawmill and simple grist mill had been in operation there since the 1820s—the early years of Fort Snelling—but when John S. Pillsbury arrived in St. Anthony in 1855, lumber was the principal commodity being produced. Only two small flourmills were in operation, producing 200 barrels per day, much of it made from wheat grown in Iowa and Illinois. Little wheat was yet grown in Minnesota, and most was being shipped to Red Wing, Winona, Faribault, and Northfield. By 1869, nine mills lined the Falls—four on the east, five on the better-managed west. But production was still only 3,380 barrels per day.

That was about to change. The northern tier of the United States was thinking big in the heady years after its victory in the Civil War. Brutal as the conflict had been, it had also opened the eyes of a largely rural nation as to what was possible when masses of people are mobilized in pursuit of a single mission. In the years after the war, it appeared that the national mission was making money.

Charles and Mary Ann arrived in Minnesota in the spring of 1869 and were "of Minneapolis" by June 4, when a handwritten contract was signed by Charles and his father (George may also have been visiting Minnesota at the time) to purchase a one-third interest in the Minneapolis Flouring Mill. It was on the west side of the Falls, on the second lot south of what is now the southeast corner of First Street and Portland Avenue S. It employed seven people and produced between 200 and 300 barrels of flour per day, making it one of the smallest facilities along the west side mill canal. Built in 1864 by Frazee and Murphy, it was owned in 1869 by Frazee, Wells Gardner, and William B. Brown, according to the Minneapolis City Directory. It was Frazee's share that the Pillsburys bought, with George furnishing $8,000 and Charles $4,000. That amount covered the purchase price of $10,000 and contributed $2,000 in working capital. Uncle John, who likely played a friendly broker's role in this initial deal, plunged in with his own cash in October 1869, buying a one-sixth share of the operation from George M. Crocker, an established miller in Minneapolis who had bought out William B. Brown in August. By autumn, the firm had a new name—Gardner, Pillsbury and Crocker —and a new salaried manager, Charles A. Pillsbury. He was to be paid $1,000 a year, plus half of the one-third share of the profits due to the father-son pair. [22]

Though only five years old, the mill Charles would operate was neither financially nor structurally sound. "The townsmen thought they had been sold a turkey, a business as shaky as its machinery," Philip Pillsbury, who knew something about mills, wrote eighty years later.[23] Charles himself would write later in life, "Up to that time, Minneapolis flour was way down at the bottom of the heap, and the mill had been losing money almost steadily. The other fellows in the business rather pitied me, and said that another poor devil had got caught in the milling business of which he would soon get enough."[24]

Charles set up his office in a small wooden shack next to the mill and threw himself into every aspect of the operation. He befriended his co-owners and employees, became acquainted with his competitors, and took particular interest in the farmers who supplied the raw material for his enterprise. Rail transport had not yet asserted its dominance and farmers and millers were not yet strangers to one another. Charles dealt personally with farmers who delivered their wheat by wagonload, and made friends in the process. He amazed his new neighbors by turning a profit in the first year.

But more than the human side of the business appealed to Charles. This New England teacher-language student-businessman developed a keen interest in milling technology. Grandson Philip, who as a young man worked alongside mill employees who had known his grandfather, attested that Charles "was always watching the milling." He soon gained an appreciation of the difficulty that confronted millers of the spring wheat that grew in the cold northern prairie. Its hard, brittle kernels and bran broke into small, rough particles when milled, unlike the fine powder produced by winter wheat grown in Missouri, Kansas, and southern Illinois. Those rough particles were small enough to survive the sifting process, which gave an unappealing speckled look to the finished product. When Minneapolis millers tried to compensate by running their millstones at high speed and pressure, the resulting heat discolored the flour—another undesirable trait.

Charles consulted his fellow millers, who suggested the problem might be traced to an inferior quality of wheat being delivered to the Falls of St. Anthony. Somehow or another, better flour was being produced in Faribault, Northfield, and Hastings. He set out to see for himself, visiting the mills in the small towns south of Minneapolis and bringing back wheat samples to test. The wheat was the same. There must be a difference in the milling practices.

He was on the right track. And after two seasons at the Falls, he had the good fortune to watch as new equipment was installed at the mill owned by his most prominent competitor, Cadwallader C. Washburn. A native of Maine, Washburn was the fourth brother in a large, remarkable family that saw two brothers elected as governors and four sent to Congress. (He himself was governor of Wisconsin at the time.) A resident of LaCrosse, 160 miles downriver from Minneapolis, Washburn never spent more than a few days at a time in

Minnesota, but his vision and investment had guided milling development at the Falls of St. Anthony since 1856.[25] His youngest brother, William, was Cadwallader's man on site at the Falls, along with his cousin Dorilus Morrison, who served as Minneapolis's first mayor.

Unlike the Pillsburys, the Washburn family had no interest in managing mills themselves. They hired that talent, and chose well. In the winter of 1870-71, Washburn managing partner George H. Christian agreed to install a machine of French design that had been tried with some success in Faribault before a flood wrecked the mill that housed it. That machine was a "middlings purifier," the invention of brothers Edmund and Nicholas LaCroix. Edmund brought one to Christian who in turn showed it to George Smith, the Washburn mill stonedresser. Smith made improvements in the design and by the spring of 1871, the new purifier was operational.

Cadwallader C. Washburn, circa 1870.

The LaCroix purifier subjected the "middlings"—the glutinous center of the wheat kernel—that had been partially ground to sifting, while simultaneously blasting it with air from below to lift and scatter the bran. Those middlings that remained, containing the most nutritious elements of the grain, were then subjected to further grinding.[26] The result was a flour that was not only whiter but also more nutritious than anything produced by earlier grinding techniques.

No one was more impressed by this new technology than Charles Pillsbury. He also fully recognized its commercial potential. Therefore, he quickly did two things: hired George Smith away from Washburn to be his head miller and bought another mill.

Next door to the Minneapolis Flouring Mill stood the equally small Alaska Mill, also known as the Taylor Bros. Mill. When it fell into foreclosure in 1870, Uncle John and nephew Charles snapped it up, renamed it the Pillsbury, and ordered that both mills be fitted with the new middlings purifier machine. The Alaska Mill workforce initially resisted the new process. A "regular war" ensued between mill employees and the new owner that "became so great that finally it was found necessary to discharge the head miller of the Taylor." Smith was put in charge of both Pillsbury mills.[27]

"It was in this matter that the pluck of the man was shown," a milling industry journalist wrote admiringly a dozen years later. "With all his small savings invested in the mill, which was yet almost an experiment with him, to invest $10,000 [on the new mill and its equipment] and change its entire system was a much bolder move than the investment of half a million would be at the present time. But the results justified his expectations."[28] The middlings purifier produced a top-grade product, much of which could bring a price of $14 per barrel in New York. Wheat then typically sold for between $.60 and $1.25 per bushel; four and a half bushels of wheat were needed to produce a barrel of flour.[29] "It can easily be seen that Mr. Pillsbury and his partners made money very fast, and it was here that he laid the foundation for his large fortune and extensive milling interests."[30]

In only two years in Minneapolis—and before his thirtieth birthday—Charles had established the business patterns that would serve him and his enterprise for the rest of his life. He was keenly interested in every aspect of both his business and that of his competition. He was eager to employ the latest technology, capable of quick decision-making and willing to trust his instincts. He was quick to recognize talent, and bold in luring it away from the competition. And he aimed for rapid growth through the acquisition of more property. Never would he be content to stand pat.

Charles also exhibited business genius in marketing. Instinctively, it seems, he understood the latter-day concept of branding. With his family's blessing, he put a single name—his own—on the milling enterprise. Beginning in 1871, the company was known as C.A. Pillsbury & Co., regardless of how many family members shared its ownership. He advertised the name heavily, becoming the first miller to place regular advertisements in the *Northwestern Miller* magazine, for example, which served the wholesale and export trade. Charles personally settled on a brand name for the flour his mills produced: Pillsbury's Best. He is credited with designing the distinctive red, white, and blue circular logo, featuring a circle of nail heads, denoting a flour barrel, and the trademark XXXX. It first appeared on every barrel and later on every bag of flour. The four "X"s, it was said, was an attempt to go one better than the XXX symbol used in medieval times to denote the flour so superior that it was reserved for the bread used in the Christian communion ceremony. Those three "X"s represented the three crosses of Calvary, according to legend.[31]

Pillsbury's Best XXXX was first used on March 1, 1873, and was duly registered as a trademark in 1875. That logo would come to be recognized around the world, and is still familiar to grocery shoppers today. It had been registered in fifty-seven countries by 1930.[32]

Charles also understood the importance of a loyal, capable workforce and set out early to secure one for C.A. Pillsbury & Co. Wages for common laborers at Pillsbury were set higher by nearly a third than elsewhere in the city—$1.90 per day at Pillsbury, compared with $1.32 on average in Minneapolis. By 1880, skilled grinders and machine tenders at Pillsbury were paid $3.25 per day, among the most generous manufacturing wages in the city. Unlike other millers, Charles made it his practice never to deduct wages for holidays or occasional brief mill closures, accidental or otherwise. "On the day before Thanksgiving, drayloads of turkeys drew up to the doors of every Pillsbury mill. No man went home that night without a fat turkey under his arm for the family feast the next day," an undated company history relates.[33] In 1883, Charles established what may have been the first employee profit-sharing plan in the Upper Midwest, and one of the first in the nation.[34] He did it, he said in 1891, out of a desire to "more equitably divide the profits between capital and labor. Of course, the continual agitation of the labor question called my attention to the subject, but there was no disaffection among my own employees, so far as I was aware."[35] As long as Charles lived, there would not be.

The nation's major markets took notice of the improved quality of flour coming out of Minneapolis under the new Pillsbury label, and wanted more. Success was sudden for C.A. Pillsbury & Co., and enabled quick recovery from disaster. On Oct. 12, 1872, a fire destroyed the Minneapolis Flouring Mill. It was rebuilt immediately, with its capacity increased by 350 barrels per day. Obtaining credit for rebuilding evidently presented no problem. The Pillsburys—John, George, and Charles continuing to invest together—added two more mills to their operation: the Empire in 1873 and the Anchor in 1875. During this period, they also sold their half-interest in their original Minneapolis Flouring Mill. From that point until 1889, every Pills-bury mill would be entirely family controlled.[36]

Some setbacks dur-ing those years were not as easily remedied. Mary Ann gave birth to the young couple's first son, named for his grandfather George Alfred, on Oct. 4, 1871. The baby boy did not live to see his second Christmas. The cause of his death on December 22, 1872, is not

The Anchor Mill.

known.[37] Count him among the many much-beloved youngsters—a huge number by modern standards—who did not survive childhood illnesses in nineteenth-century America. The awful losses were all too common, touching families in every income and social category. Similarly and tragically common were the deaths of young mothers, often in childbirth or soon thereafter.

A glimpse of Pillsbury business and family life in the sad days after little George's death is preserved in letters written by Frank H. Carleton, Charles's first cousin and his mother's nephew.[38] Frank

Carleton was a Dartmouth graduate who came to Minnesota to seek his fortune soon after graduating from college. His letters to his father, Henry G. Carleton, in Newport, N.H., were written on letterhead stationery bearing the name "Charles A. Pillsbury & Co. Flouring Mill." The first is dated Christmas Day 1872, only three days after the baby's death. The missive makes no mention of any funeral observance, but says, "I came direct to Charlie's, and he gave me a hearty reception. At present, Mr. and Mrs. Stinson are spending the winter with him. They left New Hampshire the day after election, and came directly here."

The presence of Mary Ann's parents from mid-November that year suggests that they may have been aware that their grandson was ailing, and that their daughter needed support. But it is also possible that Charles Stinson came as an investor. Frank Carleton avows that Stinson had acquired property in what became downtown Minneapolis, as had George A. Pillsbury. "The First National Bank of Concord has considerable money invested here, some of it in the mill," he wrote.

Young Frank's enthusiastic assessment of his cousin Charlie's enterprise is notable for its directness: "I find Charlie engaged in the extensive manufacture of flour. He has three mills—and in all together they consume (or will, when the damage done by the fire has been repaired) a million bushels of wheat per year. He turns out each day from his two mills, anywhere from 175 to 225 barrels of flour per day. At present, millers are doing well. I think Charlie is worth from $30,000 to $40,000 now. At least, he is so estimated by the prominent men. In addition to his share in the mills, he has a regular salary of $1,500 from three men, i.e. G.A. Pillsbury, J.S. Pillsbury and Woodbury Fisk—making $4,500 per year, certain. There have been some bad times in the flour business, but the flour manufacturers in this place are all rich." He went on to estimate the net worth of John S. Pillsbury at between $200,000 and $400,000, and described the Pillsbury hardware business as "extensive... wholesale and retail." He estimated Mahala's brother Woodbury Fisk's net worth at half that amount. Such news must have made jaws drop in hardscrabble central New Hampshire.

During 1872 when the family was a threesome, Charles, Mary Ann, and baby George became affiliated with the city's fastest-growing Congregational Church, Plymouth. Founded in 1866, the Minneapolis parish at first used but later dropped the name "First," perhaps out of deference to the First Congregational Church that was flourishing in St. Anthony with the vigorous support of parishioners John and Mahala Pillsbury. But like many things in Minneapolis, Plymouth Church was overtaking its St. Anthony counterpart. Located at Fourth St. and Nicollet Av., it was only the second church in the city to install a pipe organ, in 1868. (The first, at First Universalist Church, was a gift of Cadwallader Washburn in 1866.)

Charles Stinson and his daughter Mary Ann Pillsbury, perhaps during Stinson's Minneapolis stay in the winter of 1872-73.

Mary Ann joined Plymouth Church by transferring her membership from her home church in Dunbarton, N.H., on May 5, 1872. Evidently, she had not joined a church in Montreal. What may be the only surviving personal anecdote about her early days in Minneapolis concerns her attendance at Plymouth Church, some months or maybe years before she officially joined the congregation. "Mrs. Pillsbury often recalled the rustling and fluttering in the pews of old Plymouth Church the first Sunday she appeared wearing her sealskin sacque (a short, loose-fitting coat.) It wasn't new, but it was the first sealskin coat the parish ladies had ever seen," reported a magazine decades later, likely drawing from a story Mary Ann later told to one of her sons.[39]

A week before Mary Ann joined Plymouth Church, Charles was elected a trustee of Plymouth Society, the congregation's fund-raising arm and alternative membership category. Like John at First

Church, Charles held membership in the society, not the congregation as a whole, for his whole life. Charles's bent for leadership in community as well as business affairs is evident in the minutes of Plymouth Society proceedings in 1872. At the meeting at which Charles was elected, the building committee resolved to continue raising money for a new church but not to proceed until $35,000 was pledged. Charles got busy, and by November 1872, "C.A. Pillsbury reported to the trustees that $21,000 had been pledged" toward the $35,000 goal.[40] The gift that put the fund drive over the top: $10,000 from Charles A. Pillsbury.[41] A new church was open for worship at Eighth and Nicollet in October 1875.

Such zeal for building community institutions likely was considered unremarkable by the Pillsburys and other recent transplants from New England. They brought with them what has been described as a "civic consciousness in which pride and a kind of inverted humility were mingled." A historian would describe the young town's civic spirit this way:

> *Social and cultural institutions grew as luxuriantly as they had in the fertile ground "back East," and the local inhabitants watched with pleasure the evolution of a "polished and refined society" at the Falls. They were inordinately proud that the new towns were "peopled from the colleges, court-rooms, pulpits, counting rooms and workshops of the East." Affirming this identification, the "Minnesota Republican" claimed: "We are Yankees by birth and profession, by inclination, education, habits and twang.*[42]

Among the civic institutions these Yankees brought to Minnesota were robust state and local governments, fueled by lively and broadly participatory politics. As the 1870s reached their midpoint, Pillsbury participation in politics was intensifying.

(top) Bridge Square in Minneapolis, 1873. City Hall is on the left.
(bottom) The house John and Mahala built in the late 1870s.

Chapter Three

Our Dear Governor

Life was good for the John Pillsbury family in the 1870s. His nephew Charles had joined him in Minnesota, he and Mahala had become prominent residents of St. Anthony, and in 1877 or thereabouts they began construction on a grand Victorian house at 1005 SE Fifth St. The completed structure was adorned with graceful porches, a stylish porte cochere, ornate fixtures, and an expanse of lawn that ran to eight city lots—ample for the frolic of their four children.[1] A municipal drinking water system had come to Minneapolis in 1871,[2] and the new Pillsbury house undoubtedly took advantage of it.

The bustling Twin Cities—that meant St. Anthony and Minneapolis until 1872—were playing host to an increasing array of lectures, concerts, and other events, both ecclesiastical and secular, many of which engaged the family. The Pence Opera House on the west side of the river offered almost nightly meetings and performances. When St. Anthony and Minneapolis finally merged, the suddenly-much-larger city became a place of greater significance overnight and a destination for entertainers and authors on regional and national tours.

The family circle of the Minnesota Pillsburys was also swelling. Charles and Mary Ann made their home on the Minneapolis side of the river, and on most Sundays they crossed the Hennepin Avenue Bridge for dinner with John and Mahala. Regular dinner guests also included Mahala's brother Woodbury Fisk, his pretty young wife Mary, a native of Maine, and their daughters Lizzie and Mary.[3]

John's first cousins Thomas and George Andrews, who had followed John to Minneapolis in 1855, also would have been frequent visitors—not least because Thomas was married first to Mahala's sister Lizzie, and after her death, to a second sister, Mary.[4] Mahala's brother John and his wife Sarah were on hand long enough in 1870 to be recorded as residing with John and Mahala in that year's federal census. The census-taker wrote that John Fisk was "without employment."

And sometime in the summer or fall of 1870, brother George dispatched his second son, Fred Carleton, a recent high school graduate, to join Charles and John in Minnesota.[5] Fred was ten years younger, taller and fairer than Charles. Fun-loving and sweet-natured, he was barely eighteen when he came to Minneapolis, eager to make his mark in the region Americans still called the Northwest. John put him to work in the hardware store. "The young clerk rapidly made friends for himself and the firm, for he attended strictly to business, treated everyone courteously and impressed all who came to know him as one of the finest types of young businessmen in the city," noted a paper written about thirty-five years later by an unknown author who evidently knew Fred personally. "He had no desire for public office, always refusing to entertain political ambitions urged upon him by his friends."[6]

John's business was booming. The family's original venture, J.S. Pillsbury & Co., had become the region's leading wholesaler and retailer of hardware and industrial equipment of all kinds. Its specialty was the equipment needed for the milling of both timber and grain, but the wares it stocked were much more extensive. Advertising from the 1870s boasts of merchandise including "Boston Belting Co.'s rubber belt and hose," French and German plate and window glass, "P. Jewell & Son's leather belt," and assorted English and American shelf iron and steel materials.

Minnesota's growth after the Civil War resumed its pre-1861 rate, and the hardware trade expanded apace with the state. The state's population grew 64 percent in the 1860s, and an astounding 77 percent in the 1870s.[7] That circumstance gave John Pillsbury the opportunity for a profitable venture, but seizing and capitalizing on that opportunity was his own doing. "It is significant that from the first, Mr. Pillsbury was successful," a journalist who knew John well wrote shortly after his death. "It is said of him that in these early days, he held his trade because he never misrepresented the quality or value of his goods, and because he was uniformly courteous to people of every class and condition, and very early manifested those warm sympathies which so enriched his later years."[8]

The store by 1871 had moved from its original St. Anthony location to downtown Minneapolis—39 Bridge Square, just west of the Hennepin Avenue Bridge.[9] It was positioned between sawmills (upstream) and flour mills (downstream), in the midst of burgeoning retail and residential districts on both sides of the river. It was across the street from City Hall and two blocks from the city's first subscription library, the Athenaeum, where the Pillsburys were undoubtedly enrolled.[10] John customarily walked across the bridge to work.

By the mid-1870s, hardware and flour milling were by no means Pillsbury's only business ventures. As soon as he was clear of the debt caused by the 1857 fire, John began investing heavily. The chief object of his acquisitions was timberland in northeastern Minnesota. The extent of his holdings at their peak has never been established precisely, but an 1883 account describes the Pillsburys as "among the most extensive owners of pine lands and manufacturers of lumber in the Northwest." In 1880 Charles Pillsbury set up the Gull River Lumber Company, perhaps in concert with his father and uncle, ten miles west of the newly-founded railroad town of Brainerd, and at its height the Gull River mill produce 175,000 board-feet daily during the sawing season."[11]

John also invested in Minneapolis banks, and would eventually be a director of five of them. Following the lead of his brother George, he bought a stake in railroads, and would become a director in three rail firms.[12] He bought a large enough share of the struggling St. Anthony Falls Water Power Co. to be a director and secretary of that chronically troubled concern in 1870.[13] Due largely to ill-management, the St. Anthony firm increasingly took a back seat to the Minneapolis Mill Co., its counterpart on the west side of the Mississippi, but it remained a leading force city development on the east side of the river. In 1870 it offered for sale a thousand city lots and various riverside mill sites "for the manufacture of lumber."

Business was good—but for a son of Captain John Pillsbury of Sutton, N.H., business was never sufficient for a good life. Public service was also necessary. That's why, as he had since 1863, John stayed attentive to the governance of the University of Minnesota. And in odd-numbered years—state election years in that period—his name was on the ballot for election as state senator from St. Anthony District 4. He won each election handily. Each January (the Legislature met annually during these years, and state senators served two-year terms) John would rent a room at the stately four-story Metropolitan Hotel at Third and Washington Avenues in St. Paul and settle in for two intense months of lawmaking and politicking.[14] Perhaps he deemed the ten miles between the Capitol at Tenth and Wabasha in St. Paul and his St. Anthony home too long and unreliable to traverse twice a day during Minnesota's most inclement months. No doubt the experienced senator had also become aware that a good share of the Legislature's real business took place after hours in the capital city's hotels and restaurants. John Pillsbury was a man of modest tastes; he would not have boarded in St. Paul merely to join in frivolity. "He was not a politician, and never adopted the unworthy methods of some politicians, but was quiet and unobtrusive in all his habits," a lifelong friend said of him years later.[15] But as chair of the powerful Senate Finance Committee beginning in 1868,[16] he could not remain on the sidelines even if he wanted to. That position of responsibility put him in the thick of things.

Much of the political action in the early 1870s in state government was within Pillsbury's own dominant Republican Party. The Democratic Party had a stronghold in St. Paul and a popular leader in Henry H. Sibley, the Dakota War general who was chosen to be Minnesota's first governor, but it was otherwise confined to the role of loyal opposition at the statehouse as well as in the local governments taking shape throughout Minnesota.

The Democrats' state platforms and those of the Grand Old Party were often quite similar. Minnesota Democrats were not much enamored of "states' rights," the segregationist rallying cry voiced by Democrats in the states of the former Confederacy that Minnesota Democrats would vigorously oppose in the twentieth Century. Third parties were still decades away from having much influence.[17] But one colorful populist, Ignatius Donnelly, attracted a following that at times took on the characteristics of a third party, as Donnelly went his mercurial way in and out of the Republican fold over several decades.

The fault line that divided Minnesota Republicans in the 1870s tended to be generational.[18] The larger of two factions was made up of New England and mid-Atlantic pioneer stock. They were men (women could not yet vote) who came to Minnesota during its territorial days, launched it into statehood, and sought to maintain their grip on its levers of power. The group's champion was the venerable Pennsylvania native and former Whig congressman Alexander Ramsey, Minnesota's first territorial governor and second governor after statehood, who was serving the second year of his second term in the U.S. Senate in 1870.

Not every Republican was pleased by Ramsey's political longevity. Younger men, many of

Alexander Ramsey, circa 1870.

them Civil War veterans, farmers, and small business owners, believed they were being denied the political opportunity they deserved. They found ready allies among the ranks of new immigrants, many of them Scandinavians who brought with them an appreciation for broadly participatory democracy and vigorous government. Organizationally, the upstarts drew strength from the Grange movement, a national network of local social and political clubs in which farmers and small business folk—both men and women—gathered to advance their mutual interests.[19]

These younger Republicans grumbled about a Ramsey "dynasty," and, in 1873, rallied around one of their own for governor: Cushman Kellogg Davis, a St. Paul lawyer born in New York and reared in Wisconsin. The Ramsey group promoted William D. Washburn, youngest brother of Wisconsin governor and St. Anthony Falls milling magnate Cadwallader C. Washburn. William had been a one-term state representative in 1871 and surveyor-general for the state during the Civil War (an appointment arranged by another older brother, President Lincoln advisor Elihu Washburne.[20]) Handsome and charismatic, William Washburn's rise was promoted not only by old-line Minnesotans but also by national party leaders who believed the prominent Washburn name guaranteed electoral success. (Four Washburn brothers ultimately served in Congress; two were governors.) But the advantage of a familiar name was not persuasive to a majority of delegates to the 1873 Republican state convention. Davis was the better orator, and bested Washburn for the party's endorsement on the fourth ballot. Still, the GOP rank-and-file was slow to warm to Davis. He won election as governor by a narrow 4,460-vote margin out of 77,022 votes cast.[21]

Cushman Davis in the early 1870s.

Where state Sen. John Pillsbury stood as his party feuded is not entirely clear. His age, background, and social and political standing gave him natural ties to Ramsey and his crowd. While the Pillsbury name in the early 1870s was not yet associated with "big business," the family's entrepreneurial reach was rapidly lengthening. So might have been John's association with the large multi-state enterprises that younger Republicans increasingly viewed with suspicion.

But as a merchant and miller, Pillsbury had common cause with the younger group on a major issue. Like them, he had a love/hate relationship with the railroads. While Minnesotans clamored for more and better rail transportation, by the early 1870s they were also suspicious that they were being charged unnecessarily high rates to ship their produce to eastern markets and import finished consumer goods to the state. Many believed that whole cities and states were charged discriminatory rates, while other communities where railroad owners had business interests received discounts. Davis made state regulation of railroads a major theme in his campaign.[22] In principle if not in every particular, Sen. Pillsbury likely agreed.

Pillsbury and Davis saw eye-to-eye on another matter of importance to the state's future. In the same year in which statehood was granted, the brand-new state constitution was amended to allow the state to issue $2,275,000 in bonds to finance a loan to railroad companies. In exchange for state-backed financing, rail interests promised that a network of track would be built quickly in the as-yet undeveloped state. That promise was not kept in the aftermath of the Panic of 1857. The railroads took the money, but laid little track. Their default was plain by 1860. Angry Minnesota legislators not only refused to service the debt owed to bondholders. They also attempted to make repudiation of the railroad bonds binding state policy. They submitted to voters in the 1860 general election a constitutional amendment requiring that no state funds be expended to retire a debt that had proven so fruitless, and that no tax could be levied in the future for that purpose without prior voter approval. The amendment was approved. But forward-thinking state leaders soon saw the error of that vindictive policy. It seriously impaired the young state's ability to raise the borrowed capital required to build its infrastructure. Investors no longer trusted Minnesota. In John Pillsbury's eyes, the state had chosen an indefensible, intolerable position. But as one among many state senators, he lacked the clout to change the policy. John undoubtedly cheered Gov. Davis as he tried unsuccessfully to convince the Legislature to initiate a repeal of the ill-advised constitutional prohibition.[23]

Pillsbury played a bit part in the great political drama of the 1875 legislative session, and his contribution to that episode suggests that he may have been adroitly maintaining positive associations with both the Ramsey and the Davis camps. On Jan. 14, only one week after the session commenced, the Legislature took up its constitutionally mandated duty to elect a U.S. senator. (Popular election of U.S. senators did not commence until 1914.) Sen. Alexander Ramsey's second term ended on March 4, 1875. He wanted a third term. But Gov. Davis wanted his seat. An acrimonious two days of balloting were required within the Republican caucus before Ramsey was chosen over Davis as its candidate. Sentiment was also split within the "non-Republican" caucus of Democrats, independents, and third-party legislators. Their far-from-unanimous choice was Ignatius Donnelly. When those two candidates vied before the entire Legislature on Jan. 19, caucus ranks did not hold. Votes for both Ramsey and Donnelly fell well short of the seventy-four votes needed to elect a senator. Davis came in third in the initial balloting. Balloting continued on succeeding days, then weeks, in an atmosphere of increasing acrimony and frustration. As January turned to February and the daylight noticeably lengthened, supporters of first Donnelly, then Davis and Ramsey, asked the principals to withdraw and sought out possible dark-horse candidates who would allow their names to be floated for the seat. Among those found willing to be nominated: John S. Pillsbury.[24] He wasn't the winning horse. On Feb. 19, the Senate seat finally went to the chief justice of the state Supreme Court, Samuel J.R. McMillan of Stillwater. But the notion that the respected veteran state senator from Minneapolis East might consent to serve in statewide office had been planted in the right political minds.

Governor Davis surprised Minnesotans after the 1875 legislative session adjourned with an announcement that he would not seek a second term. He wanted to go to Washington and was only interested in the governorship as a stepping stone to the Senate. Failing to achieve that goal, he wanted to return to the more lucrative practice of law and bide his time. (His patience would be rewarded; he was elected to the U.S. Senate in 1887 and served two terms.) In the weeks after Davis's announcement, when Republican clubs and Republican-leaning newspapers around the state talked about the governor's race, they frequently mentioned John Pillsbury. By the time the state convention assembled on July 28, enthusiasm was so widespread that Pillsbury was endorsed for governor on a single ballot, by a party more united than anyone involved in the Senate battle six months earlier could have predicted.[25] His election followed in November with similar ease, "as a matter of course," wrote his friend and neighbor, University of Minnesota president William Watts Folwell.[26] Pillsbury defeated Democrat D. L. Buell of Houston County by a 12,000-vote margin out of 84,000 votes cast. He became governor so naturally, one observer wrote three decades later, that the office was won "without any effort upon his part or any of the usual accompaniments of candidacy and canvass."[27] Anyone who knows Minnesota politics would advise against taking such comments at face value. His admirers more likely were saying that John Pillsbury was so skillful politically that he made his election look easy.

John made a major business move in 1875, perhaps because he was running for governor and recognized that he stood a good chance of winning. Then again, the move may simply have been in recognition of the flour bonanza that had come to Minneapolis. John understood business timing, and knew that the time had come to maximize his holdings in milling. Whatever the reasoning behind the move, John decided to sell his hardware business after twenty years in the trade. Its new owners were brothers Thomas and Edwin Janney and their brother-in-law Samuel Moles, who had entered the retail hardware business in Minneapolis in 1866. Janney and Moles Hardware was situated in downtown Minneapolis on Washington Avenue between Nicollet and Minnetonka (now Marquette) Avenues, about three blocks from J.S. Pillsbury & Co. Acquiring the Pillsbury firm allowed the Janneys to expand into the wholesale business. New partners came and old ones retired and died, until in the twentieth century the store was known as Janney, Semple, Hill & Co.[28] Its Pillsbury acquisition allowed it to claim at the time of Minnesota's 1958 statehood centennial that it was the only Minneapolis retailer to have been in continuous operation since territorial days. It became part of the Coast-to-Coast Hardware chain in 1960, and finally disappeared in 1965.

John quickly invested his proceeds from the store's sale in another flour mill, the Anchor. Built in 1874 with a 500-barrel-per-day capacity, it was acquired solely by John and then leased to C.A. Pillsbury & Co. A few years earlier, it would have been one of the larger mills on the Minneapolis waterpower canal. But in 1874,

Cadwallader Washburn raised the ante. He started construction that year on a 3,000-barrel-per-day behemoth that would be known simply as the Washburn "A," about a block away from the cluster of Pillsbury mills.[29] That separation would prove fortuitous a few years later. For now, John, Charles and young Fred—who took a one-seventh interest in the milling company when his uncle sold the hardware business—intently eyed every Washburn move. They aimed to do more than simply keep up with the competition. They intended to beat it.

But beginning on Jan. 7, 1876, John had larger concerns. He became governor at a time when much of the state was thriving, and demanding more public amenities and services from their government. To better meet that demand, Gov. Pillsbury sought to set the state's credit rating to rights. His inaugural address urged payment of the 1858 railroad bonds that the state was still constitutionally bound to repudiate. Proceeds from the sale of

Gov. John S. Pillsbury, 1878.

state lands could retire the debt, he said. He recommended a number of cost-saving measures for state government, including shortening legislative sessions from sixty to forty calendar days, switching from annual to biennial sessions, limiting the printing of minutiae in public reports, and the elimination of one or more state offices. Notably, he also urged shrinking the Legislature from two chambers to one.[30] He would not be the last in his family to favor that change.

Pillsbury's inaugural address boasted about a "vigorous commonwealth of 600,000 people equipped with all the appliances and comforts of civilized life."[31] But circumstances in the state's southwestern quadrant were not nearly that positive. For three straight years, beginning in 1873, crops, orchards, and gardens in several dozen counties had been wiped out by a massive invasion of Rocky Mountain locusts—the detested grasshopper. It had become a recurring plague of biblical proportions, one so severe that it strained the imaginations and credulity of Minnesotans who did not experience it for themselves.

Periodic mass invasions of locusts native to the eastern foothills of the Rocky Mountains were known to European-American settlers since explorer Jonathan Carver's warning about the swarms in his "Travels" in 1767. He considered them "septennial," genetically programmed to return to the northern Mississippi watershed every seven years. In truth, the insects were not that predictable. But Carver had it right when he wrote that they "do a great deal of mischief."[32] They "ate every green thing" when they came to the Red River Valley in 1818 and 1819,[33] and were similarly voracious in 1851 in the Red River Valley and in 1856 and 1857 in the northern Mississippi region. Minnesota River valley crops were devoured by invasions in 1864 and 1865.

The 1870s infestation began on June 12, 1873. "My younger brother and I were in school that day . . . and about two o'clock the great cloud of grasshoppers came down," recalled one settler. "We rushed out of school and started home. We had to hold our hands over our eyes to keep them from hitting us in our eyes."[34] The swarm made a whirring, mechanical sound that some witnesses described as a locomotive, others as the sound of a thousand scissors all cutting at once. In her autobiographical novel, *On the Banks of Plum Creek*, Laura Ingalls Wilder describes being barefoot as a child on her family's homestead near Walnut Grove, Minnesota, unable to step anywhere without crushing a grasshopper.[35]

Before the year was out, the vermin had infected thirteen counties in the state's southwestern corner, and done an estimated $3 million in damage to crops, mostly wheat. The state's wheat harvest was only down 2 percent in total that year—a testament to a bountiful harvest in counties spared by the bugs. But in the worst affected western counties, wheat yields dropped by almost one third, and oats, barley and corn took similarly large hits.[36] The infestation's distribution was not uniform. Some farms and even whole towns were unscathed. But where the grasshoppers lit, whole fruit trees, clothing hung out to dry, hatbands coated with sweat, and even the wooden handles of hoes and forks were consumed—the latter, twentieth-century entomologists explained, because they were

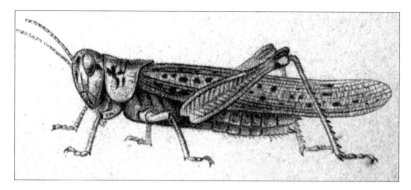

A Rocky Mountain locust, as sketched in an 1877 federal entomology report.

coated by a residue of salt from human perspiration. [37]

When word of the blight reached Minneapolis and St. Paul, Minnesotans did what they've always done when natural disaster strikes within the state's borders. They organized to collect and distribute relief supplies. Henry Sibley, who had been the state's first governor but no longer held elected office, took charge of the relief committee of the St. Paul Chamber of Commerce, and set out to determine how many people were in need of both provisions to get through the winter of 1874 and seed for the next season's crop. A canvass by county officials that first year of the plague found 600 families in need of assistance. Sibley distributed all the donations he had, found them insufficient, and went to Gov. Davis to request more from state coffers.

Sibley probably approached the governor reluctantly, knowing full well that state coffers had been under strain since the national panic of the previous year, which had depressed prices, incomes—and tax collections. Though the downturn was less worrisome in Minnesota than in Eastern states, a wave of government fiscal restraint was being felt. The government assistance Sibley was seeking also ran against the grain of the belief, widely held at the time, that hard work, not charity, was the rightful guarantor of self-sufficiency, if not prosperity, and that easy bail-outs squelched individual ambition. Those ideas applied particularly to farmers. Though an industrial boom was on the horizon, Americans still held that farmers were a "chosen people," the nation's agents of development and destiny. [38]

At government-financed poor farms and poorhouses, it was presumed that lazy indigents were being put to work. Other assistance could be left to private individuals and organizations. Natural disasters provoked a more generous response, but even here, it was customary for governments to parse victims into two categories: the "deserving," afflicted through no fault of their own, and "paupers," whose poverty was considered their own fault and whose squalor government aid would only encourage. Sibley ran headlong into those attitudes at the 1874 Legislature. He persuaded lawmakers to provide a mere $5,000 for the necessities of life for grasshopper victims. Disbursements were to be in the form of supplies, not cash, so as to control how taxpayers' dollars would be used by the needy.[39] Notably, legislators provided five times as much, $25,000, for the purchase of seed by farmers whose seed grain was lost to locusts.[40] Legislators were more interested in restoring farmers' self-sufficiency—and in supplying raw material for Minnesota's burgeoning flour industry—than in keeping the afflicted and their children adequately fed.

The Legislature was also acting out of the optimistic view that locust invasion was a one-time phenomenon. It was not. Eggs laid in 1873 hatched early and abundantly in 1874, and that year's devastation was worse. More than twice as many counties were affected, and by the winter of 1874-75, Sibley was back at the governor's door. Between 1,200 and 1,500 families were "totally impoverished" as a result of locusts, he reported. This time, Davis asked the state's county boards of commissioners to contribute relief funds. Ramsey County put up $5,000. But only eight of the state's other 86 counties followed its example. The 1875 Legislature was slightly more generous than its predecessor: $20,000 for provisions, $75,000 for seed. But rigid rules limited the distribution of provisions to those in the most abject circumstances, and as a result, some of the funds went unspent.

As John Pillsbury was campaigning for governor in the summer of 1875, 19 counties were again watching and despairing as clouds of locusts devoured their crops. By year three of the infestation, the southwestern corner of the state was losing population and the stubborn souls who remained were in great duress. W. W. Folwell would remember that in the affected areas, "generous neighbors had divided their substance with the less fortunate until whole communities had been reduced to a common destitution."[41] Pillsbury served on a relief committee appointed by Gov. Davis, and heard testimony on the crisis before his Senate Finance Committee. He had to be conversant with the dire circumstances locusts were causing. Had John been running for governor in the twentieth century, a relief and recovery plan for that distressed region almost certainly would have been a prominent part of the gubernatorial campaign. But this was a different time. If John made the grasshopper blight an agenda item in his campaign, he did so in a way that warranted no mention in a history of the Minnesota Republican Party written twenty years later.[42] Pillsbury also avoided the subject in his 1876 inaugural address.

But the hoppers were back with a vengeance in 1876, and could no longer be avoided. Forty counties were hit in two waves. The first, out of Canada, destroyed the rich wheat crop in the Red River Valley; the second, out of Dakota Territory, afflicted west-central counties. The governor made at least one harvest visit to the stricken fields.[43] As a businessman in the milling business and as a humanitarian, he had to be moved by what he saw. Yet in an address at the end of August, Gov. Pillsbury made clear his distaste for "weakening the habit of self-reliance" by providing government handouts. There was no hint of the possibility of a special session to appropriate more relief dollars. Instead, he sought to step up efforts to eradicate the problem at its source. He made the grasshopper Minnesota Public Enemy #1. Farmers were urged to plow infested fields thoroughly to destroy locust eggs; crush newly hatched larvae with rollers; burn piles of straw and prairie grass near hatching grounds. Scaring the critters away with "loud and discordant noises made by striking tin vessels and by shrieking and yelling with the voice" was also deemed practical.[44] Perhaps out of awareness that these were feeble measures—the last, laughably so—Pillsbury invited his fellow Midwestern governors and the region's leading entomologists to a summit on the scourge which convened in Omaha, Nebraska, on Oct. 26, 1876. The event was widely covered in the press and resulted in a popular pamphlet—but unfortunately, it produced no additional insights regarding how to keep the locust swarms away.

The governor may have felt a nagging sense of futility after the Omaha conference. Later in life, he told an interviewer that upon his return he dispatched an aide to the western part of the state to provide him with an update on conditions there. Not satisfied with the report and increasingly disturbed by letters he was receiving from impoverished farmers, Pillsbury decided to head west to see for himself, alone and unannounced. He traveled by horse and buggy, and was at times on horseback, much as he had been ten years earlier while raising money for the University of Minnesota. "He first went to Worthington, traveling incognito, and from there, though the weather was severely cold, drove into the country," the interviewer wrote. The governor sought out the writer of a letter that had particularly moved him: "This farmer was scantily clothed, as was his family, and their food consisted of nothing but potatoes." Others he met had sold or consumed all their livestock.

In one notable case, while the governor was questioning a proud sufferer, who had more than once refused proffered aid, a little child, whose tender limbs were exposed through her tattered garments, suddenly entered the room. "You refuse help for yourself," said the governor, "but how about your children?" The poor man struggled hard for self-control, and, catching the child in his arms, exclaimed in broken accents, "My children, my children! Oh God, help my poor children!" The governor, too deeply affected to prolong the interview, pressed a bank-bill into the parent's hand and hurried away: and it is needless to add that further succor speedily reached that suffering household." [45] Starvation was stalking the prairie that winter. "As he drove from house to house, he left small amounts of money, thus giving temporary relief." [46]

John returned home for Christmas a man conflicted. He had been raised on both the gospel of the Good Samaritan and the Puritan work ethic. He wanted to relieve human misery, but feared creating a dependency that would only prolong it. Somewhere on the long ride to Minneapolis, his compassion overtook his restraint. He had to do something more. He devised a plan that would only minimally involve state government. On Dec. 20, 1876, he issued a "State of Minnesota Executive Department Appeal" to "the pastors of the several religious denominations; to the officers of the various charitable and benevolent associations; and to the humane and philanthropic, individually and collectively, throughout the state of Minnesota."

The message threw the moral authority of his office—but not the contents of the state treasury—into an enlarged relief effort. He went to some length to convince his fellow Minnesotans that the locust victims had run afoul of a natural disaster not of their own making. His appeal read in part:

> *Repeated applications for relief have been made to me for months past, by persons claiming to be sufferers from grasshopper ravages in various frontier counties of this State. Although these appeals were apparently supported by various concurrent representations, they were received with some distrust on account of the abuses frequently resulting from the practices of unauthorized and unworthy solicitors of public aid.*
>
> *In order, therefore, to ascertain beyond question the actual condition of these people, I have visited many of them in their homes, and verified by personal intercourse and observation the worthy character of the sufferers, and the urgent necessity for their speedy succor for impending and extreme destitution.*
>
> *Many localities in the frontier counties of the southwestern portion of this state have sustained an almost total loss of crops for four years in succession, and the people who have suffered these constant ravages have been compelled to mortgage not only their farms but their entire stock and household goods to procure means to avert starvation from their families. Most of the improvident and unscrupulous persons who were disposed to resort to begging and to trade upon the distress of their neighbors have been forced to absent themselves, and those who remain are among the very best people in the state. Indeed, their humble pride and noble spirit of self-dependence, as evidenced by their indisposition to reveal the full extent of their poverty, appeal to the worthiest impulses of our common nature.*
>
> *Instances are not infrequent of strong men reduced to extreme poverty, who, in behalf of still more destitute neighbors, persistently disclaim any need of aid for themselves; while the spectacle of parents who maintain themselves in faith and hope, but break down at any allusion to their half-naked children, is such as to touch the hardest hearts. Many of these people are living upon a single article of food—in some instances flour, in others potatoes, and not infrequently bran or shorts.*

They possess, variously, from 20 to 50 pounds of flour per family, or a like quantity of inferior food, as their sole dependence until the coming of another crop. Unless relieved, they must reach the point of starvation before the winter is half gone.[47]

Gov. Pillsbury invoked the season, then asked the state's churches to set aside a day during the Christmas celebration to collect contributions for the sufferers. He asks individuals and associations to "do what they can." Money, clothing, and foodstuffs are all welcome, he wrote. He closed with a personal vow: "I propose, myself, to revisit the destitute localities, to personally distribute the contributions, and to carefully seek out the most necessitous and worthy recipients."

If Pillsbury ever doubted the power of a governor's bully pulpit, those doubts were erased in the days following his appeal. He rented one storeroom, then another, to contain the outpouring of goods that

First Lady Mahala Fisk Pillsbury.

came to his office in response. He enlisted his best lieutenant, Mahala. Together, they and their household staff—and, undoubtedly, their four school-aged children and other relatives, employees, and friends—spent evenings and weekends sorting the donations and preparing them for railroad shipment west. "The idea of personal work…seems to have been one of Gov. Pillsbury's prominent traits," a journalist would later write of this episode.[48] Personally sorting contributions and packing them for shipment west appealed to his ideal of servant leadership. The task was not small, which likely made it all the more satisfying of Pillsbury's work ethic. Provisions sufficient for six thousand families were gathered.[49]

If these trying times took a personal toll on John Pillsbury, he gave no visible sign of distress. That wasn't his nature, a New Hampshire acquaintance would say when they were both old men:

He always possessed the happy faculty of doing his work eas-
ily; he never got excited, and always commanded his temper. In the
most excited crowd, he never lost his self-poise, and was always quiet
and unruffled. Nor could such labors have fallen to more capable or
willing hands, or have been more assiduously and conscientiously per-
formed. While the most paternal of all Minnesota's executives, Gover-
nor Pillsbury was happy in extending timely aid to the people without
undermining their self-dependence. He elevated their moral sense while
relieving their personal wants.[50]

Good as his word, John made another trip on horseback or perhaps in a one-horse rig to the state's southwestern corner in January.
On that trip, his great-nephew Philip Pillsbury related decades later,
the governor came upon a settler on foot with no overcoat near Windom, the Cottonwood County seat. Questioning revealed that he had
no means to buy a coat. Pillsbury gave the man his own coat, and rode
coatless to a Windom hotel—a heroic and dangerous act in January
on the Minnesota prairie. That episode was widely recounted, and was
dismissed as "romantic" by one latter-day historian.[51] But the Pillsbury
Company's archives include a letter from E.E. Gillam, a Windom merchant, to Philip Pillsbury in 1946 that confirms the story.

I was a boy here in the years of our grasshopper days. When our
crops were destroyed for four years and your grandfather (sic) was our
good governor. Some of the settlers out on these vast prairies were cold
and hungry. Our dear Governor Pillsbury came here at Windom
alone one time and went out in the country to call on some of our
settlers to find out conditions for himself. He was coming back from
his visit to the homes late in the afternoon, and it was a very cold
day in January when he met a man with an ox team and saw that
the man did not have an overcoat on. He stopped him and talked
with him and found that the man had no overcoat and no money to
buy one with. Your grandfather took off his coat and gave it to him,
and came into town without his overcoat.
Shortly after this visit a car of flour and meat also clothing came
from St. Paul for the settlers. I was one of a group of boys at the depot

*where this car came, and quite a crowd of people were getting relief
that day, and there was rejoicing. . .*

*An old lady who now lives on a farm out quite a ways from
Windom called on me one day and said to me, Mr. Gillam, . . . I
want to say that was true what you said about the overcoat, because I
was the hired girl in that little old hotel at the time, and I waited on
the governor at the supper table that evening after he came back.*[52]

Tales of Gov. Pillsbury's personal philanthropy traveled far, and
gave him a reputation for compassion in the face of disaster. But
despite his personal generosity, he remained opposed to employing
state government as a relief agency. He asked the 1877 Legislature to
finance bounties for dead grasshoppers, an entomological commission, a reward for best design of a machine of steel and tarpaper to
dig out and eradicate locust eggs (a "hopperdozer"), and authorization for townships to levy a tax to pay for locust-retarding firebreaks
and ditches. He did not ask for an appropriation for direct aid to
the victims.[53] But the Legislature provided anyway: $5,000 more for
relief; $75,000 for seed grain loans; abatement of penalties for late
property taxes in affected counties; and permission to the counties to
conduct referenda to levy a tax for grasshopper destruction measures.
Pillsbury approved of offering loans, not grants, for seed grain because
he believed it "preserved the respect of the beneficiaries," his friend
Folwell explained.[54]

In April, as the weather warmed and locust eggs began to hatch,
Gov. Pillsbury did one more thing that lived long in Minnesota memory. At the urging of religious leaders, and in keeping with old New
England practice, he declared a state day of fasting and prayer for an
end to the grasshopper trouble. April 26 was designated for Minnesotans "to withdraw from their ordinary pursuits and in their homes
and places of public worship, with contrite hearts, to beseech the
mercy of God for the sins of the past, and His blessing upon the wor-
thier aims of the future." The official proclamation called on citizens
to "humbly invoke, for the efforts we make in our own defense, guid-
ance of that hand which alone is adequate to stay the 'pestilence that
walketh in darkness and the destruction that wasteth at noonday.'"[55] A

summons to prayer by the state's chief executive would have been roundly criticized in the mid-twentieth century, and it met with a decidedly mixed reaction at the time. But where the grasshoppers had ruined crops for four straight seasons, Pillsbury's day of prayer was welcomed, and widely observed. "The different religious denominations joined together in the observance of the day; there was no clash of creed; all sectarian differences were lost sight of temporarily," an observer would recall a few decades later.[56] But in Minneapolis, at the ever-busy Falls of St. Anthony, only the Pillsbury mills fell silent on the appointed day. "No miracle was wrought," Folwell would record.[57]

That, however, is not the legend that survived. In the southern third of the state, the warm spring day of prayer was followed a day later by a sudden storm of sleet and snow. In some portions of the state, a late-season freeze killed young grasshoppers. "In some sections it is reported that all the young hoppers have been frozen to death and the eggs are rotten," the *Faribault Republican* reported.[58]

The April storm was a foretaste of a wet spring. More eggs rotted in the ground, while crops got a good start. Meanwhile, an invention called a "tar-pan" was proving effective at dislodging and catching young locusts when it was dragged by rope over growing grain. It was the sort of breakthrough Pillsbury had been hoping for—one that would allow him to provide meaningful assistance, short of dependency-inducing handouts. He telegraphed county officials: He would personally supply the materials for tar-pans if they would provide for their assembly and distribution out of county funds. Twenty-nine counties eagerly agreed. Soon 56,000 pounds of sheet iron and 3,000 barrels of coal tar were on their way to western county seats, courtesy of Gov. Pillsbury's personal donation and the unspent balance of relief funds appropriated by the Minnesota Legislature. Railroads were persuaded to ship the materials without charge.

Maybe it was the tar-pan, or the heavy rains, or the late spring freeze, or the day of prayer. For whatever reason, locusts were decidedly fewer in number in the summer of 1877, and they were also behaving differently. Reports reached the Capitol of swarms of young locusts rising from their hatching fields and forming a high-flying cloud that moved westward *en masse,* rather than merely hopping to an adjacent acre. The Rocky Mountain locusts were heading home.

In the minds of many of his fellow Minnesotans, Pillsbury and his day of prayer had been the motivating force. That summer, he was unanimously re-nominated for a second term by his Republican Party amid "unusual harmony and good feeling."[59] The 1877 harvest produced the largest wheat crop yet seen in the Gopher State. And in November, Pillsbury swamped his Democratic opponent, W. L. Banning, winning nearly 60 percent of the vote. A poem written twenty-two years later about the end of the grasshopper scourge quotes John Pillsbury as saying of the aftermath of his day of prayer: "And the very next night it turned cold, and froze every grasshopper in the state stiff; froze 'em right up solid, sir. . . Well sir, that was over twenty years ago, and grasshoppers don't appear to have been bothering us very much since." The poem took on a life of its own, to the distress of John's friend and defender, William Folwell. "From an intimacy of thirty-five years, the author does not believe that Governor Pillsbury ever talked in that style," Folwell sniffed.[60]

More mundane affairs of state also occupied a large amount of the governor's attention, and may have been a welcome diversion from worry about marauding clouds of insects. Perhaps because he was a businessman, not an attorney, John enjoyed studying the evolving bureaucracy in Minnesota government and proposing ways to improve it. He promoted several constitutional changes aimed at more efficient government—line-item veto of spending bills (approved by the voters in 1876); two-year terms for state representatives and four-year terms for state senators (1877); biennial rather than annual sessions of the Legislature (1877); the creation of a state board of canvassers to supervise and certify the counting of ballots after an election (1877)[61] and a move to biennial elections (initiated in 1879 but not enacted until 1883.) [62] In 1878, he supported financing of the fourth and final addition to the state's first Capitol. What started as a plain, unimposing structure in 1853 had become a gracious statehouse, with north, south, east, and west wings and a central lobby topped with a bell tower and a modest dome. At Pillsbury's urging, the 1878 Legislature created the Office of the Public Examiner,

Minnesota's first state Capitol showing the addition in 1878.

an in-house auditor of financial records at state agencies, state-chartered institutions, including banks, and local governments. The first occupant of the office, a St. Paul banker named Henry Knox, soon proved the position's worth. Sloppy, inaccurate, and dishonest bookkeeping were all in ample supply, especially in county courthouses. Knox went about the state, visiting every bank, institution, and office in his jurisdiction, and wrote orders for correction that had the weight of the governor's full backing. By 1881, Pillsbury could report to the Legislature, "No single act of legislation in this state has ever been productive of more good in purifying the public service . . . than the creation of this Office of Public Examiner."[63]

It was a strong record, and earned John an honor none of his seven predecessors had been given—his party's nomination for a third term. "His businesslike administration had given general satisfaction throughout the state," noted an 1896 Minnesota Republican Party history.[64] Even St. Paul Republicans, who initially were wary of a merchant-miller from their municipal rival Minneapolis, had come to appreciate Pillsbury's even-handed administration of state government, "showing as much interest in his official conduct in the welfare of St. Paul as in that of his own city," the same source said. A two-term limit for Minnesota's governor was set in tradition, not law. The pattern could be freely broken. Still, some in his party grumbled that three terms were too many and that other leaders deserved a chance. Pillsbury won a first-ballot endorsement at the GOP convention, but he had to fend off four other candidates to do so.

In rural areas, one other factor cut into Pillsbury's support among his fellow Republicans. He had become incessant in pressing the Legislature and the voters to finally honor and pay the holders of the railroad bonds the state had issued in 1858. In Honest John Pillsbury's mind, not honoring a contractual debt was shameful, "far more damaging to the state than grasshoppers," he told the 1878 Legislature.[65] He took that message to every political assembly, church meeting, civic club, and business gathering he attended.[66] But in the Minnesota countryside by the late 1870s, resentment of the railroads had become as habitual as complaints about the weather. Paying off the bonds would not have enriched the railroads, who had already long since received their money—a fact that may have been lost on some opponents of Pillsbury's position. But it would have removed a blot on Minnesota's credit-worthiness and enabled more borrowing—most likely, the idea's critics reckoned, for the further benefit of railroads. That prospect lacked popular appeal. In 1877, the state's voters were given a chance by the Legislature to erase the old debt via an exchange of state land for bonds. The voters refused by more than a 3-to-1 margin. But even overwhelming popular sentiment against his position would not silence John Pillsbury. He shrewdly told the 1878 Legislature that the voters had merely disapproved of the *method* by which the bonds would be repaid, not the repayment itself. He pressed on. By the 1879 fall campaign, there was some reason to believe that his message was winning support. The Democratic Party and its gubernatorial candidate, Edmund Rice, remained curiously silent on the subject during the campaign. "They were not willing to openly antagonize Gov. Pillsbury's proposition for the settlement of the railroad aid bonds," Republican historian Eugene Smalley wrote. More likely, they weren't sure that the issue would be a winner for them. John won his unprecedented third term with 500 more votes than he had received in 1877.

The Legislature did not meet in 1880; John's biennial session amendment had gone into effect. (He was not one to lightly call the Legislature into special session. For example, to avoid calling legislators back to St. Paul, Pillsbury advanced money to the state from his own funds to rebuild the state asylum for the insane in St. Peter after it was damaged by fire in the winter of 1880.[67] He was similarly generous in 1879, when legislators inadvertently failed to appropriate operating money for the state prison. Pillsbury loaned the state the requisite $50,000, rather than calling a special session.[68]) He recognized that the 1881 session was probably his last chance to persuade the state to do right by its indebtedness. This time, he made it personal. In his message to the Legislature, he pleaded, "In the name of law, justice and honor, as the last public utterance I may make to you, I implore the people of Minnesota and you, gentlemen, their honorable representatives, to seize this last opportunity before it is too late, to wipe this only blot from the fair name of our beloved state." [69]

The Legislature was of a mind to agree with the governor, and put the matter to rest. But the 1860 constitutional amendment repudiating the bonds complicated matters. On March 2, during the last week of the regular session, the House and Senate passed a bill allowing the five justices of the state Supreme Court to function as a "tribunal" to rule on the validity of the 1860 amendment. Should any or all of them refuse—a real possibility, since the Legislature cannot order the Judiciary to act and the mission being created was quite unconventional—the legislation empowered the governor to appoint other judges in their place. The high court indeed refused and it was July 26 before Pillsbury found five willing district court judges to meet. But the constitutional validity of that panel, and of the law authorizing it, was immediately challenged by, oddly, the attorney general, William J. Hahn, whose job ordinarily would be to defend the Legislature's action. This move forced the matter back before a reluctant state Supreme Court. The justices finally found their voices, and ruled that the law of 1881 was constitutional because the amendment of 1860 was not. It was in conflict with the U.S. Constitution's provision barring states from interfering with the obligation of contracts, the justices said. The 1860 amendment was tossed out, and the Legislature was directed to honor the state's 1858 debt. Pillsbury, who had gone to extremes to avoid special sessions, was only too pleased to call his first and only special session of the Legislature on Oct. 11, 1881. His message to the Legislature made a moral appeal: "... it cannot be possible that an intelligent and progressive people with moral and religious convictions can refuse the final payment of an honest debt. An individual who does this while able to pay justly incurs the scorn of his honest neighbors. What must be thought of a prosperous state which does it, using its sovereignty as its shield?"[70]

With a fair amount of foot-dragging, finger-pointing, and alleged but never proven bribe-taking, the Legislature finally approved "an act providing for the adjustment of certain alleged claims against the state." The bondholders had agreed to accept new Minnesota state bonds, redeemable after ten and before thirty years, at one-half the face value of the old ones. The new bonds were to be retired with the sale of the same state lands that the voters of 1877 refused to sell. As a nervous Legislature expected, resistance from some of those voters emerged. A Minneapolis attorney sought an injunction to forbid the delivery of the new bonds to the bondholders. Pillsbury's response to that threat, in the last days of his governorship, reveals that he was not only an honest politician, but also a canny one.

> *There was no time to get these bonds engraved on steel, as required by the rules of the New York Stock Exchange, and they were hastily lithographed in St. Paul. Governor Pillsbury carried them over to his house in Minneapolis in a tin box, by installments, and signed then at home at night. He was especially anxious to get them signed and have the transfer made before his term should expire in January 1882. The holders of the old bonds sent them secretly to St. Paul in a private car, and they were conveyed to the state Capitol in an old trunk, so that the hostile lawyer should not know when or how they reached the governor's office. When the new bonds had all been signed and the exchange had been made, the new bonds were placed in the old trunk, a hack was called, and Governor Pillsbury directed his porter to carry out the trunk and place it on the hack. Inside the hack were the representatives of the old bondholders, who made haste to get out of the state as soon as possible with their securities.* [71]

Folwell said his friend performed this duty "with greater satisfaction than any in his long period of public service." [72]

The bond story would not be complete without mention of one more drama that coincided with it. On March 1, 1881, at about 9 p.m., four days before the Legislature's scheduled adjournment and while discussion of the bond redemption bill was dominating evening floor sessions, a terrifying cry rang through the newly remodeled Capitol: "Fire!" Moments later, "pieces of burning timber came down through the ceilings. The whole dome and roof were on fire."[73] Staff and legislators rushed out of the building, grabbing what furniture and state papers they could. Fortunately, the Historical Society's collection was in the basement, and was largely spared, thanks in part to legislators who grabbed what files they could as they rushed out of the building.[74] But the Capitol's second-floor library was a near-total loss. The cause of the fire was never known, but given the intensity of debate in the session's final days, it was of suspicious origin.

The city of St. Paul had recently completed a large indoor market building just three blocks from the Capitol, in what remains the heart of downtown St. Paul. Retailers had not yet moved in. While the Capitol was still smoldering, the city offered that building to the state as a temporary headquarters. Gov. Pillsbury quickly accepted. Market Square was so quickly adapted for lawmaking purpose that the Legislature was able to meet in official session the next day and act on the bond bill. It served as the ad hoc state Capitol for twenty-two months. Before the regular session ended on March 5, Gov. Pillsbury arranged for plans to be hastily drawn for a new Capitol on the same Tenth and Wabasha site, and secured the Legislature's authorization to proceed with reconstruction. Once again, he went to considerable lengths to avoid a special session.

A third term for a governor had been unprecedented in the young state. A fourth term was unthinkable—or was it? Some accounts say that Pillsbury was ready to retire to private life in the summer of 1881. But his friend Folwell tells a slightly different tale: "He was not indifferent to the proposition" of running again.[75] On Sept. 7, 1881, the *St. Paul Pioneer Press* launched what was likely a Pillsbury-authorized trial balloon, announcing his candidacy. But the instant reaction was not positive, and a few days later, Pillsbury formally announced that he would not seek a fourth term. He left elective office on Jan. 10, 1882, returning to private affairs that Folwell claimed "had suffered during his already long incumbency." One would have needed only to glance at the Pillsbury enterprises on either side of the Falls of St. Anthony in 1882 to question that claim.

George A. and Margaret Pillsbury in the 1870s.

Chapter Four

The Builder

The sense of living in two places at once must have been intense for George and Margaret Pillsbury in 1877. At the time they were residents of Concord, N.H., the capital city of their home state and their home for a quarter-century. They were deeply engaged in community affairs. George was Concord's mayor that year at age sixty-one. He had retired from the railroad executive's post that drew the family to Concord in 1851 and from leadership roles at the two banks he helped found in the 1860s. He had stepped down after a number of years on the city's school board and had also ended the second of two stints in the Legislature.[1] In addition to being in charge at City Hall, George sat on a number of governing boards. Both he and Margaret were much involved at First Baptist Church. The Concord Board of Trade, Centennial Home for the Aged, and the Orphan's Home in nearby Franklin were all prominent on George's agenda, and also much on Margaret's mind as she helped guide the household's philanthropy.[2] It may have been her idea for George and Charles to provide the new Baptist Church in Concord with an organ in 1875, priced at $4,000.[3] George as mayor may still have been wrapping up the special assignment given him by the City Council in 1876. He took on a role that later would have been assigned to a city assessor, evidently a new position in the 1870s. His mission was to appraise all the real estate in the city for purposes of taxation. The delicate task required a personal visit to every residence and business in Concord.[4] Only someone of widely admired judgment and pleasing personality would be tapped for such politically sensitive work.

Yet the scale of these local commitments notwithstanding, George and Margaret must often have turned their attention to Minneapolis, where their two sons, Charles and Fred, were flourishing. A year earlier Fred had found a bride there, a Massachusetts native named Alice Thayer Cook (who also was known as Alice Goodwin, taking the surname of her stepfather, Dr. David Goodwin).[5] They were married at the brand-new Church of the Redeemer (later called First Universalist Church) in Minneapolis on the evening of Oct. 19, 1876. Margaret and George were on hand for the occasion, according to an account that took up two full columns on the *Minneapolis Tribune's* society page.[6] Fred was making what his parents hoped was a smooth transition from junior-associate status in his Uncle John's hardware business to junior-owner status in the flour milling company that bore his elder brother's name. Grandchildren for George and Margaret were arriving quickly now and the first among them were their own namesakes. Charles and Mary Ann became parents of Margaret Carleton on July 18, 1876; Fred and Alice welcomed George Alfred on Dec. 12, 1877.[7]

George was undoubtedly proud and delighted when his brother and former business apprentice was elected—and reelected—governor of Minnesota. He had to be enthusiastic, too, about son Charles's first bid for elective office. The young miller won a Minnesota Senate seat in the 1877 election that saw John handily reelected. George followed his sons' business careers with the interest not only of a father, but also an investor. He was a co-owner and senior advisor of C.A. Pillsbury & Co., the fastest-growing and most innovative milling concern at the Falls of St. Anthony. George had invested not only in the company's mills, but also in parcels of land in what was quickly becoming downtown Minneapolis. He had taken Margaret to visit the place at least twice. The May 1, 1875, census found both of them, and Fred too, residing temporarily in the household headed by Charles and Mary Ann. They were back for Fred's wedding the following year. Throughout the 1870s, George and Margaret undoubtedly followed the young city's progress as closely as newspapers and letters from the Falls of St. Anthony allowed.

The idea that George, Margaret, and their adopted teenaged daughter Minnie might move to Minnesota may well have been "what-if" conversation for some years in the gracious Gothic revival house they built in 1855 at 39 Rumford St. in Concord, but the talk evidently turned serious in 1877, as the pull of family and business in Minneapolis grew stronger. Two events that took place in New Hampshire that year may have tipped the balance. Minnie completed eighth grade—often an endpoint or breakpoint in a young woman's formal education in those days—and Susan Wadleigh Pillsbury, the family matriarch and a widow for more than twenty years, died at age eighty-four.

Little is known of Susan or of her influence on her one daughter and four sons, but it's a good guess that she encouraged them as community servants. She was both the daughter and the granddaughter of men who held elective office, and grew up in a family every bit as civic-minded as the Pillsburys. Her role in George and Margaret's lives is a matter for speculation, though the record suggests that she was closest not to George, her second son, but to the baby of the family, Benjamin Franklin Pillsbury. Born in 1831, Benjamin was four years younger than John and more than fifteen years younger than George. Until age forty-one, he was a bachelor farmer and lumberman who lived with his mother. For many years, they evidently were alone together at the big house at the crossroads in Sutton where Susan and Captain John raised their family. No names of hired hands appear on census records; Benjamin evidently provided all the labor the modest farm required. Benjamin's share of its value was pegged at $4,900 in the 1870 census; his mother's share of the homestead was listed at only $900—both middling sums in comparison with the holdings of some of their neighbors and kinsmen.[8] But Benjamin's responsibilities for the family's home place did not deter him from community involvement. A history of the region published in 1893 reports, "He was selectman and town treasurer quite frequently." Another tells us, "He served as a public officer longer than any other citizen of Sutton of his time. Like his brothers, he was possessed of the best business judgment, great energy, and financial ability."[9]

In 1877, Benjamin was sent to Concord as a state representative from the Sutton area. (While he was there, his late sister Dolly's son, Charles Cummings, served as the House of Representatives sergeant-at-arms. Dolly, the Minnesota Pillsbury brothers' only sister, had died in 1858, at age forty.)[10] Benjamin finally married in 1872, and brought his bride, Susan Wright, to the house he shared with his mother. That they chose to remain in Sutton largely out of devotion to Susan can be surmised from this fact: Less than a year after her death, and soon after the 1878 New Hampshire legislative session adjourned, Benjamin and his wife pulled up stakes and left the state.

Benjamin Franklin Pillsbury.

Their destination, unsurprisingly, was Minnesota. But it wasn't the Falls of St. Anthony. Instead it was Granite Falls, 125 miles west of Minneapolis, where C.A. Pillsbury & Co. had acquired a run-down mill through foreclosure. It had been the little town's first mill, built by town founder Henry Hill. With ownership of the mill came rights to much of the town site as well. John Pillsbury, the family's persistent recruiter, played his usual role. Sell your lumber business in Sutton and come to Minnesota, Gov. John urged Benjamin and Susan. You can take charge of the Granite Falls mill and continue to lead the rural life you love. Granite Falls was a place of promise, the site of one of two waterfalls on the

Minnesota River and by then a decade and a half removed from the bloody Dakota Conflict. Benjamin and Susan accepted the invitation. They had no children, but came in the company of Susan's nephew, Fred Gillingham. With the proceeds of the sale of their home and lumber business in Sutton, they invested in land and lumber milling in Granite Falls, and in an impressive new two-story house atop a hill overlooking the city. They arranged for its construction before they arrived in the town for good in September 1878.[11] The Pillsbury name attached to a modern-day residential addition in Granite Falls refers not to the more famous Pillsburys of Minneapolis, but to Benjamin. [12]

At 39 Rumford Street in Concord, talk of moving west must have picked up in earnest after Susan Wadleigh Pillsbury died. She was the last of George and Margaret's parents to pass.[13] If word of Benjamin's intention to head to Minnesota followed soon after Susan Pillsbury's funeral, it probably added one more reason to move. George must have realized that if he did not decamp for the west, he soon would be the only member of his family of origin still living in New Hampshire. He and Margaret were loath to spend their old age far from the people they loved most. Sometime late in 1877 or early in 1878, they decided "after much consideration, and with deep reluctance" that they, too, would become Minnesotans.[14]

The weeks that followed the announcement of their plans were a time of high emotion and activity for George, Margaret, and Minnie. When word spread in Concord that the mayor was not only retiring from public life, but moving to Minnesota, "it drew forth strong and widespread protests from the citizens and neighbors whom he had served so long, for they felt the state could ill afford to lose such a man," said an account written four years later.[15] His neighbors shortly set to work to give the Pillsburys a memorable sendoff. An account written only a year later describes the exertions of the Pillsburys' friends and admirers:

Probably no person ever left the city who received so many expressions of regret as Mr. Pillsbury. Complimentary resolutions were unanimously passed by both branches of the city government and by the First National Bank, the latter testifying strongly to

his integrity, honesty, and superior business qualities. Resolutions
passed by the First Baptist Church and Society were ordered to be
entered upon the records of each organization. The Webster Club,
composed of 50 prominent businessmen of Concord, passed a series
of resolutions regretting his departure from the state. A similar tes-
timonial was also presented to Mr. Pillsbury, which was subscribed
to by more than three hundred of the leading professional and
businessmen of the city, among whom were all the ex-mayors then
living, all the clergymen, all the members of both branches of the
city government, all of the bank presidents and officers, 26 lawyers,
20 physicians, and nearly all the businessmen in the city. On the
eve of their departure, Mr. and Mrs. Pillsbury were presented with
an elegant bronze statuette of Mozart. Such tributes, however wor-
thily bestowed, could but afford great gratification to the recipient,
showing as they did the great esteem in which he was held by his
fellow citizens.[16]

With those tokens of their neighbors' regard packed into their
trunks and rich memories tucked into their hearts, George, Margaret,
and Minnie boarded a train headed west in the late spring or early
summer of 1878. Margaret left behind one kinsman with whom she
had a special bond, her brother Henry, but she knew she would see
him from time to time in Minnesota. Henry's son Frank was among
the young New Hampshire men who had heeded the siren song of
the Falls of St. Anthony and settled in Minnesota for good.

Upon their arrival, George, Margaret, and Minnie undoubtedly
lodged in the comfortable house Charles and Mary Ann had built
a few years earlier at 927 Second Av. S. Though that house offered
ample accommodations, playing the role of elders in a multi-genera-
tional household was not what George and Margaret had in mind
when they left New Hampshire. They selected a lot about a block
away, at 225 South Tenth St., and hired an architect to design for them
an elegant three-story Victorian mansion, to be built of New Hampshire granite and surrounded by a trim wrought-iron picket fence.[17]
It would be twice the size of the house they left behind on Rumford
Street in Concord.

The house George and Margaret built in Minneapolis.

That winter, while they were still living with Charles and Mary Ann, George and Margaret became grandparents again. To the great relief of both parents and grandparents, fraternal twin brothers Charles Stinson and John Sargent arrived in robust health on Dec. 6, 1878. The new house was ready the following summer, and it immediately became the headquarters of their clan, which was growing rapidly.

Margaret contented herself with domesticity and service to the First Baptist Church, one of the oldest congregations in her new home city. The Pillsburys became attached to and active in that parish almost immediately upon arrival. But that was only the beginning of George's activity. He had relocated, not retired. Officially, he took the title vice president at C.A. Pillsbury & Co. Unofficially, he became the firm's ambassador to the community, throwing himself and the Pillsbury name into a wide range of good causes, business ventures, and civic projects. The sight of George Pillsbury's horse and buggy, scuttling about the still mostly-unpaved streets of Minneapolis en route to an appointment or meeting, became an everyday occurrence.

The operation of the Pillsbury mills remained Charles's domain and chief focus, although he, too, had taken on community responsibilities. In addition to serving in the state Senate, Charles moved into leadership of the Plymouth Congregational Church Society,[18] and partnered with two other city-building visionaries, George Brackett and Charles M. Loring, in establishing the first free medical clinic for the Minneapolis poor. (It would grow into today's giant University of Minnesota-Fairview Hospital.)[19]

The presence of his wise and capable parents in Minneapolis was likely a help and comfort to the 36-year-old miller in eventful 1878. But the exact date of George and Margaret's arrival in Minneapolis is not known, and we can only guess if they were on hand for what remains to this day the biggest industrial accident in the city's history. On May 2, 1878, at 7:20 p.m., Charles was likely finishing dinner with Mary Ann or playing with little Margaret when three tremendous booms shook the city and rattled dishes as far away as Saint Paul. Many people in the Twin Cities believed they were experiencing an earthquake. That windy spring night, the Pillsburys may have been among the many Minneapolitans who bolted from their houses, ran into the street and peered toward the river. If so, then the sight of a massive cloud of billowing black smoke above the mill district likely set Charles sprinting to see for himself what had happened. The mighty Washburn A Mill, largest of the eighteen mills at the falls and the pride of the Washburn Co., had exploded, taking five smaller mills with it.

Folwell's account, written decades later, conveys the drama of that night:

> At 7:20 o'clock a roaring sound, like that of a tremendous thunderclap, was heard far and wide over the city. Distant buildings were shaken and glass was shattered in windows many blocks away. Persons in and near the mill district saw an immense column of black smoke, with flames darting through it, rise from the Washburn A Mill. They also saw the roof of the mill heave upward and then drop, carrying the successive floors with it, and the walls crumble and fall outward. The walls of two other mills, the Diamond and the Humboldt, standing west and south, were seen to collapse and their roofs and floors fall to the ground in ruin. The three other mills [Pettit-Robinson, Galaxy and Zenith] standing across the canal a little

The aftermath of the Washburn A Mill explosion, May 1878.

more distant, were not exploded but were a mass of flames in the course of a few minutes and were completely consumed.[20]

Eighteen men died that night, fourteen at the Washburn A Mill; one each at the Diamond, Humboldt, and Zenith mills; and one man who lived nearby, Jacob Rhodes.[21] Just one workman at one mill, Fred George at the Zenith, survived. He was sucked out of the burning Zenith by the force of the explosive updraft from the mills across the canal that fed the waterwheels. He was tossed into the canal, badly burned, but able to climb into the arms of rescuers over the debris that littered the waterway. He was scarred for life.[22] Had the three rapid-fire blasts and subsequent inferno occurred one hour earlier, when the larger day shift was giving way to the smaller night crews, hundreds of lives would have been lost.

The explosion had cost the city at least a third of its milling capacity. The cause of the conflagration was never precisely determined, but the minute particles of flour dust floating in oxygen-rich air were almost undoubtedly to blame. At the time it was a common sight in the mill district on warm evenings to see workers sitting in front of their buildings, lighting matches and smoking cigarettes. [23] The investigation that ensued after the Washburn A disaster added much to millers' knowledge of the imperative to control dust and ban open flames of any kind from the premises.[24]

Charles, Fred, John, and—if he was in the city—George, all probably raced to the smoldering scene on the Mississippi's west bank, and may have lingered late into the night examining the wreckage. If Charles was true to form, he was also on hand early the next morning. The Pillsburys' first concern was undoubtedly for those who lost loved ones. In a small city in which rivals were also acquaintances and friends, they would have grieved alongside the families whose breadwinners were killed and their fellow mill owners whose facilities were destroyed. But those emotions would not have dulled their consciousness of the competitive opportunity that disaster had handed them. None of the five Pillsbury mills was damaged. In the short run, demand for their product—and the price it could command—would be greater than ever.

But so would be the imperative to fit their mills with the latest and most efficient milling equipment. Within forty-eight hours of the explosion, the question "Would C.C. Washburn rebuild the A?" was answered in the affirmative. The former Wisconsin governor arrived at the scene of the still-smoking ruins late on May 3, after spending the morning at the University of Wisconsin-Madison, formalizing plans for his gift of an observatory to the school. The next day, after seeing to funeral arrangements for the men who died, Washburn himself paced out a massive addition to his own B Mill, and announced that a new Washburn A would soon rise again. A few years earlier, Washburn had formed the Washburn Crosby Company by making a full partner of his able Minneapolis manager, Maine native John Crosby, who was married to his brother William's wife's sister.[25] Following the disaster, he bought the site of the blasted-out Diamond Mill and made plans to extend the Washburn A from First St. to Second St., doubling its size. He aimed to make it the largest flour mill in the world.[26] "Undeterred by the devastation all around him, he was calmly planning to double his production," Washburn's great-great-grandson would relate 125 years later.[27]

Minneapolis legal pioneer and historian Isaac Atwater wrote fifteen years later that the Washburns' impulse to rebuild responded to "something in the Minneapolis atmosphere so stimulating to her citizens that they will not permit ruin to stalk unchecked. Fire cannot burn it or drown it." That noble invocation of Minnesota resilience has considerable local appeal. But to the area's compelling spirit must be added this fact: In the 1870s, the profits to be made in the milling industry were enormous, and due to improvements in technology and economies of scale, a large, up-to-date mill could pay for itself in a year.[28] The market for Minneapolis flour had gone global in 1877, when Washburn began selling in Liverpool, England. Demand for the high-quality Minneapolis product built quickly in Britain.[29] Washburn could scarcely afford not to rebuild bigger than before. And the Pillsburys intended to more than keep up with the competition.

Later that year, Charles traveled to Europe for a few months to see the latest in milling technology for himself. He and other millers at the Falls of St. Anthony had been aware for some time that the premier European flour manufacturers in Budapest were replacing their ancient millstones with steel rollers.[30] In fact, a few years earlier Charles and the manager of the Washburn mills, George H. Christian, had jointly sponsored an investigative trip to Budapest by W. D. Gray, of a Milwaukee-based flourmill machinery company, to bring back all the information he could about the roller process. Gray reported that by this process, the wheat passed through six or seven pairs of rollers, set successively closer together and made to rotate against each other to break the wheat. After each pass the grain was sifted, then run through the next pair—hence the name "gradual reduction" process.[31] Gray was convinced that the steel rollers greatly improved mill productivity and would eventually become the world standard.[32]

Gray brought several sets of Hungarian chilled steel rollers back with him for experimentation, and both Pillsbury and Christian had them installed to be used as a first step in the manufacture of flour, to crack the wheat kernel. The rest of the grinding was left to time-honored millstones, probably because the equipment Gray brought to Minneapolis was not well adapted to the hard-kernel spring wheat of the northern American prairie.

An account preserved in company files said, "Mr. Pillsbury and his associates realized that these first crude rolls needed great improvement before the whole milling process could be safely entrusted to them. He therefore ordered his machine shop foreman to put the rolls through the most rigid tests" in an experimental shed that stood near his first mill on Sixth (now Portland) Avenue South. "The big Pillsbury experimental shed was constantly a place of mystery to other Minneapolis millers. 'What has Charlie Pillsbury got now?' they asked one another whenever a fresh shipment of machinery was seen to go into the shed for testing. [Pillsbury] got his machinists busy changing the style, depth and design of the corrugations [of the steel rollers.] Virtually hundreds of different kinds and combinations of corrugations were made and tested—zig-zag cutting edges, spiral lines, ovals, semi-circular, stair-step effect, wavy lines."[33]

No one else at the Falls of St. Anthony pursued roller technology with as much vigor. Perhaps the others lacked the capital. More likely, the bonanza that traditional milling was producing in the 1870s kept their curiosity in check.

But the Pillsburys recognized that the Washburn A disaster had put that firm in the position to install the latest technology on a large scale—and Washburn-Crosby had the capital to do so. They had also been privy to W.D. Gray's report and had received some Hungarian rollers. It's no wonder Charles felt the need to see an all-roller Hungarian mill for himself.[34]

Charles's assumptions about the competition were right to this extent: At the Washburn C Mill,[35] experimentation began in 1879 on all-roller milling. But Charles was giving the Washburns more credit for innovation than they deserved. The new Washburn A would open in mid-1880 with millstones, not rollers, for grinding grain. Nor did Charles's trip to Europe convince him once and for all that roller milling was feasible for grinding the local wheat. Among the experts that he consulted locally on the issue was William de la Barre, a very able Austrian engineer who had arrived in Minneapolis at C.C. Washburn's behest as Washburn A dust was still settling. His talent would be a boon to enterprise at the Falls of St. Anthony for the next half-century. De la Barre recalled an exchange with Charles after the latter's return from Europe. The "starting of the Washburn A" places the conversation in early-to-mid 1880:

> *"Soon after the starting of the [rebuilt] Washburn A, Charles A. Pillsbury and his brother Fred C. Pillsbury called at my home one day while I was eating dinner. Charles A. Pillsbury said that he would like me to answer just one question, if I thought it was fair to do so. . . 'Just tell me,' said he, 'from what you know about this Hungarian way of milling, if, in your opinion, we will all have to come to it. Consider the question well, as a good deal depends on it.' I told the Messrs. Pillsbury that I was fully convinced that a change would have to be made from the old way to the new by all the mills, sooner or later. Mr. Pillsbury looked at me sharply for a minute, then shook hands with me, saying, 'Many thanks to you. I believe you are right.'"[36]*

The Excelsior Mill, built by the city's first mayor, Dorilus Morrison, and purchased by the Pillsburys in 1878, was chosen to inaugurate all-roller milling for C.A. Pillsbury & Co. It became the first all-roller mill at the falls in the spring of 1881.

The Archibald Mill at tiny Dundas, in the Cannon River Valley, can claim bragging rights as the first all-roller mill in not only the state, but the nation. At the time, the valley was a premier milling region, and flour from Faribault, Dundas, and Northfield was among the finest in the nation, due largely to the fact that David Faribault had invited French milling experts to improving his middling purifiers.[37] E. T. Archibald later hired W. D. Gray, the milling machinery expert Pillsbury and Washburn had sent to Budapest a few years earlier, to outfit his mill with the new roller equipment. Ever on the alert for information, Charles sent his head miller, the aptly named Jim Miller, to Dundas to inspect that facility while it was still under construction. Miller brought back ideas that later benefited the Excelsior retrofitting.

He was sold on roller milling, but some of his fellow mill managers were not. A story was told by John Foley, a long-term Pillsbury employee who ended his career in the Pillsbury B front office, that Charles G. Hoyt as head miller of the B and the Anchor had little faith in the newfangled rolls. He was so sure the steel contraptions would be a failure that he ordered his men to retrieve the millstones as fast as Jim Miller threw them out of the Excelsior, and store them in the Anchor's basement. He laughed with his friends over the fun he would have when Jim wanted them back after the roller process proved a bust. But it was Jim who had the laugh on Charlie. Hoyt would be tossing out his own millstones a year or two later. [38]

Roller milling was only a part of the giant business step the two pairs of Pillsbury brothers were contemplating in 1879. As they watched the rise of the new Washburn A, they contacted leading local architect Leroy S. Buffington and asked him to design a mill that would be much larger than any other they owned—and larger, too, than the Washburn behemoth rising on the ruins of the original Washburn A. With one structure, George, John, Charles, and Fred aimed to more than double their company's milling capacity.

The west side of the falls was already crowded with mills. But that would not deter them. They aimed to put the Pillsbury A Mill on the river's east side, on Main Street in old St. Anthony. It would be less than a block from the original J.S. Pillsbury & Co. hardware store, and also close to the site of the first commercial grist mill at the falls, which went up in 1851. Situating the Pillsbury A on the city's less prosperous east side was Gov. John's idea, and needed selling to his skeptical kinsmen. For John, the location decision turned on loyalty to his neighbors. He wanted the mill "built where it would benefit East Side working men."[39] He went on to make an unusual request

The Pillsbury A Mill.

of architect Buffington: He wanted the new megamill to include a library. The workers of old St. Anthony didn't have a conveniently located library of their own, and that bothered the son of book-loving Captain John Pillsbury. "I have always had a great interest in the people of the East Side," the governor explained. "There are people still living there—working men and men of moderate means—who were my neighbors when I first came to St. Anthony. I have felt like doing all I could to benefit them."[40]

The library did not come to fruition in the Pillsbury A, though John would not forget his idea for a working people's library on the East Side. But beginning in the spring of 1880, the mill rose according to Buffington's plan. The building would house two side-by-side, separate units, each capable of operating independently. With dimensions of 175 feet by 115 feet, and at 116 feet tall, it would be an imposing blue limestone cube on the outside and a thoroughly modern flour factory inside. Rollers would do all of the milling, with the refinement of the best available middlings purifiers—100 of them, at a price of $125,000, an amount large enough to warrant a story in a St. Paul newspaper.[41] The plant would also include the novelty of a passenger elevator, to prevent worker fatigue climbing up and down stairs. "Its precautionary measures against fire are most perfect," the *Northwestern Miller* reported, with a nod to every millers' biggest worry after 1878.[42] The building was designed with four large "risers" running from bottom to top of the building, and to them on each floor was attached a hundred feet of fire hose. Every floor also had at least four fire extinguishers.

The most newsworthy feature at the A was its lighting plan. It would be the first building in the city to employ electric lights. The *Stillwater Gazette* of April 6, 1881, excitedly reported, "C.A. Pillsbury Co have determined to light the great Pillsbury A Mill by electricity, and have closed a contract with the Brush Electric Light Co. of Cleveland, Ohio for one of their No. 7 machines with a capacity of eighteen lights. They will place two lights on each floor of the mill, sufficient to brilliantly illuminate the entire building from basement to top." The facility's price would be $650,000 by the time it was finished in 1882; two years later, after more improvements, it was reported that $1 million had been invested in the A.[43]

Electrical power would soon be the rage, but water power was still the crucial moving force for Minneapolis mills. The A Mill's power requirements necessitated the digging of a new east-bank canal by the St. Anthony Water Power Co., the city's oldest utility. Starting near Second Avenue, it ran 400 feet parallel to Main Street, and was 18 feet wide and 16 feet deep when it was done. The digging began in early 1880. Before it was completed, the chronically troubled water power works changed hands, bringing two of Minnesota's leading entrepreneurs into commercial proximity for the first time. The new owner of the east-side riparian rights was James J. Hill of St. Paul. He had purchased his Minneapolis stake for $467,000, and took personal interest in the completion of the "improvement" the A Mill required.[44]

The A Mill was built by local contractors Gunn, Cross & Co. But their work and decisions governing it proceeded under the watchful eye of the eldest member of the firm. Charles may have been the family's chief miller and marketer, but his father was its chief builder. George supervised construction.[45] For him, it was a grand scale reprise of a recurring role he had played as a public official in New Hampshire, overseeing the building of schools, a prison, a home for the aged, and other large facilities. Charles had such confidence in his father's construction expertise that he returned to Europe at least once more while the A was being built, likely for two reasons: to continue his study of new-process milling techniques and technology; and to sell flour. Pillsbury's Best XXXX flour closely followed Washburn-Crosby's Gold Medal brand into European markets. Washburn had hired a young dynamo, William H. Dunwoody, to market his flour in Europe.[46] That move undoubtedly pricked Charles' competitive spirit and propelled him to action. By 1882, it was said, "There is not a European market in which [Pillsbury's] flour is not sold extensively and given the highest quotations."[47]

The spring days in 1881 leading up to the midsummer opening of the first half of the A Mill should have been heady and happy ones for the family. Their enterprise was flourishing. Construction was proceeding apace at the falls. Each week's edition of the milling industry's mouthpiece, *The Northwestern Miller*, contained another admiring account of the new mill's size, style, and innovation. "In point of elegance it will probably excel anything yet attempted," the April 8 issue enthused. But the weekly's April 29 edition brought Pillsbury news of a different sort:

> *The household of Mr. C.A. Pillsbury, the miller, has been thrown in deep sorrow this week by the loss of their only daughter, Margery, an unusually bright and amiable child, who died of membranous croup on Tuesday evening. She was about five years of age.* [48]

The loss of a second child and their only daughter must have been devastating to Charles and Mary Ann, though having an extended family close at hand offered some consolation, and Charles no doubt found solace in work and the company of his associates. Mary Ann may have felt more isolated in her grief, especially during Charles's absences. Her father had died in 1878 in New Hampshire, and if her mother came to visit her in Minneapolis following her daughter's death, there is no surviving record of it. Census reports show that the household included two younger women in the early 1880s, both named Mary, one of them likely a nanny for two-year-olds John and Charles.[49] Those toddlers became the household's focus. The absence of almost any record of Mary Ann Stinson Pillsbury's Minneapolis life suggests that she chose a home-dominated existence, eschewing community attachments, for the rest of her days.

Mary Ann Pillsbury in the 1880s.

Despite all the interest the A Mill's construction generated, the start of flour production in its east half on Tuesday, July 5, 1881, was not noted in the *Minneapolis Tribune*'s news pages the following day. Neither do company records show that Charles and George sought press attention during those first, perhaps tentative days, while construction was still in progress on building's western side. But careful readers of the newspaper's advertisements might have caught a change in the C.A. Pillsbury & Co. display ad that ran every few days in the morning Minneapolis newspaper. On July 5, the Pillsbury notice listed the Anchor, Excelsior, Pillsbury and Empire mills, and said, "Capacity, 2,000 barrels per day." On July 9, it named the A among its mills and boasted: "7,500 barrels per day."[50]

The opening of the A Mill, hard on the heels of little Margery's death, would have provided emotional highs and lows sufficient to make 1881 "the best and worst of times" in Pillsbury family memory. But the year wasn't over. Ten days after the A's start of operation, half of the town of New Ulm, a mid-sized town a hundred miles southwest of Minneapolis, was smashed to pieces by two massive tornadoes. Twenty people were killed.[51] Gov. John S. Pillsbury, serving his final year in office, had to leave business matters unattended for weeks as he mobilized aid for the stricken survivors.

November started happily enough. John and Mahala's twenty-fifth wedding anniversary was marked on Nov. 3 by about forty friends and family members, who surprised them at their home that evening, bearing silver gifts and food for an impromptu celebration.[52] But the month ended in sorrow. Fred and Alice set out for New England to visit family and friends, leaving their two children, George, almost four, and Harriot, almost two, in the care of other family members and a nanny. "Hardly had they reached Boston," the *Northwestern Miller* reported on Dec. 2, "before they were informed by telegraph that their little four-year-old son was dangerously ill. Though hurrying back, they did not reach home until after the little fellow they called Georgie had succumbed to diphtheritic croup, after an illness of only four days."[53] He died on Nov. 24—Thanksgiving Day. Alice was two months pregnant at the time of her son's death; the following May, she would give birth to another boy. He was given his paternal grandmother's and his mother's maiden names: Carleton Cook.

Just one week after Georgie's funeral, disaster struck again at the Falls. The headline in the next edition of the *Northwestern Miller*: "Four large mills in Minneapolis destroyed Sunday morning Dec. 4."[54] Three of the four went up in smoke—the B, owned by C.A. Pillsbury & Co., and the Excelsior and Empire, both leased by Charles's company. The Minneapolis Flouring Mill—Charles' first mill, which he later sold to Crocker, Fisk & Co.—exploded with terrible destructive force. Four men died—two of them Minneapolis firefighters, killed when the Minneapolis mill's front wall fell on them; the other fatalities were a laborer and a millwright. Six men were injured, four of them firefighters.[55]

The fire started in the basement of the B Mill, only recently enlarged and upgraded, and spread so rapidly that the workman who left to sound the alarm just outside could not re-enter the building to fetch his wallet. Charles stood alongside the firefighters and millworkers as dawn broke over the ruins that chilly Sunday morning, and arranged for a large breakfast to be served to the firefighters who continued to douse the embers.

There was no question that the mills would be rebuilt. Insurance covered at least a portion of the losses, which were estimated at more than half a million dollars.[56] Among the facilities that needed to be replaced was Charles's own office, which sustained water and smoke damage and broken windows. It may not be a coincidence that soon thereafter, the company's headquarters moved away from the mills, to the Windom Block on the corner of Washington and Second Avenues.[57] The company had grown into a major corporation, employing hundreds of workers and selling its products across the seas. The time had come for a fitting corporate headquarters—and one safely removed from the hazards of the industry.

From their new offices, the Pillsburys could look with pride to the pivotal part they were playing in the transformation of the flour milling industry, which helped place Minneapolis among the nation's burgeoning manufacturing centers in the last decades of the nineteenth century. The expanded Washburn and Pillsbury milling factories at the Falls of St. Anthony were part of a larger shift in American industry away from small, nearly autonomous producers to corporate mass production, made possible by improvements in technology and an expanding railroads system.[58] The change brought with it a population boom, and the city that straddled the Falls of St. Anthony gained 120,000 residents in the decade after the A Mill's construction.[59] Mass production of flour also spurred agricultural development in the rest of the state, as the hard spring wheat of the northern prairie took rank in world markets over the winter wheat of Kansas and Missouri.[60]

Modern scholar W. Bernard Carlson described developments in the Minneapolis milling district in the 1870s and 1880s:

> *The story of how flour milling in Minneapolis became a big business can be summarized quite simply: recognizing that there was both a huge supply of wheat and an equally huge demand for flour, Washburn and Pillsbury stepped forward and developed the technology (roller mills) that would allow them to match supply with demand. Along the way, they found it most profitable to process flour on a large scale and quickly; this led them to build a large business organization with managers and engineers who could coordinate operations. To protect their investment in equipment, both Washburn and Pillsbury integrated backward toward the wheat farmer, and forward toward the consumer.[61]*

Engineering that kind of vertical integration was primarily Charles's responsibility. Whether by conscious decision, unwitting preference, or mere force of habit, his father concentrated on the family's integration with the city of Minneapolis. In 1880 George became vice president, and a year later, president of the Minneapolis Board of Trade. In any other city, this organization would have been given the name Chamber of Commerce, but in Minneapolis that name had already been claimed by the grain trading organization that would eventually be called the Minneapolis Grain Exchange. (The names would not be sorted out until the mid-twentieth century.)[62] The large firms had not been involved when this organization of millers and independent wheat buyers was formed, but the Pillsburys joined in 1882, and two years later George also became *that* organization's president. In the early 1880s, he also said yes to the vice presidency of the Minnesota Loan & Trust Co. and of Manufacturers' National Bank,[63] and became a trustee at First Baptist Church, an officer of the Young Men's Christian Association, and president of the region's Baptist Union.

And as he had done in New Hampshire, George became involved in local Republican politics. Already in 1881, he was mentioned as a possible candidate for the city council. (In those years, Minneapolis city council terms lasted only one year; mayoral terms were two years long.) He opted for, and won, a school board seat instead. The city council talk turned serious two years later. George's name was on a ballot again, this time to serve as one of three Fifth Ward aldermen (city council members.) He was also one of three election judges in his own precinct, the Second. The party endorsements listed behind his name on the April 3, 1883, ballot reveal much about the issue that would dominate George's public life for the next three years. He was the candidate of both the Republican and the Prohibition parties.[64]

How to control liquor sales was the dominant issue in city politics in the mid-1880s. That alcohol would be at the forefront of civic concerns at that time of rapid population growth says a good deal about the values and priorities of nineteenth-century Minneapolitans, and about their view of government's rightful role in their shared life.

The boomtown was hobbled by inadequate public transportation, understaffed and overcrowded schools, unpaved and, at times, impassable roads, limited sewers, too few parks, and a too-meager library. The city's leaders weren't blind to those problems. Several of those subjects appeared in the policy platforms of both the Republican and Democratic parties. But to judge from the reporting in the city's dominant newspapers, the *Morning Tribune* and *Evening Journal*, the primary challenge facing municipal government was to control the rampant growth of saloons in the city. Between 1882 and 1884, during the second mayoral administration of Democrat Albert Alonzo "Doc" Ames, the number of liquor-selling establishments grew from 252 to 515, and the constabulary needed to police those businesses and their patrons grew from 33 to 86. Too many of the saloons were operated by "gamblers, bunko men, keepers of bawdy houses," the *Journal* charged.[65] They paid a mere $100 to obtain a license to operate. If city ordinances existed to restrict their hours of operation, they were evidently not enforced. The editors complained about liquor being sold at all hours of the day, every day of the week, including Sunday. The latter was a serious breach of cultural norms in Protestant Minneapolis, where Monday newspapers published synopses of Sunday sermons and the clergy threatened a boycott of the newspapers when they began publishing Sunday editions.[66]

When the newly elected 1883 city council met for the first time on April 10, their first order of business was to elect their own presiding officer. George was nominated and quickly elected president after leading 13-6-1 on a three-candidate straw ballot.[67]

In choosing George, the new council seemed to be committing itself to a change in direction on at least one issue—the expansion of the city parks system. The previous council had been outspoken opponents of efforts by the city's Board of Trade (including George Pillsbury) and local legislators (including state Sen. Charles Pillsbury, then chair of the Senate Finance Committee) to add more city parks and establish a Minneapolis Board of Parks Commissioners. The city's commercial leaders were convinced that the metropolis springing up all around them deserved a first-rate park system, yet opportunities to acquire property were slipping away. The tax-averse city council rejected such pleas throughout the late 1870s and early 1880s, but as Minneapolis became more influential at the State Capitol, parks advocates began to explore other avenues to the same end. When Minneapolis businessman Loren Fletcher, a former business partner of fervent parks proponent Charles M. Loring, became speaker of the Minnesota House in 1883, the moment for an end run to the Legislature had arrived.

The council howled in protest at what it considered an attempt to usurp its authority. Its members understood that granting a state charter to a city park board and allowing it broad powers to levy taxes, condemn property, issue bonds, and otherwise conduct its own affairs would diminish the council's freedom to do those things. The council complained that the city's voters had never asked for and didn't really need the expansive parks system that the Board of Trade and its legislative allies envisioned.[68] But the council was misreading the minds of voters in a city that would more than double in population between 1880 and 1885. People in crowded living conditions longed for more picnic grounds, ball fields, and open spaces. They regretted seeing streets and houses encroaching on the river and the handsome lakes on the city's southern and western sides. The more the council resisted, the more the Board of Trade and legislators sought to circumvent it, and give the new park board real autonomy. Creation of the Minneapolis Park Board was approved by the 1883 Legislature, with the condition that city voters agree. They did, with a 1,315-vote margin of victory in the April 3, 1883, election.[69] The composition of the first board was spelled out by the Legislature; subsequently, its members would be elected, establishing a political power center to rival the council. The tension thus created would still be felt in the twenty-first century.

On the roster of that first Minneapolis Park Board was John S. Pillsbury. He remains the only Minnesota governor whose subsequent career included a stint on the Minneapolis Park Board. How many parks-resistant city council members lost their seats in 1883 is not known, but it is telling that the new council was sufficiently pro-parks that it handed its gavel to the president of the park-loving Board of Trade.

As council president, George was back in territory he knew well, municipal administration. He was in his element, dealing again with police staffing, sewer adequacy, street maintenance, and other routine city business. Street paving was beginning in earnest in Minneapolis in the early 1880s, and the sewer system was being extended as rapidly as possible to accommodate the city's exploding population. George's expertise in construction raised his profile at City Hall. He was also the most visible Republican counterweight to Democrat Ames, the current mayor. That made him an obvious man for Republicans to rally around for mayor in the 1884 election.

But George did not encourage his own candidacy. He told a pre-convention meeting on Feb. 29 that he had months earlier suggested to two others, J.T. Wyman and G.A. Camp, that they pursue mayoral bids. But Camp withdrew in Pillsbury's favor, and Wyman's support faltered at the March 6 convention. George was so diffident about the prospect of a mayoral bid that he was not in attendance at the convention. Charles came, authorized to speak for his father. He came to the podium to say that while George did not want to run, it was the opinion of both father and son that Wyman could not be elected. A straw vote was taken after that mixed message was delivered. George was in the lead—and in second place was not Wyman, but Charles A. Pillsbury! The announcement of the straw-ballot result sent Charles scurrying back to the podium. He would not run for mayor, he said in terms much less equivocal than he had used to describe his father's position. He said "his business has been so large that his physicians had warned him to take more rest, or he would go to pieces," the *Evening Journal* reported.[70] Someone had given Charles important advice.

The day belonged to George. When it was time for the formal vote, he won his party endorsement by acclamation. A delegation was sent to fetch him, and found a willing candidate who vowed to "do what I can for the interests of the city." The decidedly anti-Ames editorial page of the *Evening Journal* enthused, "Here's our next mayor!" Pillsbury was hailed as a friend of the working man and of all people, regardless of national origin. But both the *Journal* and the *Morning Tribune* were more vigorous in vilifying Ames for his "wide-open" saloon policy, "corruption," and "thug rule." The March 7, 1884, *Journal* said of George: "One good thing about the Republican candidate for mayor is that he doesn't need any lengthy biography in the news-papers. Everybody knows him, and knows him favorably." That famil-iarity was essential to this candidacy, for another reason: George did no personal campaigning.[71] He practiced the placid politics of small New England towns, where good reputation, willingness to serve, and mild exertions of friends and party on one's behalf were sufficient to win one of the many local and state elective offices that needed to

Minneapolis Mayor George Pillsbury.

be filled. Ames was a more vocal candidate, but he was handicapped by a divided Democratic Party. A personal feud between the mayor and Democratic First Ward alder-man M.W. Glenn had gone public, with Glenn openly accusing Ames of tolerating gambling and bribe-taking by police officers. The Democrats' intraparty strife helped propel George to victory on April 1 by the widest margin yet seen in a city election—6,000 votes.

The Republican election night celebration in 1884 was itself notable. The winning candidate again was not in attendance. Neither were his two sons, even though one of them was a leading state sena-tor whose presence at such an important party function would have been expected. His younger son, Fred, a man with a keen eye for horseflesh and a passion for racing, had spent Election Day meet-ing at the Nicollet House hotel with people interested in forming a Northwestern Racing Circuit.[72]

The political habits George had acquired in New Hampshire would not quite do in Minneapolis, however. As the orchestra con-ducted by Frank Danz (the precursor of the Minnesota Orchestra) performed at the Republican party at Windom Hall, someone sug-gested that if George would not come to them, they should go to him. Spontaneously, a parade assembled, the next day's *Journal* reported:

"Headed by Danz' band, the throng marched by way of Nicollet Avenue, the ranks being constantly increased as the column advanced. Along the line of marchers, shout after shout was sent up, and campaign songs were sung with a fervor indicative of the happy feeling because the right had triumphed. Fully 3,000 people assembled about the spacious grounds of Mr. Pillsbury's residence, which was brilliantly illuminated. Mr. Pillsbury appeared and was introduced by Alderman M. W. Glenn as 'the next mayor of Minneapolis, and the man who had received the largest and handsomest majority of any man ever elected to the office.' After the cheering had subsided, Mr. Pillsbury delivered a short address in which he said the people had done their duty, and he thanked them for the honor conferred. The result, he thought, was not brought about by party but by men of all parties who desired a change in the city government. He thought the 'wide-open' policy had been condemned, and he would endeavor to administer the duties falling upon him in a manner that would meet public approval.

"C.A. Pillsbury said, 'Gentlemen—you all know I am too tired to talk. All you want to know is something about the man you elected mayor. I am well acquainted with him. He is a man of few words. When I was a boy and acted badly, I heard from him. All I have to say is that when certain institutions in the city hear from him, they will do well to pay close attention to what he says.'" [73]

George claimed a mandate to clean up the city's saloons, and set out quickly to do so. His first message to the city council promised an overhaul of liquor licensure and measures to keep permission to sell liquor out of the hands of "vicious people." [74] On April 12, by unilateral decree, he ordered a halt to the sale of alcohol on Sundays. Only days later, he took to the council a major proposal: increase the cost of liquor licenses to $500 per year. He further proposed to restrict licenses to only those portions of the city in which residents did not object to saloons as neighbors, and where police forces could readily patrol. He asked the council to grant him the authority to draw the licensure boundary, which soon took the name "patrol limit." The mayor frequently credited his son Charles with conceiving the zoning idea. It was enacted. Irate saloonkeepers promptly took the mayor and city council to court to fight the new restrictions—and lost. The Supreme Court said in June 1884 that the limit was constitutionally permissible, though the council, not the mayor, ought to draw the patrol limit's boundaries. The patrol limit proved durable. A geographic restriction on liquor sales became a fixture in Minneapolis, adjusted slightly but not finally eased until well into the twentieth century. It must have been satisfying to Mayor George that the city attorney who successfully defended the patrol limit in court was Frank Carleton, Margaret's nephew.[75]

The policy quickly produced its intended effect. The number of licensed saloons in Minneapolis dropped dramatically, from 515 to 298, while the annual city revenue derived from liquor licenses nearly tripled. That success alone should assure Mayor Pillsbury a second term, the *Journal* editorialized in March 1886. But the mayor himself was again ambivalent about putting his name on the ballot. His reasons don't appear in newspaper accounts, but they can be readily surmised. George was a few months away from his seventieth birthday in the spring of 1886. His health was good but his attention was divided. C.A. Pillsbury & Co. remained profitable, but business was not as strong as it had been in the boom years of the 1870s. Bumper crops depressed wheat prices as the Minnesota countryside became well populated with farms and farmers. George's brother and sons were interested in diversifying the family's investments. They were eyeing an industry he knew well, railroads. His counsel was undoubtedly in demand—and not just by family members. George was a leader in the Minneapolis Chamber of Commerce. Ever the builder, he was president from 1883 to 1885, during the building of the first home for the exchange, complete with a trading floor, at Fourth Ave. and Third St. (Today's Grain Exchange complex is a twentieth-century reconstruction on the same site.)

In addition, George was increasingly caught up in Margaret's passion: church-related philanthropy. They took great joy in charitable giving, and, along with John and Mahala, resolved to do as much of it in their own lifetimes as prudence allowed. The city's First Baptist Church had a major claim on their time in 1885 and 1886. George also headed that organization's building committee, overseeing construction of the handsome Romanesque-Gothic revival structure that would be a landmark at Tenth and Hennepin for generations.[76] Perhaps taking their cue from the satisfaction John and Mahala derived as nurturers and benefactors of the University of Minnesota, George and Margaret developed a college interest of their own. They were drawn to helping little Minnesota Academy, a struggling Baptist college that originated in Hastings in 1854, closed in 1868, then reopened in Owatonna in 1877. They made arrangements to pay $30,000 for construction of a women's dormitory and gymnasium, which would rise in 1886. It would be the first of a number of major gifts to what soon would be renamed Pillsbury Academy.[77]

As his clan's patriarch, George also had to be much affected by the family's joys and sorrows. On Oct. 8, 1884, George and Margaret were on hand at John and Mahala's home as their eldest daughter, Addie, married her former classmate at the University of Minnesota, attorney Charles Webster. The happy occasion was reported in rich detail by the *Morning Tribune,* which raved about the candlelight, "choice cut flowers and autumn foliage" and "sumptuous repast."[78] Not quite seven months later, the same newspaper reported Addie's death, at age twenty-five, after what was evidently a brief illness. "The spirit of the beautiful bride has returned to God who gave it. . . Tears are falling from every eye," the April 5 edition said. Five months later came a second wedding in John and Mahala's home. Their second daughter, Susan, who had been a bridesmaid for her late sister 11 months before, was married to attorney Fred B. Snyder, who had been a groomsman for Charles Webster. The *Tribune* described the occasion as "quiet but elegant," attended almost exclusively by relatives[79] —signaling to readers that the Pillsburys were still grieving for the bride they had lost.

It had to lift the whole family's spirits when Fred and Alice announced that another baby was on the way. Helen Margaret would be born on Aug, 27, 1886, two days before her Grandpa George's seventieth birthday. Later that year, George and Margaret's adopted daughter Minnie, who had made something of a name for herself as a declamation artist at clubs and meetings,[80] married a native of old St. Anthony, Burt B. Townsend, a furniture dealer.[81] No record exists of a lavish wedding, raising the suspicion that George and Margaret may not have approved of the match. An item in the *Minneapolis Tribune* on Aug. 12, 1888, provides more grist for such speculation. It reports on the business failure of furniture dealer Townsend, whose total debt was more than double his assets, and whose sixty-seven creditors were led by George A. Pillsbury, at $13,500. Burt and Minnie had one child, a son named for Margaret, Sprague Pillsbury Townsend, born in 1894.

George's reluctance to seek a second term, but refusal to decisively decline renomination, led to a replay of 1884 at the 1886 Republican city convention. George showed up this time, but gave a speech "in the attitude of a man in deep trouble," the *Tribune* reported the next day, leaving his backers believing that while he said he did not want a second term, he was open to a draft. That's what they engineered— but not before indulging in another attempt to recruit Charles for the office. Charles' "polite but firm" refusal to run "had much the effect of a wet blanket" on the convention. When George finally consented to be the party's standard-bearer in the April 6 election, the response was "three not-very-vigorous cheers for Mayor Pillsbury, as the delegates were tired."[82]

The city's Republicans evidently remained listless in coming days, despite the exhortations from the two Republican newspapers for businessmen to hit the hustings on behalf of the mayor. No such fatigue afflicted Doc Ames and his well-financed allies, the city's liquor merchants. Ames may have been a physician, but by the 1880s, his vocation was politician. His comeback mayoral bid in 1886 was his fifth try for the office; he had also run unsuccessfully for lieutenant governor, Congress, marshal, and—in 1877—the state Senate, when his opponent was Charles A. Pillsbury. George and the Republicans set out to use the liquor issue to their advantage, thinking that it had been a winner for them in 1884. But Ames better understood the urban machine politics of the day, which were quite different from those of rural New Hampshire. He chalked up his loss in 1884 to a personal feud with Alderman M. W. Glenn, a fellow

Democrat, and did what he could to win Glenn back by promising him the plum position of postmaster. With a Democrat, Grover Cleveland, in the White House for the first time since the Civil War, and mayoral recommendations crucial to such appointments, the promise was plausible enough. Early in the 1886 campaign, Glenn announced

his support for Ames over George Pillsbury.

Ames also accurately identified Pillsbury's political weak spots, and tailored his campaign to the flood of newcomers to the city. The claim about George made two years earlier by the *Journal*, that "everybody knows him," was no longer true. All that many Minneapolis residents knew was that George was a rich old man backed by big business. Ames, twenty-six years George's junior, unabashedly played the age card, referring to George in his frequent stump

Albert Alonzo Ames, circa 1887.

speeches as "that old woman."[83] Saloon owners and their allies, the liquor distillers and distributors, also made sure the newcomers knew that George's policies were driving up the price of a drink. That knowledge was imparted with the offer of cash to voters who chose Ames, the newspapers implied. The liquor industry "is spending a fabulous sum of money" to defeat Pillsbury, the *Journal* warned on April 2. "A huge effort to naturalize foreigners and persuade workingmen against Pillsbury are being made. In the face of these energetic, sleepless, day-and-night efforts for the overthrow of law and order in Minneapolis, our businessmen are listless, careless and neglectful." The *Tribune* pulled out all the rhetorical stops on election day: "It is astonishing that the truth about (Ames) has been told so gently and sparingly in this campaign. His personal conduct while in the mayor's chair was indecent and outrageous. The mere proposition that he should be accorded the office again is an insult to the city. . . He and his gang have waged a campaign of prejudice and vituperation."[84]

George must have perceived in the days before the election that things were not going well. He broke with the pattern of his political lifetime on April 3 when he gave his first-ever campaign speech to the Sixth Ward Republican Club in a heavily Scandinavian area of the city. Again, liquor licensure was his theme. The *Evening Journal* did its part to make the most of the occasion, publishing a long excerpt of his remarks:

"If you think low (liquor) licenses and an increase in saloons is for the best interest of the city; that it will be better for your wives and children; think it will enhance the value of your homes; that it will better enable you to lay by from your hard earnings more money against a rainy day; that you can better educate your children and make them more respectable and your homes more happy, then there is no doubt for whom you ought to vote. If, on the contrary, you think differently, you cannot doubt as to your duty as a good citizen. Principle and not men should be your motto."

Implying that his opponent was doing otherwise, George added: "I never once paid one dollar to influence any man to vote against his own conviction."

The *Journal* pitched for Pillsbury again the day before the election, publishing a front-page column that allowed the mayor to answer questions readers had submitted. One question revealed how ethnic and class biases were being used by the Ames campaign to sow political discord. "Have you ever distributed any portion of the profits of your milling business among those confiding ignorant foreigners and others of the lower strata?" one question asked. George answered with words that would make his heirs proud: "I deny the imputation that laboring men are of that kind, and I consider the insinuation an insult to that class of people." He explained that C.A. Pillsbury & Co. distributed a share of its profits to all of its employees, from head miller to roustabout, without reference to class or nationality. (Our story will detail that company policy in the next chapter.)

The city's voters ended George's term as mayor, and his long career in politics, in that election. His margin of defeat in 1886 was comparable to his margin of victory in 1884—5,182 votes. A week later, George wrapped up his mayoral service with a lengthy "debriefing" to the city council, painstakingly conveying information about the details of city administration that he had been keeping in his large mental portfolio for three years.[85]

Among his mayoral achievements was the construction of the first Washington Avenue bridge across the Mississippi, linking downtown with the University of Minnesota campus. As mayor, he had also served on the city's first Library Board, which had been created by legislative action in 1885, modeled after the 1883 maneuver that had created the city's Park Board.[86] That high-powered group of library stewards included such local notables as lumberman and arts patron T.B. Walker, streetcar developer Thomas Lowry, and University of Minnesota president Cyrus Northrop. Notably, George took pains to praise city employees, whose ranks had grown considerably during his tenure. He then passed the torch to Ames, who would go on to lose another reelection bid in 1888, come back one more time—as a Republican—in 1900, and be convicted of bribe-taking in 1903. His conviction was tossed out on appeal, but the city's police chief—the mayor's brother, Fred Ames—and a half-dozen other Ames cronies served prison time. Muckraking journalist Lincoln Steffens probed the corruption in his administration in a widely read *McClure's* Magazine article, "The Shame of Minneapolis," which exposed the city to national scorn. A century later, Ames would be remembered as the most corrupt mayor in city history.

As the *Tribune* lamented on April 7, 1886: "Elections do not always go by reason."

When Exposition Hall opened in 1886, it vied with the Pillsbury A Mill as the biggest tourist attraction on the east side of the Minneapolis stretch of the Mississippi.

Chapter Five

Flour and Iron

In January 1884, *Lippincott's Magazine*, Philadelphia's erudite monthly journal of literature and science, told its readers about the amazing development of an industrial powerhouse to the northwest: Minneapolis. Lippincott's reporter, F. E. Curtis, dubbed it "a Floury City," and observed that a million-dollar megamill had been built on the east side of the Falls of St. Anthony little more than two years earlier, vastly increasing both the city's milling capacity and its international renown. The Pillsbury A Mill was "a noble building," Curtis said, citing its world-leading production capacity: 5,200 barrels of flour and 180 tons of "offal" (by-products) per day, produced from the contents of 110 railroad carloads of wheat delivered daily. "Four days' product would load an ocean steamer," he reported. It often did. By 1884, daily shipments of barrels branded "Pillsbury's Best" and "XXXX" were arriving at Europe's principal ports, where the flour inside them was acclaimed for its outstanding quality. "The mill employs 200 men, is illuminated by a 40-light electrical machine, has a complete fire apparatus, more than fifteen miles of belting, and many other things that excite the wonder of the visitor," purred the magazine scribe, clearly impressed.[1]

It's likely that during his visit to the city, Curtis had been escorted through the Minneapolis milling empire's east bank fortress by the man who knew and sold it best, Charles A. Pillsbury. He stood— or rather, he moved, incessantly—at the center of his business. His eyes, hands, and lively mind were engaged in very nearly its every aspect. "He has a remarkable faculty for mastering details, and greatly aids himself in this by a thorough system of reports of every part of his system," the editor of the *Northwestern Miller*, William C. Edgar, Charles's friend, admirer and sometimes critic, wrote a few years later. "Not a day passes without his being able to tell at a glance as to the firm's gain or loss, and the same system is carried into every branch and department of his mills."[2]

Charles was forty-one in January 1884, though he retained the vigor of a younger man. His hair was still wavy brown, though his forehead had grown more prominent and strands of gray had begun to lighten his chin whiskers. He still possessed the modest tastes and friendly manner of the New England country schoolteacher he had been twenty years before, yet he had attained as close to celebrity status as the young Midwestern city of Minneapolis could bestow. His every move was the subject of newspaper social notes and community gossip. And as Minneapolis became more established on the international scene, Charles also began to develop a reputation in business circles around the country and in Europe. An undated account preserved in Pillsbury corporate archives, evidently circa 1890, noted the contrast between the man's manner and his role:

"Charles A. Pillsbury is, on one sense, a common man. He is approachable, direct, interested in the duties and responsibilities of citizenship, a friend to his employees, a good neighbor, a helper of the deserving poor. In another and broader sense, he is indeed an uncommon man. He handles affairs of magnitude and a business involving many millions of dollar a year with the grasp of a master. He keeps his fingers on the pulse of the commercial world, and his word has weight in every civilized land under the sun." [3]

Charles was a captain steering his industry through a revolution. Better than perhaps anyone else in the nation, he seized the opportunity presented by the post-Civil War expansion in both the supply of wheat and demand for high-quality bread. His vision for the company that bore his name was that it would position itself as fully as possible between the farmer and the consumer, using economies of scale and technological innovation to turn wheat into commercially dispensed flour in a way that minimized cost and maximized quality. He would then employ what today would be called mass marketing to sell it to the world. [4]

In keeping with that strategy, C.A. Pillsbury & Co. went into the grain elevator business in 1882, in partnership with Charles S. Hulbert, a New York-born grain merchant ten years Charles's senior. The associates changed their company's name from Pillsbury & Hulbert to the Minneapolis and Northern Elevator Company three years later. It eventually owned and operated forty-seven elevators and warehouses in Dakota Territory and thirty-three in Minnesota, along the Great Northern Railway line owned by St. Paul's James J. Hill. The locations of those elevators, and by one account 120 others, were chosen by Pillsbury, Hulbert, and perhaps a few of their associates, likely including Hill. Those decisions determined the sites of scores of small towns in western Minnesota and eastern Dakota Territory, soon to become North and South Dakota. Few twenty-first-century inhabitants of those three states realize that key features of their local geography were decided at the Falls of St. Anthony as part of a master plan for the region's economy. [5]

But the path to hegemony in grain distribution being charted by Pillsbury and Hulbert soon faced a formidable obstacle. A new entrepreneurial species was emerging in Minneapolis to compete with them. Grain "warehousemen" Frank Peavey, George Van Dusen, and W.W. and Sam Cargill had never operated a mill, but they found in grain storage and shipment a niche in the milling industry, and exploited it for all they were worth. One curiosity is that none of those grain handlers claimed control of the barrel manufacturing that was flourishing in Minneapolis ancillary to the mills and terminal elevators. Instead, beginning in 1874, the "coopers," or barrel-makers, of Minneapolis created a cooperative union and shared the proceeds of their labor. This groundbreaking arrangement lasted for more than thirty years, and is cited in the annals of U.S. labor history as a rare success story among early craft cooperatives. One reason for its success might have been the support the union had from Charles Pillsbury. "Mr. Pillsbury made the giant cooperative cooperage (barrel works) industry of Minneapolis possible," one early account said.[6]

As their enterprises grew in the 1870s, Charles and the other Minneapolis millers increasingly chafed at the high cost of transporting their finished product to eastern markets. They believed they were being gouged by Chicago-based lines, which provided the only rail link from the Falls of St. Anthony to the east. William D. Washburn, then a Republican congressman and C. C. Washburn's youngest brother, was the first to put his money behind a plan to establish a new rail route to the east via Sault Ste. Marie, Michigan, avoiding Chicago. He'd been publicly urged to do so as early as 1873, in a speech in Minneapolis delivered by another Washburn brother, Gov. Israel Washburn of Maine, the eldest of that remarkable family. Ten years were to pass before William acted on Israel's advice and organized the Minneapolis, Sault Ste. Marie & Atlantic, which quickly became known as the Soo Line. Washburn was the line's first president; its vice president was Charles A. Pillsbury.[7]

The family's rail holdings expanded in mid-1885 when Charles purchased controlling interest in the Minneapolis, Lyndale and Lake Minnetonka streetcar line, better known locally as the Motor Line. Brother Fred was installed as the line's vice president the next year; he would go on to be its president before the line was sold in 1887 to Thomas Lowry, who would be the prime human propeller of the city's streetcar system for the next two decades. The Motor Line was a technologically up-to-the-minute steam-driven system linking Lakes Calhoun, Harriet, and Minnetonka to the west. It also connected Minnehaha Falls, in the southeast section of Minneapolis, to the city's industrial heart at St. Anthony Falls. Charles paid $360,000 to purchase the company's debt, which included bonds previously held by William D. Washburn.[8] The two rail ventures showed how these two business rivals were also capable of common endeavors—and of those, railroads were only the beginning.

Charles's keen attention to what was happening in his mills inspired him to further innovations—as did a downturn in wheat prices, which began a long slide in 1882. One problem in particular—the unreliability of waterpower in the variable Minnesota climate—piqued his interest. In the winter of 1884 he began to convert

William D. Washburn in the 1880s.

the A Mill from waterpower to steam, giving the big plant more consistent year-round capability.[9] An account of that decision kept in company files illustrates how quickly Charles could act to improve his mills: "Low water was bothering at the time and the idea of introducing steam as auxiliary power came into his mind one morning before he was out of bed. On reaching the office he used the telegraph so effectively in obtaining an estimate of the cost and requirements that by noon he had the plant ordered, the expenditure on which was $75,000. The improvement was arranged for with such expedition that all partners in the firm were not aware of the move until they were advised of its consummation later in the day."[10]

Other Minneapolis mills soon followed suit. They also followed Pillsbury's lead in installing of both electrical lighting and telephones. The Pillsbury mills were among the first ten subscribers to the city's first telephone exchange, the Northwestern Telephone Co., in 1878. No other mills were on the initial list. Charles was said to take particular pride in bringing electric lighting to the A mill, and hence to the entire milling district. It gave the Pillsbury A the look of an illuminated castle, and was such an attraction on summer evenings that a door-keeper was hired to "keep snoopy tourists out." The story was told in 1890 of an exchange between Charles and the state's first territorial governor and second state governor, Alexander Ramsey. "When that tempting dish, oysters on the half-shell, was served, the ex-governor was heard to remark to the big miller that he was the first one to introduce oysters into the state of Minnesota. To this, Mr. Pillsbury replied: 'We are both pioneers in certain respects then, for I was the first to introduce electric lights in the Northwest, placing them in our A mill.' "[11]

As early as 1875, Charles made space and hired staff for a test kitchen, or "doughing room," in which flour of various grade blends were tested for all manner of attributes important to home and commercial bakers. By the early 1880s, the blending of wheat grades to achieve desirable baking results had become the latest thing in mills in England, and Charles was fascinated by the prospect of doing the same himself. He was among the nation's leaders in mixing low- and high-grade wheat in his test kitchen to achieve optimal gluten strength. He took great interest in the test kitchen's work, concerning himself with such details as the room's lighting and equipment. By the decade's end, he had E.C. Hughes, the electrician at the A Mill, testing the baking of bread "in a tin cylindrical case heated via a wire through which current is passed." It was the first electric oven in Minnesota.[12]

Little about his mills or his men escaped Charles's attention. He impressed a visiting journalist in the mid-1880s when, in response to a question, he produced from his desk a "yield book" that allowed him to quickly determine the amount of "bran, shorts, screenings and Red Dog" byproducts produced in the manufacture of a barrel of flour.[13] An 1885 account described his work habits:

> *C.A. Pillsbury and Capt. Holmes [H. W. Holmes of Sidle, Fletcher, Holmes & Co., owners of the Northwestern Mill, whose corporate board members included Fred C. Pillsbury] are early birds," said a grain trader. "Go to their offices any morning except Sunday, and you will find them there at 7 o'clock, buried in business. Their work has grown to such enormous proportions that they are compelled to do this. Getting down early, they are able to do a vast*

amount of work in the two or three hours that elapse before the long procession of callers descends upon them. They must give the bulk of the day between 10 a.m. and 4 p.m. to parties who approach them on all sorts of errands – flour buyers, flour sellers, elevator builders, grain dealers, representatives of local business, charity, church and social organizations, canvassers and what-not. Both men are of temperate and regular habits, using neither tobacco nor stimulants, and there are no harder workers in the country, nor do I know of two men who can turn out as much business in a given time. They come nearer to making every minute count than anybody I know of, and not one of the men in their employ averages as many hours per day the year around as they do. While they do not spare themselves, they are, so far as their employees are concerned, kind and indulgent almost to a fault. [14]

Indeed, the manner in which C.A. Pillsbury & Co. demonstrated its regard for its employees became the talk of the town in the mid-1880s. The company had long paid wages higher than their non-milling competitors, and reaped the benefit of employee loyalty in return. For example, the average daily wage for grinders and machine tenders at Pillsbury was $3.25 in 1880, compared with $2.15 for carpenters, $2.17 for engineers, and $2.45 for machinists at other firms in the city. [15] For that generosity, Pillsbury expected the same hard work he required of himself. In 1887, he penned his advice to young men seeking a business career: "When a young man commences a business life by working in the employ of others, let him strive not simply to earn his salary and to give satisfaction to his employers, but let him aim to do all he has strength to do and to earn his salary many times over. In my first business years, it was no uncommon thing for me to work all night until breakfast time, a thing I was not expected nor asked to do. If a young man will follow the rule of trying to make his services many times more valuable than his salary, either his employer or someone else will appreciate him . . . My experience is that between natural ability and hard work, the latter will always win. When the two are in combination, nothing can prevent success." [16]

Beginning in 1883, the company went one step further in employee compensation—a step taken by no one else at the falls and by few other employers in the country, if any. Pillsbury established an employee profit-sharing plan. It was initially available to employees with five or more years of service, but was eventually extended to those with at least two years' tenure. Given that the A Mill alone employed 375 men in the latter half of the 1880s, the number of Minneapolis households that benefited from the profit distribution undoubtedly ran well into the hundreds. For the rest of that decade, those households and, it seemed, the whole city, would anxiously await word each October about the year's profits and whether and how they would be shared.

Indeed, flour milling profits were generally "drab" in the 1880s, and payouts were not guaranteed.[17] Three times between 1883 and 1890, no payments were made. "It has been known for some time that the dullness of the milling business would this year preclude the usual division of profits by C.A. Pillsbury & Co among their employees, and the firm has written a letter to their men notifying them of this fact, frankly giving as the reason that they made no money last season," the *Northwestern Miller* reported on Oct. 8, 1886. "The letter urges the employees to be vigilant in the interest of their employers, as a matter of mutual benefit, and notifies them that the profit division plan will be continued in force the present year."

On Sept. 18, 1888, the arrival of profit-sharing checks totaling $40,000 in Pillsbury pay envelopes was acclaimed by the *Minneapolis Tribune*. The payout "strengthened the bond of union and mutual respect which for some years has notably existed between the firm and their workmen....The eyes of American workingmen and employers in all parts of the country have been turned to this the great flour milling firm in the world, to see if the system was to be a success or a failure. Now its success seems assured, and it is hardly to be doubted that in the near future, many large firms employing hundreds of men will see the wisdom of the policy and adopt the same course."[18]

That assessment proved overly optimistic. Employee profit sharing caught on elsewhere very sporadically and slowly. But for the sons and grandsons of Capt. John Pillsbury of Sutton, N.H., allowing

The Palisade Mill.

all those connected to their business to share in its rewards was only natural. The Pillsburys were in Minnesota to make money, to be sure, but it was money to be used to build a better life for everyone associated with the enterprise, employees and neighbors alike. Money was the means to the end they sought, not the end itself.

To the Pillsburys, profit-sharing was also what simple fairness demanded. After all, Charles would say, his employees were responsible for the high quality of Pillsbury's Best. "The public generally gives the managers of the mills too much and the employees too little credit for the high reputation of Minneapolis flour," he said, adding that his head millers had been with him for so many years and were so experienced that it was impossible for them to turn out poor flour.[19] In 1891, Charles told the journal *The Review of Reviews* that he was attracted to a "plan which would more equitably divide the profits between capital and labor." He acknowledged that sour management-labor relations in other industries were giving rise to the labor union movement at home and abroad. "The continual agitation of the labor question called my attention to the subject," Charles said, "but there was no disaffection among my own employees, so far as I was aware." As long as Charles lived, there would not be.

Charles was not the family's only innovator in the 1880s. Fred, never as driven in matters of business as were his father and brother, nonetheless had curiosity and creativity sufficient to conceive of an experiment with "offal," the part of the wheat kernel unused for flour: hulls, bran and germ. Offal was long considered a by-product of little or no value. Some early Minneapolis mills simply dumped it into the Mississippi. By the 1880s, it had some resale value as animal feed, enough to warrant construction of a "bran house" adjacent to the Pillsbury A from which to sell and ship offal to farmers on the East Coast. There was little local market for the stuff.

Fred C. Pillsbury in the 1880s.

Fred believed bran was under-appreciated as livestock feed. It could be a better moneymaker if its value as a superior stock-fattening and milk-producing agent could be demonstrated, he thought. The idea likely sprang from Fred's attraction to things agrarian and equestrian. More than his father, brother, or Uncle John, Fred favored country life. His interests may have more nearly matched those of his younger uncle, Benjamin, by then a lumberman, farmer, and land dealer in the Minnesota River town of Granite Falls. The *Northwestern Miller* magazine noted in June 1884 that "most everybody is aware that Fred Pillsbury is a great lover of fine horseflesh," and that he excelled at buggy racing.[20] About that time, he bought a small herd of Holstein cattle and conducted a controlled experiment at the farm owned by the University of Minnesota's College of Agriculture, near the state fairgrounds, where Fred loved to race. Some of the cattle were fed a ration of hay and wheat bran; the bran was denied to

Fred and Alice Pillsbury's home, 1888.

others. He kept careful records of the animals' growth, under the tutelage of Prof. E.D. Porter. The conclusion, as reported by the *Northwestern Miller*, supported Fred's hypothesis: "The economy of using bran as an article for feeding stock will depend, like any other food, upon its cost in the local market and the value of its product; but it would seem if dairy and stock men of the Atlantic states can afford to pay the first costs at the mills, profits of middlemen and transportation for 1,500 miles, Minnesota farmers might find it profitable to retain this by-product of their mills for their own advantage."[21] With the Pillsbury name backing the notion that cattle would fatten more quickly and produce more milk on a bran diet, bran sales soared. By 1889, the A Mill's bran sales exceeded $200,000.[22]

But once again, family tragedy followed hard on the heels of triumph. Just as Fred's work with bran as livestock feed was gaining acclaim, his daughter Marian, only two-and-a-half, took ill with scarlet fever. She died on Jan. 10, 1887. The *Northwestern Miller* reported the "deep sorrow in the family" as it extended its condolences on another beloved child lost to a nineteenth-century scourge.[23]

Fred, Alice, and their surviving children settled into a grand new house later that year, at Tenth St. and Third Av. S, very near the homes of both George and Charles. The home's location attested to the closeness of the Pillsbury family. So did newspaper society columns during the 1880s which describe New Year's Day receptions and Thanksgiving dinners in which the entire Pillsbury clan participated, including married daughters and sons-in-law.[24]

Thus it seems likely that the whole family—or at least, both pairs of brothers—counseled closely with each other in the late spring or early summer of 1889 when a major business opportunity arose. Wealthy British investors were stalking the American Midwest in search of investment opportunities. They were the Gilded Age's version of modern-day multinational corporations. In fact, it might be said that they, not their great-grandchildren, invented economic globalization. Several American breweries were the first to fall into British hands. The quality of Minneapolis flour and the boomtown it had spawned at the Falls of St. Anthony next caught the Brits' attention. In the eyes of the Minneapolis boosters at the *Northwestern Miller*, the prospect of British ownership represented a threat—a view that would only intensify with the passage of time. In 1925 the magazine described the arrival of British capitalists in Minneapolis in 1889 as "a danger" that "cast its shadow over the Falls.[25]

But to the principals of C.A. Pillsbury & Co., the British interest in buying their mills and paying Charles a handsome salary to run them looked like opportunity, not a danger. It might have seemed a safe haven in the storm that the flour industry had become. "After the prosperous years of the introduction of roller milling there came a pause—a period of depression," an industry historian would write three decades later. From 1883 to 1887, flour prices declined steadily, competition among millers intensified and profits fell. "On the other hand, the growth of Minneapolis flour exports to English markets, the wide publicity secured by C.A. Pillsbury and other Minneapolis millers, the large amounts of English capital seeking investment—all these combined to make such a purchase seem desirable to the English."[26]

When British investors first offered to buy Minneapolis mills is not clear. But by July 4, 1889, the presence of three Englishmen in town with an interest in flour and waterpower was public knowledge, thanks to the reporting of the *Northwestern Miller* and the city's newspapers. They first approached the heirs of C.C. Washburn, who had died in 1882, and of John Crosby, who died in 1887. Washburn-Crosby still had some family owners, including Cad Washburn's brother William and nephew John Washburn. But the firm was controlled by William Dunwoody and James S. Bell, a very able flour salesman Dunwoody had hired to replace Crosby the previous year. Cad's daughters and sons-in-law were willing to sell, but Dunwoody, Bell, and John Washburn were not. For them, Washburn-Crosby Co. was more than an investment. It was their careers.

That was not the attitude of wheeler-dealer William Washburn. By 1889 he owned but a small share of his late brother's firm, but he had a small two-mill flour company of his own, consisting of the Palisade Mill at the falls and the Lincoln Mill twenty miles upstream in Anoka. As a newly elected U.S. senator, sent to Washington by the Minnesota Legislature that spring, and a man prone to living well beyond his means, William was more than happy to convert those mills to cash. He also had considerable interest in the west-side water-power company known as the Minneapolis Mill Co. He was keen to put it on the block as well.

The British courtship lasted through the summer and into fall as options deadlines were set, then extended, and vague reassuring statements were made to the public. In September, the *Tribune* reported excitedly that a Minneapolis businessman visiting London was astonished to see former Gov. John S. Pillsbury and Sen. William Washburn entering a bank there together, "as if by appointment."[27] On Oct. 29, the deal was done. Pillsbury-Washburn Flour Mills Co., Ltd., was born on Nov. 1, 1889. Its holdings included the three Pillsbury and two Washburn flour mills, two elevator companies, and the capital stock of both the Minneapolis Mill Co. and the St. Anthony Falls Water Power Co., which had been in James J. Hill's hands since 1880. That made Pillsbury-Washburn far and away the largest enterprise at the falls, controlling more than half of the flour output of the city of Minneapolis, plus approximately 170 grain elevators in Minnesota and the neighboring Dakotas, which had only very recently been granted statehood. The firm could produce 14,500 barrels of flour per day. At its managerial helm was the man believed to be paid the largest salary of any industrial manager in the United States—Charles A. Pillsbury. In addition to a $15,000 annual minimum employment contract, plus the opportunity to earn bonuses that would put his actual earnings at several times that amount, Charles came away from the sale with his share of the family's total proceeds: $4,325,000, of which $3,225,000 was paid in cash and the remainder in debentures, preferred stock, and ordinary shares. At a time when workers at Pillsbury mills considered themselves fortunate to bring home $1,000 a year, these were princely sums indeed.[28]

Pillsbury-Washburn had about 300 stockholders, and was capitalized at just under $8 million. Four Brits headed the board of directors: Richard H. Glyn, a banker; J. Flower Jackson, a hops merchant; Sydney T. Klein, a flour merchant; and E.T. Rose, an investment banker. A "committee of management in America" was also formed, headed by Charles and including John S. Pillsbury and William Washburn.

Foreign ownership of the many of the leading mills at the falls, not to mention the water power companies on both sides of the river and elevators throughout the Upper Midwest, was not exactly a welcome prospect to proud Minnesotans. News reports immediately questioned whether the six hundred Pillsbury employees would continue to enjoy annual profit-sharing payments under the new arrangement. (The initial answer, through 1891, was yes.)[29] When "Honest John" returned from London, he became the chief dispenser of reassurance to the community, telling inquiring local journalists that he expected "the most gratifying results" from the new arrangement. The *Tribune*'s editorial page tried to stoke enough civic pride to overcome jitters. "When conservative English capital, after searching the United States over, finds Minneapolis the most promising field for investment of many million dollars in manufacturing, there is cause for congratulations," the paper said.[30] Still, skepticism ranged as far as Washington, D.C., despite the involvement of Minnesota's junior senator in the deal. Within a year, Charles was summoned to testify before a U.S. Senate subcommittee investigating the effects of foreign corporate acquisitions on the American workforce. When he was asked why he and his partner-relatives sold to the British syndicate, his answer was simple: The Englishmen had offered a good price; and the family felt "it had too many eggs in one basket"[31] and should unload some of them.

Charles may have been candidly describing his family's anxiety about the flour business. But in truth, by 1890, the Minnesota Pillsburys had a number of profitable business holdings apart from milling. Their ventures included, among others, extensive timber holdings, rail, banking, and shares of an underwear knitting mill founded by George D. Munsing (its Munsingwear union suits and, eventually, polo shirts would become world famous.) A year earlier, John Pillsbury was one of three incorporators of the Minneapolis Heating & Power Co., the city's first electrical utility. It would grow up in the twentieth century as Northern States Power Co., the region's primary supplier of electrical power. He was also a co-owner and director of the Minneapolis Stock Yards and Packing Co. George and Charles were both directors of Northwestern National Bank, the city's largest; George was soon to become its board chairman. John would take the same leading position at First National, the second-largest bank in the city, and was a director at two other banks. Fred joined him on the First National board of directors. Today, these two banks exist in Minnesota as Wells Fargo and U.S. Bank, respectively. [32]

Timber lands and lumber mills had been among Pillsbury holdings in Minnesota since the 1860s, when John was both selling and buying parcels of University of Minnesota land to retire its disabling debt. The extent of those holdings by the late 1880s is not known, but they included considerable property near Brainerd and more to the northeast. The Pillsburys established the Gull River Lumber Co., about ten miles west of Brainerd, not long after John sold his Minneapolis hardware store. An account written late in John's life says he headed the "very extensive business" at Gull River for nearly twenty-five years. Land sale records in Duluth show a large number of purchases by John in September 1883 and throughout 1884. In 1889, exactly when John was negotiating with the Brits over purchase of C.A. Pillsbury & Co., he also was launching the Gull

Lake and Northern Railway Company, a railroad link from northern forests to his Gull River mill. [33]

The buzz among landowners and speculators in northeastern Minnesota in the 1880s wasn't just about the money to be made from still-bountiful stands of giant white and red pine. It was also about minerals. As early as 1865, Minnesota had experienced a mini-gold rush, when a few golden nuggets were found near Lake Vermilion. Gold fever faded almost as rapidly as it has appeared, but University of Minnesota geologists began a more thorough assessment of the area's mining potential during the 1870s. In 1883, R. D. Irving, chief geologist of the Lake Superior Division of the U.S. Geological Survey, announced his conclusion that south and west of Lake Vermilion, in an area named Mesabi after an Ojibwe legend about a sleeping giant, a substantial iron formation was likely to be present. Conditions there matched those of the already proven Gogebic district in northwestern Michigan, he said. At the time, more than ten thousand acres of Mesabi land were owned by John, George, and Charles Pillsbury. [34]

John had to be aware of the possibility of substantial iron deposits on his land, but he evidently received that word with skepticism. Little else could explain what may have been his only rash business move in a lifetime of astute capitalism. On March 10, 1890, he signed an agreement with prospector Russell M. Bennett granting him half of the mineral-rights proceeds from the family's Mesabi holdings if Bennett found on them a confirmed iron ore deposit of at least ten thousand tons within five years. Their initial understanding, reached in late 1889, was sealed only with a handshake. [35] Bennett had already acquired a partner who could provide crucial resources he lacked—financing and mineral exploring expertise. Shortly after the March 10 deal was struck, Bennett signed a contract with John M. Longyear of Marquette, Michigan, a man fifteen years his senior and an experienced explorer and assayer of mineral deposits. Bennett agreed to a 50-50 split of his share of the mineral proceeds he stood to acquire from the Pillsburys, should he and Longyear find the requisite amount of ore on Pillsbury land.

It's remarkable that a man as young as Bennett—he was only twenty-five at the time—would be able to win the confidence of a businessman as savvy as John Pillsbury (not to mention John Long-year) after what amounted to a cold call in 1889. Bennett evidently projected competence, reliability, and drive. A robust, adventuresome fellow, the son of a deceased Minnesota steamboat operator, Bennett had been financially on his own for more than a decade and had made his way with aplomb in a vari-ety of places in the American West.[36] His sojourns took him to Mexico, brought him into personal contact with the Apache leader Geronimo, and linked him by marriage to the Davis family of Saginaw, Michigan, where his mother moved after being widowed. That family was part of Wright & Davis Co., which owned even more timberland in northeast-ern Minnesota than the Pillsburys did. Bennett counted among his personal friends a man who had been his father's friend and steam-

Russell M. Bennett, circa 1915.

boat-company colleague in the 1860s, James J. Hill. That connection may have opened Pillsbury doors. In 1888 and 1889, Bennett was working as a "timber cruiser" on land owned by the Pillsburys. He probably was not in direct Pillsbury employ, but collected his pay from a logging company that was under contract with Pillsbury to harvest timber on the land.

Timber cruisers were, in essence, logging scouts. Working alone, Bennett traversed the deep woods with a tent, a coffeepot, flour, coffee, a rifle (with which to shoot his dinner,) a small hatchet, and a note-book and pen to record his findings. Using the hatchet, his job was to mark trees he considered suitable for harvest the following season, and to keep detailed account of their location.[37] The work attuned him to nature and gave him plenty of time to dream and scheme. He probably spotted more than a few outcroppings of red rock amid the trees.

John Pillsbury may have been skeptical about claims that his rich timberland was even richer under the surface. Then again, he may have seen the value of hiring someone with Bennett's pluck and perseverance to scour the largely roadless and densely forested countryside on his behalf. In any case, when a find of fifty thousand tons of iron ore was confirmed in 1892, honest John Pillsbury, man of his word, signed a deed giving Longyear and Bennett claim to half of the mineral rights on ten thousand acres containing some of the richest iron deposits anywhere on the planet. More than a hundred million tons of ore would ultimately come from those Mesabi holdings.[38]

John was said to be disgusted with himself, and apologetic to George and Charles, for having agreed to terms so generous to Bennett. "Well," he conceded, "if I was damn fool enough to sign the option, I will live up to it."[39] Bennett's nephew would recall years later: "The saying got about quite generally, and its beneficent effect on the commercial morality of his day is hard to estimate. It is a sermon in a sentence."[40] Time proved that Pillsbury's remorse was unwarranted. The Mesabi Range had ore sufficient to make all three families—Pillsbury, Bennett and Longyear—prosper for generations to come. As of this writing, their three-way split of Mesabi Range mineral-rights proceeds has continued without interruption for more than 117 years.

The gain from the sale of C.A. Pillsbury & Co. to British businessmen was invested in several business ventures. But a portion also went into a residential upgrade for Charles, Mary Ann, and their twin boys, and into a flurry of philanthropy. Charles's new business partner, W. D. Washburn, owned the grandest house in town, Fair Oaks. Built in 1883, it was a palatial eighty-room mansion atop the highest hill south of downtown, between Twenty-second and Twenty-fourth Streets and Stevens and Third Avenue S. Across the street to the south stood Villa Rosa, home of the city's first mayor, mill investor, and Washburn cousin, Dorilus Morrison. (His home would become the site of the Minneapolis Institute of Arts.) And across Stevens to the west stood an elegant yellow limestone mansion owned by the president of the Minneapolis school board, retired manufacturer J. W. Johnson, built by local architects Franklin Long and Frederick Kees between 1885 and 1887.[41]

Highland Home, 2200 Stevens Av. S.

Long and Kees were building the Lumber Exchange, a downtown landmark at Fifth and Hennepin, at about the same time. After completing Johnson's Highland Home, their next projects were the Minneapolis Courthouse and City Hall between Third and Fourth Avenues and Fourth and Fifth Streets, and the Minneapolis Public Library, a gracious building at Tenth and Hennepin that was lost during the demolition craze of the mid-twentieth century. (Charles helped underwrite the latter project with a $5,000 gift.) Johnson's massive Romanesque house was deemed "restrained" in style—an assessment that could only be justified in comparison with the castle that stood across the street.[42]

Fair Oaks, Villa Rosa, and Highland Home were considered "out in the country" in those years.[43] In 1890, Johnson, contemplating a move to California, was willing to sell. He was also eyeing investment property downtown, and observed that commercial activity was crowding close to the northeast corner of Tenth Street and Second Avenue, site of the yellow brick home of the Charles Pillsbury family. Charles, meanwhile, was attracted to Johnson's more prestigious address and its proximity to his new business partner—even though it meant moving a dozen blocks away from his parents and brother. A $125,000 transaction was negotiated that included a land swap. In April 1890, Charles, Mary Ann, and eleven-year-olds John and

Charlie took possession of Highland Home and its adjacent carriage house and stable. They moved in with their household staff (a coachman, nanny, cook, several maids and likely a gardener/handyman) and animals that included three horses, a cow (affluent people didn't "trust the public milk in those days," young John later explained in an interview) and two St. Bernard dogs. They then set about filling the mansion's vast interior spaces with furniture and art purchased in Chicago, New York, and Europe. Among the receipts stored in company files are ones reading "Spaulding & Co., Chicago, three vases, $1,850" and "M. Knoedler & Co., 170 Fifth Av. New York, two paintings, $3,500."[44] The modest taste of Mary Ann and Charles's New England youth was a thing of the past; it had given way to refinement and touches of opulence.

But it was not in Pillsbury nature to spend a windfall entirely on personal gain and comfort. They always had been generous givers to church and civic causes. With the profits from the sale of C.A. Pillsbury & Co., the family's philanthropy moved to a higher plane, setting a new standard of generosity for affluent Minneapolitans.

The remarkable run of Pillsbury giving began at the state Capitol on April 16, 1889, at an unusual joint meeting of the University of Minnesota Board of Regents, on which John had served since 1863, and a House-Senate conference committee considering capital investments for the coming biennium. The legislative session was in its waning days, and lawmakers were in a quandary over how to respond to a fervent request from the regents. The university was outgrowing its meager facilities, and lacked the modern science laboratories required to compete with the major public universities that were gaining prominence in Ohio, Michigan, Illinois, and Iowa—not to mention Methodist-affiliated Hamline University in St. Paul. The legislative panel was in sympathy with the request, but it had already agreed to bond for $100,000 for a science hall, and could afford no more. When a fire seriously damaged the half-completed building in 1888, the regents determined that a fireproof science hall was essential—and so was an additional $150,000 for its construction.

What happened next was recounted later by journalist Rollin Smith of the *Northwestern Miller*:

No one knew what to do; but finally, Mr. Pillsbury rose, and in the quiet manner peculiar to him, spoke to those assembled. He began with the early days of the university, and briefly reviewed its history and showed its present needs. Then he said, "As the state has not the funds, I wish to help this university myself. I have had the intention of leaving something for it. I think I cannot do better for the state, which has so highly honored me, and the university I so much love, than by making a donation for the completion of this building; and I propose to erect a complete science hall, at an expense of $150,000, more or less, and present it to the state." The Legislature was in session at the time, and the offer of Mr. Pillsbury was received with much enthusiasm, and each house spread on the records resolutions of gratitude.[45]

An account written in 1893 included more of John's remarks that day:

All I ask is to know that these land grants be kept intact, and this institution be made one that this great state may be proud of; that may be adequate to the needs of the state, an honor to it, and a lasting monument to the progress which is characteristic of this state now, and in the years to come – some assurance that when I am dead and gone this institution shall be kept for all time, broad in its scope, powerful in its influence, as firm and substantial in its maturity as it was weak and struggling in the days that saw its birth.[46]

Whether a verbatim account or an artful reconstruction, the threat to which these remark refer was real. One possibility being bruited in 1889 was that the University of Minnesota would be divided into two or more institutions, geographically separate from one another. Such a move had proved politically irresistible in other Midwestern states, where land-grant agricultural and technical "state universities" were established to rival the first public universities established in the state. John considered such a division a mistake for Minnesota. It would dissipate or destroy the synergies made possible when academic disciplines are pursued in close proximity—something

Pillsbury Hall, University of Minnesota.

Minnesota's university, with its limited resources and comparatively remote location, could ill afford to squander. (Those who witness the dynamic interactions between biology, medicine, agriculture, and environmental science on the university's Twin Cities campus today may agree that he was right.)

A few months after John's dramatic announcement at the Capitol, university president Cyrus Northrop—the second man to hold the post, and, like the first, personally hired by John—paid tribute to his institution's most faithful steward, and described well the Pillsbury attitude about money: "He has shown himself wise in estimating money at its just value—not for what it is, but for what it can do—not as something to be held and loved and gloated over, or to be expended in personal aggrandizement and luxury, but as something which can work mightily for humanity; which can reinforce even the educational power of a sovereign state; which can enrich human minds and can thus lift up into the true greatness of a noble citizenship the sons and daughters of the whole Northwest." [47]

While John was making news with the gift of the building that would take the name Pillsbury Science Hall at the University of Minnesota, George was stepping up his donations to Pillsbury Academy in Owatonna. By April 1889, his gifts had reached the $200,000 mark. That caught the attention of the *New York Times*, which reported the brothers' largess on April 28. It praised these "sons of New Hampshire," active "on behalf of education." George would go farther the next year, as president of the American Baptist Educational Society. At its Chicago meeting in May 1890, the society accepted a $400,000 fundraising challenge issued by John D. Rockefeller of Standard Oil Co. Rockefeller would donate $600,000 if the Baptists would raise a $400,000 share, and use that money to found a first-class college in Chicago, on 20 South Side acres donated by retailer Marshall Field. George came home to Minneapolis enthusiastic about prospects for a school that he said was likely to be called the University of Chicago.[48] He became a member of that prestigious institution's first governing board, and would serve for four years. He likely contributed generously to meet the challenge Rockefeller had set forth, though records are not clear on the matter. It is known that in 1891, he established an endowment of $5,000 so that Pillsbury Academy graduates in Owatonna could continue their study at the University of Chicago.[49]

Personal charity—the aiding of acquaintances, friends and relatives in need—was also a priority for the Pillsburys of Minnesota. One such gift in September 1890 bears noting because of the likely role Mary Ann Pillsbury played in arranging it. Her role must be surmised but the circumstantial evidence strongly indicates a measure of wifely influence over the family purse that no other surviving story reveals.

In May 1890 the former Anoka County attorney, George Washington Morrill, went missing. He had an active legal practice in Anoka, built in large part as a real estate attorney after he lost the elective prosecutorial post in 1880. (Morrill, a Democrat, could not survive the Republican sweep in that presidential election year.) He packed a valise, told his wife he was headed to the Twin Cities on a business errand, and disappeared, never to return again. Foul play was alleged, either on his part or the part of someone who knew that some portion of his legal mission that day was the cashing of a large check, intended to retire a mortgage.[50] His disappearance left his wife, Olive Ireland Caldwell Morrill, and their two children bereft of income, and with a mortgage owed to Anoka financier Winthrop Young. Olive Caldwell Morrill happened to be the third cousin of

Mary Ann Pillsbury, the daughter of her father's second cousin. Less than four months after attorney Morrill's disappearance, on Sept. 16, the mortgage on Olive's house was paid and the house was purchased by Charles A. Pillsbury.[51] Her lodging was secure.

The elder Pillsbury brothers' next wave of giving went in a different direction—eastward, to their home turf in New Hampshire. Chapter Two told of the first of their tokens of appreciation to the communities that raised them—a Civil War soldier's memorial statue, made of granite and thirty-two feet tall, erected a stone's throw from the white clapboard house in little Sutton in which George and John spent their boyhoods. It was dedicated on Sept. 1, 1891, with George, Margaret and Minnie, and John and Mahala, in attendance—but with Charles, who had been of military age in the 1860s but had opted for work in Canada instead, conspicuous by his absence. George wrote a letter one month before the dedication apologizing for Charles's decision to stay away, explaining that "the critical outlook as to the future of our business matters was such that he did not think it prudent" to travel to New Hampshire just then.[52]

Civil War memories meant a great deal in Sutton, which sent 164 of its 1,431 citizens to the Union Army when President Lincoln's call came. The tiny town overflowed with people on the monument's dedication day, as "an enormous milling, chattering and laughing crowd of townspeople, ex-residents, and guests from neighboring towns followed (former) soldiers toward the statue."[53] George's political career had produced little evidence of a gift for oratory. But on that day, as his heart overflowed with memories and emotion, he paid eloquent tribute to his hometown and its Civil War sacrifice. "I believe Sutton is credited with having furnished over 150 soldiers during the late struggle; and I would have this monument commemorate not only the valor of those brave men who responded to their country's need, but I would have it represent the courage and the patriotism of those mothers, wives, and sisters who surrendered their dearest gifts—their sons, husbands and brothers—to their country," he said.[54] Knowing that his son had not been among them must have weighed on George's heart.

The Pillsbury brothers were undoubtedly mindful too, that day, of the many friends and relatives whose physical remains resided in Sutton's cemetery. In 1891, that resting place included a relatively fresh Pillsbury grave. Benjamin Franklin Pillsbury, the brother four years younger than John who had lived the longest in Sutton, then emigrated to Granite Falls, Minnesota, had died on October 28, 1890. He was only fifty-nine years old, and evidently had been in good health until shortly before his death. He had been elected a member of the Granite Falls City Council earlier that year. B.F. Pillsbury & Co. owned and operated one of the largest and best-built grain elevators in western Minnesota;[55] his ventures also included a lumber and building supplies business. The *Granite Falls Tribune* business news items in 1888 referred to a new lumber yard, a large stock farm, and some of the finest Hereford cattle and Percheron horses in the state, all bearing Benjamin Pillsbury's name.[56] The C.A. Pillsbury & Co. flour mill in Granite Falls evidently was not included in that company's sale to British investors in 1889. It's likely that by then, the mill was the property of B.F. Pillsbury & Co. But with Benjamin's death, it was sold to the W.W. Pinney family of New London, Minnesota. Susan Wright Pillsbury retained control of her late husband's other businesses until her death on April 27, 1900.[57]

Of note is what happened to the Pillsbury house after her death: It was sold to the Granite Falls mayor, Andrew J. Volstead, who briefly lived there. In 1903, he was elected to Congress, where he went on to sponsor the constitutional ban on the sale of alcohol known as the Volstead Act. George A. Pillsbury would have smiled to know that his younger brother's house had a connection with the Father of Prohibition. When brothers John and George returned to New Hampshire in the fall of 1891, they likely paid their respects at the graveside of the little brother they had lost the year before.

The soldier's monument was the first of three gifts George and Margaret would dedicate in New Hampshire that fall. Next came the Pillsbury Free Library, a charming Richardson Romanesque structure on Main Street in Warner, kitty-corner from what had been the Pillsbury general store in the 1840s. It was situated on land donated by Nehemiah Ordway, another prominent native son who had gone

131

on to serve as governor of Dakota Territory from 1880 until 1884. Building a library was actually Ordway's idea, George confessed at the dedication. His original thought had been to build a high school. But he learned that Warner already had a relatively new high school, donated by other local benefactors, Mr. and Mrs. Franklin Simonds. George chose well. He gave Warner a lovely, lasting community asset, designed by one of Minneapolis's best architects, Harry Wild Jones. Jones was the University of Minnesota's first professor of architecture and the designer of such Minneapolis landmarks as Butler Square, Lakewood Cemetery Chapel, and Folwell Methodist Church (now the Scottish Rite Temple at Franklin and Dupont Avenues), as well as some of the finest Minneapolis homes of the 1890s.

George's intention was to provide an attractive and functional space to house books that the community either already owned or would supply. But having no library before, Warner had no books to house—a fact that came to light in correspondence between Mayor A. P. Davis and George in the months while the building was under construction. George suggested that the city tax itself for library operations, proposing a levy equal to one-fifteenth of 1 percent of the town's property valuation. The mayor strenuously balked, and George backed down—with Margaret's intervention, evidently. She allowed that she had been of a mind to create an endowment for the library's future operations, and that given the need for books, she would offer the sum she had in mind not as an endowment, but for immediate expenditure on the collection. She also tapped her two sons for gifts earmarked for book purchases.[58]

Not only does Pillsbury Free Library still stand, it thrives: in 2006 it was named Library of the Year by the New Hampshire Library Trustee Association.

George paid tribute to Margaret's munificent spirit when the library was dedicated on Oct. 2 and did so again three days later, when the Margaret Pillsbury General Hospital was dedicated in the state capital, Concord, the city where they had raised their family. Again, George tapped a Minneapolis architect for the job—Warren Dunnell, whose practice was devoted to designing hospitals, schools, and churches. (The next year, Dunnell would build First Baptist Church

in Owatonna, a church closely associated with Pillsbury Academy.) [59]
The naming of the hospital for Margaret was George's salute to his
wife in honor of their fiftieth wedding anniversary, which they had
celebrated on May 9 in Minneapolis with a festive party for family
and friends. It was a public acknowledgement of how deep their
partnership had been. As Concord Mayor Henry W. Clapp, who had

known them both for many
years, said on dedication
day, "Mr. Pillsbury has forever welded with his own
the name of the loved companion of his earthly life,
who, by her counsel and
co-working, has gone hand-
in-hand with him in all his
good works."[60] It was also
the gesture of a man whose
thinking about women's
roles and status was shifting,
if only slightly, as the wom-
en's suffrage movement
took root in the nation. "I
am extremely well pleased
to know that you have on
your board so many culti-

Four generations: Mahala Pillsbury with her
mother, Sarah Goodhue Fisk Lougee, her
daughter Susan Pillsbury Snyder, and grandson John Pillsbury Snyder, in 1891.

vated and Christian women; I hope this will ever be the case," George
said as the hospital on Turnpike Street was dedicated on Oct. 5. "I
believe they can do more, in many cases that will be treated here, than
those of the other sex."

John and Mahala, who had been present at the first of the three
dedications in Sutton, were absent for the two in October, for sad
reason. Bad news arrived two days after the Civil War memorial was
dedicated, while John and Mahala lingered in New England with
Freeman A. Fisher, a Minneapolis contractor (he built the Masonic
Temple and the original Chamber of Commerce building) whom
they had engaged to build a town hall for Sutton.[61] Their elder

surviving daughter, Susan Pillsbury Snyder, died suddenly on Sept. 3, evidently of the kidney malady then called Bright's Disease. The twenty-seven-year-old wife of Fred Snyder and mother of little John Pillsbury Snyder had been "ailing somewhat," the *Minneapolis Tribune* reported the day after her death. But not until twenty-four hours before she died was her condition considered serious. "She was one of those universal favorites, of great strength of character and intelligence, combined with those gentler and sweet graces, which made her presence sought by all," the *Tribune* said.[62]

Strong as John and Mahala were, this loss was a painful blow. The next June, when their surviving daughter, Sarah Belle, whom everyone called "Sadie," married attorney Edward Cheney Gale, son of wealthy real estate developer and city pioneer Samuel Gale, the occasion was "quietly and unostentatiously celebrated... owing to the fact that the bride's family is still in mourning," the *Tribune's* society columnist reported.[63] Two weeks later, when the brick-and-granite Pillsbury Memorial Town Hall was dedicated in Sutton as a tribute to his parents, John was overcome with emotion during his address, and handed his text to brother George to finish reading.[64]

By then, the Pillsburys had suffered fresh, sharp sorrow. Fred Carleton Pillsbury—young, handsome, promising—had come home from a horse-buying trip to Kentucky on May 7, 1892, feeling fatigued and unwell. On May 15, at age thirty-nine, he died of "diphtheria of the most radical and malignant type."[65]

Fred's death triggered in all who knew him the painful mix of regret and grief that accompanies the loss of an active, able adult in his or her prime. Fred seemed to be on the verge of great things. The sale of C.A. Pillsbury & Co. two and a half years earlier had made him a wealthy man about town—or, in his case, about countryside. He took great interest in his farm, a 120-acre livestock operation at Lake Minnetonka southwest of the lakeside village of Wayzata. His love for horses drew him frequently to racetracks and to other states on shopping missions.[66] He could have chosen a life of ease.

But Fred was a Pillsbury. In 1890, he ran for the Minnesota House of Representatives, as a Republican in a city district that was trending

Democratic. In a fifteen-candidate free-for-all to fill four seats, Fred came in fifth. It was his only bid for elective office. That same year, his friend William C. Edgar, the editor of the weekly *Northwestern Miller*, touted Fred as a candidate for mayor "whose election would ensure for the city a clean, firm, strong business-like administration."[67] But Fred had watched his father get burned in city politics; he opted that year for a legislative race instead. Had he lived longer and watched the Ames machine take a nasty toll on his city's civic well-being, he might well have decided eventually to seek the office himself.

In the State Agricultural Society, Fred found a venue other than elective office in which to satisfy his inborn desire for public service. This modestly named organization was already a major player in Minnesota economic and cultural life in the late 1880s because of its biggest and best-known enterprise, the Minnesota State Fair. Both the fair and the society that runs it predate statehood in Minnesota. The first fair was at Fort Snelling in 1854. The fair acquired its lasting home near the Ramsey-Hennepin county line in 1885, when Ramsey County commissioners donated their 210-acre poor farm for use as a fairgrounds. Tom Lowry quickly put a streetcar spur to the site, and the Great Minnesota Get-Together was on its way to becoming one of the largest state fairs in the nation.

The Pillsburys had long appreciated the commercial value of the fair. In 1871, Pillsbury, Crocker & Fisk, the tiny company that preceded C.A. Pillsbury & Co., won the fair's First Premium Award for its Minnesota Snow Flake flour, the brand name used before the launch of Pillsbury's Best. That same year, J.S. Pillsbury & Co. won the Second Premium prize for its National brand hand corn planter. The latter achievement was front-page news in the weekly *St. Anthony Falls Democrat*.[68] By the late 1880s, with the fair installed at its permanent Falcon Heights home, C.A. Pillsbury & Co. was a regular vendor and exhibitor. Fred was elected the Agricultural Society's president in 1890, and became one of the event's most active promoters. When his brother Charles was in Washington that January and called on President Benjamin Harrison, he passed along to the Republican president an invitation from Fred: Come to the 1890 Minnesota State Fair. "The president gave encouragement for belief that he would accept the invitation," the *Northwestern Miller* reported,[69] likely quoting Fred, who as a personal friend of the editor was a regular visitor at the weekly publication's office. But Harrison evidently had no great interest in visiting the North Star State. He not only stayed away from the 1890 fair, but also declined to show up two years later, when Minneapolis was host to the Republican National Convention that nominated him for his unsuccessful reelection bid.[70]

One other community institution occupied a good deal of Fred's energy during his last years. Along with his brother Charles and uncle John, Fred had been a founding member of the Minneapolis Club in 1883. Its first permanent clubhouse, at Seventh Street and Sixth (now Portland) Avenue, had been the home of former Minneapolis mayor A.C. Rand, who along with seven other members of his family drowned when their steamer yacht was swamped in a sudden storm on Lake Minnetonka on July 12, 1885. That house quickly became inadequate. When club members set out in 1891 to build a new clubhouse at the corner of Sixth Street and First (later Marquette) Avenue, Fred was a member of the "house committee" that contracted for the services of architect William Channing Whitney, and oversaw other arrangements. Though there's no record that Fred's father George was ever a member of the club—making him an exception among both the nineteenth- and twentieth-century male members of his family—the family's master builder undoubtedly took an interest in his son's role at the city's premier social institution and offered his advice. Fred paid particular attention to the clubhouse's interior décor. A history of the club written in the 1920s said of Fred's service: "It was owing to his unremitting efforts that the appointments of the new house were exceptional in quality: linen, made to order, containing the monogram of the club, was imported from Scotland; the china, of a special design, was imported from France; the decorations and all the new furniture required were furnished by (John Scott) Bradstreet [the city's leading interior designer], and when the club took possession of its new premises in May 1892, they presented a dignified and attractive appearance with an added quality of comfort which was most satisfactory." Sadly, Fred's death came only a few weeks before the new clubhouse opened. [71]

In business, Fred became more independent of his relatives after the sale of C. A. Pillsbury & Co. In about 1887, he had invested in the Northwestern Mill, whose management was in the hands of Sidle, Fletcher, Holmes & Co. (Holmes was the aforementioned milling manager whose appetite for work was equaled only by that of Charles Pillsbury.)[72] In 1891, Northwestern was one of six mills that combined as the Northwestern Consolidated Milling Co., under the financial leadership of a lumberman named Jim Miller and with a brand-new flour brand name, Ceresota, to take to market. The combination made Northwestern the second-largest milling company at the falls, behind Pillsbury-Washburn but larger than Washburn-Crosby. Northwestern's facilities included some that have survived handsomely into the twenty-first century, including the Crown Roller Mill, now an office complex, and a 1908 brick grain elevator that in the late twen-

Alice Thayer Cook Pillsbury and her children, circa 1892. Left to right, Carleton, Alice, Harriot and, in front, Helen.

tieth century was home to the Whitney Hotel. The new company's three managing directors included Fred C. Pillsbury and Albert C. Loring, the exceptionally gifted son of pioneering Minneapolis merchant and parks developer Charles M. Loring.[73] The connection Fred established with Loring would serve the Pillsbury family well in years to come.

No one, probably least of all Fred, thought the sore throat and fatigue he experienced on May 8 and 9, 1892, were anything serious. On May 9, he checked on the progress of the nearly completed Minneapolis Club. On May 10, he went to his office at Northwestern

Consolidated and checked in at Pillsbury-Washburn, too. But by May 12, his sore throat was unbearable. The *Northwestern Miller* described it as "an ulceration." His physician—his father-in-law, Dr. David Goodwin—recognized trouble, and sent for a skilled colleague in Red Wing, Dr. Charles Hewitt, to consult on the case. By the time Hewitt arrived on May 14, Fred's decline was irreversible, and even he knew it. "After a manly battle against the most discouraging odds, (he) became completely reconciled to the inevitable," the *Tribune* reported on May 16. "His sufferings were intense." Conscious almost until the end, Fred begged to be allowed to see his son and three daughters. That grace was denied him, his friend William Edgar reported. Alice, her parents, and George and Margaret were afraid that his condition was contagious. Those five adults stood watch as Fred died. Charles, traveling on business in the East, had been summoned, but he did not arrive until May 16.[74]

A private funeral was held, owing to worries about the contagious nature of the disease that took Fred. He was buried at Lakewood Cemetery near the small graves of his daughter Marian and son George and the side-by-side headstones of the two Pillsbury brides, Addie Webster and Susan Snyder. They were the first to occupy a prominent hill overlooking Lake Calhoun, where today the family plot is marked by a tall, stately column adorned with four sets of overlapping initials—G.A.P., J.S.P., C.A.P. and F.C.P.—and a sad-faced statue of a woman holding a cross and a book under one arm. It's tragically ironic that among the lives signified by those initials, the first to come to rest on that hill was also the youngest.

The impact of Fred's untimely death on his family was clear and profound. His widow, Alice, married E. W. Paige, "a flour jobber prominent in New York City," in 1903, and left Minnesota the following year.[75] A 1911 *Minneapolis Tribune* society note placed her in Pittsfield, Massachusetts, and in 1937, the family's most authoritative genealogy placed her in Pasadena, California. It was there that she died in 1940; her remains were returned to Minnesota to lie next to Fred's on the Lakewood knoll. Curiously, the name Paige was omitted from her gravestone. None of Fred and Alice's three daughters remained in Minnesota as adults. Each married and raised a family elsewhere. Harriot, the eldest, married Harold Osgood Ayer, a Dartmouth-educated chemist, and lived first in Savannah, Georgia, then in Pasadena. There, she raised twin daughters, Alice and Ann, born in 1903.[76] Her large home in Pasadena is now the site of Pacific Oaks College. Helen Margaret married Robert Daniels Bardwell in 1907, raised two children, and spent her adult life in Massachusetts. Alice, the youngest, married Stanton W. Forsman and raised four children in Pasadena.[77]

Carleton Cook Pillsbury, Fred's only son to survive childhood, returned to Minneapolis after attending Lawrenceville School in New Jersey. His father's death two days after his tenth birthday may have left him with the deepest psychological wounds. As a young adult, Carleton's name would be associated in newspaper columns with Minnesota's earliest and fastest automobiles, all-day golf outings, and notable parties. His cousin, four years his elder, would tell of getting calls from the city jail at odd hours, asking him to fetch an inebriated Carleton and get him home safely.[78] He was hospitalized in August 1910 for an undisclosed ailment, sent home, and found dead a day or two later at his home at fashionable 2445 Park Av. He was only twenty-eight years old.

How Fred's death affected Minnesota is a matter for speculation about opportunity lost. In the late 1890s, generational change was coming fast in the industries that anchored the young state's economy. It would prove to be a bumpy transition, perhaps made more so by the absence of a leader of Fred's age and caliber at a time when he was needed most.

Charles A. Pillsbury in the 1890s.

Chapter Six

Big Miller

When the Minneapolis Club was nearing its fortieth birthday in 1920, sixty-four-year-old William C. Edgar, a devoted clubman and editor of *Northwestern Miller* magazine, compiled his recollections of that favorite gathering spot of city leaders. Lavish occasions stood out in his memory: There was the dinner honoring Vice President Theodore Roosevelt in 1901, twelve days before an assassination made him president; the breakfast for President William Howard Taft in 1909, attended by some who would lose their lives on the *Titanic* three years later; the legendary gathering of city leaders on January 10, 1911, at which Dorilus Morrison's son Clinton proposed to donate his father's home, located diagonally across the street from the Pillsbury mansion, as a site for a Minneapolis Institute of Arts, if sufficient additional funds could be raised. An astounding $335,500 was pledged within ninety minutes that day, with W. H. Dunwoody's impressive $100,000 gift leading the way.[1]

The night Edgar may have remembered most fondly (though he got the date wrong in his reminiscences) was August 24, 1897.[2] On that day, more than a hundred leaders of local milling and elevator businesses and of the city's Chamber of Commerce (today's Grain Exchange) attended a sumptuous six-course feast "in Celebration of the Long Delayed Triumph of the Bull." It was an all-male affair—a situation for which the host apologized, blaming the limited size of the room. The menu, which included Amontillado, whisky, cigarettes, and cigars, seemed chosen with male guests in mind. Among the more unusual guests was "a splendid white bull, decked with flow-ers," Edgar recalled. The beast was goaded into the dining hall "to the tremendous plaudits of the bulls of the grain market who were pres-ent." (Not being housebroken, the bull was then paraded out again, quickly.)[3] The occasion? After a long run of depressed prices, the "bulls" were finally running again in the wheat market, with the price of wheat topping $1 a bushel. The evening's jovial host was Charles A. Pillsbury. The gathering was as welcome and as rare as a perfect spring day after a long Minnesota winter.

Judging from infrequent mention in newspaper society columns, Charles and Mary Ann did not entertain often. Charles was "not at all inclined toward society," Edgar would write of him in 1899. "He lived quite a domestic life, never being so happy as when enjoying the companionship of his wife and twin sons."[4] But when the Pillsburys did entertain, they partied on a grand scale. On November 5, 1884, they sponsored a "brilliant" reception and dinner for hundreds of friends that filled the entire parlor floor of the West Hotel, the city's finest.[5] A large employees' gathering at their home on March 23, 1887, received notice in the *Northwestern Miller* two days later.[6] On the twenty-fifth anniversary of his graduation from Dartmouth, Charles hosted a dinner "complimentary to the Class of 63" in Hanover that featured an extravagant menu: littleneck clams, salmon, lamb, beef, sweetbread patties, chicken croquettes, "upland plover," and a large variety of side dishes and desserts.[7]

But infrequent as they were in the 1880s, such large-scale gather-ings all but ceased for Charles and Mary Ann during the early years of the following decade, due to personal tragedies and such business difficulties as the Panic of 1893. The flour market had become fully national and international, and consolidation led to intense compe-tition. All the milling companies in Minneapolis were struggled to adapt to changes in the industry. One after another, the small-scale producers disappeared. The remaining large producers, Pillsbury-Washburn among them, were under relentless pressure to drive down production and transportation costs to stay in the game.[8] The market for their product ceased its rapid growth, and stopped growing at all in the depressed years of 1893-94. Meanwhile, the supply of wheat swelled with the rural population in western Minnesota, where native prairie had nearly all given way to tilled acres. Charles told the *New York Times* in January 1892 that were it not for demand from Europe, the 1891 bumper wheat crop in the United States would have made wheat "so cheap that it would not have paid to market it."[9] Beginning at about that time, milling capacity at the Falls of St. Anthony exceeded demand—a condition that would prove stubbornly enduring.[10] Pillsbury-Washburn surpassed its profit goal in 1890 but then experienced a yearly decline for the next four years. The steady income generated by the company's waterpower holdings kept it barely in the black. A slight rebound in profits occurred in 1895 and 1896, but the company's British owners weren't seeing anything close to the returns on their investment they had anticipated when they bought the Minneapolis concern in 1889. Understandably, they closely questioned and second-guessed their well-paid American managing director.[11]

They weren't the only ones. Charles Pillsbury's reputation as a friend of the Minnesota farmer came under public attack in 1892, when a pamphlet entitled "Gigantic Conspiracy" gained widespread circulation. It linked Charles to a grain-buying ring which had "for years robbed and despoiled the farmers of the Northwest" by depressing the price paid at elevators for wheat. Its author was C.C. Wolcott, a minor figure in the Minneapolis grain elevator business whose firm came in for frequent mention in local newspapers in connection with bad-debt litigation.[12] Those who knew Charles's wheat market preferences found Wolcott's accusation risible. "That his whole course of business has been to the contrary is known to anyone who is even slightly acquainted with facts," editor Edgar wrote in Charles' defense. "The most frequent and bitter complaint made against Mr. Pillsbury by the millers of the country is that he has systematically caused the price of wheat to be inflated beyond reasonable limits. It is unquestionably true that during the last ten years the farmers of Minnesota and the Dakotas have received millions of dollars more for their wheat than they would have gotten had it not been for Mr. Pillsbury's well-known partiality for the bull side of the market. If Mr. Pillsbury is not a friend of the farmers, in that he has always put money in their purses, frequently at his own expense, then he is nothing."[13]

But farm incomes were down, and many farmers, lacking Edgar's "insider" perspective, were susceptible to the imputation that their hardship was caused by greedy capitalists in fancy offices in Minneapolis. Consolidation presented industry leaders with what appeared to be an opportunity to set prices at every grain elevator in the region, and farmers suspected those prices were being intentionally suppressed. The fact that Charles Pillsbury was a major stockholder in two of the state's biggest elevator companies fueled their suspicion that he was a ringleader in an "elevator combine."[14] And his image was further tarnished when Pillsbury-Washburn moved its headquarters to the prestigious new Northwestern Guaranty Loan Building at Third St. and Second Ave. in 1891. At twelve stories, it was the city's first skyscraper, and was also home to Fred's Northwestern Consolidated Milling

The Northwest Guarantee Loan Building, later known as the Metropolitan Building.

Co.[15] The massive building contained a concert hall, Turkish baths, a rooftop promenade, elegant iron scrollwork, and a top-floor restaurant. Not long after Pillsbury-Washburn moved in, they fitted their quarters with a large bakery test kitchen. Charles put great store in the work done there to both maintain Pillsbury's Best reputation for high quality, and to develop new products. Among those was Vitos, which emerged in 1897 as the first ready-to-cook breakfast cereal produced by Minneapolis mills. Competition-conscious Washburn-Crosby Co. soon followed suit, and made a more durable contribution to the breakfast cereal market.[16]

The "Conspiracy" smear got the Minneapolis business brotherhood's attention—and got Charles' goat—when it was reprinted in the *St. Paul Globe* newspaper. Charles was never described as a man with a hot temper, but he could be fierce in defense of his own reputation or the good name of his company. He sent a stern open letter to the *Globe*, offering to open to them the company records that would refute any charge that Pillsbury-Washburn elevators were gouging farmers. The offer was backed by a vow that he would give $10,000 to the state Democratic Party if his side of the story was not borne out by the evidence.[17] There's no record that he or any other Pillsbury of that era ever made such a donation.

What's notable about this episode is not so much Charles's pique as the response of his peers. They rallied as if a member of their own families had been attacked. The day after the *Minneapolis Tribune* reported Charles' indignant response to the *Globe*, a petition addressed to Charles was circulated in milling offices at the falls. Two hundred signatures were quickly gathered under these words:

"We the undersigned members of the Minneapolis Chamber of Commerce, desiring to show our confidence in your eminent fitness for the office, and feeling that, at the present time when so unwarrantable an attack on your business career has been made by unprincipled parties for the furtherance of their own ends, an expression of this kind is due you from your business associates, who hold you in high esteem and REQUEST that you reconsider your decision in this matter, as given in former years, and accept the Presidency of our Chamber." [18]

After leaving the state Senate in 1886, Charles had spurned repeated suggestions that he run for elective office. He remained involved at Plymouth Church and several local charities but stayed out of top leadership. He enjoyed taking the lead in responding to trouble, sending more than five hundred barrels of Pillsbury's Best to Lynn, Massachusetts, after an 1889 fire nearly destroyed the manufacturing city,[19] and making the first and largest gift, 112,000 pounds of flour, to an 1891 relief effort when crop failure threatened mass starvation in Russia.[20] When a forest fire ravaged the lumbering town of Hinckley, Minnesota, on Sept. 1, 1894, killing more than four hundred, Charles agreed to head the state's relief commission.[21] Activities of that kind seemed to satisfy his itch for community service. But the timing and context of the 1892 invitation to head the Minneapolis grain-trading organization were too compelling to refuse. Charles gratefully accepted, and served two terms in the post his father had held a decade earlier.

Were Pillsbury's fellow millers sending a message of defiance to militant farmers, as one latter-day author hints?[22] Perhaps. But more plausible, given these Minnesotans' self-interested desire for harmony within the state's borders, is that Charles was invited to head the Chamber of Commerce out of loyalty, respect, and a genuine sense of outrage over a baseless attack on a friend. They likely also trusted that the caliber of Charles's leadership would be its own best defense. For his part, Charles drew closer to his Minneapolis business colleagues as a result of the "Conspiracy" accusation. The Bull Dinner of 1897 may have been, in part, an expression of his gratitude for their support.

Charles's surviving public comments about the whirlwind changes taking place in the milling industry[23] at that time suggests that he was just as frustrated with low prices as farmers were. He was better positioned than many of them were to comprehend the cause. Oversupply of grain and the weak national economy were the major culprits. In the months after a railroad financing bubble burst in 1893, setting off a ripple of bank failures, an estimated 90 percent of Minnesota's milling capacity went idle for a time.[24] But futures trading in the Chicago-dominated wheat market also played a role. Primitive trading of "forward" contracts began within the confines of the Chicago Board of Trade in 1865. By the 1880s, a system that would be recognizable by brokers today was in place on the exchange floor in Chicago, to be copied in Minneapolis and in other commodity-market cities around the country. The trade volume in wheat futures contracts far outstripped the actual volume of wheat grown in the country in any given year. That fact alone was enough to convince farmers that the trading in futures contracts was not a justified way to hedge against price fluctuation, as grain millers insisted it was, but was a price-eroding form of gambling. As economic historian Joseph

Santos put it, "Nineteenth-century America was both fascinated and appalled by futures trading."[25]

It seems Charles himself had a similarly schizophrenic reaction to futures trading, and so did the London owners of Pillsbury-Washburn. At the company's annual shareholders' meeting in 1891, chairman Richard Glyn boasted that the company's policy was to avoid gambling "in any way, either directly or indirectly, in the buying or selling of wheat." [26] In 1892, Charles's business partner, U.S. Sen. W. D. Washburn, sponsored "anti-option" legislation that would have effectively banned the practice of treating futures contracts as commodities in their own right, without material to back them up. Bucking the majority of his peers in the milling industry, Charles went to Washington to testify before the U.S. House Agriculture Committee against the excessive influence of futures trading on wheat prices. "I stood in the center of the wheat fields of North Dakota where the wheat could be seen as far as the eye could reach," he testified. "I thought: The man who managed or sold or owned those immense wheat fields has not as much to say with regard to the price of the wheat as some young fellow who stands howling around the Chicago wheat pit."[27]

In supporting Washburn's bill—which died in conference committee and was not revived in future years—Pillsbury not only was disappointing a good share of his fellow industrialists, but also was proposing to tie his own hands. Later in 1892, as wheat prices fell, Charles evidently changed his mind. He recommended to the British stockholders' board that they begin using futures contracts to hedge against their own large stores of wheat. His recommendation did not prevail that year at Pillsbury-Washburn.[28] Before the decade ended, it would.

Charles waded into national economic policy again in 1896 as an advocate of "reciprocity," or tariff-free trade. He headed the Minnesota delegation to the Republican national convention in St. Louis that June, and pushed a pro-reciprocity clause into the party platform. Two months earlier, he had testified in Washington before the U.S. House Ways and Means Committee in opposition to continued tariffs, telling the *Minneapolis Tribune* that "reciprocity will do the man-ufacturing interests of Minnesota more good than high tariff, for the simple reason that very few of the state's industries can be protected as well by high tariff."[29] In this matter, he did have the backing of

his peers in the milling business, so much so that when he first appeared on the Chamber of Commerce trad-ing floor after the convention, trad-ing paused and the room erupted in applause. The buzz that day, and fre-quently thereafter, was that Charles would make a fine U.S. senator from Minnesota the next time one of the two Senate seats came open.[30] When Charles paid a courtesy call on newly elected President William McKinley at his Canton, Ohio, home in Janu-ary 1897, the rumor mill had him pegged for a cabinet spot.[31]

William de la Barre in 1933.

A discouraging decade for Pillsbury-Washburn had one bright spot: waterpower. Its steady profitability underscored Charles' belief that the capacity of the churning water at the falls to generate elec-tricity had not yet been fully exploited. That view was shared by two men who stand tall in Minneapolis history: William de la Barre, the brilliant Vienna-born engineer who had managed the west-side Minneapolis Mill Company since 1882,[32] and Thomas Lowry, the president and great developer of the city's streetcar system, the Twin City Rapid Transit Company.

De la Barre had been lured to Minneapolis by C.C. Washburn in 1878, but his expertise had been at the service of the entire Min-neapolis milling industry almost from the start. Charles respected him enough to seek his advice about the conversion to steel roller mill-ing in 1880. Whether the men were personal friends is not known, but they clearly were professional allies who thought alike about the positive potential inherent in new technology. De la Barre was the professional Charles turned to in about 1894 with an idea for a new electricity-generating dam, 2,200 feet downstream from a dam that had stood at the falls for several decades. Together they explored the feasibility of long-distance transmission of electricity, and soon convinced themselves that a 10,000-horsepower hydroelectric dam could extend the benefits of electrical power throughout the city.[33]

Charles loved a new project, and likely bubbled about this one to his good friend Lowry. An Illinois native, Lowry was only a few months younger than Charles, and had settled in Minneapolis as a newly minted attorney two years before Charles arrived. The practice of law wasn't enough to satisfy the ambitious and gregarious young man, however. He served as a legal agent for eastern investors in Minneapolis real estate, and couldn't resist making some investments of his own. Before long, Lowry was a major local property owner, and he was drawn to purchase and improve the struggling horse-drawn streetcar system when he saw how reliable transit could increase the value of his property at the city's edge. His projects were nothing if not ambitious—a trait he shared with Charles. One of them was the creation of a whole new municipality, Columbia Heights, north of Minneapolis. He was a flamboyant fellow, "the smoothest, best-dressed and fastidious sort of a man" who "used to wear a silk hat and a frock coat every day to business," remembered Charles's son John.[34] Charles,

Thomas Lowry in the 1890s.

perhaps inspired by his friend, took to wearing a gray top hat too. Of Lowry, John said: "He was very aristocratic in the way he lived. But he was very democratic about knowing people."

Lowry began the electrical power conversion of his transit system in 1890. When Charles and de la Barre were ready to go to London in 1894 to sell their plans for a new hydroelectric dam to Pillsbury-Washburn's British board of directors, Lowry accompanied them. Lowry assured the Brits that if the dam were built, Twin City Rapid

Transit would be a major customer for its power. The project was approved, along with nearly $1 million in borrowing to finance it.

The ceremonial laying of the last large granite block in the new dam on March 20, 1897, must have been an occasion of pride, relief, and hope for Charles—pride in the accomplishment, relief that it was done without a financial hiccup, and hope that the distress that followed the Panic of 1893 was behind him and his city. The laying of the stone was done with a flourish, with de la Barre serving as master of ceremonies and Pillsbury and Lowry together guiding the big stone into place. The *Minneapolis Tribune* account of the day refers to Charles as "the chief of the movement which made the dam possible." Charles called the occasion one of the happiest of his life, and voiced the hope that it would lead to employment for tens of thousands of people in years ahead. He also expressed admiration for the laborers who built the dam, and gratitude for the good labor relations his firm enjoyed at a time of mounting labor unrest elsewhere in the United States.[35]

Charles had other reasons to be upbeat in 1897. His sons were happily enrolled at the University of Minnesota, in the Class of 1900. Their satisfaction in that local institution must have been a source of some relief for Charles and Mary Ann—and also for their great-uncle. John S. Pillsbury, still the university's most generous and engaged regent, demonstrated his confidence in the quality of the institution he had built by enrolling all four of his own children there. His son Alfred, who matriculated in 1885, earned a bachelor's degree in 1889 and a law degree in 1892—and played football as quarterback for seven straight seasons. His football success wasn't owing to his size. He weighed only 142 pounds during his student years. But he personally supplied the first rugby-style football ever used at the University of Minnesota. (Prior to his gift, football was played with a soccer-style ball.) Alf was clever enough to devise plays that allowed a 200-pound lineman to run interference for him—and was credited in later years with originating the offensive blocking maneuvers that became standard in the twentieth-century game. Alf was also likeable enough to be elected team captain, twice.[36] He led his Golden Gophers to their first undefeated season and first-ever conference title in 1892.[37] In university annals he is hailed as the team's first star player.

Alfred was also a star recruiter. On one occasion, while getting the team ready to play, he noticed that the team was short a man, so he recruited a student from the group of Minneapolis Central High School students who were on hand. His name was William Walter "Pudge" Heffelfinger. After playing for Minnesota for a year, Heffelfinger went on to Yale and acclaim as a football hero. He's credited as America's first professional football player, paid $500 plus $25 in expenses for his services by the Allegheny Athletic Association in 1892.[38]

As Charles's family considered where the twins would be educated, they were swayed by the preference of wealthy Minneapolitans for Yale University in New Haven, Connecticut. More than other Ivy League schools, Yale had established a Minneapolis admissions pipeline in the 1890s. An early Minnesota exponent for the school was Samuel Gale, Yale Class of 1854 and a top scholar. A lawyer, Gale moved to Minneapolis in 1857 and quickly became the city's leading real estate broker and investor. He was also keen on education, serving nine years on the city's school board and aiding in the establishment and early leadership of the Athenaeum, the precursor of the Minneapolis Public Library. Gale sent both of his sons to Yale and all three of his daughters to Smith College, an exclusive women's school in Northampton, Massachusetts. The family appears to have set a pattern that well-to-do Minnesotans followed for more than a century. Samuel Gale was Sadie Pillsbury Gale's father-in-law. The Pillsbury boys were undoubtedly exposed to his praise for his alma mater.

Neither the twins nor any of the twentieth-century Pillsburys attended Carleton College in Northfield, Minnesota, despite the fact that Plymouth Congregational Church, where Charles, Mary Ann and the twins worshiped, had been instrumental in founding it. In time Carleton developed the strongest academic reputation among undergraduate schools in the Upper Midwest, and the Pillsburys were undoubtedly among its benefactors. But when it came to educating their own, the Pillsburys preferred established colleges in the East to the new one they were building nearby.

Twins John and
Charles Pillsbury
at 2200 Stevens
Avenue South,
about 1895.

During their senior year at Minneapolis's Central High School,
Charles S. and John S. (who had taken to signing his name "John S.
Pillsbury Jr." or "John S. Pillsbury II" to distinguish himself from his
famous namesake) took entrance examinations for Yale, and passed
them "without a condition."[39] They set their caps for Connecticut,
going so far as to reserve rooms in a rooming house near the New
Haven campus.

Then Uncle John intervened. Would the young men consider
staying in Minneapolis and attending the University of Minnesota, as
his son Alfred had done? The case John made undoubtedly included a
recitation of all the Pillsburys had done to build a fine public college
on the east bank of the Mississippi. The school's reputation might be
dented if two promising young Pillsburys chose a college elsewhere.
But things more personal were said and intimated too. Young John
would recall decades later, "It was too bad that (Uncle John) didn't
have a son who was closer to him. Alfred, of course, was a young

fellow and a very, very smart boy. But I thought that we were going to the university at a time when we were more mature than Alfred when he went there."[40] The former governor was close to his great-nephews, and liked having them nearby. The twins' grandfather George, by then an eighty-year-old who had already suffered one stroke,[41] likely joined in urging them to study at home. The twins' companionship during his declining years would have been on George's mind—but so was his old bugaboo, alcohol. The younger John Pillsbury remembered his elders discussing episodes of drunken disorder by college students in Boston that had made national news. George and Margaret, staunch Baptists, would have wanted to keep their grandsons away from East Coast debauchery.

Charles came up with an offer to the twins that settled the matter. John would later describe it this way:

> My father told us that if we went here, we would be giving up our association with a lot of Eastern boys that we knew, and he said he would make a deal with us. Every time that we had a week or two weeks free from our attendance at the university, we could go anywhere we wanted to. I went to Europe five times when I was in college. This was on the condition that all of our marks had to be above grade, you see. And you can bet your life that I never flunked anything.[42]

The twins' good friend Horace Lowry was under the same kind of pressure from his parents, Tom and Beatrice Lowry, and his grandfather, Dr. C. G. Goodrich, one of the city's leading physicians. Whether Horace extracted from his parents the same travel promise that the Pillsbury twins received is not known. But the threesome enrolled together at the University of Minnesota in the fall of 1896.

Charles, John, and George undoubtedly counted the twins' decision as a personal victory in a purely familial matter. More than a century later, it takes on much larger significance. If twins Charles and John had been lost to Minnesota in 1896, the Pillsbury imprint on the state in the twentieth century would have been much diminished. When the many acts of service to Minnesota by the nineteenth-century Pillsburys are enumerated, their recruitment of the Pillsbury twins to the University of Minnesota belongs on the list.

A Pillsbury celebration may have seemed overdue in the summer of 1897. That may be why Charles backed up his prediction that the price of wheat would again hit $1 per bushel with the promise that if it did, he would treat his friends to the festive dinner at the Minneapolis Club that William Edgar remembered so fondly. As he recalled it, the "Great Bull Dinner" was conceived in connection with a wager between Charles and James S. Bell,[43] the Washburn-Crosby chief executive who was both a Pillsbury rival and friend, and whose son James Ford Bell was a great chum of the twins. When rumors of war

James S. Bell.

(the Spanish American War would break out the following year) made the market behave as Charles had forecast, he decided to pull out all the stops. On the afternoon before the dinner, he hired a brass band that paraded from Pillsbury-Washburn headquarters at the Guaranty building to the trading floor at the Chamber of Commerce building two blocks away. Its serenade stopped trading for fifteen minutes, and undoubtedly encouraged an early departure for the club by invitees. When they arrived at the dining room, the guests were awestruck by a large mass of flowers decorating the fireplace mantle, trimmed with a banner bearing the motto: "Welcome to Ye Who Feed the World." Lush bouquets of roses were on each table. Small electric lights were hidden among the greenery, creating an effect the next day's newspaper called "ingenious."[44] Guests were handed a menu card that featured a cartoon dialogue between two traders, dressed in Roman togas and top hats. The caption: "History Repeats Itself." The exchange:

Caius W. Ursa: "Well met, good neighbor Sextus! 'Tis thou who hast the latest tidings of the state of trade. How goeth the market this morning?"

Sextus J. Taurus: "The gods do smile propitious on my house this day. The latest news which cometh to mine ears is that the Greek will shortly battle with the barbarian hordes: therein they will embroil all countries; husbandmen must ere long leave the plow to follow Mars' calling. Therefore the coming crop will be much shortened. In consequence of this news the price of cereals hath gone up three several sestertii. My holdings being large, this news doth greatly cheer me, and I go from hence to mingle with my class in one great baccanalian symphony. Wilt join me?"

Ursa: "Nay! Nay! Thy words do smite upon mine ears most ominously. Disaster doth o'ertake me. I will not seek the reveler, but rather hie me to the place where sleep the dead, and mourn for wealth once mine but now departed." [45]

The evening was rich in both cuisine and oratory. Eight scheduled toasts were called for in the program, with toastmasters including Frank Peavey of the grain elevator company that bore his name, and William Henry Eustis, attorney, real estate developer, and, just then, mayor of Minneapolis.

The keynoter was the host himself. As Edgar reported in the next week's *Northwestern Miller*, Charles was "in his happiest mood." He might have been feeling the effects of some of the strong spirits listed on the menu. There's no mention in any accounts of the presence of either his uncle, who was a club member, or his father, who was not, and who would have disapproved of alcohol consumption. But Charles was fully capable of delivering a strong speech, much of which was reprinted in the next day's *Tribune*. His words reveal why he considered higher wheat prices—something many of his fellow millers resented—ample reason for a party. More than many, he understood the connection between the general welfare of his state and the prosperity of his business. The philosophy he expressed that night was bedrock Pillsbury thinking:

> *I have long been a believer that we could have no genuine prosperity in this country—and especially in this part of it—unless the farmers were liberally rewarded for the fruit of their industry. As a miller, I have never failed to make money when wheat was around a dollar a bushel, and I have never really succeeded in making any money when wheat was around 50 or 60 cents a bushel. . . .My main theory is that the prosperity of the agriculturists is the basis and*

foundation of all the prosperity. Give the farmers good, liberal prices for their productions, and their purchasing power will be so increased that the increased demand for all merchandise and manufactured goods will bring prosperity to the merchants, to the manufacturer, and through them, to the laboring men...

There are many manufacturers and businessmen who are always looking to Wall Street for evidences of prosperity. They will always look in vain. Let them look to the agricultural and laboring communities. If prosperity and contentment reign there, then it must certainly bring prosperity to the capitalist and manufacturer.[46]

The newspaper commented that Charles believed in celebrating good economic news with his friends "while they all live, for they will be a long time dead." It was a flippant but eerily prescient remark.

No one in the dining room that night but Charles and perhaps his protégé, chief lieutenant, and sales manager, forty-year-old Henry L. Little, knew that the Bull Dinner was a kind of last hurrah. Less than three months later, Charles would announce his semi-retirement. He would keep the title and some of the responsibilities of general manager of Pillsbury-Washburn, but Little would take over management of daily operations.

Another native of New Hampshire, Little had been an ambitious twenty-two year old newcomer in Minneapolis in 1879, clerking at a hardware store without compensation while waiting for a paid opening, when Charles tried to hire him as an office boy. When the young man refused, saying he wanted more active work, Charles was impressed with his vigor and offered him a traveling sales job.[47]

The two men evidently understood each other, and "clicked." "The utmost harmony exists between Mr. Pillsbury and Mr. Little," Edgar reported soothingly on November 19, 1897. "Mr. Pillsbury feels he has worked steadily and with unabated energy long enough. He is not worn out or exhausted by any means, but, like a wise man, concludes to relinquish as much as possible of the detail work and content himself with the general oversight of the enormous industry which he himself founded. . . Mr. Pillsbury remains director, and

Mary Ann and Charles relaxing outside Highland Home.

Mr. Little manager under him, the only difference being that as manager, Mr. Little will have full charge of all details and full authority to act in the absence of Mr. Pillsbury." The British board of directors approved the change after a visit to Minneapolis by one of their members, Sir William Forwood, in October. The visit confirmed what almost anyone in Minneapolis could have told him: Charles Pillsbury was a workaholic. Those who knew him best would have added that more than a quarter-century of twelve-hour days, six-day workweeks, and minimal exercise had taken a toll on his health. He was exhibiting symptoms of heart disease.

Whether Charles initiated the change in responsibility or was talked into it by his physician and/or family, is not known. But if it was his idea, he appeared to change his mind in subsequent months. He and Mary Ann left town in January 1898 with the intention of taking a long, restful trip to the Orient. He got as far as California, stayed there for a few weeks, and came home to resume a full schedule, at least initially.

One reason for his return may have been a development at the Board of Trade in Chicago. A grain trader named Joseph Leiter, adept in the ways of the futures market, was attempting to corner the May wheat market. Doing so meant driving up the price of wheat, at least in the short term, as Leiter's aggressive purchase of futures contracts made demand for the commodity appear to outstrip supply. Many years later Leiter revealed that his maneuver had been in collusion with had two silent partners in Minneapolis, Charles Pillsbury and elevator magnate Frank Peavey. Charles had promised to keep the substantial store of wheat in Pillsbury-Washburn elevators off the market, at least for a time, while Leiter maneuvered to drive up the price. Ever a fan of high prices, Charles may have been drawn to Leiter's scheme because it promised to have that effect. But as sellers moved trains and barges laden with wheat to Chicago to fulfill their contractual obligations to Leiter, the exorbitant price to which he had driven the market collapsed. His corner attempt failed spectacularly. Leiter said years later that he lost between $10 million and $12 million in the maneuver—more than the Brits had paid for C.A. Pillsbury & Co. ten years earlier—and his silent partners in Minneapolis undoubtedly suffered heavy losses as well.

A young grain broker in New York City, George Zabriskie, kept his eye on the visiting Charles Pillsbury one day in May 1898 as wheat prices on the big board in that city's exchange were in freefall. He would tell Charles's grandson fifty years later that "your grandfather showed no distress, no emotion whatsoever," as he watched the value of his assets drop more than $100,000 in an afternoon. If Charles felt remorse over participating in the kind of market manipulation he had denounced a few years earlier, he kept that sentiment to himself.[48]

That episode led to a terrible earnings year in 1898 for Pillsbury-Washburn mills, and a rift between Charles Pillsbury and the firm's British owners. The British view was that a flour company ought not also be engaged in grain market manipulation, and that it ought not maintain in its elevators overlarge stores of wheat. Charles had been told that company policy was "not to hold large stocks, but to buy our wheat and make our flour."[49] His defiance of those instructions during the Leiter affair soured the company's trans-Atlantic relations—and that made Pillsbury-Washburn vulnerable a few months later, when New York financier Thomas McIntyre sought to form a gigantic flour trust. He wanted Pillsbury-Washburn included in his family of fifteen milling companies in six cities, to be named the United States Flour Milling Co. The Pillsburys considered McIntyre's plan flawed and wanted no part of it. But they worried that London would think otherwise.

A s those storm clouds circled, the family suffered another loss. George A. Pillsbury, age 82, suffered a second stroke in the summer of 1898 and died on July 17. George was older than most of the young city's leaders, but he kept his buggy shuttling from one meeting to another when charity or community affairs called until his last few weeks. He was, from 1890 until his death, president of Northwestern National Bank, leading its governing board as it became the largest financial institution in the region. (The bank had been founded by Tom Lowry, Dorilus Morrison, and W.D. Washburn to manage the financing of the leg of the Northern Pacific Railroad from Duluth to Fargo.[50] It was the "mayors' bank." Morrison, the first Minneapolis mayor, was the bank's first president, succeeded by the first mayor of St. Anthony, H. T. Welles. George's leadership continued the mayoral pattern.) The bank board sent Margaret and her family a formal expression of condolences, praising his "excellent judgment, superior business ability and well-known financial standing. . . We feel that by his death the bank has sustained irreparable loss." Those words of lofty but somewhat customary praise were followed by a more personal passage: "He was singularly sweet, gentle, kindly and lovable, and while he was a man of firm and decided convictions, he was always tolerant of the opinions of others."[51] George went to his rest at Lakewood Cemetery not just respected, but also beloved in his adopted hometown. His resting spot was fitting; for many years, George had been president of the Lakewood Cemetery Association.[52] When the funeral procession bearing his remains arrived at Lakewood on July 20, the family was surprised and touched to see six hundred Pillsbury mill employees, their hats doffed in tribute, lining the road to its gate.[53]

George's death was not a surprise, but the loss was an added burden at a time when the family was struggling to save the family business from a combination they believed would be ruinous. Someone needed to go to London to tamp down any desire by Pillsbury-Washburn owners to sell their stock to McIntyre. Charles was not in good health; John was aging; and Henry Little was not deemed suitable for the job (or perhaps was needed in Minneapolis.) The responsibility fell to Alfred Fisk Pillsbury, the eldest male family member born in Minnesota. Alfred would recall years later that his father personally gave him the assignment.[54] That suggests that in the summer of 1898, at age seventy-one, John was still—or again—leading family business affairs, and that he had developed a degree of trust in his twenty-nine-year-old son.

Alf had left the University of Minnesota with a law degree, but he did not practice law. Instead, he took a position in Pillsbury-Washburn's purchasing department, where he had worked in the summers while he was a high school and college student. How much knowledge of the business he acquired during those summers is a matter of some question. One of his "duties" was to play baseball on the Minneapolis Chamber of Commerce team. Alf would be remembered as the team's star player.[55] After his university days, his work at

the company was overshadowed by his leisure activities, to judge from the coverage in newspaper society and sports columns.[56] He and his pals Frank and Walter Heffelfinger were regular party hosts as young bachelors. Alf was described years later as "keen on games, especially golf, bridge, and backgammon," playing each at a high level.[57] An 1896 receipt in corporate files for a $52 custom-made saddle from "Martin & Martin of New York/ London Harness Agency of London

Alf Pillsbury dressed for sailing, in about 1895.

(Harness and Saddlery Makres to the Queen)" suggests that Alf was an avid horseman too, and a fussy one.

In the summer, Alf and the Heffelfingers commuted to the city by train from a cottage they shared in what would become the village of Deephaven on Lake Minnetonka, the big, island-studded body of water twenty miles west of downtown Minneapolis. His cousin Fred had built a big summer house with rambling porches in what became the village of Wayzata, and may have been the first Pillsbury drawn to that lake.[58] But Fred's interest in country living was agricultural. Alfred's was recreational and social. He fell in love with boating—and given his sporting bent, he was a natural for racing. His sloops "Wizard" and "Hazard" were by 1897 taking the winners' cups in regattas organized by the already fifteen-year-old Minnetonka Yacht Club. A new periodical, *Yachting in Minnesota,* described Alfred in 1898 as "thoroughly devoted to the sport" and "a thorough all-round sportsman and athlete."[59] His enthusiasm for life at the lake was infectious among his kin. "A.F. Pillsbury has interested in yachting nearly every member of the Pillsbury-Washburn Flour Mills Co.," the new publication said. "Previously, his father, J.S. Pillsbury, had no particular interest in Lake Minnetonka, but this season he built one of the handsomest summer residences to be found on its shores." He chose a site in the wooded area southwest of the village of Wayzata that had been given the name Ferndale. A haven for well-to-do milling families since the late 1870s, by the 1890s Ferndale was home to families named Sidle, Semple, Christian, Bell, Heffelfinger and more. The ex-governor called his new retreat Lake Home, and painted it dark green, a color he thought suited its wooded setting. The neighbors called the place Doggone It.[60]

The *Yachting* newsletter continued: "C.A. Pillsbury too sees beauties in the lake, and finds interest in the (Minnetonka Yacht) Club's races that failed to attract him before his nephew [cousin] showed such skill on the water. Then, too, there are C.S. Pillsbury and J.S. Pillsbury Jr., [the twins] who are also members of the club." Other prominent names in the Minneapolis milling industry—Bell, Christian, Dunwoody, Peavey, Washburn—were also on the boating club's roster. Charles bought a modest, three-bedroom farmhouse not far from Ferndale Road to house the twins and their sailing friends. A fixation was taking hold.

Alfred was energetic, fun-loving, competitive, and not necessarily business-minded. But by 1898 he had taken a position in the company's wheat department, which put him in the thick of the Leiter corner attempt and the McIntyre move to create a flour trust. He was tapped to go to London along with Arthur T. Safford, manager of Pillsbury-Washburn's Buffalo, N.Y. office, and Lucius P. Hubbard, the company's treasurer. They had a twofold mission: convince the corporation's London owners to oppose the McIntyre plan; and, lest their persuasion did not take hold, buy enough shares in England so that in the event of a shareholders' vote on a motion to sell to McIntyre, the motion could be defeated.[61]

The three-man delegation left for London in late 1898. By January 1899, their mission had succeeded. The London office cabled Minneapolis on January 13 that "for the present" the English would have no more truck with McIntyre. (The Minneapolis owners of Consolidated Milling Co., the successor of Fred C. Pillsbury's firm, were not as fortunate. McIntyre got control of Consolidated in 1899. Within a year, his U.S. Flour Milling Co. was in receivership.)

Alfred wrote his father to personally report the good news. The handwritten letter John sent his son in response is the only piece of personal correspondence between the two to have survived more than a century of shuffle in Pillsbury corporate files.[62] It's an undated document, but the context places it days after the January 13 cable from London.

"Your letter was clear and concise and just what we wanted," the happy father wrote. He added that Hubbard had already returned home, and "he speaks very highly of you and your manner of dealing with Englishmen and this situation generally, as he also does of Arthur." The letter goes on to chattily weave together business and family news, telling of John's trip to Bemidji to inspect lumbering camps, the price of wheat, the profitability of water power rental fees, and the bitterly cold Minnesota weather. "My health continues good," he added—suggesting that in the not-distant past, it had not been. John signed the missive "your affectionate Father" in genuine warmth—and illustrating that among adult male Pillsburys, there was little distinction between business and personal affairs.

It said much about Charles Pillsbury's condition at the close of 1898 that he agreed to delegate to his young cousin a mission thought crucial to the salvation of the company he built. A few weeks after Alf sailed from New York (or was it Boston, where pretty Eleanor "Gretchen" Field was his special friend?) Charles and Mary Ann also set sail for Europe, but on an entirely different mission. Charles was on a quest for a cure.

In London, Paris, Vienna, and Berlin, Charles made appointments with the city's most eminent physicians. After each examination, the diagnosis was the same: heart trouble, caused by overwork and too little exercise.[63] The doctors prescribed relaxation and gentle but persistent activity, such as the walking a sight-seeing tourist would do. Belatedly, Charles took medical advice to heart. He extended his stay abroad until mid-June, and his itinerary to Egypt as well as the European continent. He and Mary Ann were in Florence for Carnival; in Rome during Lent, where they chatted with another Minnesotan visiting the Holy See, Archbishop John Ireland of St. Paul; and in Paris in April, where a surviving receipt for a $1,400 painting reveals that they did some art shopping.[64] While in London in May, they sent home a letter to journalist Edgar commenting on the agricultural bounty of the Italian peninsula—and made no mention of medical visits. Their trip to Egypt apparently coincided with a spring break from classes for twins John and Charles S. The young men joined their parents, likely in Naples, from which they sailed to Port Said and Cairo. John and Charlie took a mail steamer up the Nile to its first waterfall, while their father "loafed," rode a donkey, and examined the growing of soft Egyptian wheat and the irrigation plans for farm fields near Cairo. He told Edgar that the climate in Egypt was superior to California's, and that it was "the most comfortable place to loaf which he visited."[65]

Charles returned to Minneapolis professing to have regained his health and strength. His friends were reassured by his words, but had to notice the change in his habits. For years, Pillsbury-Washburn employees had seen their chief executive sweep off his carriage and rush into the Guaranty building well before 8 a.m., and remain there until 6 p.m. or later. Now he arrived at work after 9 a.m., and when he went home for his noon meal, he was done for the day. "It was evident to those who knew him best that his days of business activity were over," Edgar would write that fall. "While they had no thought of his immediate death, they could not but feel that he was in a precarious condition."

On Tuesday, September 12, Charles and some friends traveled to southern Minnesota on an unspecified errand that might have included a little early fall hunting. When he returned to Minneapolis on Thursday, he remarked that he did not feel well, describing symptoms of nausea. But that day and again on Friday and Saturday, he spent a few hours at the office, chatting with Henry Little and making some calls. He was said to be in good spirits then, and Saturday evening as well. He and Mary Ann played a card game and retired as usual. But he had such an uncomfortable night that a doctor was summoned early Sunday morning. He seemed to rally as Sunday progressed. He chatted pleasantly with Mary Ann and the attending physician. But at 4:45 p.m. "he suddenly gasped for breath, and died almost instantly," Edgar reported.[66] Charles Pillsbury, a few weeks shy of his fifty-seventh birthday, had suffered a massive heart attack.

Only those close enough to Charles to know about his failing heart were anything but shocked by the news that washed over the city that Sunday night and Monday morning. If Minneapolis had an indispensable citizen in the minds of its residents, it was the man whom headline writers for years had called "the big miller." The city's phenomenal growth and development through three decades had been propelled in large part by Charles Pillsbury's entrepreneurial talent and civic values. "Few among us could be more illy spared," the *Tribune* editorialized the next day. "None will be more universally and sincerely mourned."[67]

Cables and telegrams of condolence arrived from around the world in the ensuing days. Corporate boards throughout the city and the nation sent resolutions of regret. Flags at public buildings throughout the city were hung at half-mast. On Tuesday, the day of the private funeral at the large Pillsbury home, all activity at Pillsbury-Washburn mills ceased. The trading floor at the Chamber of Commerce building was hushed as the Board of Trade met to attach signatures to their formal expression of loss, then closed at noon. The family requested no flowers, but they were inundated with bouquets anyway. Employees were advised that they were welcome to be in attendance at Lakewood for the burial after the funeral. More than a thousand showed up, lining Thirty-Sixth Street (the recently numbered road to the cemetery and Lake Calhoun.) The crowd within the cemetery's gates was described a "silent throng."[68] The funeral sermon preached by the Rev. L. H. Hallock of Plymouth Church was reprinted and circulated widely. It was profuse in praise for the deceased: "His was, in very many of its aspects, an ideal life: so strong; so kindly; so genial; so masterful. Energetic, undaunted; sweetened by smiles; stimulated by obstacles; never too busy in all his eager life for a half hour every day for his mother! And always his best for his home and his family.... As long as the nations shall eat bread; as long as the edifice of commercial progress shall stand, those who laid its foundations in righteousness 'shall be had in everlasting remembrance.' Charles A. Pillsbury has gone home!"[69]

The passage of 110 years has not diminished Charles' standing. He ranks as a leading personality in the formative first 40 years of the city of Minneapolis and the economic region it anchored, establishing not only their most important industry but also much about their defining character. He thought big, acted boldly, and embraced the new. He was the prototype for the twentieth-century Minnesota business leader. His blend of business ambition with public service and private benevolence set the example future Minnesota business executives would strive to emulate. His optimism, friendly approachability, and concern for the common good were qualities Minnesotans came to expect and demand of their leaders. His reputation for integrity and insistence on high quality became key elements of the Minnesota trademark. Charles's legacy is an enormously positive one. But his death created an awful void.

Gov. John S. Pillsbury's statue at the University of Minnesota.

Chapter Seven

Two Johns

Emotion ran high on the grassy knoll at the heart of the University of Minnesota campus on September 12, 1900. Several hundred friends and alumni of the leading educational institution of the North Star State had gathered in gratitude to dedicate a handsome bronze statue. Originating at the suggestion of Minnesota's first governor, Henry Sibley,[1] the project was taken over by the Alumni Association, which raised the princely sum of $15,000 to finance the work and commissioned sculptor Daniel Chester French to execute it. French had completed an impressive statue of George Washington astride his horse in Paris earlier that year, and would go on to carve the massive sculpture of seated Abraham Lincoln at the Lincoln Memorial in Washington, D.C.[2] The subject of the statue unveiled in Minneapolis that day was not a president or a king chosen for posthumous glory. It was a modest, bald, white-bearded, seventy-three-year-old man who was seated on the speaker's platform that morning, waiting to take his turn at the podium—John S. Pillsbury. Deservedly, he was being hailed as "the father of the university."

The former governor had served for thirty-seven years on the Board of Regents, much of that time as its president or chairman of the executive committee. He had almost single-handedly rescued the fledgling institution from insolvency in the 1860s and had been the state Senate author of legislation insuring that it would continue to have an operating budget. The science hall that his $150,000 donation built was the pride of the campus. Each month, he reviewed university spending, and kept an eye open for possible overdrafts of state appropriations—"a thing he would not tolerate," recalled William Watts Folwell, Pillsbury's great friend and the first president of the university.[3] John had personally hired both Folwell in 1868 and his successor, Cyrus Northrop, in 1884—though in the latter mission he had considerable assistance from his stalwart ally, Mahala. "She gave a reception which was one of the most unique and enjoyable occasions that has ever occurred in Minneapolis," wrote an admirer seven years later. "On this occasion Governor and Mrs. Pillsbury brought together not only the educators of the city and their wives to meet Dr. Northrop, but also other prominent men of the state, and such an impression was no doubt made of the intellectual forces of the community that he was aided in gaining a correct idea of the importance of the position tendered him."[4]

The record does not indicate whether Mahala was at John's side that day on campus, at the start of the academic year. She is known to have been in fragile health in 1900 and thereafter.[5] But if she was there, she undoubtedly joined John on the platform, gazing out at the throng of admirers, which included the elderly first territorial governor of Minnesota, Alexander Ramsey, and the current governor, Swedish-born John Lind of New Ulm. Perhaps in her mind's eye she saw the absentees as well. John and Mahala had been the first of the New Hampshire Pillsburys to choose Minnesota and pour their energies into building a robust society in the young state. At their invitation, nephews Charles and Fred and brothers George and Benjamin came later and took up the same cause. Now all four were gone, as were two of John and Mahala's daughters. The first to choose Minnesota were the last of the pioneering Pillsburys still standing.

Their former son-in-law, Fred B. Snyder, had remarried but remained close to the family, and was seated on the platform with John. Susan Pillsbury Snyder's only son, twelve-year-old John Pillsbury Snyder, was also likely on hand. The Snyders had purchased a home on Twenty-second Street close to Charles Pillsbury's Highland Home. It was Fred, as president of the university Alumni Association, who had spearheaded fundraising for the statue.[6]

Also likely present, though the record does not say so, were several young adults of the next generation: son Alfred and his bride of a little more than a year, Bostonian Eleanor Louise Field Pillsbury, known to all by her nickname Gretchen; daughter and son-in-law Sarah Belle, or "Sadie," and Edward Gale (though Sadie was six weeks from delivering her first and only child, and may have been excused from public appearances for that reason), and twin great-nephews Charles Stinson and John Sargent, who had graduated three months earlier with bachelor's degrees from their great-uncle John's university.

Eleanor Louise Field Pillsbury, called Gretchen, circa 1900.

Widows Margaret and Mary Ann could have been in attendance too, though their presence is less likely. Advanced age restricted Margaret's activity. But her devoted adopted daughter Minnie Townsend lived with the matriarch, along with son-in-law Burt and grandson Sprague. They could have lent strong arms on which to lean that day. Margaret was months away from a series of debilitating and ultimately fatal strokes. She spent her last years receiving and responding generously to appeals for assistance from Minnesota Baptist congregations, being "more devoted than ever to charity" after George's death.[7] Among the parishes that were recipients of her benevolence are some still active today: Immanuel, Calvary, Elim, Fourth (now in Plymouth, MN), Tabernacle (now New Beginnings) in Minneapolis and, in St. Paul, Pilgrim, in the African-American Rondo neighborhood. Margaret's check also went to Second Baptist in Duluth.[8] When her only surviving sibling, brother Henry Carleton, died in January 1901, Margaret began to perceptibly fail. She died on March 16, 1901, at age eighty-three.

Mary Ann retreated even more from public view after the loss of her husband Charles, almost one year to the day before the statue dedication. She still paid her $2 per year dues to the Plymouth Church women's society, and contributed $104—a meager $2 per week—to the congregation in 1901. She may have been in attendance on Sunday mornings to personally put her $2 into the collection plate, but if she was, she made no lasting imprint on church records.[9] Her sons might have coaxed her to the university campus that late summer day to applaud the uncle-in-law who had redirected her life thirty-one years before. If they did, they scored a coup.

"We rejoice that he in whose honor this statue was raised is present to take part in these exercises," said Fred Snyder as the ceremony began, speaking aloud the sentiment of those in the audience acquainted with the Pillsbury story. "We desire that he should know during his lifetime how much we esteem and honor him, not waiting to say it over his ashes." Next to speak was Cushman Davis, who had been Pillsbury's predecessor as governor. (In less than three months, Davis too would be dead.)

Bittersweet nostalgia, gratitude, and a sense that his Minnesota sojourn was coming to a close must have been part of the rich mix of feelings that put a lump in John's throat that day. When the other orations were finished and the three cheers and tremendous applause for him had died down, he found himself nearly unable to speak. It took him a moment to compose himself before he could begin. The next day's *Tribune* reported some of his words: "It is nearly forty years since I became connected with this institution. I can truly say, in spite of all the adversities and discouragements which were experienced in early days, when the very life of the university was at stake, and amid all the different problems that have from time to time beset the university, that no part of my life's work has afforded more gratification and happiness than that bestowed upon this institution." For this common-school-educated man, raising a great university with the constant nurture one might give one's own child had been a labor of love.

The statue is a lasting emblem of the affection that was returned to John Pillsbury in his later years. But it wasn't just his university stewardship that won Minnesotans' hearts. As memories of the privations of the grasshopper plague receded, his gubernatorial administration was becoming the stuff of legend, and he was often acclaimed as the state's best governor. "The most paternal of all Minnesota's executives," a tribute written nearly two decades after he left office said, praising him for "extending timely aid to the people without undermining their self-dependence." [10] His role in the devel-

opment of Minneapolis's leading industry, flour milling, was seen as crucial and perhaps understood more clearly by his contemporaries after his nephew Charles's death. John had also been a prominent player in the state's lumbering, mining, banking, and rail transportation industries. Taken together, his honorable dealings had won him the nickname "Honest John."

Among the stories told about John by his twentieth-century descendents was of the day in late 1893 when, as was his custom, he walked from his house near the University of Minnesota campus

"Honest John" in 1899.

across the river to the office he maintained in the First National Bank Building. John was the chairman of that bank, which would grow into US Bank; it was the same role his brother George played at the larger Northwestern National Bank, which is today's Wells Fargo. That day, he found a long line of agitated people on the banking floor, asking to withdraw their money. The Panic of 1893 had come to the nation's Northwest. Canada native Clive T. Jaffray, whose son would go on to found a leading Minneapolis investment firm, was a nervous young bank clerk that day. He watched as the former governor arrived, spoke to some of the bank customers, and quickly assessed the situation. He asked to see their bank notes, the account records carried by the customers nearest him. Calmly, he turned each note over and signed his name. With that signature, he was backing each person's account with his own funds. Jaffray would recall watching as word of what John Pillsbury was doing spread through the crowded chamber. "The dear old governor is promising us our money!" Jaffray heard. The calming effect of Pillsbury's gesture was instantaneous. "The floor was immediately cleared," was how Jaffray would describe the moment years later. Within minutes, the run on the bank was over.[11]

Mahala in the 1890s.

John and Mahala's philanthropy also continued to awe their neighbors, and not only those connected with the University of Minnesota. For example, in 1900, their gift to the state of Minnesota of a thousand acres of cut-over pine timberland ten miles northeast of Brainerd led to the establishment of something none of them had heard of before—a "state forest," to be forever protected from logging and available for recreation. It was also the site of the state's first tree nursery and forest fire lookout tower. Today that parcel is appropriately known as Pillsbury State Forest. It is laced with trails enjoyed by equestrians and bikers in the summer and cross-country skiers in the winter.[12]

Mahala helped organize the first Minneapolis home for orphaned children, the Society for the Relief of Homeless Children or, as it became known, the Children's Home Society, while she was Minnesota's first lady. She accepted its founding presidency in 1881, a year when a typhoid outbreak was increasing the need for orphan support.[13] She led the Children's Home Society from rented quarters to its initial home at Twenty-Second and Sixth (now Portland) Avenues, then to a large new home on Stevens Avenue between Thirty-Second and Thirty-Third Streets, built for $40,000 entirely with donated funds. When Cadwallader Washburn's will provided $375,000 for a separate orphan's home in Minneapolis (today known as the Washburn Center for Children), Mahala's group shifted its focus to the care of the elderly poor women. Mahala continued as the original organization's president, even as she consented to the dictum in Washburn's will that she must serve on the board of directors of his orphan's home.[14] Mahala guided the Children's Home Society to rebirth as the Home for Children and Aged Women, which in the twentieth century would be called Stevens Square. Its charity balls became a highlight of the Minneapolis social season; the annual event raised the bulk of the $7,000 annual operating budget in the 1890s.[15] When the Home for Aged Women and Children sought to build an endowment in the late 1890s to sustain its service to indigent women, Mahala and John responded with a $100,000 donation.[16]

Mahala likely did not apply the term "feminist" to herself. But as Minnesota's first lady, she cheered enactment of legislation granting women the vote in school elections, and spoke at a rally in support of the election of the first women, Charlotte Van Cleve and Charlotte Winchell, to the Minneapolis School Board.[17] In Mahala's later years, her work in the public sphere bent in a decidedly feminist direction. She participated in organizing the Minneapolis Women's Exchange, which was part of a national network of fashionable shops where entrepreneurial women of modest means could sell home-crafted merchandise on consignment.[18] She was also among the founders of Northwestern Hospital for Women and Children in 1882 (today's Abbott Northwestern Hospital), a project spearheaded by lumberman T.B. Walker's wife Harriet. Staffed with two female physicians, Northwestern's mission was to provide health care to impoverished women and children, many of whom were suffering from pneumonia and typhoid fever.[19] The hospital stressed the value of rest, good nutrition, and cleanliness as aids to natural healing, and fostered the training of young women as nurses.

That occupational choice for young women, though comparatively new in the 1880s, was one that Mahala encouraged. She was keenly aware of the problems too often associated with the work that was most available to the poor young women from rural Minnesota who gravitated to the big city: domestic service, with housing provided in employers' homes. Too often, girls thus employed were subject to abuse—psychological, physical, and sexual. When "things didn't work out," a young worker was often abruptly tossed into the street, where worse dangers awaited. The plight of those young women had long been under discussion by the Women's Christian Association, the city's oldest charitable organization, which had claimed Mahala Pillsbury as a member since its start in 1866. Mahala and John determined in 1900 that they would do something to help dislocated domestic workers. As they dedicated Daniel French's likeness of John that September day in 1900, they could have been thinking about their latest project—a boarding house for self-supporting young women, with room to accommodate sixty tenants. They would build it for $25,000 on Second Avenue between Eighth and Ninth Street—one block from Charles and Mary Ann's old address—and give it free of encumbrance to the Women's Christian Association to operate.[20] When it opened in February 1901, it took the name Mahala Fisk Pillsbury Home for Young Women.

When that project was winding down, John announced another one. For years, he had wanted to provide a permanent library for the working people of old St. Anthony, the "East Side." He had not forgotten his father's devotion to the little lending library he helped establish in Sutton, nor the unfulfilled notion he had in 1880 of putting a library inside the Pillsbury A Mill. In the twenty years since the mill was constructed, a modest branch library collection had been amassed for the neighborhood and had been housed in several rented facilities—one of them at the corner of University and First Avenue SE. Pillsbury had in mind to build a stylish, substantial permanent home for the branch library diagonally across the street from the rented library rooms and directly across from East Side High School. He approached the Minneapolis Library Board with an offer of $75,000, the largest gift the board had received to that date, and an Italian Renaissance design by architect Charles Aldrich, who had built the University of Minnesota armory in 1896 and was working on Jones Hall on the campus that year. He proposed that it be built of striking white marble. Would the board accept such a gift? They would, most gladly.[21] The building served as a handsomely appointed neighborhood library through the mid-twentieth century, at which

The Pillsbury Library as it appeared in the 1970s.

time it was converted into a private art gallery and later an art warehouse. In recent years it has served as the headquarters of the Phillips family foundation and businesses. Its distinctive architecture and striking marble façade continue to bring charm to the neighborhood John loved.

In the summer of 1901, John and Mahala presented a gift to their dear First Congregational Church. They commissioned glass artist Walter Jones of New York to produce a pair of large stained glass windows in memory of their deceased daughters, Addie Webster and Susan Snyder. They were the first of Jones's work to be installed in Minnesota, and were considered an artistic achievement as well as a fitting memorial.[22] Their gift of memorial stained glass windows was not the first for the Pillsbury family. The Plymouth Congregational Church that stood at Eighth and Nicollet from 1875 until 1908 had two large, elegant windows donated by Charles and Mary Ann, in memory of their infant son George and daughter Margaret. The windows were considered too precious to leave behind when the Plymouth congregation moved south to 1900 Nicollet Avenue in 1908, but a parish committee deemed them unsuited to the new church's design. The windows were moved in 1916 to Wayzata Congregational Church, which was rebuilding after a fire. There they remain today, in what is now Wayzata Community Church.[23]

As digging began for the new library's foundation, Pillsbury agreed to an interview with journalist Horace B. Hudson. The result was a feature article in the *American Monthly Review of Reviews*.[24] He told Hudson, "I have always had a great interest in the people of the East Side. There are people still living there—working men and men of moderate means—who were my neighbors when I first came to St. Anthony. I have felt like doing all I could to benefit them." He looked for a site for his library in a working-class neighborhood, "very accessible for the class of people who most need library privileges." Hudson concluded that his subject was "a man of the present," who believed in doing things when need arose. "His impulse always was 'Act; act now; act effectively; act for the greatest good,'" Hudson wrote.

"I want to do these things while I am living," Pillsbury told the journalist. He apparently sensed that his time was running short.

In late September 1901, John contracted a case of whooping cough, one of a number of contagions that terrorized people before the advent of modern medicine in the mid-twentieth century. Evidently, a fit of hard coughing triggered a minor stroke that confined him to bed. Then heart failure set in. On October 12, the *Tribune* announced that the former governor was "dangerously ill." He appeared to rally but then relapsed. Early in the morning of October 18, in his own bed and surrounded by his loved ones, John Pillsbury died.

The outpouring of grief and tributes that the Pillsburys had witnessed when Charles died was more that matched two years later as John took his place in the family plot at Lakewood Cemetery. It was as if all of Minnesota paused to mourn. People "gathered in little groups in hotels and offices, factories and shops, and retold the many stores of the kindly charge that he had kept, for the God that he had glorified," the *Tribune* reported the day after his death.[25] Even the most perfunctory list of his achievements is impressive: a university established, a state rescued from debt repudiation, major Minnesota industries well launched, charitable work accomplished, all for the benefit of many. But the focus of many of the tributes published that October was more personal. They spoke of loans quietly given, kindness unfailingly shown, the inspiration of strong character softened by winsome humility and modest manners. John S. Pillsbury "saw, perhaps more clearly than most men, that good citizenship consists in more than personal probity and the right ballot on election day," wrote Hudson, whose article was published after the governor died. "Personal service is required; and such service he gave, beginning with modest labors and gradually extending this sphere of usefulness as his ideas developed and as his means increased. It is a very conservative estimate that he spent more than one-third of his life, after removing to Minnesota, in the service of the public."[26] He had not come to Minnesota just to acquire wealth. And when he did become wealthy, he did not turn to public service out of *noblesse oblige,* the notion that the wealthy owed service to lesser folk. His thinking was more democratic. It was born in the town meetings of New England, in which each adult male, as John himself described it, plays his part, "fully recognizing his rights and his duties" within the community.[27] "Each man is the equal of the other, and how the rights of each community are upheld!" he said on the day the town hall he donated to Sutton was dedicated in 1892. He believed that only if each individual did his part—and with Mahala's stalwart partnership in mind, he likely would have added "her part"—could the whole community thrive. No self-respecting citizen could neglect the needs of his community, any more than he could the needs of his family. Those with more gave more as a matter of course, not because of special obligation. Democracy's duties, he maintained, were to be shared by all.

New Englanders by the thousands carried that attitude from the granite hills of their youth to the Falls of St. Anthony. They built a democratic political culture modeled on the one they had left behind. Among them, the first John Sargent Pillsbury of Minnesota was a master builder.

For the second John Sargent Pillsbury of Minnesota, the first decade of the twentieth century suddenly looked disconcertingly different from the one he had imagined for himself. He no doubt expected to ease gradually into the family business along with his twin brother Charles Stinson, now that the two had graduated from the University of Minnesota. The real work of leading Pillsbury-

Washburn Co. would remain in their father's capable hands, guided behind the scenes by wise Uncle John and, in his most optimistic imagining, by Grandpa George for many years to come. Young John and Charles would enjoy a long tutelage, affording ample time for travel and for as merry a social and cultural life as Midwestern Minneapolis could afford young bachelors with means.

Nothing in John's childhood had geared him to expect otherwise. His was the carefree youth of a favored son in a burgeoning young city. In fact, he and Minneapolis had grown up together. The tales he told as an octogenarian to columnist Barbara Flanagan in 1959 offer residents of twenty-first century Minneapolis a fascinating glimpse of life in their city when it was new.[28] John's boyhood home at Tenth Street and Second Avenue, near the heart of today's downtown, included a carriage house and barn out back, occupied by a two-seat Concord buggy, a four-seat carriage with a fringe on the top, three horses, a cow, and a coachman. Young Johnny and Charlie spent a lot of time there.

Twins Johnny and Charlie with their St. Bernard dog.

They got to know the man who came most days to lead neighborhood cows to pasture just south of Grant Street, a few blocks away. They made a particular bond with the family coachman, John Hanrahan. Hanrahan's appeal included the fact that his brother Red was a shortstop for the Minneapolis Millers baseball team, which played at a ballpark behind the West Hotel, the city's finest, at Fifth and Hennepin. Red provided his brother and the twins with free tickets, and they took in so many games together that "I knew all the players, and they knew me," John boasted in the interview. The boys considered it a privilege to be allowed to carry Red's gear bag as they walked into the stadium with him.

When William Dunwoody at Washburn-Crosby hired James S. Bell as general manager in 1888, the boys had another reason to head to the West Hotel. The Bell family, including ten-year-old James Ford Bell, lived there—an unusual housing arrangement that was a fascination to the Pillsbury twins. Young Jim Bell, the future leader of General Mills, became Johnny Pillsbury's best friend. Hanrahan had taught Johnny how to drive a team of horses, which he could do quite well by age nine, even though he had to stand on a soapbox to put harnesses on the trotters.

It may have been to keep the horses available for adult transportation that Charlie and Johnny were given the first "safety bicycles" in the city, in about 1889. Jim Bell got one too, and the three boys tooled around town at will. They discovered they could bicycle as fast as downtown horses could trot—a discovery that likely annoyed more than one buggy driver. The kids never missed a fire when school was not in session. When they heard the bell of a fire wagon, they pedaled fast. "Every fire wagon had us behind it on our bikes," John said. The boys sometimes had a little change in their pockets to spend. "We used to get 25 cents for a haircut from mother. Then John [Hanrahan] would clip our hair with the horse-clipper, and we saved the quarter. Of course, our hair looked just awful, and we'd really get it from the family," John told Barbara Flanagan. "When we were really naughty, we'd go and hide under the mill wood at the lumber yard. Then we'd have to go home sometime."

The boys started school at the first Washington School at Fourth Street and Third Avenue, where Minneapolis City Hall now stands. It was a rough-and-tumble public school, originally built to serve the entire west-river side of the fast-growing city. "There used to be some pretty good gangs at Washington School. The first day there, I got the worst licking of my life," John remembered. "We had double desks, and it was punishment to sit a boy with a girl. As I remember, I had to endure some of that punishment." John and Charles spent only one year at the old building, which the school had more than outgrown, before moving to brand-new Washington School at 725 Sixth Street South. That address is now part of the

Hennepin County Medical Center complex. The imposing stone schoolhouse had a turret and separate entrances and playgrounds for boys and girls. John confessed to trying to sneak onto the girls' playground on several occasions.

When the family moved "out of town" to 2200 Stevens Avenue in 1890, the boys transferred to Emerson School, which still stands on LaSalle Avenue two blocks from the park that now bears Charles Loring's name. "It was such a lovely, polite school . . . It wasn't as much fun as Washington," John recalled, revealing much about his boyhood nature. But the new neighborhood had its own attractions. Diagonally across the street from Highland Home, Dorilus Morrison and his second wife threw extravagant parties at which teenaged boys could play a role. At one or more of their annual Rose Fetes, John drove a pony cart. Across the street at Fair Oaks the twins found a new chum, Stanley Washburn, son of W. D. Washburn, their father's business partner and Minnesota's U.S. senator. Together the three boys attended Central High School at Eleventh Street and Fourth Avenue South (later, the site of the city's Vocational High School.)

Their semi-rural setting and entrepreneurial natures inspired Charlie, John, and Stan to go into business one summer. They created the Fair Oaks Poultry Company. John explained to journalist Flanagan: "We boys would buy broilers at the old market—big and stringy ones. Then we'd go over to the Pillsbury A mill and buy screenings, you know, the corn and oats milled out of the flour. We'd fatten those old broilers up in the Washburn stable yard and then go out and sell them door-to-door." For a city kid, one feature of this business venture wasn't easy: "It was tough to cut off the first head," John confessed.

One of the few surviving Pillsbury anecdotes about the 1892 Republican National Convention involves Stanley Washburn and the twins. The convention assembled in the Exposition Building on the east side of the river only a few weeks after Fred Pillsbury's death. The rest of the family evidently pulled back from convention participation—but the boys did not. They were pages, serving delegates on the convention floor, and they ran a little lemonade business on the side. A man outside the hall was selling a glass of lemonade for a nickel. The boys would buy several glasses, carry them into the hall, and sell

The Hennepin Avenue Bridge leading to the Exposition Hall, site of the 1892 Republican National Convention.

them to delegates for a dime apiece. They also did a little political demonstrating—and got into trouble for it. The convention nominated President Benjamin Harrison for a second term. "But we boys were for [Maine Sen.] James G. Blaine, the People's Choice…When Blaine was licked, we were all so disgusted that we went back to the Washburn house to mope. The senator [Stan's father] had four flags flying, [one] at each corner of the house. We put them at half-mast in honor of Blaine. There was hell to pay when the senator came home and saw those flags. He had a lot of distinguished Republicans with him. I don't think I've ever seen anyone turn purple with rage except Sen. Washburn. Needless to say, we were really pummeled for that stunt."

Dancing lessons on Saturdays, torchlight parades on election nights, sledding on the big hill near Tom Lowry's house (near today's Walker Art Center), ice skating at Loring Park, debutante and charity balls at the West Hotel, Sunday dinners at Uncle John and Aunt Mahala's house, riding Lowry's private streetcar to parties in St. Paul, staying overnight afterward at the mansion of their father's friend

James J. Hill—those were among the memories that John Pillsbury cherished. He was loved but not indulged at home. He would tell his granddaughter that the first birthday party ever given in his honor occurred after his marriage.

The best of times for young John were the trips he took with his father. By the time the twins were nine or ten, they were invited with some frequency to accompany Charles on business trips around the country. John, and perhaps his brother too, went to Europe for the first time in 1890, at age eleven. Travel afforded many pleasures, the greatest likely being a larger slice of their father's attention than they were granted at home. Charles taught his sons to speak English slowly and distinctly when addressing people in foreign countries. He let them watch him in action in business conversations, giving them a richer understanding of the family enterprise than they got as summer errand boys at the Minneapolis office. When the boys joined their parents in Europe and Egypt in the spring of 1899, they were doing what they loved best with their parents. They likely expected that many more family trips would follow.

Things didn't work out that way. Upon their father's death, John set aside his notions about study in France and an eventual career in the diplomatic corps,[29] and both young men took positions at Pillsbury-Washburn; Charlie worked as a cashier, John as a clerk in the central office, then as a Midwestern states salesman. In the formal office atmosphere that was customary in those years, they may have been among the few employees at the headquarters to address each other by their first names. Even much later in life, they referred to the man who succeeded their father at the helm of the company as "Mr. Little."[30]

John and Charlie continued to live at home with their mother at Highland Home, the family's Stevens Avenue mansion. But life at home was changing. Charles had fallen in love with a Minneapolis girl with Southern roots and charm, Helen Pendleton Winston—"Nelle" or "Nellie" to those who knew her well. The story of their meeting has been lost,[31] but their families were neighbors and they probably became casually acquainted as teenagers, even though Nelle was educated by private tutors and attended a boarding school in Baltimore.

The choice of schooling reflected the family's Southern ancestry. Nelle's father, Philip Bickerton Winston, was among the few Minneapolis business leaders who did not hail from New England. Rather, he was a son of Virginia, and a loyal one. He was an officer in the Army of the Confederacy, and letters written to his sister Caroline during the Civil War reveal him to be accustomed both to slaveholding and to life's comforts. In one of them, amid news about a teacher with measles and wishes that more girls would write to him, Winston observes: "Dr. Morris told me that Pa was not at Taylorsville, but that the negroes sold remarkably well, one went as high as thirteen hundred." A letter written in 1864, when the South was suffering, told about new uniforms ordered, and asks that a comforter be sent to him via Gen. Rosser, a family friend.[32] As a lieutenant in Robert E. Lee's Army, Philip Winston faced off against the storied Minnesota First at Gettysburg.

After the war, Philip and his brothers fled the ruined economy of the South and eventually settled in booming Minneapolis, where, in 1872, they founded a construction company that specialized in building railroads. Winston Bros. Construction soon became the Bechtel Corp. of its day, raking in government and private railroad contracts, including one to build more than a thousand miles of James J. Hill's Northern Pacific Railroad. In Minneapolis, Philip wooed and wed Katherine D. Stevens, a daughter of the first U.S. settler in Minneapolis, John H. Stevens. Their daughter Nelle was born in 1878, two months before the Pillsbury twins arrived.

True to his roots, Philip Winston was an active Democrat. He served one term as mayor of Minneapolis from 1890 to 1892, and two non-consecutive terms in the state House. There, his proudest achievement was a bill assuring public school students access to free textbooks.[33] That was the kind of lawmaking that even Republican Pillsburys could admire.

In July 1901, a few months before the death of John Pillsbury, Philip Winston passed away, and was laid to rest at Lakewood on the afternoon of Independence Day. He was so highly esteemed in his adopted Yankee home that an ivy wreath was given at his funeral by

(left) Nelle in her wedding dress, December 1901.
(right) Charles S. Pillsbury soon after his marriage.

local veterans of the Civil War's Grand Army of the Republic—men
who had been his foes on the battlefield forty years earlier. Mayor
Ames, back in office once again, issued a special order forbidding
the shooting of firecrackers anywhere in the vicinity during the
services.[34]

Charles and Nelle were married in a small, simple ceremony at
her mother's Park Avenue home on Dec. 7, 1901, one day after his
twenty-third birthday. Only their immediate families were present.
After a brief wedding trip to the East—with possibly a stop in Virginia,
which Nelle considered her second and perhaps truer home—the
young couple settled into the big house at 2200 Stevens. It had more
than enough room for the bride and groom, his bachelor brother,
and their mother, but from the very first, during the summer months,
Charles and Nelle often escaped to a cottage they'd purchased on
Ferndale Road, along Lake Minnetonka's northeastern rim. In time
an understanding developed between the brothers: John and Charles
would share Highland Home while John remained single. But two
wives under one roof would not do. If and when John took a wife,
a coin toss would decide who would stay at 2200 Stevens and who
would go.[35]

Mary Ann's role in this agreement, as in so many things, is unknown. She popped up in newspaper society notes in April 1902, when she and her son John (but not Charles and Nelle) were co-hosts of a dinner party at 2200 Stevens for one of Fred Pillsbury's daughters, Harriot, who had returned to the city of her birth to be married to Harold Ayer "from the East." Mary Ann Stinson Pillsbury does not appear in the papers again until a two-paragraph notice on page one of the Sept. 26 edition reports: "Mrs. C.A. Pillsbury dies of pneumonia." She had been ill for four or five days, the notice said. She was sixty-one years old. Her funeral would be at home the following Sunday afternoon, with the Rev. Hallock of Plymouth Church officiating. Her casket was covered with white roses that day, a tribute from her twin sons.

In a span of a little more than four years, the twins had lost their Pillsbury grandparents, parents, and guiding great-uncle. Their father's younger brother, who might have been a rock for them to lean on, was gone as well. One Pillsbury great-aunt, Mahala, remained, frail and increasingly housebound. The toll of all those losses weighed heavily on their spirits, no doubt, and the sudden dramatic increase in business responsibilities was an added burden. Along with their cousin Alfred, who was nine years older, the twins had become by default the leaders of the Pillsbury family in Minnesota. A sizeable share of the Minneapolis workforce and a goodly slice of the Minnesota economy were accustomed to looking to the Pillsburys for leadership. The events that followed would test their ability to provide it.

After his father's death, Alfred opted out of Pillsbury-Washburn Co. He would manage his family's total investment portfolio instead of sharing operational responsibility for one aspect of it, he said. He kept his position on the company's board of directors, where he was a consistent advocate for fair treatment of employees and good working conditions.[36] It must have grieved him in 1903 when the company experienced its first-ever labor strike. Flour loaders, who lifted heavy bags and shoved heavier barrels into boxcars all day long, demanded an eight-hour day at the same pay that they had been receiving for 10 hours, $2 per day. When the proposal was rejected, they went out on strike. The strike affected not just Pillsbury-Washburn, but also Washburn-Crosby and Consolidated. Strikebreakers were hired and the strike was broken.[37] Alfred must have watched with dismay, knowing how sympathetic his late father and cousins were to labor.

Flour milling was only one portion of the business portfolio Alfred inherited. He had considerable timber and mineral holdings to oversee as well. He succeeded his father on the First National Bank board of directors and as an officer of Farmers and Mechanics Bank. Fred Beal Snyder, Alf's brother-in-law, was also on the F & M Bank board; he would remain for the rest of his long life in the Pillsbury family orbit, and exhibit Pillsbury-like commitment to public service. But Alf's interests as a young adult ran in a different direction. In 1903 he acquired one of the first three automobiles to appear in Minneapolis, a steam Locomobile with bicycle tires and a hand tiller. He was fascinated with sailboats and racing. He took up golf and became quite good at it. As he approached middle age, the jury was still out regarding whether business and public service would ever supplant leisure as Alfred's life focus.

Charles and Nelle responded to the depletion of Pillsbury family ranks by launching the next generation. Nelle was already pregnant with a son, Philip Winston Pillsbury, when she stood at her mother-in-law's grave in September 1902. Young Phil, namesake of his maternal grandfather, was born on April 10, 1903. Three daughters followed in quick succession: Mary Stinson, on November 14, 1904; Katharine Stevens, on December 11, 1905; and Helen Winston, on November 18, 1907. The drafty mansion on Stevens Avenue filled again with young life.

The brand-new automobile bug also bit Charles. A *Minneapolis Times* item on June 24, 1905, urged readers to come to Riverside Hill, situated approximately where the Frederick Weisman Art Museum sits now on the University of Minnesota campus, and watch the fledgling Automobile Club's hill-climbing contest. Among the entrants: Alf Pillsbury, whose $4,000 Peerless would be driven by H.D. Savage, and Charlie Pillsbury, driving his own 45-horsepower Locomobile. Charlie's car was described as a new arrival at the Winston and Walker

186

Garage (likely co-owned by one of his in-laws) with a listed value of $7,500—several times more than the average Minneapolis mill worker then earned in a year.[38]

That same year, Charles Stinson Pillsbury scaled back his work schedule at the milling company. "In 1905, Mr. Pillsbury suffered an illness which obliged him to take a three-year leave of absence from the company, during which time he regained his health and traveled extensively," a corporate publication records.[39] His absence may have begun even earlier: A September 24, 1904 social note in the *Minneapolis Tribune* said Charles, Nelle, and John were leaving on a trip south, and expected to be away through the winter. More than a cen-

John S. Pillsbury at the office, circa 1920.

tury later, Charles's nephew and grandson attest that Charles was afflicted with a mysterious physical malady that diminished his capacity to work for most of his adult life.[40] The nature of his ailment is not known. It could have been Chronic Fatigue Syndrome, now popularly referred to as "the Yuppie disease." It could have been an early manifestation of the heart disease that claimed the father's life. It could have

been that watching his father work himself almost literally to death made Charles fearful of overwork. Whatever the cause, Charles would struggle to maintain physical stamina for the rest of his life.

Of the three Pillsbury young men, John appears to have been the most focused on Pillsbury-Washburn and the larger community. He had majored in chemistry and physics at the University of Minnesota, suggesting that he was serious about understanding the heart of his family's business and grooming himself for company leadership.[41] He had been student manager of the Golden Gophers football team, developing strong relationships with his generation of future

Minneapolis leaders. That role was different in 1898 than it is today. The student manager was essentially an assistant coach, helping to negotiate the schedule, recruit players, make sure athletes attended classes and ate three meals a day. Pillsbury initiated training-table meals that the team consumed together.[42] When John graduated, he enlisted in the Minnesota National Guard and served from 1900 until 1904, holding the position of battalion adjutant with the rank of first lieutenant. [43]

He aided, and may have spearheaded, the creation of a significant and lasting memorial to his parents. As members of Plymouth Congregational Church, Charles and Mary Ann had been "in heavy sympathy" with the congregation's mission work among the city's poor and its newcomers.[44] As early as 1879, Plymouth had opened a drop-in service center for the poor at Third Avenue and Second Street. In 1880, the center added a free kindergarten. As the city's disadvantaged population drifted southeast to Cedar Riverside, Plymouth's mission work did too. In 1883, it became the Plymouth Kindergarten and Industrial Association, with its own building at 1416 Second St. S. It offered kindergarten, industrial classes for women, sewing classes for girls, and a day nursery.[45] When the settlement house movement reached Minnesota in the 1890s, the Plymouth ministry added more services, took the name Bethel Settlement House, and struggled to keep up with increasing demand. Prostitution, crime, alcoholism, and disease were all major problems for the growing population of immigrants, vagrants, and unskilled laborers that Bethel served. By 1904, its clients numbered more than a thousand per week.[46]

Whether the proposal to donate a new building for Bethel House originated with John, Charles, or someone else at Plymouth Church is not known. But the idea took hold of both brothers. In April 1905, they donated $40,000 to build what became known as Pillsbury House at 320 Sixteenth Av. S. The brothers proposed that a $20,000 matching fund be raised for the building's maintenance. Within six weeks, pledges exceeding that amount were in hand, and construction began. The new facility made possible the addition of a health clinic, a women's employment office, home economics and art classes, citizenship training for men (women's voting rights were still fifteen years away) and boys' and girls' clubs. The latter work was conducted in affiliation with the YMCA and YWCA, national organizations whose presence in Minneapolis was winning John Pillsbury's notice. Soon thereafter, John and Charles became trustees of Pillsbury Settlement Association, the agency that operated the house. Upon opening, Bethel was rechristened Pillsbury Settlement House. It's the root from which grew today's Pillsbury United Communities, a leading nonprofit social services agency in south Minneapolis.[47]

Y et there were also times when John's attention wandered from the problems and opportunities Minneapolis had to offer. He itched to travel. When the chance arose in January 1904 to join three other young Minnesota men on an extended trip to east Asia, he grabbed it. Along with M.B. Koon, a local judge; J.B. Gilfillan Jr., the son of another judge; and L. S. Gillette, the son of a machinery manufacturer, John set sail from San Francisco on Jan. 25. They were in Yokohama on Feb. 19—nine days after outbreak of the Russo-Japanese War. Rather than being alarmed at that turn of events, John was enthralled. The Minnesota foursome went on a houseboat tour of the interior of China in mid-April, sailing to Beijing. When the group's intended departure date arrived, John and Gilfillan decided to stay on for ten more weeks.[48] They went to Tokyo and made connections with Western journalists; among the friends John made there were future literary notables Jack London and Richard Harding Davis. "They were chafing under severe restrictions, and while being entertained at elaborate tea parties and concerts, felt completely bottled up, longed to get closer to the fight," John said many years later.[49]

In Shanghai the Minnesotans reconnected with an eager young reporter for the *Chicago Daily News*, Stan Washburn. John's old Fair Oaks neighborhood chum had based himself in the Chinese port of Chefoo (now Yantai) and operated a shuttling dispatch boat for his and other American newspapers, gathering daily reports from the Japanese Navy and running them back to waiting reporters on shore. Among those who filed reports, unsolicited, to newspapers back home was John Pillsbury. He finally returned in late August, and was sought after for interviews about his observations. His admiring description of the Japanese war machine is more chilling in post-World War II hindsight than it likely was for its original readers. In Hiroshima, John said, he saw ninety-two troop-transport ships in the harbor being loaded with troops that would soon be dispatched to do battle with Russia. "It gave one an idea of the marvelous development of Japan in the past few years," John said. In later years, John would refer to this period in his life, perhaps a bit wistfully, as his "war correspondent days."[50]

He made an even longer trip in 1905-06, embarking from San Francisco aboard a ship dubbed *The Mongolian* for a trip around the world. This time his traveling companion was Charles Heffelfinger, a member of a large Minneapolis family that prospered in the footwear manufacturing and grain storage businesses. The October 29, 1905, *Tribune* social column reporting their imminent departure lamented, "What will the smart set do without its two most popular bachelors?"[51] John was indeed in demand in upper-crust social circles. Monday night theater parties, Friday night orchestra dates, Saturday night card parties, and a raft of balls, dances, and club events filled his social calendar when he was in the city. A night spent quietly at 2200 Stevens with Charles and Nelle, playing with his little nephew and nieces, was a rare one for John. But if he had a special girlfriend or favorite companion in those years, her identity was not passed along to future generations.

That began to change in the fall of 1907. John was driving a primitive Packard one afternoon outside the heart of the city—it might have been around Lake of the Isles, which had only recently been created by dredging marshland west of the city—when his vehicle began to give him trouble. He stopped, crawled under the machine to assess the problem, then peered out at the sound of a horse-drawn carriage approaching. John recognized the driver. It was distinguished English-born Edmund Pennington, president of the Soo Line Railroad. John had taken his father's place on the Soo Line board of directors. Beside Pennington sat Eleanor Jerusha "Juty" Lawler, a strikingly beautiful young woman. She was a newcomer to Minneapolis, having spent most of her teenaged years in St. Paul or away at boarding schools. Pennington was her new stepfather. She would later recall that John seemed too preoccupied with his vehicular difficulty that day to truly notice her.[58] About that, she was wrong.

Eleanor saw John again two weeks later at a theater party, at which he was chosen (perhaps not coincidentally) to be her escort by their

mutual friends, Mr. and Mrs. Larry Day. "That evening each girl acquired a special beau who continued his attentions throughout our debut season," Juty reported years later. Beginning in November 1907, Minneapolis newspaper society columns began recording with some frequency the presence of "Miss Jerusha Lawler" at parties attended or hosted by John S. Pillsbury.[52]

But the roller-coaster pattern of luck that had coupled glad events with trouble or tragedy held firm for the Pillsburys in 1908. Just as new joy

Eleanor Jerusha Lawler, 1907.

was entering John Pillsbury's life, trouble engulfed him at Pillsbury-Washburn Co. In July, John, Charles, and Alfred Pillsbury were summoned to a meeting with representatives of the city's three leading banks—First National, Northwestern, and Security. Each of those institutions had a long personal history with the Pillsbury family. Representing First National that day was its vice president, Clive Jaffray, who as a young clerk fifteen years earlier had watched former Gov. John Pillsbury single-handedly quell a run on the bank. Jaffray had been tipped off by a golfing buddy he would identify only as a "prominent grainman" about reckless wheat speculation by C.A. Pillsbury's hand-picked successor, Henry Little. The banker believed the tip was credible and wanted to share it with "the three Pillsbury boys." The news seemed to surprise them.[53]

Though Alfred and Charles had been quite removed from the business, and might well have been surprised that day, it's unlikely that John was entirely unaware of the situation. He had been on the job at Pillsbury-Washburn since his return from travelling in 1906, first in sales and later in the treasurer's office. He was also a leading stockholder of the company. He knew a good deal about the lean profits his industry had endured in the previous twenty years, and was close enough to daily operations to recognize that Little's attempts to make gains on the futures market were failing badly. When the situation became dire, John would have wanted the company's local lenders made aware of it. They were, after all, Pillsbury businesses too. It's not inconceivable that Jaffray's golf course tipster was John Pillsbury himself.[54]

Family lore is more definite about how the next shoe dropped. Just as the bankers and the "Pillsbury boys" were discussing a financial rescue plan for a company that was almost out of cash, John became aware of a deeper problem. Henry Little had borrowed more than $1 million on notes issued in the company's name, but not recorded on its books. Little and another trusted associate of Charles A. Pillsbury, Charles Amsden, had signed the unrecorded notes. In the modern era, their action would have been deemed a criminal offense. In 1908 Minneapolis, the proper place for a twenty-nine-year-old major shareholder and mid-level employee to go with such a discovery was not to a prosecutor, but to his family and its closely affiliated local bankers. That's what John did. It was a courageous move—an act of disloyalty to his boss, but loyalty to the integrity for which the Pillsbury name stood. "Dad believed very strongly in telling the truth," John's youngest son attested. The revelation quashed the family's plan for a $1 million rescue from their own funds.

On Sunday, August 9, a front-page story in the *Minneapolis Tribune* announced that the city's largest milling concern, Pillsbury-Washburn, was in receivership. That action had been taken in court on the motion of four Minneapolis banks, one St. Paul bank, and one stockholder, John S. Pillsbury. The motion had alleged "bad management, mismanagement, and management that has steadily decreased profits... and rendered bankruptcy imminent," the newspaper reported. It added that its reporters failed at efforts to obtain details about the

Twins Charles and John at work at the Pillsbury Company.

alleged mismanagement. The court had appointed three receivers: Minneapolis attorney Albert C. Cobb, representing the banks; Fred C. Pillsbury's former Consolidated partner, Albert C. Loring, reputedly the shrewdest milling manager in the Flour City; and Charles S. Pillsbury, "who is a shareholder in the company but has never been in any way connected, either as director or managing agent or otherwise, with the administration of (the company's) affairs." The receivers' attorney and "spokesman" was a close-mouthed Frank Carleton, Charles A. Pillsbury's cousin. Such matters were kept within the family.

Receivership is akin to the modern-day Chapter 11 bankruptcy. It allowed the company to continue operations until it was either reorganized or sold. Bankruptcy, on the other hand, would have led to a quick forced sale of the company's assets to satisfy its creditors, and an end to Pillsbury-Washburn. Receivership would cause only minor disruption to workers and local vendors, including the banks, the *Tribune* reported. Most of the company's debt was owed to unspecified banks on the East Coast. "It is believed that the company will be upon a new and sounder basis within a year or so," was the reassuring news.[55]

But the paper was unable to explain why a company that grossed $22 million the year before was unable to raise the cash necessary to pay its bills. The next day, the *Tribune* revealed that the Pillsbury mills had been silenced on Saturday, August 8. They would reopen on Tuesday, August 11, under receivers' management. Henry Little had submitted his resignation two weeks earlier, the paper disclosed.[56] He would leave town for good within days.

The newspaper did not immediately reveal the whereabouts of Alfred, the one Pillsbury who still sat on the company's board of directors. Had the reporter inquired, he would have learned that Alfred was in London, on a mission not unlike the one on which his father had sent him ten years earlier. Alfred's role was to convince the company's London owners that receivership, not bankruptcy, was in their interests as well as those of Minneapolis. He was accompanied on that errand by the company's attorney, W. W. Paine. Together, they successfully argued that the company was worth more intact, with its skilled workforce and mills remaining productive, than it was idle and on the block.

To varying degrees, John, Charles, and Alfred had been neglectful of the company their fathers had built, or too trusting of Little and Amsden, the men their fathers had left behind in the front office. Perhaps they assumed that the aging W. D. Washburn, who had been elected chairman of Pillsbury-Washburn's American management committee when Alfred's father died, was as competent a businessman as their Pillsbury elders had been. Recent scholarship reveals how mistaken such an assumption would have been. Washburn also contributed to the cash crunch that came to a head in the summer of 1908.[57] The Pillsbury boys may have put themselves too far from the heart of the company to detect or do much about managerial misdeeds.

But when crisis arose, the three young Pillsburys rose to the challenge. With income flowing from timber holdings and the mining operations on the Mesabi Range, they did not need to revive the mills for their own sakes. But they cared enough for the company, its employees, and the business reputation attached to their name, that they were willing to invest their inheritances in the company's rescue and reorganization. They had built positive relationships with the bankers and businessmen of Minneapolis, to whom they were able to turn in genuine trust when trouble arose. And they were able to bring Albert Loring, the city's best milling brain, to their side, astutely recognizing that he "was the one man of all we had to have."[58]

Together with Loring, the Pillsbury boys hatched a plan not only to return Pillsbury milling to an even keel financially, but to bring it firmly within Minnesota hands once more. They would establish Pillsbury Flour Mills Co., based in Minneapolis and capitalized at $2,250,000—their own funds. That firm would lease the Pillsbury-Washburn mills, paying the British company rent plus a share of its profits. Negotiating a deal that would provide the Brits with enough restitution of their own losses to permit the company's survival, while addressing the often mixed imperatives of a divided British ownership board, required months of delicate transatlantic interchange. It required the skill of a diplomat.

John Pillsbury had once dreamed of entering the U.S. Foreign Service. In May 1910, after a fashion, he got his wish. At this critical juncture, it was John, not Alfred, whom the family sent to London to cut a deal that would discharge the receivers and set a new course for Pillsbury-Washburn and the new operating company. He was there for four months, as dissatisfied British board members delayed decisions repeatedly in hopes of extracting a more favorable deal. His absence from Minneapolis meant he was not on hand to pay his respects as the last of Minnesota's pioneering Pillsburys, Mahala Fisk Pillsbury, slipped away in June. Her death at age seventy-eight was not unexpected; she had been housebound for a number of years. It had to make John feel quite alone to be so far from home as his much-esteemed great-aunt was laid to rest. Her grand Victorian home would shortly be offered to her husband's beloved University of Minnesota for use as a president's home, for an annual lease price of $1.[59] It would serve as the president's official residence for the next fifty years.

Through it all, John maintained his characteristic grace and equanimity. He also demonstrated anew his ability to rally support from his friends. James J. Hill, the Minnesota railroad tycoon in whose home John had been an occasional post-party overnight guest a decade earlier, kept a London attorney on retainer. Hill directed the barrister to take John under his wing in London, providing assistance significant enough to be recounted to John's children decades later. John gradually won the confidence of the company's British owners. On Aug. 3, 1910, a resolution discharging the receivers was agreed to; eighteen months and fifty documents later, the final paperwork was signed.[60] Pillsbury Flour Mills Company was the new mill operator at the Falls of St. Anthony, with Albert C. Loring as its president, Alfred and Charles S. Pillsbury as vice presidents, and John S. Pillsbury as secretary-treasurer and Loring's "chief lieutenant."[61] The public embarrassment of criminal proceedings against Little and other company officers was avoided.

Matters of diplomatic ability aside, John may have been chosen to represent the family's interests in London because he was neither married nor burdened by parenthood. But John could no longer be said to be unattached. Someone very special was waiting when he came home.

Chapter Eight

Homemakers

Eleanor Jerusha Lawler was unlike any other young woman John Pillsbury had met—and that's saying something. For years, wherever he went, young women had schemed to make his acquaintance. His good looks, charm, and fortune made him a magnet for feminine attention, and he returned the interest. He had a reputation for shifting his focus from one debutante to another, year after year. John's list of female friends must have filled one of the black address books that socially active people kept in those years.

Juty Lawler's beauty alone would have turned John's head. She was tall, slender, fair-haired, and wide-eyed, and moved with regal bearing. But if looks were sufficient to win his heart, John would not have remained single as he approached his thirtieth birthday. He was in a position to be choosy about a lasting relationship, and he exercised that option well.

When John met Juty in 1907, he must have been surprised to find in a woman nine years his junior such evident intelligence and wide-ranging interests. Though only twenty, she possessed maturity beyond her years. Juty was socially confident yet sufficiently reserved, especially as compared with gregarious John, to project an appealing air of mystery. She did not laugh easily, but she appreciated John's vibrant humor. John learned that she had recently returned from an extended tour of Europe in the company of her widowed grandmother and namesake, Jerusha Wilcox Sturgis; that she had been educated at a French-language convent school in Italy; and that, like him, she loved to travel. He might have been intrigued by her somewhat cool initial response to his attention. He would learn later that when they met, she was considering becoming a nun.[1]

As he learned her story and that of her family, John had to be struck by its parallels to Pillsbury history. Both Juty and John sprang from families with deep New England roots. Both were steeped in New England values, prizing integrity, personal responsibility, loyalty to family, and service to community and country. They had both experienced a mix of family triumph and tragedy, and it had had shaped their personalities in ways they themselves were not, perhaps, fully aware.

Juty had fascinating family tales to tell. One English forefather, Thomas Dudley, came to North America in 1630, ten years before the first Pillsbury arrived; within four years he was governor of the Massachusetts Bay Colony. As such, he appointed a committee to establish a college in Cambridge; in 1650, he signed into law the charter for Harvard College. Juty's ancestors were American history-makers, as committed to public service as the Pillsburys. Many of them expressed that commitment through military service. One was an officer in the Continental Army who crossed the Delaware River and took part in the battles of Trenton and Long Island with Gen. George Washington; another was with Washington at Valley Forge. Her great-great-grandfather and his brother were part of a 1796 surveying party in what became Ohio. They founded a settlement at the mouth of the Cuyayoga River and named it after the party's leader, Moses Cleaveland. (The place's spelling would later be simplified.) A kinswoman was married to Ralph Waldo Emerson's cousin Daniel, who had officiated at her grandparents' wedding. Another relative was a congressman from Indiana and speaker of the U.S. House of Representatives in the 1840s.

Juty's grandfather, Samuel Davis Sturgis, graduated from West Point in 1846. His reconnaissance of the Mexican Army later that year was instrumental in the U.S. success in the Battle of Buena Vista during the Mexican-American War. He was captured before the battle, but the Mexicans released him unharmed eight days afterward. Sturgis was in Sacramento during the Gold Rush, led commands at frontier outposts in New Mexico, Kansas, and Dakota territories in the 1850s, and became chief of cavalry for the Army of the Republic during the Civil War.

Samuel's son Jack was killed in June 1876 with George Custer at the Battle of Little Big Horn, in what is now eastern Montana. Gen. Sturgis was then commander of the Fort Meade Cavalry Post in present-day Meade County, S.D. Two months after Jack died, the town of Sturgis, S.D., was founded and named for the fort's popular commander and his lost son. A statue there today honors Gen. Sturgis.

Juty—Eleanor Jerusha— would be named for her beautiful, brave grandmother, Jerusha Wilcox Sturgis, who endured frontier Army life, raised eight children, and led three of them on a daring midnight escape from Fort Smith, Arkansas, to St. Louis when a Confederate attack was imminent during the Civil War.

Juty's parents were fun-loving Ella Maria Sturgis and handsome John Dinan Lawler. Ella was a skilled markswoman and equestrian as well as a gifted actress, the belle of the military posts at which she was raised. John was the eldest son of a large and affluent Catholic family. They met in 1886 in Prairie du Chien, Wisconsin,

General Samuel Davis Sturgis.

where Lawler had been raised in a comfortable house that had been originally built for President Zachary Taylor. Ella was visiting a married sister who lived there. John and Ella Lawler were married later that year after a whirlwind romance and decamped to Mitchell, S.D. He owned considerable land in and around that town on the James River, and was a major investor in the town's bank. He would shortly become the bank's president and Dakota Territory's treasurer (South Dakota would not become a state until 1889.) His political involvement made him a likely contender for governor of the new state. The couple's daughter, Eleanor Jerusha, was born in Mitchell on Aug. 31, 1887, the first of four children.[2]

Juty Lawler was not a typical Dakota girl. Her mother disliked their dusty little prairie town, and felt ill at ease with other Mitchell wives, who spent their days in their kitchens and washhouses instead of their parlors. Ella sought to shield her daughter from the community's unrefined ways and, by her standards, inadequate schools. Grandmother Jerusha, a widow after 1889, took particular interest in her namesake and invited the little girl for long visits. They went first to Washington, D.C., where the Sturgises had moved when the general was appointed commander of the Soldier's Home, then to St. Paul, where son Sam Sturgis was a military officer assigned to Brig. Gen. Wesley Merritt, who then headed the Army's Department of Dakota.[3]

Ella Sturgis Lawler Pennington, at age 45.

Because of her grandmother's connections, little Juty was invited to the White House to play with President Benjamin Harrison's grandchildren. She attended a small private kindergarten in St. Paul and learned at her grandmother's side to read, spell, curtsey, play chess, and appreciate Tennyson. After returning home to Mitchell, where her family lived in the fanciest house in town, Juty's mother discouraged her from making friends with other local children and sought to supplement her public-school lessons. The lonely little girl's favorite playmate was her father. She was "compelled to dress in white dimity with a pink or blue sash, and wait quietly on the family porch" until her father came home for a game of croquet.

Life abruptly changed for Juty Lawler on Feb. 18, 1896. On a business trip to Sioux City, Iowa, John Lawler was stricken with a massive heart attack and died. A special train was arranged for the family to take from Mitchell to Sioux City to retrieve John's body and take it to its rest in his hometown, Prairie du Chien. Juty, age eight, would always remember that "the seats were hard and stiff and there was no place to lay one's head and try not to remember what had happened." The bond between fathers and eldest daughters is often close, and theirs had been no exception. A light had gone out in her life, one that in some ways was never rekindled.

Her granddaughter Sarah's assessment, years later, was that Juty had been traumatized by the loss of her father. "She was her father's favorite. Her sister was her mother's favorite. There's a psychological term, mirroring, having parents who mirror back to you, say 'That was a very good thing you did.' She lost the parent who would mirror back the good in her, and was left with an overly stressed mother. She told me once that when her father died, no one thought it was the kind of thing to talk about with children. She said, 'I learned right there and then, it does no good to tell people how you feel.'"

Grief made Juty Lawler self-reliant and self-contained. In future years she would be considered shy. It may have been more accurately said that she was emotionally wary.

After her husband's burial, Ella Lawler moved her four small children to St. Paul, into the orbit of her mother and two siblings, sister Mamie and brother Sam (whose Army career would soon dispatch him elsewhere.) Juty's education continued to shift with some frequency between public school and private lessons, as the fatherless family was increasingly forced to balance high cultural standards and ambition with modest means. Juty discovered that she preferred public school and the friends she made there. But when a friend of the family, the Rev. Thomas Tecumseh Sherman, son of Civil War Gen. William Tecumseh Sherman, recommended that Juty and her sister be educated at Sacred Heart Convent in Chicago and offered to watch out for them, the girls were shipped to boarding school. The next year, it was another Sacred Heart convent school—Maryville, in St. Louis. There, Juty blossomed academically, athletically, and socially. Several years at Maryville were followed by a year at Trinita dei Monte, yet another Sacred Heart school in Rome, Italy, which served as a finishing school experience. Juty shared part of that experience with her Grandmother Sturgis, who wintered in Rome during the year her favorite granddaughter was studying there. Following that year of study the two went on a sight-seeing tour of Europe, including Paris, and London, and a glamorous steamer trip home.

When Juty returned to Minnesota in 1907, home was no longer St. Paul, but Minneapolis. Ella Sturgis Lawler had married Edmund Pennington during Juty's year abroad. Pennington, Ella's senior by twelve years, was head of the Soo Line Railroad, which made it possible for the Lawler family's to put their financially pinched years behind them. Juty took to Pennington immediately, and described him many years later as "one of the finest men I have ever known, and a devoted stepfather."[4] They moved to 1004 Summit Avenue, a stately red-brick mansion on Tom Lowry's hill southwest of downtown. More than a hundred years later, it is still one of an elegant neighborhood's finest houses.

Had Juty Lawler come of age one generation later, she almost certainly would have arrived in Minneapolis intent on establishing a career, perhaps as a teacher, artist, or social worker. The capable young woman was tempted by that notion in 1907, even though a career of her own would have been a radical departure from the norm for a young woman of her social standing at the time. She admired the purpose-filled lives of the nuns who had taught her at various convent schools, and considered the pursuits of Minneapolis debutantes and young wives frivolous and dull. But the more she saw of John Pillsbury, and the more she learned about his ideas and interests, the more smitten she became.

As he struggled to save the milling company that bore the family's name in 1909 and 1910, John and Juty carried on an intermittent but persistent courtship. While he was in London or on the East Coast meeting with financiers, "we were always in close touch with each other," Juty would recall. They did not always see eye-to-eye. She described their personality differences as springing from her preference for the company of select individuals, while outgoing John liked people more generally. "We argued about many things—religion, children, and life generally—but we were in love, so eventually we came to an understanding."[5] They were married at the Pennington mansion on Dec. 5, 1911—almost ten years to the day after Charles and Nelle were married, and one day before John's thirty-third birthday. Roman Catholic Archbishop John Ireland of St. Paul officiated. The formality of the occasion can be gleaned from Philip W. Pillsbury's recollection, many years later, of attending as an eight-year-old, and being required to wear a white velvet suit adored with gold buckles.[6]

The two travel-lovers had a long, luscious two-month honeymoon trip to Italy, Spain, Paris, and London. One memorable episode took place aboard a small boat during a terrible storm off the coast of Naples. An Italian oarsman sought to extort a large sum of money from the young Americans. John refused, and the exchange ended in a flurry of fists that left the boatman sprawled in the bottom of the boat and the honeymooners leaping to safety on the pier.

John Pillsbury Snyder in the 1920s.

But that nautical adventure was nothing compared to the one experienced a few months later by John's second cousin, John Pillsbury Snyder. By 1912, the quiet, mechanically gifted grandson of Gov. John S. Pillsbury was twenty-four, a University of Minnesota graduate, and the proprietor of an automotive garage in downtown Minneapolis at 407 South Tenth Street. He was also a bridegroom. On January 22 of that year he had married Nelle Stevenson, daughter of wholesale clothier Thomas W. Stevenson, in the Stevenson home on fashionable Portland Avenue.[7] Following John and Juty's lead, they too set off for an extensive European honeymoon, spending more than two months abroad. Their return was booked on a brand new mega-ship that set sail from Southampton, England on April 10, 1912—the *Titanic*.

John and Nelle retired to their first-class stateroom at about 10:30 on the fateful night of April 14, and John quickly dozed off. Nelle was awake to feel the big ship shudder and hear a sound that, to her Minnesota ears, was akin to that of a canoe being pulled over a lakeshore's rocky bottom. She woke John. He threw on a bathrobe, stuck his head outside their stateroom door, and was advised by a steward that the ship had struck an iceberg. But, he was assured, all was well, and the ship would be pursuing its charted course. That satisfied Snyder for the moment. But as he prepared to return to bed, the couple heard a friend of the occupants of the neighboring stateroom bang on their door in alarm. Nelle "urged me to get up when I wanted to go back to bed," John wrote to his father on April 24. "If it hadn't been for Nelle I am sure that I never would be here now."[8] The newlyweds decided to dress—warmly, with extra sweaters—and proceed to the ship's deck. They expected to hear reassurance there, and to return shortly. John even locked the stateroom door, and left money and his jewelry case lying on a table.[9] Nelle had the presence of mind to grab her jewelry case and tuck it inside her clothing.[10]

The scene they found on deck was a calm one—a testament to the faith many passengers placed in the ocean liner's much bal-lyhooed "unsinkability." Deck hands were preparing lifeboats for use, John would recall a week later, but had trouble convincing passengers to climb aboard. "The drop from the deck to the sea in the little boat looked more dangerous than the *Titanic*," he told a *Minneapolis Tribune* reporter. "Everyone was talking about how the first lifeboat to be lowered from a ship in times of wrecks generally tips over." An officer appeared and pleaded with the crowd to cooperate, then began barking orders. Still, most of the slowly assembling passengers initially refused to climb into the small crafts. John and Nelle did not. Their Minnesota familiarity with small boats may have been what saved them. John figured his boating skills, acquired during boyhood summers on Lake Minnetonka, would be helpful to the young crew.

"We were almost the very first people placed in the lifeboat," John wrote to his father. "We hit between 11:40 and 11:50 at night." Their boat was the first to leave the doomed liner. As John and the other men aboard took their turns at the lifeboat's oars, and Nelle used her fashionably large hat to help bail out the little craft,[11] they watched with horror as tragedy unfolded before their eyes. The *Titanic* was not unsinkable, and the supply of lifeboats was about a third short of that needed to save the lives of all 3,547 passengers. That night, 1,517 would die. Among them was another prominent Minneapolitan, millionaire grain trader and business investor Walter D. Douglas, a member of the Cedar Rapids, Iowa, milling family whose mill became part of the Quaker Oats Co. in 1901.

It was said later, as the story of the Snyders' *Titanic* rescue was told and retold in Minnesota, that John was one of the few men allowed into a lifeboat because he and Nelle were on their honeymoon. That was the explanation gossips gave for John's survival while Douglas perished. Walter helped his wife, Mahala Dutton Douglas, and Mrs. Douglas's maid, Bertha Lavery, climb aboard a lifeboat. Douglas was reported to have said as they pleaded for him to stay with them, "I would not be a man or a gentleman if I left the *Titanic* while there was a woman or child on board."[12] Mrs. Douglas, an exuberant personality, consented to a newspaper interview as she changed trains in Chicago on April 20. She said her husband told her: "I must be a man."[13] The *Tribune* had already commented: "Mr. Snyder can well consider himself as one of the luckiest men in the world, as he was one of the few taken from the sinking ship. At least fifty husbands were separated from their wives, and in only one or two cases, among them being Mr. and Mrs. Snyder, were husband and wife saved together."[14]

John himself did not credit his honeymooner status for his survival in the days after the disaster. Instead, he explained, the "women and children first" protocol had not yet been invoked as the first boat was being filled and dropped to the sea. Several other men were on board his lifeboat, like him at the direction of the crew. When John and Nelle returned to Minneapolis on April 21, he was appalled by wild stories about their experience that had been published in the hometown newspaper. Among them was an account from a New York newspaper quoting Snyder saying that crew members aboard his lifeboat had shot three passengers who had become disruptive. No such shooting—and no such interview—occurred, he said emphatically. In fact, he considered the conduct of the young crew exemplary.

Though he did not say so to the newspaper, John Pillsbury Snyder was also troubled by the accusation, often uttered indirectly but still made clear to him, that his survival was evidence of unmanly conduct on his part that night. Family members attest that he was bothered by survivor's guilt for years afterward. According to his granddaughter, John spoke about that traumatic night in the North Atlantic only at considerable urging, and then revealed few details. Nelle Stevenson Snyder was more open with her grandchildren, acknowledging that she and John had been participants in a significant episode in maritime history and ought to share their story. She praised her husband's boat-handling skill and his calm demeanor that night, and assured her descendants that any embarrassment on his part was unwarranted. Psychologists today would say that such guilty feelings are commonplace among survivors of a fatal disaster, and often arise despite the absence of any misdeeds. But "survivor's syndrome" was neither named nor understood in the Minnesota to which John and Nelle returned.

Carrying that burden, John and Nelle built an elegant, double-staircased home at 2118 Blaisdell Avenue, in a block also occupied by another prominent young Minneapolis business family, G. Nelson and Grace Dayton. The five Dayton sons, who would grow up to build the Upper Midwest's most prominent retail business, became childhood playmates of the three Snyder children: John Pillsbury Jr., born July 10, 1913; Thomas Stevenson, born March 12, 1915; and Susan Pillsbury, born Feb. 25, 1918.

The boys' Snyder grandparents, Fred B. Snyder and his second wife, Lenora Dickson Snyder, lived a block away with their teenage daughter Mary. In keeping with what had become a Pillsbury pattern, John and Nelle Snyder also bought a large summer house on Lake Minnetonka, on what was then known as Lookout Point. The house had been built in 1905 for the president of First Minneapolis Trust Co., and designed by architect William Channing Whitney, who also designed the St. Paul mansion that would become the Minnesota Governor's Residence. The spacious dwelling considerably stretches the image conjured by the phrase "summer cottage."[15]

Nelle Pillsbury and her
daughters, from left,
Helen, Katharine,
and Mary.

John and Juty also faced a housing issue after their wedding. Highland Home, the imposing mansion on Stevens Avenue, had been home
to both John and his brother Charles for twenty-two years. Charles's
wife Nelle and their children had been sharing the house with John
for a decade, though their trips to Florida in the winter and long stays
at Lake Minnetonka in the summer kept the young family and the
bachelor uncle residentially separate for a good part of the year. But
Juty's arrival changed everything. The twins had resolved years earlier
that a coin toss would determine which of them would relocate when
both of them were husbands. Sometime in 1911 or 1912, a coin was
flipped. John won.[16] Juty would often say with a wry smile in later
years that she wasn't sure the opportunity to live in a rapidly aging
mini-castle that came complete with a German-speaking staff could
properly be described as "winning,"[17] but the place did hold special
charms for young children. The next generation of Pillsburys would
recall fondly the old mansion's tower (great for climbing and hiding),
the carriage turntable built into the floor of the carriage house (great
for twirling friends), the big lawn in back (great for touch football) and
the hill on which it stood (great for bicycle coasting and sledding.)[18]

Charles and Nelle Pillsbury's mansion, 100 E. Twenty-second St.

Charles and Nelle bought a lot nearby, at 100 East Twenty-second Street, and took their brood of grade-school children on an extended trip to Europe while architects Hewitt and Brown designed and supervised the building of a tastefully elegant house of mixed classical style. Juty could not suppress a tinge of envy as her brother-in-law and his family settled into the latest, nicest addition to a neighborhood that had become a Pillsbury compound. Alfred Pillsbury had moved into the Fair Oaks neighborhood in 1903 and built a Tudor revival house, designed by architect Ernest Kennedy, at 116 East Twenty-Second Street on the northwest corner of Stevens Avenue. Built of locally quarried limestone, it stood immediately east of Charles and Nelle's house, and across Stevens Avenue from another new house being built in 1912. Alfred's sole surviving sister, Sarah Belle (Sadie), her husband Edward Cheney Gale, and their twelve-year-old son, Richard Pillsbury Gale, was joining the cluster with an Italian palazzo-style mansion. The Gale house, which became the property of the Minneapolis chapter of the American Association of University Women in 1947, would be deemed the most handsome house still standing in the Fair Oaks neighborhood in the late twentieth century.[19]

Other grand houses nearby were also occupied by families associated with the success of the Minneapolis milling industry: the

Crosbys and Christians of Washburn-Crosby Co., the Morrisons and their in-laws the Van Derlips of the Minneapolis Mill Co.; and the Washburns themselves. Until William died and his wife Lizzie moved East in 1912, they lived in the palace that gave the neighborhood its name. But a pall hung over Fair Oaks and its Frederick Law Olmstead-designed grounds in William Washburn's last years, as creditors —possibly including Pillsbury-Washburn Company's British investors—came after the elderly former senator for unpaid debts. In 1910, it was announced that Fair Oaks would be donated to the city of Minneapolis upon William's death for possible use as a museum. The gift was likely part of an arrangement with the city to quietly conceal unpaid property tax bills.[20] The house was given to the Minneapolis Park and Recreation Board in 1914, used as a recreation center during World War I, and found to be too expensive for taxpayers to maintain. The largest house ever built in Minneapolis was razed in 1924. Today, only an unusual depression in the middle of Fair Oaks Park marks its location.

The 1910s and 1920s were relatively tranquil for the Pillsbury twins and their cousins, in business and also domestically. John Sargent Jr. was born to John and Juty on October 28, 1912, almost eleven months after his parents' wedding. Fourteen months later, on December 22, 1913, came Edmund Pennington, named after Juty's step-father. John and Juty had been on a trip to Russia the previous spring, with John Jr. in the care of his grandmother, when Juty learned of her second pregnancy. She suffered through cravings, then rejection, of caviar during her first trimester, while learning a great deal about the last days of czarist Russia and the motives behind the Bolshevik Revolution soon to follow. On the way home, she and John visited Paris and arranged for a black cocktail dress, a simple, elegant sheath, to be made for her by famous fashion designer Coco Chanel and shipped to Minnesota. (Juty was photographed in 1972 beautifully wearing the same dress at age eighty-five, at her son John Jr.'s sixtieth birthday party. See page 343.[21])

The couple's first daughter, Ella Sturgis, arrived on October 11, 1915. She was the only child in the family born in a hospital, "much against my wishes and tradition," Juty would write decades later. The reason for the shift to Northwestern Hospital, which had been founded as a maternity care center with the considerable support of Mahala Pillsbury, went unstated.[22] On April 4, 1917, came Charles Alfred, namesake of his famous grandfather. A second daughter, Jane Lawler, was born Feb. 13, 1920—the only child in the family not to be given a first name shared by a grandparent or great-grandparent. Just seventeen months later came the baby of the family, George Sturgis. Born on July 17, 1921,[23] George alone among the six children was born at the family's Lake Minnetonka home, as a spectacular midsummer thunderstorm crackled outside. The 1920 census, evidently taken in the weeks before Jane's birth, found two parents, four children under age seven, and six female servants, five of them born in Norway, Sweden, or Germany. The household also included a chauffeur who lived elsewhere.

The household and childrearing staff no doubt made it easier for John and Juty to maintain an active social life. Newspaper society columns attest to an abiding closeness between the Pillsbury brothers and cousins as they entertained together and shared social events.[24] John and Juty also hosted frequent business dinners, chaperoned dances for young people at the Pillsbury Settlement House, and attended activities at the Minneapolis Club, where John served as president in 1911.[25] In those years and for some decades thereafter, the Minneapolis Club was the gathering spot during "the season" for almost-weekly pre-concert or pre-theater dinners among the city's financial elite. John and Juty were regular attendees.

John, following in the footsteps of his uncle Fred, had served on the 1908 committee that oversaw the construction of the Tudor-style house at the corner of Second Avenue and Eighth Street that still serves as the club's headquarters. That design featured a "women's door" at the rear, under a porte-cochere that would be reviled as a symbol of sexism in more recent times. When it was added it was no such thing. John told *Minneapolis Star* society columnist Barbara Flanagan that putting a door at the rear of the clubhouse for female guests was Eleanor Jerusha Lawler's idea. The two were dating at the time, and when John showed her the plans for the new clubhouse, she advised him that the entrance on Second Avenue was inadequate for well-dressed women in a winter climate. Expensive ball gowns deserved the protection of a covered entrance, she thought. The notion that the "front door" was restricted to male use arose by custom, not by original intent.[26]

In July and August each year, the young family left the sultry city for breezy Lake Minnetonka, as was the custom of many Minneapolis families who could afford to do so in those days. At first, John and Juty used a small farmhouse that Charles and Mary Ann Pillsbury had acquired in the 1890s for the recreational pleasure of their then-teenaged sons. The family quickly outgrew the rustic three-bedroom structure, however, and they began a search for suitable property upon which to build a new lake house, large and elegant enough for formal entertaining. [27]

In February 1914, Washburn-Crosby stalwart William H. Dunwoody died; his wife Kate followed him in death a year later. They left behind a farm a few miles west of the lake and lakeside land on a narrow peninsula known in the early days of white settlement as Starvation Point, so named because a trapper had died of starvation there. Later, the peninsula took the name Orono Point, after the Maine birthplace of its owner, Minneapolis civic leader George Brackett. Nowadays it's known as Brackett's Point.[28] Juty and John were interested in the Dunwoody property, but they had come to no definite decision when, in the summer of 1915, a real estate agent approached John at the Minikahda Club golf course, near the northwest corner of Lake Calhoun. He informed John that another party was poised to purchase the Dunwoody farm, and if the Pillsburys wanted it, they needed to act immediately. Impulsively, John said he would buy it, and agreed to sign the requisite papers the next day.

When John returned to the Lake Minnetonka farmhouse that night and told Juty what he had done, a bad case of buyer's remorse set in. "I'm not a farmer. Why do I want a farm?" he lamented to his wife. He would not consider reneging on the verbal agreement he had made—Pillsburys were people of their word—but he couldn't sleep, so at 3 a.m. he and Juty boarded their Packard runabout and drove the dark country roads north of the big lake, discussing their options as they watched the early summer sunrise.

At one point Juty asked John whether he knew any of the trustees of the Dunwoody estate personally. Indeed, John had often played golf with Charlie Bovey, the son of a pioneering Minneapolis lumberman and a member of the Washburn-Crosby firm. Bovey lived close to the Pillsbury lake house during the summer months, and John telephoned him later that morning to discuss the situation. During the conversation that followed Bovey came up with the marvelous idea of summoning a number of their Lake Minnetonka neighbors of similar ages and interests to his office at 11 a.m., to hear "an exciting proposal."[29] The Dunwoody farm ought to be converted into a golf course, Bovey proposed. All that was needed was for a group of investors to buy it from John Pillsbury, whose verbal agreement the day before made him the property's putative owner, even though he had as yet neither signed a document nor paid a single dollar for it. The recruited investors agreed; the financing and incorporation of the group was arranged, and Woodhill Country Club was born. As Juty wrote seventy years later, "it has been a great blessing to Lake Minnetonka ever since."

The remaining Dunwoody property on Brackett's Point was still available and still desirable in John's eyes. It shared the narrow peninsula with the home sites of three other prominent families. The peninsula's tip, where George Brackett had lived, had passed into the hands of the E. L. Carpenter family, and would stay there for years to come. But north of the Dunwoody land stood property owned by Dr. Amos Abbott (Abbott-Northwestern Hospital bears his name today) and Pierce Howe, owner and operator of a large chain of grain elevators and lumber distributors. Both were friends and contemporaries of William Dunwoody, which meant that it was possible for the young couple to envision that those properties too would go on the market in a few years. The prospect of being able to acquire most of the peninsula before many years passed, thus gaining a measure of privacy at the socially busy lake, sold a hesitant Eleanor Lawler Pillsbury on the purchase. Brackett's Point, she told friends and family, was "south a ways" off the county road. The directional description morphed into a name that stuck.

Southways.

Construction of Southways, under the keen eye of New York architect Harrie T. Lindeberg, began in 1916. But it slowed and then stopped completely in 1917, as the war effort consumed the labor and materials of the domestic construction industry. The delay gave Juty and Lindeberg, two strong-willed people with definite but conflicting ideas, time to work out their differences—or at least most of them. Lindeberg appeared to let her win a fight over whether the large living room he wanted would be paneled in butternut, as he preferred, or plastered and painted a green color of Juty's choosing. She won that fight, and only much later learned that the paneling preferred by the architect had been installed beneath the plaster for a future decorator to find. Likewise, she did not know he had finished the third floor as a ballroom until 1920 when the family moved in.[30] It would become the scene of ping-pong matches, teen dances, pajama parties, and more raucous fun than Lindeberg may have envisioned.

Southways was considered a landmark on Lake Minnetonka even before the roof, which was made of stones from the Cotswolds in England, was completed, due to its situation on the lake, its size, and its many unique design touches. Prominent iron artisan Samuel Yellin of Pennsylvania made the wrought-iron door with a peacock design. Minnesota woodcarvers were commissioned to create banisters featuring carved owls that Pillsbury children would break time and again as they slid down the stairs. Juty called upon Elsie deWolfe of New York, whom she had met on a transatlantic steamer, to decorate the powder room. DeWolfe, a pioneer of interior design in America, shared Juty's love of French décor and desire for light, bright, flower-bedecked rooms. One thing Southways lacked until much later was a swimming pool. John Pillsbury held that no household on a lake, no matter how full of youngsters, required a swimming pool for water fun.[31]

The property came with both a greenhouse, which the Dunwoodys had used to grow orchids, and a gardener, whom the Pillsburys retained. During World War I, coal was in short supply, and using it to heat a greenhouse seemed almost unpatriotic. Juty "farmed out" the orchids to friends during winter months in the war years. But when the war was over and Southways was completed, its garden and greenhouse became points of particular interest to the lady of the house. Juty set aside a small room adjacent to the garden entrance for flower arranging, and when the Lake Minnetonka Garden Club was organized in 1926,[32] she was a founding member. She and the other founders were creating much more than a hobby club: they approached horticulture as a serious discipline. The club helped found the University of Minnesota Landscape Arboretum in rural Chaska, and set a high standard in anything they did—like Juty Pillsbury herself.

Juty was the unquestioned mistress of Southways, manager of its large staff, and dominant force in her children's lives, exhibiting administrative ability worthy of her military-general grandfather. Her children had nurses when they were babies and governesses when they were a bit older, all carefully screened and closely supervised by their mother. The Pillsbury children were encouraged to be physically active and creative, but they were also required to learn French, music, and social graces. They maintained a full schedule of lessons and activities which included swimming, bicycling, tennis, riding, hockey in the winter, and sailing in the summer. A friend chuckled seventy years later at the memory of the answer one Pillsbury boy gave when he was asked on a Saturday whether he could go sailing—their favorite summer activity—the next day. "We can't," Eddy Pillsbury was

John and Juty with their children, 1922. Baby George is on his mother's lap. Other children, from left, are Ella, John Jr., Chuck, Jane and Edmund.

said to reply with a long face. "We have polo on Sundays."[33]

One governess popular with the children was dismissed because Juty believed she was spoiling seven-year-old George. Between-meal snacking was not allowed, though the children learned that if they befriended the three cooks employed in the big industrial-sized kitchen at 2200 Stevens, extra cookies could be had.[34] As soon as the children were old enough to join their parents at the dining-room table for dinner—which always consisted of formally served soup, an entrée, and dessert—they were expected to exhibit proper manners. Mealtime disruptions were never tolerated. Dinnertime formality was so rigidly adhered to that George did not experience his first self-serve buffet dinner until he was in college. Family evenings together were quiet affairs, with Father working on his beloved stamp collection, Mother reading nearby, and children attentive to their homework. One family employee later recalled that when the impulse for a song struck, or one of the children's lessons included piano practice, it wasn't unusual for the family to gather around the piano to sing along. John and his brother Charlie, both mandolin players and singers in college, were always eager to take up a tune.[35]

When war broke out in Europe in the summer of 1914, the news had a personal dimension for the Pillsburys. Their cousins John and Nelle Snyder happened to be vacationing in Austria at the time. As the violence and international tension grew following the assassination of Archduke Franz Ferdinand by a Serbian nationalist, they decided to cut their trip short for safety's sake.[36]

Three years later, when the United States entered the war, John Snyder, aged twenty-nine, was one of two males in the extended Pillsbury family who were close to prime military age. Snyder's draft card, dated June 5, 1917,[37] included the fact that he was the sole support for a wife and two children, and the proprietor of a thriving business. He likely could have avoided Army service, had that been his desire. Instead, he was commissioned a lieutenant in the Fourth Minnesota infantry.[38] In December 1917, he was promoted to the rank of major and assigned chief draft aide for the state of Minnesota, to work in concert with Gov. J.A.A. Burnquist, a great supporter of the nation's war effort. That position makes it unlikely that his service took him away from Minnesota for any prolonged period. A May 1918 news account places him in Minneapolis, charged with overseeing the assembly of 629 drafted men in the city and sending them for training to Camp Lewis, Washington. Each of the city's wards—by then there were thirteen, as there are today—had a quota to fill.[39]

The other potential soldier was Richard Pillsbury Gale, like Snyder a grandson of Gov. John S. Pillsbury. Gale turned seventeen the year America entered the war. The doted-upon only child of a couple that had tried unsuccessfully to have more children, Richard wanted for nothing as a child. "Anything that could be bought, he had," his son said of Richard's upbringing.[40] But the one thing he needed was not yet available in 1917. When Richard was interviewed at an Army recruiting office, he told the officer about his occasional dizziness, overwhelming thirst and frequent fatigue. A physical examination revealed that Richard suffered from Type I diabetes. In 1917, diabetes was a death sentence. His parents were devastated. Their lives revolved around their son. Richard did not become a soldier. Instead, he was subjected to the standard treatment of the day for diabetes—a carefully restricted diet, fresh air, exercise—while he and his parents began a worldwide quest for more effective treatment and a cure. Their search would be rewarded in dramatic fashion five years later. In 1921 and 1922, a four-man research team at the University of Toronto discovered that diabetes is a shortage of the pancreatic hormone insulin, and that injections of extracts of pancreatic tissue would replace the missing hormone and control diabetes indefinitely. Among the first Americans to receive insulin injections in the summer of 1922 was Richard Pillsbury Gale. He traveled to Boston for weeks of what was still experimental treatment, and may have been the houseguest of his uncle Alfred's in-laws, the Fields. Insulin was the miracle the Gales had been praying for. Richard's health improved quickly; within two years he would be married to a beautiful, socially prominent St. Paul soap manufacturer's daughter, Radcliffe-educated Isabel Marion Rising, known to her friends as Pete.

World War I struck the rest of the Minnesota Pillsburys only a glancing blow. It temporarily curtailed their ability and desire to travel abroad but boosted their incomes. Pillsbury Flour Mills Co. and other Minneapolis millers had their best years in more than a decade, and demand soared for the ore extracted from Pillsbury-owned land on Minnesota's Mesabi Range. In the competent hands of Albert Loring, and with Alf, Charles, and John Pillsbury providing financial backing as needed, the company had been steadily regaining ground that had been lost during Pillsbury-Washburn Co.'s receivership. All three Pillsburys had official positions in the company. Of them, John was the most involved in operations, directing the sales department for a number of years, scouting for expansion opportunities, and functioning as the corporation's secretary-treasurer. [41] Together, John and the man he always respectfully called "Mr. Loring" oversaw the upgrading of the Pillsbury test kitchen and laboratory and the rebuilding of the A Mill, where dry rot and vibration had taken a serious toll on the 1881 wooden skeleton.

The high standards for flour quality set by Charles A. Pillsbury were reasserted. So were steady profits. Pillsbury Flour Mills Co. shareholders received at least a 7 percent dividend each year from 1911 forward. (The string would only be broken once, in 1924, through more than seventy-five years.)[42] When the federal government asserted wartime control over the nation's food production in 1917, Albert Loring was chosen head of the northwest district of the U.S. Food Administration Millers' Committee, which set profits and coordinated the production of nearly a third of the flour mills in the United States.[43] That relationship brought the Pillsburys into contact with future president Herbert Hoover, at the time the nation's chief food administrator. John's role included functioning as something of an ambassador for the company to the rest of the milling industry and to the local business community. He was an officer in the Millers National Federation and in the Minneapolis Chamber of Commerce, following in the footsteps of both his father and grandfather in the latter role.

John Pillsbury is personally credited with developing one line of business for Pillsbury Flour Mills Co.—semolina, or "macaroni wheat." Pasta had an auspicious start in the United States. It is believed to have first come to this country in crates in the tow of Ambassador Thomas Jefferson, returning from four years in France in 1789. Jefferson also brought home a pasta machine, which he proceeded to modify to improve its performance. By World War I, pasta was in big demand among Americans, especially the large Italian-American immigrant community. But much of it was imported from Italy. With the outbreak of war, the export of Italian pasta was interrupted and American manufacture of pasta soared. During the war the number of U.S. firms turning out dried and boxed macaroni, spaghetti, linguini, and the rest grew from 373 to 557.[44] But many of those producers complained about the quality of the product they were able to make with American-milled flour. Pillsbury heard the lament and determined to do something about it. He described how he proceeded on a radio broadcast in 1940:

> Durum wheat…was also called macaroni wheat. It was rust resistant, so (American) farmers planted it, but it was unsuitable for

bread flour. This wheat became a drug on the market, until some of the millers finally found that it was being exported in large quantities to southern France and Italy.

I became very much interested in this, myself, and after considerable investigation I found (the Europeans) were making excellent semolina, which is a very hard granular flour used in the making of macaroni, spaghetti, et cetera. Due to my personal acquaintance with an American macaroni manufacturer, I discovered that most of the good macaroni in this country was being imported from Italy and France, and that he had imported semolina, himself, which doubtless was made partly from our durum wheat, and was successful in making the very best quality of macaroni in this country.

Pillsbury went on to describe his efforts to see the machinery being used in European semolina mills first hand, and gather samples of the product at various stages in its manufacture. As a result of these investigations, within a year Pillsbury was producing semolina flour in Minneapolis equal in quality to the best imported products. [45] John Pillsbury, the milling executive who had wanted to be a diplomat, had again scored a coup in a foreign land to the benefit of his family's enterprise and his home state. The local pasta-maker to whom Pillsbury refers might well have been James T. Williams, who developed thin-walled, quick-cooking Creamettes macaroni in 1912 and put that brand name on the Minnesota Macaroni Co. when he bought it in 1916.[46]

Business took John to London many times after World War I, while Pillsbury Flour Mills Co. continued to lease the mills at the Falls of St. Anthony from British-owned Pillsbury-Washburn Co. But the principals on both sides of the Atlantic were dissatisfied with the arrangement. The Pillsbury-Washburn investors were beginning to despair at ever achieving the return they anticipated on their original investment, and began to think in terms of cutting their losses. Meanwhile, Loring and the three Pillsburys wanted to expand and geographically diversify their own company, without British entanglement. They used their own funds in 1921 to acquire a new mill still under construction in Atchison, Kansas, and a year later they announced that a large new side-by-side mill, modeled on the Minneapolis A, would be built in Buffalo, New York, to better serve Eastern and European markets. That move should have been a signal to observers of American milling trends: Minneapolis was losing its grip on Pillsbury's Best production. But what Minneapolis boosters at publications like the *Northwestern Miller* saw and hailed instead was the deal sealed on June 27 and announced on July 4, 1923: "Again Completely American." In a complicated transaction, Pillsbury-Washburn Co. ceased to exist, and its debts were erased. Pillsbury Flour Mills Co., the operating company, became the wholly owned subsidiary of the new Pillsbury Flour Mills, Inc. It was incorporated in Delaware, but for all practical purposes, it was a Minnesota company, thanks to John, Charlie, and Alf Pillsbury.

Juty Pillsbury, 1930.

In 1919, Juty and the couple's two elder sons, John Jr. and Eddy, accompanied John on his first long stay in London since the end of hostilities. The ocean-going adventure and prowl around historic London was great fun for the six- and seven-year-olds, and likely sealed in them the love for travel that John and Juty shared. But as the family grew to six children in the early 1920s, travel abroad became more difficult.

Charlie and Nelle had long passed Minnesota's coldest months in Palm Beach, Florida, far from wintry blasts. Early in their marriage, John and Juty also began annual treks to the Sunshine State. Their pattern in those years was to travel south after the New Year's holiday. Much of the family's household staff and any children who were not in school joined them. One staff member recalled that John would go south first, by train, accompanied by the butler, one maid, and one cook. They would set up housekeeping for the rest of the family, who would drive south with the family's chauffeur and one or more other maids or child care providers. "We changed trains in Jacksonville, Florida, and had to wait there awhile," cook Agnes Magney later recalled. 'Mr. Pillsbury was sitting on a luggage truck that was empty and he said to me, 'Come up and sit on this luggage truck too.' He was such a people's man. I climbed up and he told me so many interesting things about the South." The Pillsburys occupied rented quarters during their first several winters in Florida. In 1922, while John was in London for two months, Juty met with architect Marion Wyeth. Together they made plans for construction of La Chosa, a Spanish-style villa that would be the family's winter headquarters for decades to come.[47]

The family's commitment to annual Florida stays may have been what definitively answered the question, "Would this John S. Pillsbury seek elective office?" The answer was no. Despite the fact that his father, his grandfather, his great-uncle, several cousins, and two of his sons took the Minnesota political plunge, John never did. Neither did his twin brother Charles, whose health was never up to the exertions a campaign would require. It may be that for John, the question never truly arose—though he was a sufficient presence and financial contributor to the state and national Republican Party that at some point he was probably entreated to enter the arena as a candidate. He and Juty were friends of Coolidge administration Secretary of State Frank B. Kellogg, a Minnesotan; acquainted with President Coolidge and more so with his Iowa-born successor, Herbert Hoover; and huge patrons of the Minnesota GOP's boy-wonder governor elected in 1938, Harold Stassen. It may be that John's frequent absences from Minnesota for reasons of both business and pleasure made him rule out political responsibilities that would tie him down. It may also be that a wife, who confessed to preferring the company of "individuals" to groups of people, recoiled at the thought of assuming the highly visible role voters were coming to expect of a candidate's spouse.

Juty relished her political independence after the vote was granted to women in 1920—even though she had not been keen about the idea of women's suffrage as a young woman. Juty's mother was the local chapter president of an anti-suffrage association, and her cousin-in-law Gretchen Pillsbury was an active member.[48] Juty shared their conviction that if given the vote, too many women would only vote the way their husbands dictated rather than think for themselves. Ironically, Juty would never have allowed herself to be so influenced by anyone, spouse or otherwise. But, she told her son George in a revealing bit of self-analysis, she always assumed she was different from other women. Her political independence was such that in the 1928 presidential election she voted not for Republican Hoover but for Democrat Al Smith.[49]

But while John spurned suggestions that he should run for elective office, two others in the family surprised their acquaintances by entering the political arena. John Pillsbury Snyder, the auto garage proprietor who seemed much more interested in Italian cars, golf, and hunting than politics, agreed to run for the Minnesota House in 1926. His granddaughter believes he was persuaded to do so by his father, Fred B. Snyder, then well on his way to surpassing his father-in-law John S. Pillsbury as the longest serving regent in the history of the University of Minnesota.[50] Fred had enjoyed his one term in the House and one in the Senate at the turn of the twentieth century, and believed his son would similarly gain from the experience. Fred likely was also interested in securing another dependable vote when university funding bills arrived on the House floor. Helen Snyder Waldron says her great-grandfather's nudge did not kindle enduring enthusiasm for public service in his son. John Pillsbury Snyder didn't get a kick out of politics, and though he was elected, he served just one term.

A political announcement in October 1925 may have been a bigger shock to some. For the first time in thirty-nine years, the name Pillsbury would be on the roster of Minneapolis city officials. Alf Pillsbury had accepted appointment to a vacancy on the Minneapolis Park and Recreation Board.

Alfred Pillsbury's house on Lake Minnetonka, built by his father.

Chapter Nine

Late Bloomer

In one sense, Alfred Pillsbury and the Minneapolis Park and Recreation Board of the 1920s appear made for each other. Though he was destined for corporate leadership, trained as a lawyer, and much occupied in the management of his family's investments, business was not Alfred's passion. Recreational sports made Alf Pillsbury light up. The University of Minnesota football star, yachtsman, auto racer, and eager golfer was a small, wiry man with stamina that belied his size. He loved physical activity and the thrill of competition, particularly if it took place outdoors. And by the 1920s, the Park Board's work of putting the city's lakes and parkways into public hands was winding down while pressure for more organized youth activities was increasing. It's understandable that Alf would gravitate to an organization that was struggling to provide more opportunities for outdoor recreation.[1]

It might also be said that the Park Board gravitated to him. When his imposing house went up on the corner of Stevens Avenue and Twenty-second Street in 1903, its neighbors were the grand homes of other milling families. By 1925, two large plots in Alf's neighborhood were owned by the Park Board—Fair Oaks Park, where the Washburn mansion had stood, and the campus of the Minneapolis Institute of Arts, formerly the Morrison estate, Villa Rosa. The city's Society of Fine Arts owned the museum. But in a unique and creative arrangement, the land it sits upon was and is still today park property. The institute's most stable funding source is a property tax levy, first collected only in Minneapolis, later in all of Hennepin County. The tax was authorized by the Legislature, collected by the Park Board

Alfred Pillsbury in the 1910s.

and passed directly to the Minneapolis Institute of Arts. Alf had been present at the creation of the Institute of Arts in 1911. He served as a member of the board that chose McKim, Mead and White of New York, the architects who had just completed a major addition on the Metropolitan Museum of Art in New York, to design an elegant home for fine art in Minneapolis. At the museum's grand opening in 1915, some of the art on display was on loan from Alfred Pillsbury. By the mid-1920s, he was the Art Institute's most committed and engaged patron.[2]

In saying yes to the Park Board when the death of commissioner Jacob Stoft created a vacancy that the board could fill on its own authority, Alf was also doing something he had done often in his adult life: He was following in his father's footsteps. As a former governor, John S. Pillsbury had been among the first members of the city's Park Board, created by action of the Minnesota Legislature (or, more accurately, by a handful of shrewd Minneapolis legislators) in 1883. Alfred had taken his father's place on the boards of the First National Bank and the Farmers & Mechanics Savings Bank, and his cousin Charles's place on the board of Tom Lowry's streetcar com-

Gretchen Pillsbury, circa 1920.

pany, Twin City Rapid Transit.[3] In business matters, be it flour, timber, mining, or banking, Alfred's leadership provided a reassuring element of continuity in the minds of his kin and community.

Still, Alf's willingness to assume a *governmental* office, even by appointment, came as a surprise to many of his contemporaries. He "contrived to be undramatic," one observer wrote of him years later.[4] Alf seemed to dislike the limelight as much as he loved sporting competition. In 1925, when he assumed to Park Board post, Alf was fifty-six years old, and had hitherto exhibited no interest in public office or in political matters generally. He and his intellectually gifted wife, Gretchen, had no children. Readers of the *Minneapolis Tribune* society column were accustomed to seeing the couple's names in connection with dinner parties at their mansion in the city, bridge luncheons at Ferndale, and Gopher football boosters' excursions. The couple made frequent trips to Europe and to Boston (where Gretchen's family, the Fields, remained headquartered), often in the company of Gretchen's relatives. Contemporaries described him variously as "a man of simple tastes and no pretensions"[5]; and as a man who lived "quietly and with no demand on his part for acclaim."[6]

But as years passed, increasing evidence appeared in the local press that Alfred Fisk Pillsbury indeed possessed some of his family's public spirit. He and Gretchen were consistent backers of the Home for Children and Aged Women, which Alfred's mother Mahala had helped found and led as president for many years.[7] Gretchen was an officer in the group. She was also active in the Minnesota Society for the Prevention of Blindness, serving as its president.[8]

The Alfred Pillsburys were often mentioned in connection with leadership of the Church of the Redeemer,[9] then located downtown on Eighth Street on a corner now occupied by St. Olaf Catholic Church. That Universalist congregation, which had nine hundred members at its peak, claimed in its flock many of the city's oldest and most prominent families, including such names as Morrison, Eastman, Washburn, King, Chowen, and Crosby.[10] Alfred had been raised at First Congregational Church, on the city's east side. Gretchen likely drew him into the Universalist community. She was active in Redeemer's congregational life from the early days of her marriage; by 1906, she co-chaired the committee that headed the Women's Association Publishing Fund.[11] Alfred may also have been attracted by the charismatic personality and erudite preaching of Marion Daniel Shutter, the church's pastor for forty-eight years and the author of a respected history of the city published in 1923. Shutter was among the first clergymen in the city to proclaim from the pulpit that faith and evolution could coexist, and that spirituality should not be limited by dogma.[12] The message resonated with a Pillsbury whose quiet nature and sporting interests masked intellectual depth. "He is a devout student and advisor in many civic and philanthropic interests," a profile written in 1932 reported, "and he is unusually well-read and an interesting and adept conversationalist on most any subject."[13]

In 1913, Alf was elected vice president of First Universalist's board of trustees.[14] His neighbor at 2105 First Avenue South, Caroline Crosby, the daughter of Washburn milling partner John Crosby, was by then head of Unity House, the parish's busy settlement house serving the city's poor. Gretchen took a seat on Unity House's governing board.[15] The settlement house at Seventeenth Avenue North and Third Street had a popular playground program for small children, at a time when most city parks lacked such amenities.[16] Of that, Pillsbury was in a position to take note.

An association at First Universalist Church may have made Alf favorably disposed to say yes to the Park Board when its members approached him about filling the vacant seat. Among the active members of the congregation, until his death in 1922 at age eighty-eight, was Charles M. Loring.[17] Hailed as the "father of the parks" by his contemporaries (that epitaph is carved into his tombstone at Lakewood Cemetery), Loring was also the father of the man at the helm of Pillsbury Flour Mills Co., Albert Loring. Charles had been the city's first Park Board president and its tireless booster. His donations to the parks included land, a warming house at the park that bears his name, an artificial cascade at Glenwood (later Wirth) Park, and the trees and markers to honor the city's World War I war dead, planted along what became known as Victory Memorial Drive.[18] Alf undoubtedly respected the work Loring had done to give Minneapolis a park system that by the mid-1920s was winning national recognition. Alf may have been gratified to be following in Charles Loring's footsteps on the board.

The Park Board appointment that Alfred accepted in 1925 ran until June 1929, at which point he ran unopposed for another four-year term.[19] It was the perfect way for a shy guy to ease his way into long service in elective office.

With a two-year interruption from mid-1935 to mid-1937, Alf served for nineteen years on the Park and Recreation Board, and was its president for three years from 1931 through 1934. The Republican Pillsbury finally experienced the harsh side of politics on June 10, 1935, when he lost his bid for a fourth term in an election that produced a Farmer-Labor Party rout at City Hall. At the time, that left-leaning, prairie populist party, unique to Minnesota, was in its heyday, and its champion, Floyd B. Olson, was governor. A new Farmer-Labor mayor was elected on the day Alf was unseated, and four incumbent Republican City Council members also got the boot. Alf lost to Farmer-Laborite Edwin Hendricks by a vote of 5,531 to 3,969. His late Uncle George and cousin Charles, staunch Republicans and founders of the city's patrol limit policy, would have been appalled by the voters' decision that same day to enlarge the district where liquor sales were allowed. Only two years after the end of Prohibition, the voters in a referendum granted liquor licenses to thirty-six bars and one new liquor store.[20]

But Alf's return to private life was short-lived. In the 1937 city election, Hendricks sought and won a seat on the City Council, creating another mid-term vacancy to be filled by Park Board appointment. They invited Alf back.[21] He would win two more elections, in 1941 and 1945, before leaving the board of his own volition (and at the advice of his physician) in 1946.

If Alfred Pillsbury was indeed a voice for expansion of recreational facilities in city parks during his long tenure on the Park Board, it must be acknowledged that his efforts met with little success. In 1944, national consultant Liebert Weir surveyed the city's parks with a critical eye to their capacity to meet the recreational needs of a population approaching a half-million people, and found them wanting as measured against other cities of similar size. This was despite—or perhaps because of—the unusually large size of Minneapolis's park system. In the quarter-century leading up to 1930, the system had tripled in size to more than 5,000 acres. Under the domineering leadership of Theodore Wirth, park superintendent from 1906 until 1939 (and de facto superintendent for much of the decade that followed) resources were consumed dredging lakes, paving and plowing roads, and purchasing property not yet included in the Grand Rounds scenic byway originally proposed by Horace W. S. Cleveland in the 1880s. Wirth had been hired to fulfill a vision of beautiful parks and parkways surrounding the city's signature lakes—a vision dating back to the nineteenth-century. He held true to that assignment, and as a result (at least according to an analysis published by the city's Foundation for Parks in 2008) budgets for recreational equipment were often given short shrift. Wirth himself lamented as much. Indeed, he had proposed the first purchase of playground equipment when he was new to the city in 1906. But his proposed budgets never included a surge in resources for recreation or a comprehensive plan to acquire them. Instead, Wirth often implied that the responsibility to provide places and equipment for play and games resided more broadly with other municipal institutions—churches, schools, clubs—rather than with the Park Board. Wirth and Pillsbury were associated for the entire time that the latter sat on the Park Board, and were sufficiently close that when, in the mid-1940s, Wirth wrote his memoir, Alfred financed its publication. Wirth's ideas about parks undoubtedly swayed Pillsbury's.

When Alf was Park Board president in 1933, he was clearly of a mind to urge more spending on recreation. He said in an annual report that he considered its provision "just as vital as any function of government, not excluding that of the apprehension and conviction of criminals and the education of our youth."[22] But by then the Great Depression was in full swing, with Park Board revenues dropping by a whopping 62 percent between 1931 and 1933. No other part of city government took a hit as hard. In 1934, a special levy for playgrounds was eliminated as tax delinquencies mounted throughout the city. The entire playground instructional staff was laid off that year. Maintenance deteriorated to such a degree that 64 percent of lights in city parks were out of service.[23] Federal Works Progress Administration money came to the rescue in 1935, funding 243 recreation workers—more than the city had ever employed before. But the federal money was not a permanent solution to the city's recreational needs. Scarce resources for city parks would be a persistent problem for the remainder of Alf's tenure on the board.

The Depression also took a toll on what had been the city's grandest neighborhood, by altering the semiannual migratory pattern of many of the city's well-to-do residents. The Pillsburys and many of their neighbors had long been in the habit of abandoning their palatial in-town houses each June to take up residence for two to three months at sometimes equally elegant, and far breezier, houses on Lake Minnetonka. Rail transportation in the 1890s had made it possible for breadwinners to commute to the city while their spouses and children spent entire summers lakeside. The paving of Highway 12 between Minneapolis and Wayzata during the 1920s made it easier still. But during the lean 1930s, maintaining two houses was no longer affordable for some, and no longer desirable for others. John and Juty Pillsbury—or perhaps more accurately, their children—were in the latter category. In 1936, after several years of spending their children's school winter breaks at their beloved Southways, they closed Highland Home for good and joined a growing crowd of affluent families who lived at the lake year-round. The house that Charles and Mary Ann proudly purchased in 1890 would meet with a wrecking ball in 1937. Today the city's First Christian Church occupies the site.

"They did it at the begging of my brothers," Ella Pillsbury Crosby later attested.[24] "They wanted to be (at the lake) in the winter for ice boating and hockey. We girls [Ella and her younger sister Jane] felt kind of trapped, because we didn't drive yet. I loved living in the city, where we had sidewalks, a corner drugstore, and neighbors." She cherishes girlhood memories of walking across the street to the Art Institute on Sunday afternoons, hand in hand with her father, to examine the latest additions to the museum's growing collection. But by the mid-1930s, the Pillsbury children were all away at boarding schools—the boys at Yale or St. Paul's School in Concord, New Hampshire; the girls at Foxcroft Academy in Middleburg, Virginia, then Vassar College for Ella and Finch College for Jane. Pleasing them when they were home from school was important to John and Juty. So was their own freedom to travel, with fewer worries about residential upkeep back home.

It's possible that the move to the lake would have happened earlier, were it not for John Pillsbury's reluctance to put more distance between himself and his twin brother. Charlie and Nelle were often absent from the city. Yet they maintained their townhouse at 100 East Twenty-second Street, next door to Alfred and Gretchen, throughout Charlie's life. The twins had very different interests and personalities. Charlie was a bridge player and raconteur who seemed happiest in the company of women; John preferred golf, football, and the company of men. Both were involved in governing the Minneapolis Symphony Orchestra, but sitting through long concerts was more Charlie's than John's idea of fun. While both loved to travel, they did not vacation together—perhaps because John's trips were of shorter duration, and often involved Pillsbury Co. business, while Charlie and Nelle afforded themselves long, leisurely stays away from home.[25] Nelle and

The Charles S. Pillsbury family: parents are seated; chidren from left are Mary, Philip, Katharine and Helen.

Juty Pillsbury, almost ten years apart in age, were friendly but not close. Charles and Nelle bought a country estate called Cismont in her beloved Charlottesville, Virginia, in November 1929—at a time when few other Americans were displaying such financial muscle. The Virginia residence put more distance between the twin Pillsburys and their families.

But the brothers were genuinely fond of one another, John's daughter recalls, and relished each other's company. They had a bond that the two families of cousins did not share. An age gap and the distances imposed by governesses, lessons, boarding schools, and the formality of their respective households kept Charles's four children and John's brood of six from becoming close companions. Philip, the first of the Minnesota Pillsburys born in the twentieth century, was educated at exclusive all-boys Blake School through eighth grade. He likely started there when William McKendree Blake's boys' prep school, founded in 1907 when Phil was four years old, was still in a downtown Victorian house. It moved not far from the Pillsburys' Fair Oaks neighborhood, to 1803 Hennepin Avenue, in 1911. It then split, with junior high and high school taking up residence on an expansive campus in suburban Hopkins, while "Little Blake" for younger grades met at Twenty-third Street and Colfax Avenue. When Phil reached seventh grade, he had a long commute each day, likely assisted by the family's chauffeur.

Blake would eventually be considered among Minnesota's finest high schools, more than adequate to the academic needs of students heading for Ivy League colleges. But it may not have had that reputation in 1916, when Charlie and Nelle were deciding on the educational path their only son would take. Charlie was a proud graduate of Central High School, the Minneapolis public school that was walking distance from the Fair Oaks neighborhood. But Nelle was a product of Virginia aristocracy and Eastern boarding schools. It may have been her influence that landed young Phil at Hotchkiss School in Lakeville, Connecticut, in 1916. It was a feeder school for Yale, and a place where Phil could hone both his academic and athletic abilities. A strong, stocky young man—perfectly built to don a Santa suit and entertain (and scare) his younger cousins each Christmas—Phil loved music and sports, and excelled at football. Nevertheless, he went to Hotchkiss reluctantly, and battled homesickness at boarding school. "I remember hiding a bath towel in my suitcase just to have something with me from home. That first year at Hotchkiss, I never washed it," he told a reporter nearly sixty years later.[26]

Yale took notice of Phil's athletic ability. He enrolled in 1920—the first Minnesota Pillsbury to do so—and was the standard-setter for the family's next two generations. He took a guard's position on the football team under coach T.A.D. Jones, and was part of the 1923 team, often considered the best in Yale history, that went undefeated.[27] Phil was an all-American guard in water polo, no doubt the legacy of a childhood spent at Lake Minnetonka, and also excelled at racquet sports. In later years he became a national champion in squash. But Phil was more than a jock. He played the violin, sang in the glee club, and was one of the seven Whiffenpoofs, the Yale *a capella* vocal group founded in 1909. (Roaring '20s vocal and movie star Rudy Vallee was two years his junior in the group.) Though not an honor student, Phil's grades were described as "creditable."[28] His major: pre-med.

Phil's three sisters followed him to prep school and college in the East, enrolling one after the other at Smith College in Northampton, Massachusetts. Eventually all three of them settled in the East, unlike

Phil the Yale athlete.

brother Phil, who stayed tethered to Minnesota. As a college student, he spent summers in Minneapolis, doing odd jobs in various Pillsbury mills.[29] After graduation in 1924, he paid his respects at headquarters in the Metropolitan Building, then reported for duty to the supervisor at the A Mill. Teach me the trade, he said. Like his grandfather before him, Phil Pillsbury wanted to know all there was to know about an industry he aimed to lead one day.

For the next four years, Phil learned the skill and the art of milling grain into flour, from the receipt of grain to the shipment of milled products. He took a turn at nearly every job in the A Mill,[30] befriended his coworkers, and won their respect. Tales were told years later of his arrival for the night shift wearing black tie and tails, having been at a symphony concert beforehand. He'd endure good-natured ribbing, and likely return it in kind, as he changed into his dungarees before taking his place in the mill. In later years, he would proudly show off his scarred hands—the mark of a miller. He lost the tips of three fingers in Pillsbury mills. "The reason you stick your hand in there in the first place is that you learn to tell by the feel of the flour whether the machine is working properly," he would explain.[31]

At any given time, Phil's parents might have been at Lake Minnetonka or in Florida, Virginia, or Europe, depending on the season, but while he was learning the milling trade, young Phil went home each night to his parents' house at 100 East Twenty-second Street. His younger cousins and Uncle John offered him occasional diversion, but the family member to whom he drew closest during his bachelor years in Minneapolis was childless Alfred, his grandfather's cousin, whose house stood immediately to the east. The older man had much to teach about the family and their businesses, and the younger man was eager to learn. Alfred loved football, and Phil had played on a celebrated Yale team. Both of them appreciated good music, and regularly attended Minneapolis Symphony Orchestra concerts. Phil was an avid reader and ready conversationalist; later in life he would become a noted book collector.[32] When Phil's parents were away, the young miller was a frequent dinner guest at Alf and Gretchen's house. Alfred, who had quietly given $50,000 to help pay for Memorial Stadium at the University of Minnesota in 1924, had claim to one of only four seating boxes added in 1928 to the stadium already nicknamed "the Brickhouse."[33] (The other three were reserved for the governor, the president of the university, and the Board of Regents.) Phil was a frequent guest in Cousin Alfred's box at home games. (John's sons and their friends also occasionally enjoyed the privilege.) Alfred took an interest in the young man's personal investment decisions. Phil had purchased a great deal of Pillsbury stock on margin. When its value declined after the stock market crashed in October 1929, he needed help in meeting his margin calls. Alfred helped cover Phil's commitments. The older Pillsbury's investments were more diversified and thus better cushioned from the Wall Street collapse. Family lore has it that Alfred saved Phil from bankruptcy and embarrassment.[34] Phil had become a director of Pillsbury Flour Mills, Inc. in 1928 at age twenty-five, making him the youngest director in company history. A personal bankruptcy two years later would not have looked at all good.

In 1928 and 1929, Phil's milling education took him for extended work stints in Buffalo, N.Y. and Atchison, Kansas, where the company's operations had expanded in the 1920s. In 1930, he transferred to the sales department, and in 1932, to an assignment in Chicago that would last for three years. When he moved back to Minneapolis in 1935, it was with a bride. On July 5, 1934, he married Eleanor Bellows of Minneapolis, daughter of Henry A. Bellows, then manager of a ten-year-old radio station whose call letters—WCCO—were the initials of its founding owner and sponsor, Washburn-Crosby Co. Eleanor was ten years Phil's junior, and despite leaving Smith College after only two years, a person of quiet depth and ability.

With Phil moving on and Alfred passing his sixty-fifth birthday, society gossips likely speculated about whether Alf and Gretchen would remain at 116 East Twenty-second Street, or join the exodus to year-round living at their house at Lake Minnetonka. Alf's Park Board defeat in 1935 afforded him the opportunity for a move to the lake, should he have been so tempted. But by then a powerful tie bound him to the Fair Oaks neighborhood. Alf had long had a seat on the board of directors of the Society of Fine Arts, and had relished watching its Institute of Arts grow a short distance from his home. What many Minneapolitans did not yet know is that Alfred and Gretchen had become world-class art collectors. They had turned the

Eleanor Bellows, 1931.

lower level of their home into a sizeable gallery, under considerable security. Their stunning array of Oriental jades, bronzes, porcelains, and terra-cotta figurines was amassed with the intention of eventually donating it to Alf's neighborhood museum.

If sports had been Alfred Fisk Pillsbury's passion in the first half of his life, art and art collecting lit up his later years. Initially, he likely accepted a seat on the Society of Fine Arts board of directors not because of great passion for art, but—as in so many of his activities—because his father had served there before him. Gov. John S.

Alfred admiring
a Chinese bronze
piece from his
collection.

Pillsbury enjoyed having beautiful paintings and objects in the house
that would eventually become home to University of Minnesota presidents. But the Minnesota pioneer acknowledged that he bought fine
art for aesthetic pleasure, not to establish a systematic collection.[35]

Alfred and Gretchen were similarly casual buyers of art until they
took a prolonged trip to Japan in the late summer of 1919.[36] Less than
a year had passed since an armistice brought World War I to an end,
and the market for luxuries such as fine art was still in retreat. The
Pillsburys were in the Oriental art market's returning vanguard, and
in a position to take advantage of still-depressed prices and abundant
offerings. On the trip to Japan, Alfred would relate years later, he
was "captivated by the strange beauty of things he saw there." The
objects that made the biggest impression had been carved in jade in
China, centuries earlier. "To the average eye, these make no quick
appeal," an Art Institute Bulletin said of them, decades after Alf and
Gretchen brought them to Minneapolis. "The lovely pale ivory of
a chickenbone-jade dagger; the rare mottled blue of a scepter; the

watery, blue-flecked green of a symbol of rank, or the matte white of a graceful belt hook, are outside the experience of many Western-ers in the field of jade. But they ripen with acquaintance, bringing new and unexpected pleasure."[37] It would not go unnoticed that the subtlety of the Pillsbury jades had a parallel in the quiet personality of their collector.[38] The first arrival in what would become a large migration of ancient Asian art to Minnesota came home with Alfred and Gretchen in late 1919.

Gretchen was undoubtedly Alfred's most important partner and advisor as he schooled himself to become far more than a buyer of pretty souvenirs. The daughter and the sister of chief justices of the Massachusetts Supreme Court, Gretchen was a stylish, sophisticated woman and devoted wife, capable of opening her husband's eyes to the world. She was an accomplished speaker of French, and her knowledge of contemporary American, British, and French drama was such that she lectured widely on the theater not only in the Twin Cities but also in other sections of the United States.[39] In an era of greater opportunity for women, she almost certainly would have had an academic career, or possibly one on stage. Younger relatives remember that a visit to Alf and Gretchen's house was an impressive occasion, always preceded by the stern admonition "Don't touch!" Their household art displays were not childproof.

Beginning in 1921, Alf's growing addiction to art collecting was abetted by another wise counselor. Russell A. Plimpton came to the Institute of Arts as its director when he was only thirty years old. He would hold that post for the next thirty-five years. With deft diplomacy, he guided a number of affluent Minnesota art lovers to shape their personal collections in ways that would eventually benefit the Institute as well. Three Minnesotans with milling backgrounds were his particular students—Augustus Searle, James Ford Bell, and Alfred Pillsbury.[40] Plimpton was willing to be not only their adviser, but also their purchasing agent, negotiating with art dealers and bro-kers for the best prices and rarest finds.

Plimpton's efforts to eventually amass a permanent collection for the young museum via the personal purchases of patrons demanded persuasive skill and a great deal of patience. But he discovered he need not simply wait for the Grim Reaper to deliver art to the museum's door. The Minneapolis Society of Fine Art had a long tradition of calling on the city's art owners to lend pieces of interest for public displays of six months or longer. Gov. John Pillsbury had loaned some of his paintings for that purpose while the Society's galleries were still confined to a portion of the Minneapolis Public Library. Alfred lived close enough to the Institute of Art that he and/or his butler or chauffeur could simply tote "loaners" down the street, past the marble pillars and into the museum's galleries for display.

By the mid-1930s, Alfred Pillsbury's name was well known within the rarified world of ancient Asian art collecting. A 1932 Pillsbury company in-house publication took note of the extent of their corporate treasurer's impressive collection. It said that its jade objects alone exceeded 450 in number, and dated from 2,000 B.C. to 200 A.D. His Chinese porcelains included especially rare monochromes, and examples of the Kang-Hsi and Ch'ien Lung dynasties.[41] He was exposing Pillsbury employees to bits of world history and culture that they might not otherwise have known.

Alf shipped several pieces on loan to an exhibit in London in 1935, the year in which he became president of the Society of Fine Arts. In 1937, he sent twenty bronze objects—four Shang, sixteen Chou—down the street for Minneapolis museum visitors to see. The Japanese invasion of China in July of that year generated new interest in relics that demonstrated the durability of the Chinese culture. The December 1937 *Bulletin* of the Minneapolis Institute of Arts featured on its cover a Chinese bronze ritual vessel of the Yi type, decorated with designs characteristic of the Shang period, circa 1,400 B.C. The ancient object was "lent by Alfred F. Pillsbury," the *Bulletin* explained, crediting him for providing "invaluable material for the study of one of the oldest Chinese arts."[42] The original understanding was that the objects would be back at 116 East Twenty-second Street in a year or less. But a 1939 *Bulletin* announced that they were still on display, and that Alf had sent more pieces to join them. The first group contained vessels and representations of birds and animals; the new loan included ceremonial swords, dagger hilts, and chariot fittings. Two years later, the *Bulletin* referred to the lot of bronzes as "the Alfred F. Pillsbury Collection," a permanent part of the Institute. "One only has to look at them to know, with absolute certainty, that China will survive," the April 5, 1941 *Bulletin* assured.

A 1948 issue of the Institute's *Bulletin* was devoted entirely to the Pillsbury collection. It said in part:

> . . .*no one is more modest in the role of collector than Mr. Pillsbury. In assembling the archaic jades, the Wei and T'ang tomb figurines and T'ang potteries, the monochrome porcelains, the Persian potteries, the Khmer Buddhist sculpture, and finally the great Chinese ritual bronzes, he has given himself up to a pleasure which is in no sense purely selfish, since a great part of his enjoyment has come from sharing the fruits of his collection with others. His generous long-term loans to the Art Institute have made these beautiful—and, in this region, rarely encountered—objects available to all who care to look at them.*
>
> *In a way, also, they make Mr. Pillsbury the friend of everyone who knows his treasures because they reflect to an unusual degree the personality of the man who assembled them. It is no accident that they are of uniformly high quality; that they are subtle and understated; that they reveal a profound feeling for form and color; and that they are spiced by a sly humor which is the more effective for its infrequent intrusion. In assembling his own collections Mr. Pillsbury has given free rein to his personal tastes; a liberty he never permitted himself as President of the Society of Fine Arts. In doing so he has shown himself to be possessed of the qualities he admires so much in the works he has collected; qualities which, strangely enough, are to be found almost exclusively in the arts of the East: economy of expression, an intense awareness of form, and a something beneath the surface which lures the beholder to special, happy discoveries.*[43]

In the final decade of their lives, Gretchen and Alf "almost ran the Art Institute as if it were an extra room in their house," a cousin would recall years later.[44] He was an almost daily presence at the museum, poking his head into administrative offices, inquiring about acquisitions, participating in donor solicitations, and generally making himself useful. He was not above picking up a scrap of litter, answering a lost visitor's question, or—while he was in his 70s—helping to unload a shipment of precious art. *Minneapolis Star* journalist Barbara Flanagan recalls visiting the Institute in 1948 to interview Plimpton about the touring "Berlin Masterpieces" exhibition that was about to go on display. She arrived at the museum to find objects for the exhibition being removed from packing cartons by several workers, one a slight but physically fit man of senior years. She was asking him for directions to Plimpton's office when the museum director appeared to escort her there. "Do you know whom you were speaking to?" he asked the young

Bruce Dayton.

journalist as they walked away. "No," she said. "That was Alfred Pillsbury," Plimpton said. In 1948, he was seventy-nine years old.

In that year he voluntarily took the new title of Chairman of the Society of Fine Arts board of trustees, having completed more than twelve years as its president. For some years already, he had been looking ahead, setting the table for the time when he would no longer be on the scene. For example, in 1942 he personally recruited a young family friend to join the governing board of the Society of Fine Arts. Bruce Dayton had recently graduated from Yale and would soon be on his way to military service, to be followed by a career at the region's dominant retail enterprise, The Dayton Company. Bruce was known to the Pillsbury family in the 1930s as the earnest young man who dated John and Juty's daughter Jane. A dozen years later, he was known as the financial wizard among the grandsons of George Draper Dayton, the founder of the department store that bore the family name. At a social occasion in 1941, Bruce confessed to Alf a fascination with art. Alf replied mysteriously, "Young man, I have something in mind for you."

The following year, while stationed with the Army in Pendleton, Oregon, Bruce learned that Alf had engineered Bruce's election to the Society of Fine Arts board of directors.[45]

When Bruce returned to the Dayton Company in 1946, Alf called with a request. Would Dayton serve as the board's treasurer? There was a practical reason for him to make that request of a man so new to the board, Alf confessed. Bruce was the only board member whose work obligations kept him in Minnesota year-round. The other board members all spent Minnesota's coldest months elsewhere.[46] Dayton said yes to that request too. The same acquisition bug that bit Pillsbury in 1919 attacked Dayton. Just as Alfred Pillsbury was Minnesota's premier collector of fine art in the first half of the twentieth century, Dayton has undisputed claim to that title in the second half. In 2009, the *New York Times* called Dayton "the dean of American corporate arts philanthropy."

A sense that his own time was short must have laced the grief that befell Alfred on November 2, 1946, when his beloved Gretchen died at age seventy-four. Two years earlier, in November 1944, he lost his sole surviving sister, Sarah Belle "Sadie" Pillsbury Gale. Bereft of the company of two women he loved, Alfred became preoccupied in his last years with the eventual disposition of his estate. He went so far as to travel to North Dakota to interview one younger member of the family, his namesake and great-nephew Alfred Pillsbury Gale, to determine his needs and worthiness.[47]

He also made a major gift—$75,000—to the congregation that he loved. Alf served as president of the Church of the Redeemer for fifteen years, beginning in 1935. Those were lean years for what had once been a leading religious force in the city. In 1941, two years after its longtime pastor Marion D. Shutter died, the dwindling congregation sold its downtown building and decamped for a number of years to a house at 4600 Dupont Avenue South to consider its options. Alf was described by the senior pastor's wife, Mildred Olson, as "a very shy man" who became better known to his fellow parishioners during the years when the church was using a cramped house as its home. He led the congregation in a rebuilding program that led to construction of a handsome red-brick house of worship at 5000 Girard Avenue South, near Minnehaha Creek. He helped lay the cornerstone on May 23, 1948, and was on hand for the church's dedication on October 23, 1949. His gift was so prized by the church's pastor, the Rev. Carl Olson, that when his successor arrived in 1963, the letter Olson left in his desk for his successor to find was one from Alfred, accompanying his check for $75,000.[48] That successor, the Rev. John Cummins, said that every year between 1946 and 1971, a check from the Minneapolis Foundation for $600 would arrive from the estate of Mrs. Alfred Pillsbury. Gretchen's will provided for twenty-five years of support for her church after her death.

For Alfred, the end came on March 12, 1950, when he was eighty years old. He was eulogized in the *Minneapolis Star*: "Friendly, modest, sincere and generous—those were the characteristics Minneapolis knew in Alfred F. Pillsbury."[49] The value of his art collection was pegged at $1 million; to no one's surprise, it was headed to a permanent home at the Minneapolis Institute of Art.[50] His will made provisions for longtime household employees and left his Fair Oaks mansion to any male Pillsbury who would live in it. The bulk of his estate went to his sisters' sons, Richard Gale and John Snyder, and to the young cousin whose career he had helped launch, Phil.

Chapter Ten

A Personal War

More than generational change came to the Pillsbury Company when thirty-seven-year-old Philip (Phil) Winston Pillsbury moved into the CEO's office at the Metropolitan Building on May 7, 1940. The corporate board of directors may have appeared to be honoring tradition by choosing a grandson of Charles Alfred Pillsbury to take charge. In reality, by making Phil the youngest man to head a milling company in America,[1] the board was calling for a shakeup.

The 1930s were difficult years for most American industries. But a weak economy was only one of the troubles faced by Pillsbury Flour Mills Inc. In the years since its reorganization in 1911, the company had repeated its mistake of the 1890s. It became overly dependent on one man—in this case, Albert C. Loring. He was "the quintessential flour miller,"[2] in the tradition of Charles A. Pillsbury. A hands-on manager, Loring personally controlled much of the operation. The board of directors gave Loring full rein and did too little planning for leadership succession. When Loring died suddenly on Dec. 11, 1932, the void at the top was enormous.

None of the three Pillsburys who served as directors wanted to succeed Loring as CEO. Among them, John S. Pillsbury might have seemed the logical choice to assume the post. He had worked most closely with Loring as vice president of sales, and had been the company's ambassador to the community, serving terms as president of the Minneapolis Club, the Chamber of Commerce, and the Grain Exchange. He may have been a reluctant businessman in his youth, but by the time he'd reached his middle years John was devoted to Pillsbury & Co. When he wasn't traveling, seldom did a workday go by when John did not put in an appearance at his Metropolitan Building office. But at age fifty-four, more than comfortably well off and with six children in their teens, John had little desire to lengthen his workdays or confine himself to Minneapolis. After much consideration, he declined the role of chief executive in favor of a newly created position, chairman of the board.

Albert C. Loring, 1927.

Instead, Loring's role was assumed by two non-family executives in fairly quick succession. The first was Harrison Whiting, elevated from the position John had held for many years, vice president for sales. Whiting pressed ahead with a plan begun under Loring to provide longtime employees with accident and health insurance and "life annuities," or pensions, via Equitable Life Insurance Society, and life insurance through local Northwestern National Life, on whose board Alf Pillsbury served.[3] The Pillsbury Co. was among the first in the nation to provide in this way for its employees, whom Phil Pillsbury called "the family." But Whiting's four-year tenure was also marked by resistance to a New Deal effort to finance agricultural subsidies with a processing tax on flour milling (a matter taken successfully by the nation's millers to the U.S. Supreme Court) and labor strife in Minneapolis. A deadly truckers' strike in the city in 1934 spawned similar, if less violent, outbreaks in other industries, as workers sought employer recognition of their right to organize and bargain collectively for wages and benefits. Whiting was in the process of negotiating an end to a strike at the Pillsbury A Mill, and had agreed to improved vacation allowances and pay for workers, when the mills were idled by management. Then tragedy struck. He was thrown from his horse while riding with his wife and died on October 3, 1936.[4]

After Whiting came Clark Hempstead, who had been the firm's general counsel. As a lawyer, he may have been well positioned to complete the company's negotiations with its newly organized workers. But he was neither a manager nor a marketer. The devastating 1936 drought in the Midwest spurred the downsizing of Minneapolis operations, a process that had already begun on Loring's watch. In 1930, Buffalo, New York, had surpassed Minneapolis as the nation's leading flour-producing city. By Hempstead's second year as CEO, Minneapolis's flour production ranked in third place behind Kansas City and was dropping fast.[5] In 1938 Pillsbury Flour Mills Inc. was in the red for the first time (figured on an annual basis) since 1908. While the profit picture improved slightly in 1939, bleak earnings in 1940 had the non-family board members calling for new direction under a new leader. Alfred Pillsbury had one in mind.

Phil Pillsbury had been climbing the corporate ranks steadily since his return to Minneapolis from Chicago in the late 1930s.[6] As he deepened his involvement in the company during that decade, his father Charles steadily withdrew from it, though he was said to remain a sought-after source of business advice.[7] Chronic health concerns, never fully specified to his nephews,

Charles S. Pillsbury in about 1930.

plagued Charles. In May 1939, his counsel was forever lost. Charles checked into St. Mary's Hospital in Rochester for a "serious abdominal operation," performed by Mayo Clinic physicians on Saturday, May 20. An afternoon newspaper report that day said that the patient had come through the procedure, later identified as a gall bladder operation, in satisfactory condition. The next morning, Charles died at age sixty. His wife and twin brother were among those at his bedside—suggesting that his death was not totally unexpected. At the hour that Charles's funeral commenced at Plymouth Congregational Church, where he had been a lifelong member, every Pillsbury mill in the nation ceased operation in a show of respect. Phil would say years later of his father's influence, "He wanted me to make good use of all the energy I had."[8]

Less than a year later, Phil and Eleanor suffered another loss. Eleanor's father, Henry Bellows, died suddenly at home four days after Christmas in 1939, at age fifty-four. He was a man of wide interests and accomplishment, and might have acted as Phil's adviser in corporate leadership, had he lived. Bellows, a Harvard Ph.D. renown for his intellect, was by turn a classics professor at the University of Minnesota, translator of ancient Icelandic sagas, author, journalist, music critic, Minnesota National Guard colonel, manager of brand-new WCCO Radio, radio industry lobbyist, founding member of the Federal Radio Commission (later the Federal Communication Commission), vice president of CBS Radio, and publicist for General Mills.[9] Eleanor's mother, the daughter of a Harvard chemistry professor, had died four years earlier, at just forty-six. The loss of her parents while still a young adult undoubtedly drew Eleanor into a tighter Pillsbury orbit. It may also have inspired a rush to make her own mark.

When Phil became Pillsbury's president in 1940, his father and father-in-law were gone and his aging cousin Alfred was retired. His uncle John, now sixty-one, had begun to shift his focus from business to civic and philanthropic pursuits. It was as if the entire previous generation of Pillsburys had tossed Phil the keys to the family bus and moved to the rear or disembarked altogether. But Phil was ready to drive. By 1940, he had already accumulated sixteen years of solid experience, touching on nearly every phase of the company's operation. Among his teachers had been the company's "indispensable man," Albert C. Loring, who took a personal interest in the Pillsbury scion. "He was responsible for the last eight years he lived of giving all his knowledge and experience in background to me," Phil would say of Loring decades later. "While working in Minneapolis, hardly a day went by over those years that I did not spend a great deal of time in Mr. Loring's office, sitting in on meetings and hearing the wise counsel of his words."[10] Loring even taught Phil to appreciate a good cigar. A corporate history would attest, "No one was as well equipped as Philip to revive the organization."[11]

Phil aimed to see Pillsbury diversify and grow again (an objective applauded by his mentor Alf Pillsbury, who said he would rather "die from over-expansion and action than to suffocate from rotting."[12]) In 1940, 90 percent of the company's sales were from flour.[13] Phil intended to change that. He started with the acquisition of a large West Coast miller, Globe Grain and Milling Co., only weeks after he became CEO. His next move was one his grandfather would have applauded: He expanded the company's research laboratory in Minneapolis and ordered its head to report directly to him with findings that would lead to new consumer products. He was tired of watching as competitors moved into the lucrative field of home baking mixes and ready-to-eat products, and was determined to catch up. He also took note of the success the competition was having in selling flour in smaller packages. Consumers had been showing since the 1920s that they preferred to buy flour in easy-to-carry five- and ten-pound bags. Yet until Phil's presidency, Pillsbury's Best was sold predominantly in 25–, 50– and 100–pound sacks. It was, Phil would say later, an attempt "to stay in the buggy whip business," and he lost little time making the change to lighter packages.[14]

Next, recalling the contribution of his great-uncle Fred, Phil formed Pillsbury Feed Mills, Inc. as a separate division, and enlarged and modernized its production of livestock feed. Perhaps to signify the company's fresh start and to accommodate growth, Phil also engineered the company's 1942 move out of the elegant old Metropolitan Life Building to a newer, similarly named Metropolitan Bank Building at 608 Second Avenue South. It was the beginning of the end for the city's first skyscraper, which would meet with a wrecking ball in 1960 (to the abiding consternation of preservationists.) But the move gave the company new prominence closer to the modern heart of downtown Minneapolis. In 1946, the new building would become Pillsbury property, and would take the name Pillsbury Building.[15]

Phil sacking souvenir bags of flour, June 5, 1944.

Phil had inherited his father's gregarious nature and his grandfather's love of the flour business, and he applied both to the company's service. He spent a considerable share of his time building personal relationships with employees, trying to court major customers, and cultivating ties with industry peers and government and civic leaders. His "personal corporate diplomacy" likely contributed much to the improvement in labor relations that the company witnessed in the 1940s and beyond. Like his grandfather before him, Phil Pillsbury prided himself on being a good employer. Employees welcomed him as a blast of new, energizing air.

The relationships and skills he had acquired as an apprentice at the A Mill paid lasting dividends, giving him immediate credibility with the craftsmen who ran the mills.[16] While head of the company, Phil proudly maintained a membership acquired years earlier in the Association of Operative Millers, the master millers' craft guild. "He can reach into a grinding machine, pull out a handful of half-finished flour, and tell from the feel and the look of it whether the rolls are adjusted correctly," a corporate release from the 1950s boasted.[17] Phil got a kick out of demonstrating to visitors at the company's seventy-fifth anniversary celebration in 1944 that he still knew how to operate the machines that filled flour sacks. Small sacks of flour that he personally filled were sent home with guests as souvenirs.[18] Leftovers of the giant cake baked for the occasion went to Pillsbury Settlement House, to be consumed by the hungry kids who attended after-school programs there.[19]

The company's diamond anniversary observance at the A Mill was undoubtedly more subdued than it would have been on a date other than June 5, 1944. The focus of the city, state, and nation that day was not on industrial history. It was on the war in Europe. That day, Allied forces made a triumphant entry into Rome. But grim anticipation was mounting for the news that would come the following day. The Allies landed on the beaches of Normandy, France, on June 6—D-Day. Americans were riveted to their radios during those pivotal days of the war.

Unlike the first World War, World War II meant much more than distant strife for the Pillsburys of Minnesota. It was personal. By 1942, all six of John and Juty's children were in some way engaged in the all-out war that erupted with the Japanese attack on Pearl Harbor, Hawaii, on December 7, 1941. The eldest, John Jr., was a lieutenant commander in the Navy who operated what a Pillsbury publicity release delicately described as a "photographic squadron against the enemy" beginning in the summer of 1943. This was dangerous reconnaissance work that would win him a citation for distinguished service in December 1944. "The numerous details of administration to which Lt. Cmdr. Pillsbury accurately attended in making liaison with base operations authorities at advance bases from which the squadron operated, and his providing the pilots with the latest verified information on friendly and enemy forces, contributed immeasurably to the success of the squadron's operations against the enemy," his citation read.[20]

A 1935 graduate of Yale who had been the No. 2 man on the school's prestigious heavyweight crew for three years, John Jr. came home to Minneapolis to give the family business a hesitant try. Within a year, he decided it was not for him. A bright man with natural

leadership qualities, he wasted no time dithering about his options. He promptly enrolled at the University of Minnesota Law School. He did so as a married man.

On June 11, 1936, at St. James Church in New York, John Jr. married Katharine "Kitty" Harrison Clark, an only child and daughter of Donaldson and Katharine Harrison Clark of New Haven, Connecticut and New York City. She had been a schoolmate of John's sister Ella at

Katharine Clark Pillsbury, 1937.

Foxcroft in Middleburg, Virginia, graduating in 1934. Like several dozen other Pillsbury school chums would do through the years, Kitty had stopped at Southways that summer on her way west with a friend.[21] The pretty, slim brunette made a lasting impression on that stopover.

An exchange with her future father-in-law during her stay made a tale perfect for retelling at family gatherings in years to come. John's bother George related: "My father was standing by the fireplace wearing a beautiful star sapphire stickpin. Kitty went up to him and said, 'Mr. Pillsbury, that would make a wonderful ring.' He jokingly said, 'Well, the only way any girl is going to get it is if she marries one of my sons.' " John Jr. and Kitty stayed in touch through the ensuing year and a half. He asked Ella to invite Kitty to come to Minnesota for Christmas in 1935. It was then that they became engaged. "When they announced their engagement at Southways, the first thing Kitty did is go up to my father and say, 'Where's that star sapphire?' He immediately gave it to her." Years later, it was stolen—a loss the family still laments.

When John Jr. graduated from law school in 1940, he joined Faegre & Benson, already then a leading Minneapolis firm, with the intention of practicing corporate, real estate, and mineral rights law, racing sailboats in the summer and iceboats in the winter, and launching the next generation of Pillsburys. John S. Pillsbury III arrived first, on Nov. 30, 1938, and shortly acquired a lasting nickname, "Jock." He was followed by Donaldson Clark Pillsbury on Sept. 14, 1940, and Lynde Harrison Pillsbury on July 12, 1943. The couple's only daughter and her mother's namesake, Katharine Clark Pillsbury, was born on Sept. 5, 1945—one day before her father pulled into Tokyo Bay aboard the aircraft carrier *USS Ticonderoga* to witness the start of American occupation of defeated, still-smoldering Japan.[22]

John and Juty's second son, Edmund Pennington Pillsbury, loved flying almost as much as he loved racing sailboats. Eddy was the family's best sailor and most intensely competitive all-around athlete.[23] His zeal for sailboat racing helped inspire John and Juty to take over sponsorship of the Eastover Cup Race. It was an annual event on Lake Minnetonka originally sponsored by the Pillsburys' Brackett's Point neighbors, the Carpenter family. The event was renamed Southways Race and grew into a major competition involving four hundred sailors. The winner's prize was a sterling silver cup, donated by the Pillsburys. The event's attractions included a chance to spend a portion of a summer day at Lake Minnetonka's premier estate. An outdoor luncheon on Southways' thirteen-acre grounds kicked off the event.[24] Eddy won the cup for the first time when he was only thirteen years old.[25]

Eddy followed his brother to Yale, graduated in 1936, and took a trip around the world before settling in at the Pillsbury Co. For him, the family business was a good fit. When he joined the Minneapolis Chamber of Commerce (now known as the Grain Exchange) in 1939, company publicists noted that he was the fourth generation of Pillsburys to take a place there. That same year, Eddy married a California girl with a Minneapolis pedigree, Priscilla Keator. Born

Adele Priscilla Howe on November 7, 1915, she was the daughter of L. Vernon Howe and namesake of her mother, Priscilla Rand Howe, both members of prominent Minneapolis families. They divorced when their daughter was small. In the early 1920s, Priscilla's mother married Benjamin C. Keator, an executive of the John Deere Co. who adopted Priscilla and her sister and moved the family to Portland, Oregon, not long thereafter. About ten years later, Keator's work took them to the San Francisco area. Priscilla maintained her Minnesota connection by spending girlhood summers at the Lake Minnetonka homes of her grandparents. Her Howe grandparents' house was next door to Southways (and would eventually be purchased by the Pillsburys); her grandmother, Suzanne Rand, had a summer place nearby. Priscilla met the Pillsbury kids at summer parties and made a lasting impression on the second son. [26]

Eddy and Priscilla were married on December 14, 1939, at the Episcopal Church of St. Matthew in San Mateo, California. The event provided a memorable adventure for the two youngest Pillsbury children, Jane, then twenty, and George, eighteen, both of whom were studying in the East at the time. At the suggestion of both the groom and brother Chuck, they decided to fly to California on their own to surprise the rest of the family. Passenger airline service in 1939 was a far cry from what it would become after World War II. Direct flights from New York City to San Francisco were scarce; non-stop flights were non-existent. Fearing that a northerly route would almost guarantee weather delays, George and Jane booked an American Airlines flight that stopped in Nashville, Tennessee, and several other places before terminating in Los Angeles. There, Jane and George planned to catch a United Airlines flight to San Francisco.

On the first leg of their trip, they were seated in a four-seat Pullman-style compartment with a charming middle-aged man who introduced himself as Mr. Smith. They chatted amiably, Smith allowing that he had a passing acquaintance with Phil Pillsbury and revealing that his final destination was Atlanta, where he would attend the December 9 premiere of the movie blockbuster *Gone with the Wind*. The Pillsbury kids fretted aloud that bad weather might make them miss their connecting flight. Smith wished them well and got off the flight in Nashville. George and Jane's worries were justified. They were indeed late arriving in Los Angeles, and were certain that they had missed their connection. Instead, as they prepared to deplane, an American Airlines official boarded the aircraft and called out, "Mr. and Mrs. Pillsbury?" They were advised that the Mr. Smith they had met was C. R. Smith, president of American Airlines. He had teletyped ahead to United Airlines in Los Angeles, asking for a personal favor: Would they please hold their flight to San Francisco until the young people named Pillsbury had made their connection? The American official escorted them across the tarmac to their waiting flight, where they were greeted by a nonplussed United flight attendant. "Now, who the hell are you?" she asked. She evidently was expecting celebrities, not college kids, to be responsible for her flight's delay.

Eddy and Pris were living in Pasadena[27] in 1941 when war erupted. He had already worked through a series of assignments in the Pillsbury Co. grain department in Duluth, Buffalo, and Minneapolis—positions that appeared to be schooling him for eventual corporate leadership. But he had also been schooling himself to fly small airplanes, taking flying lessons and using a private plane for corporate assignments. When war erupted, he sought to enlist in the Navy or the Army Air Corps (the future U.S. Air Force.) To his chagrin, neither would take him. Eddy was nearsighted and wore glasses—a common condition that was nevertheless sufficient in those years to scuttle a bid to serve as a military pilot. Instead, he became a civilian flight instructor in an army aviation program at Thunderbird Field in Phoenix, Arizona.[28] Among his students were Chinese officers sent from Chiang Kai-shek's army to learn how to fly.[29] Priscilla joined him there, and their family grew. Their first two children were their own namesakes—Priscilla Rand, born March 8, 1941, in Los Angeles, and Edmund Jr., on April 28, 1943, in San Francisco. A second daughter, Joan Keator, was born on September 19, 1945, in Evanston, Illinois.

Eddy was joined at the Pillsbury Co. in the late 1930s by a third cousin, John Pillsbury Snyder Jr.[30] The oldest child of *Titanic* survivors John and Nelle Snyder, John Snyder Jr. was a classmate of

John and Juty's family gathered for this portrait a few days before Ella's wedding. The children, from left, are George, Eddy, Ella, Jane, John, and Charlie.

John Pillsbury Jr. at Blake School and Yale University '35, and found a professional home in the business his great-grandfather helped found. He served in the office of the Chief of Ordnance of the U.S. Army in 1942, then became a lieutenant in the Navy Reserve through the end of the war.[31] John P. Jr. united two old Minneapolis families when he married Anne Morrison in 1936. She was a descendent of first Minneapolis mayor and early miller Dorilus Morrison. The Snyders had two daughters and a son.

When war broke out, John and Juty's elder daughter, Ella, was married and a young mother. Her wedding on July 21, 1937, to Thomas Manville Crosby united two of Minnesota's most storied milling families[32]—a harbinger of things to come. Crosby was the son of Franklin Muzzy Crosby and grandson of John Crosby, who joined the Washburn milling enterprise at the Falls of St. Anthony in 1877 and lent his name to the Washburn-Crosby Co. Franklin Crosby had followed his father into the milling business, and was by 1937 an executive at General Mills.[33]

Tom Crosby's mother, Harriet McKnight Crosby, also had a long Minneapolis pedigree. Her father was Sumner McKnight, a lumberman and banker whose timber business operated in several states.[34] Tom was born in 1914 and grew up a few blocks from the Pillsburys at 2120 Park Avenue. The youngest of seven lively children, he met his future wife when both of them were three years old, and Mrs. Crosby called Mrs. Pillsbury to inquire about a play date. "Juty, I'm sure you must have somebody that's three years old…" she began, uttering words that years later would be a source of mirth at wedding and anniversary parties.

Like the Pillsburys, the Crosbys decamped to year-round lake life in the late 1930s, but not before hosting an opulent bridal dinner in honor of Tom and Ella's wedding in July 1937. Eighty guests gloried in the sight of multiple silver wine coolers overflowing with stunning white cut flowers.[35] Those flowers stood out in memory when Ella's wedding day arrived while workers at the city's florists were on strike. John Pillsbury would not hear of crossing a picket line to obtain posies for his daughter's wedding. But one guest was somehow able to get a bouquet sent to Plymouth Congregational Church as a wedding-day gift, and it was quickly converted to the bridal bouquet and carried down the aisle. Nature provided the decoration for her wedding reception at Southways. She was the only Pillsbury child whose wedding reception was at the lakeside mansion.[36]

Ella (whose mother preferred that she be called by her full given name, Ella Sturgis) had completed three years at Vassar College when she ended her formal education to become Mrs. Thomas Crosby. Tom, a 1937 Yale graduate, briefly took his bride to New York City for a stab at Columbia Law School before following his father and grandfather to General Mills. He rose quickly in leadership ranks there, though his progress was interrupted by a tour of duty with an amphibious armored company of Marines in the Pacific theater. Meanwhile, Ella was busy with babies: Thomas Manville Jr. was born on October 9, 1938; David Pillsbury came on April 18, 1940; Eleanor Lawler was next, on June 26, 1942. Three more Crosby children were born after the war: Mary Eugenie on

November 1, 1946, Lucy Sturgis on March 14, 1948, and Robert Franklin on January 9, 1954.

While attending Finch College in New York, Jane Lawler Pillsbury met and fell in love with Stanley R. Resor, the son of Stanley B. Resor, the president and chairman of the J. Walter Thompson advertising agency. Stanley Jr.'s mother, Helen Lansdowne Resor, was also deeply involved in the business, and is widely considered the creative genius behind the early broadcast advertising that made the agency famous. Stan Resor was a Yale man, as his father had been before him, and a 1939 classmate of Chuck Pillsbury, who played a matchmaking role. Stan was working toward a specialty in corporate law at Yale Law School when war interrupted both his studies and the couple's wedding plans. He joined Yale's Reserve Officer Training Program and prepared for artillery service. In the spring of 1942 he found himself at Ft. Bragg, North Carolina, unable to obtain permission for a long nuptial leave—so the wedding party came to him. Jane and Stan were married at St. Michael's Church in Charleston, South Carolina, on April 4, 1942, and the reception took place at nearby Yeaman's Hall. With war on everyone's mind, it was a subdued affair.

Charles Alfred Pillsbury, the namesake of his famous grandfather, experienced a fair amount of social discomfort at Jane's wedding. Three of his girlfriends showed up, and he had a terrible time keeping all of them happy, his younger brother George recalls. One of them was Kathleen Kennedy of Hyannis Port, Massachusetts, the sister of future American president John F. Kennedy.[37] Kathleen was a particular friend, so much so that she had visited the Pillsburys at Southways, and Jane and Chuck had been guests of her family at their large estate on Cape Cod. Jane would later recall enjoying the company of handsome Joe Jr. and John Kennedy, the two older Kennedy brothers, while finding their little brother Teddy a nuisance.

It's possible that Chuck had more experience handling such situations than brother George knew. The third Pillsbury son was always eager for fun and adventure and was accordingly popular among the ladies. Among the brothers, he alone briefly ran into academic difficulty at St. Paul's School, the preparatory academy in Concord,

N.H. favored by the family. It wasn't that Chuck lacked academic ability. He just preferred sports to studying. His interests at school ran to hockey, football and crew—so much so that he won the SPS All-Around Athlete award upon graduation. After a somewhat delayed 1939 graduation from Yale, Chuck was granted a trip around the world—a family tradition. But Hitler's troops invaded Poland on Sept. 1, 1939, and Chuck came home early with war on his mind. He briefly tried his hand at banking. But a few months at Northwestern National Bank, where his great-grandfather George had been president, were enough to convince him that banking was not for him. He had no interest in working for the Pillsbury Company. In late 1940, he

abruptly announced to his surprised family that he would join the Navy Air Corps. He expected the United States to enter the escalating war in Europe, and wanted to be ready to participate as a pilot. On December 2, 1940, he was off to Pensacola, Florida, for flight training.[38]

His decision was not unanimously well received by his family. Older brother John Jr. had signed on with fellow-Minnesotan Charles A. Lindbergh's America First movement and was

Navy Lt. Chuck Pillsbury, 1942.

staunchly opposed to U.S. involvement in what he regarded as other nations' wars. He considered participation in U.S. military buildup folly (a view he fully reversed after Pearl Harbor was attacked.) Eddy would probably have been more sympathetic to Chuck's decision, but he was in California, removed from family discussion circles. Young George was at Yale, in an environment that encouraged internationalist thinking. One of George's classmates at both St. Paul's School and Yale was Nick Biddle, whose father, Anthony J. Drexel Biddle Jr., was U.S. ambassador to Poland in 1939 when the Nazi war machine invaded. Several of his friends had spent the last pre-war summer in Europe.[39] They convinced George that American might would soon be needed to contain German aggression. John S. Pillsbury Sr., whose military experience had consisted of four years in the Minnesota National Guard, was supportive and very proud of Chuck and, eventually, of all of his sons' military service.[40] Like any mother, Juty worried.

Chuck was promoted to lieutenant on March 1, 1943. His training had taken him from flying boats to torpedo bombers and finally to fighters, and he shipped out as a fighter pilot on the aircraft carrier Bunker Hill for service in the South Pacific. That fall the *Minneapolis Tribune* reported that sons of two prominent Minnesota industrialists, Pillsbury and *St. Paul Pioneer Press* owner Bernard H. Ridder, were involved in the same Pacific engagement—Chuck as a fighter pilot, Ensign Bernard H. Ridder Jr. as a junior officer on the aircraft carrier that Chuck's squadron was protecting. Both were unharmed, the newspaper reported.

But bad news was just ahead. *The Minneapolis Star Journal* announced to the community on November 21, 1943, that Lt. Charles A. Pillsbury was "missing following combat action in the Southwest Pacific." His plane had not returned from a mission over Bougainville, where Japan had constructed naval bases in 1942 and Americans were attempting to neutralize them. As described in a 1997 book and a web site devoted to stories about Pacific theater wreckages, "Chuck and his wingman, Ensign Bob Hogan, flew an independent course up the jungle-obscured trail and managed to flame five trucks. At about 1300, just before the pair reached Kahili, Hogan idly cut to starboard to pass around 400-foot Kangu Hill. He saw Chuck swing left around the same prominence. Though Bob neither encountered nor saw any signs of anti-aircraft fire, that was the last he saw of Chuck."[41]

It fell to John Jr. to notify other family members, including the brother who was closest to Chuck, George. He was in Cambridge, Massachusetts, as fall turned to winter in 1943. Twenty-two and only recently graduated from Yale with a major in mathematics, George had enlisted in the Marine Corps and was studying at the Army/ Navy School of Radio Radar, run jointly by Massachusetts Institute of Technology and Harvard. He had completed basic training at

Parris Island, South Carolina, and Quantico, Virginia, and was happy to be back in New England, where he had many acquaintances and friends. He was having an end-of-the-day drink with a friend of both brothers at a favorite bar when the bartender surprised him by announcing that he had a long-distance call. John had called George's roommates and learned from them where George could be reached. George said later about that difficult moment. "I was so glad that I had a friend with me who knew Chuck when I heard the news."

The family immediately feared the worst. As days turned into weeks, months, and ultimately years with no news of Chuck's fate, they became resigned to his death. John Sr. admitted as much in a kindly, sorrowful letter to editor Virginia Crenshaw of *New South* magazine in Atlanta, Georgia, dated October 3, 1944, evidently in response to her mention of Chuck in an article. "I am sorry to say that I do not think there is any chance of this boy turning up, as he was shot down in a fighter plane over a very heavily defended Japanese position, at tree-top level," John wrote. "He was flight officer of a large naval fighting squadron, and his squadron for several days made every effort to locate some signs of where he crashed."[42]

A few months earlier, John hand-delivered a letter concerning Chuck to the company's publicity department. Dated June 27, 1944, it was attached to a copy of Chuck's Air Medal citation. The father was sending it along to keep corporate files complete, and was not seeking publicity, he emphasized. "I don't want this published unless the newspapers take it as purely a news item, and not because they want to cooperate with us or because I want publicity on the matter," he said. He was keenly sensitive to the fact that many other families had sustained losses equally painful.[43] The citation, signed by Secretary of the Navy James Forrestal, praised Chuck "for meritorious achievement while participating in aerial flight as flight officer during combat against enemy Japanese forces in the Solomon Islands Area" from Oct. 27 to Nov. 21, 1943. "Contributing materially to the high combat efficiency of his squadron by a thorough and skillful supervision of less experienced pilots, Lt. Pillsbury courageously led numerous strafing missions deep into hostile territory although constantly subjected to intense enemy antiaircraft fire. His expert airmanship and tenacious devotion to duty throughout numerous hazardous patrols and escort missions in this vital war area were in keeping with the highest traditions of the United States Naval Service," the citation read.[44]

Not knowing with certainty what fate had befallen Chuck was especially hard on Juty. She soldiered on with a full schedule of social and civic activities and household management chores, all of which were more demanding during the war years. But family members say that late at night, when the big house was quiet, she would walk the hallways in grief and despair.

Twenty-five years passed before her prayers for closure were answered. On September 4, 1968, a surveyor named Don Smith was examining the boundaries of a Catholic mission on Bougainville when, about 400 meters off an isolated road, he came upon Chuck's plane. His remains were still in the cockpit, badly burned. The family received word that a bullet was found in Chuck's skull—news that was a comfort to Juty. She took solace in the thought that Chuck had died a quick death, and had not been killed by the fire that engulfed the cockpit after the crash. His remains were returned to

Marine Lt. George Pillsbury, 1944.

his sister Jane because, by then, she was well connected to Washington military brass. Chuck's remains were later interred on the knoll at Lakewood Cemetery where so many Pillsburys rest. (Jane's husband, Stan Resor, had risen to the position of U.S. secretary of the Army. He took the position in July 1968—likely recommended by his Yale classmate Cyrus Vance, who held the same position in John F. Kennedy's administration and went on to serve President Jimmy Carter as secretary of state.[45])

In 1944, with Chuck missing in action, John and Juty's hearts must have been heavy as their fourth son George headed into harm's way in the South Pacific. While the young men in the clan were

The Pillsbury women of the mid-twentieth century: from left, Eleanor Bellows Pillsbury, Priscilla Keator Pillsbury, Katharine "Kitty" Clark Pillsbury, Ella Pillsbury Crosby, Eleanor Lawler Pillsbury, and Helen "Nelle" Winston Pillsbury.

overseas, their wives, children, and a company of nurses and nannies congregated at Southways to wait out the war, and beginning that summer and continuing until V-E day the following spring, the household was lively. Worry loves company, especially the company of babies and toddlers. The grandchildren gave the lakeside mansion and its grounds a workout, and undoubtedly gave their elders welcome distraction.

Pregnant Jane was the first arrival at Southways, in late 1943 or in early 1944. Her husband Stan was by then a captain on the artillery staff of an Army armored division in Europe, and Jane decided she wanted to deliver her firstborn in Minneapolis, not at an Army base hospital. Stanley Rogers Resor Jr. arrived on July 25, 1944, and came home to Southways a few days later.

Within a few months, the household swelled to include John Jr.'s wife Kitty and their three sons, Jock, Don and Harry; Ella with Tommy Jr., David and Eleanor; and little Priscilla Rand and Eddy Jr. The latter two came unaccompanied by their parents, who remained in Arizona, but in tow of a nurse who "had worked in India with an Army family," Juty wrote decades later. "Every evening she appeared in a long black gown that still carried with it the smells of India." In stark contrast was Ella's nurse Esther, a well-trained professional "always dressed in her perfect uniform." Kitty recruited Louise Owen, "entirely reliable

Juty with Eddy's children Priscilla and Ted at Southways.

and most helpful," though she had never before cared for small children. Those three joined a household staff that typically ran to five or more servants, including a cook named Anna whom Juty remembered with particular appreciation. She "understood the situation and was most sympathetic."[46] The situation included limited trips into the city due to gasoline rationing, and many frosty corners at Southways, coal being in short supply. Kitty, an only child who had not been exposed to some childhood diseases, came down with chicken pox along with the youngsters. Convalescing in chilly rooms did not hasten her recovery. But togetherness trumped physical discomfort, Ella recalled years later. "We had fun," she said. Shortly before the war, Ella and Tom had built a new house on Long Lake Road, about five miles from Southways. But when he was away as a Marine lieutenant in the anxious winter of 1944-45, even a few miles of separation from the rest of her family was too much.

How Juty coped with 1944's combination of grief, household disruption, and community need says much about her character. Instead of turning inward, she pushed herself to greater service of others. She tolerated minor domestic commotions, decisively addressed major ones, and took on new responsibilities outside her home. She had agreed to serve as Hennepin County Red Cross vice chairman and head of its Roll Call, which involved recruiting new financial donors. But that assignment wasn't enough. "I always seemed to be called away (from fundraising meetings) to help one of my children at an important moment," she would say years later to justify her decision to become more than a fundraiser. Wanting to participate in the war effort more directly, Juty decided to become a nurse's aide. As she later put it, she had taken on a profession that "would make me helpful anywhere.... It enabled me to step out of the framework of my background to be simply an individual."[47] Four decades earlier Juty had considered a career in social work. Now that idealistic young woman was back. Juty worked at both private and public hospitals, preferring Minneapolis General Hospital (now Hennepin County Medical Center), then crowded with wounded veterans in various stages of convalescence. Her exchanges with some of them created lasting memories. She would tell decades later about the man who slipped cookies into her uniform pocket because "she looked hungry." Another man, hearing that she had twelve grandchildren, counseled her that she should not be working with so much family responsibility. She should be on welfare, he said; with years of experience collecting relief himself, he could "fix it" for her to go on the government dole too.

Though she may not have thought about it in such terms, the satisfaction Juty found as a nurse's aide matched the experience of many women during the war who took jobs that had formerly been available only to men. Those female war workers were sowing seeds for the women's movement that would blossom twenty-five years later, and Juty's stories about her wartime experiences would one day help her granddaughters widen their view of their own opportunities.

For his part, John Sr. was demonstrating anew the family tradition of combining business with political and civic responsibilities. He remained attentive to Pillsbury Company matters, though with the passage of time his confidence in the young nephew he had helped put in charge grew. Phil was laying plans for new products, new marketing strategies, and new acquisitions after the war, even as he served on a number of wartime food industry advisory councils[48] addressing the nutritional needs of both the civilian and military populations. The foods laboratory Phil had revitalized was instrumental in developing products for the Army's K and C rations as well as for people in refugee housing and prison camps around the globe. [49]

As John reached his mid-60s, an age when others seek more leisure, he was busier than ever. If the Minneapolis home-front war effort had a figurehead, it was John Pillsbury. He was widely known and liked in his hometown. A personality sketch done several years before the war described John's appeal: "He is an outstanding personality. To meet him is to know him as he is, and to like him for what he is. J.S.'s office door is always open. He likes people. He enjoys talking with you and is appreciative of your viewpoint. His contacts are many.... . He is an organizer, a promoter, a finance expert, a salesman, a qualified executive and a man."[50] Another journalist, writing soon after the war, painted an even more vivid picture:

"He's this kind of man: Say that Chiang Kai-shek was coming to Minneapolis with the Chinese Communists, and President Truman ... and the whole world depended on the result of it, and some Minneapolis man must be in charge to make them all feel kindhearted and genial and honorably fair to each other, who would it be? John Pillsbury, of course."[51]

John was sought-after by a host of wartime causes, from WAVE recruitment[52] to Navy support rallies[53] to a fundraiser that auctioned off six pairs of scarce nylon stockings from the stage.[54] He had a keen sense of the whole city's needs, having been active in the settlement house he helped found in honor of his parents and serving on the leadership team of the Council of Social Agencies (a precursor of the United Way) beginning in 1926. When the federal war bonds drive came to town in 1942 in search of local leadership, John said yes. Acceptance made him responsible for recruiting more than a hundred other Minneapolis fundraisers and organizing them into working teams. With so many men in the military and their wives burdened with double duty at home, that was a formidable task—but one John said he enjoyed. "It's

The leaders of Hennepin County's war bonds drive, John Pillsbury and Clarence Chaney, May 1945.

just a matter of choosing smarter people than yourself to do it, then you take the credit, " he told Minneapolis journalist Brenda Ueland soon after the war ended.[55] (Brenda was the daughter of Clara Ueland, founder of the Minnesota League of Women Voters.) He went on to say that he liked "that chairman job" because it gave him a chance to become acquainted with "a hundred fellas I didn't know before. I'd say that's what I like best—knowing people."

John was in earnest. He headed not one war bond drive, but seven in all before the war ended. His name was at the bottom of personal letters on letterhead reading "United States Treasury War Finance Committee of Hennepin County" that made emotional appeals for the purchase of war bonds. "The more you invest, the shorter this war will be. The fewer young men will die," an April 12, 1943 letter for the second bond drive promised.[56] Another drive in the following year featured an appealing photo of six Pillsbury grandchildren under the sales pitch aimed at parents and grandparents with the slogan "Bonds for Babies."[57] A publicity photo for the seventh and final drive, published by the afternoon *Minneapolis Star Journal* on May 14, 1945, shows John and his co-chairman, Clarence F. Chaney, in a small powerboat emblazoned "BUY WAR BONDS" on chilly Lake

Minnetonka. The caption said the men planned to use the boat to "make personal calls on their neighbors." They aimed to raise a daunting $80.1 million from Hennepin County through June.

That same month, John also agreed to chair a national group of sponsors for construction of what became the Mayo Memorial Medical Research Center at the University of Minnesota.[58] University Hospital and its medical school had grown tremendously since John's father, Charles A. Pillsbury, helped establish it in the 1870s. The family's interest in the hospital's work had been avid ever since, and would remain so in generations to come. Soon thereafter, he also became the Minneapolis sponsor of the Eye Bank for Sight Restoration, Inc., a national tissue bank for cornea transplants, a new procedure developed to restore eyesight to soldiers with corneas damaged during the war.[59]

John had been instrumental in the decision that despite shortages of money and personnel, the Minneapolis Symphony Orchestra would maintain a regular performance schedule during the war years. He took the lead in a special fundraising campaign that raised $122,500 to avoid cancellation of the 1943-44 concert season. "John S. Pillsbury looked upon the [threat to the] orchestra as a war emergency," a Minneapolis newspaper reported. His fundraising strategy was to solicit gifts from companies headquartered elsewhere but with Minneapolis operations, using the pitch that "good music in Minneapolis is an asset to the company in which they are financially interested."[60] It was pure Pillsbury philosophy about corporate responsibility.

Notable about the Minneapolis Symphony's governance during the war was the emergence of female voices on the board of directors. One belonged to Eleanor Bellows Pillsbury, Phil's wife, who advocated for establishing a permanent endowment to better shield the arts organization from occasional emergencies.[61] Her innovative idea would catch on after the war.

Republican John Pillsbury's enthusiastic support for a war effort headed by Democratic president Franklin D. Roosevelt is to his credit. But it also reflects the American people's willingness to put national unity ahead of partisanship in the 1940s—a capacity that eroded substantially in subsequent years. Make no mistake: John Pillsbury was a loyal and active Republican in the run-up to the war. But his involvement in a crucial meeting of influential Republicans supporting an increase in U.S. aid to besieged Great Britain put him at odds with many isolationists in the GOP—including his eldest son.

In early 1940, John and Juty were one of two Minnesota couples that participated in a dinner meeting of national party kingmakers at the home of Ogden Reid, owner of the *New York Herald Tribune*. The other Minnesotans present were John and Elizabeth Cowles, then owners of the *Minneapolis Star Journal*. Also in attendance were both of the leading GOP presidential contenders that year—anti-New Deal crusader Wendell Willkie and Ohio Sen. Robert Taft. So was Robert Kerr, Lord Lothian, ambassador to the United States from Britain as it faced mortal threat from Nazi Germany.[62] The evening unfolded as something of an audition for the two candidates, as Lothian made the case for U.S. intervention in the war in Europe. In response, Willkie sided with Lothian, and evidently passed the group's test. Taft, an outspoken isolationist in 1940, appeared visibly angry, Juty would recall years later. [63] Taft made an excuse and left the party early; Willkie went on to be the nominee; and before the party ended, John Pillsbury bragged to the assembly about the rising star the party had in the young governor of Minnesota, Harold Stassen. It was likely no coincidence that Stassen was soon openly supporting Willkie, and was assigned a prime speaking slot at that year's Republican National Convention.[64]

But the leading politician in Minnesota's Pillsbury family in the 1940s was not John or any of his immediate family. It was Richard Pillsbury Gale—a farmer, investor, art collector, school board member, legislator, and a member of Congress representing Minnesota's Third Congressional District for two terms. The grandson of Gov. John S. Pillsbury, Richard is the only one of the Minnesota Pillsburys whose political ambition took him to Washington D.C. He won election in 1940 after serving a single term in the Minnesota House of Representatives and three terms on the Mound School Board.

At midlife—in a pattern similar to that of his Uncle Alfred—Dick Gale found himself increasingly drawn to public service. His political career likely bloomed late because he was distracted as a young man by his health. At a stage in life when other men establish professions, Dick battled diabetes. For his health's sake, he took up a regimen of outdoor physical exertion that set a pattern that endured even after newly developed insulin finally brought the disease under control in the early 1920s. He found satisfaction in working at the farm that his mother Sadie Pillsbury Gale established west of Lake Minnetonka. Sadie and her husband Edward Gale, a prominent attorney, book collector, and scholar, led increasingly separate lives after their only child was grown. They maintained their elegant house in the Fair Oaks neighborhood, next door to their Pillsbury kin, but Sadie spent the year's warm months at her "summer house" in St. Bonifacius and at the farm she called Upland, near Minnetrista.

This was no hobby farm. It was a productive operation, complete with orchards, gardens and livestock. The farm was served by a year-round caretaker, hired hands as needed, and one outdoor-loving heir to the family fortune.[65] Dick found a calling on the land. After graduating from Yale in 1922, he took classes in agriculture at the University of Minnesota's farm campus in St. Paul,[66] situated on land near the State Fairgrounds that his grandfather had helped the university acquire.[67] With Sadie's backing, he established his own farm, called Wickham, west of Dutch Lake. The place was donated to the public in 1999, and is now known as Gale Woods Farm. Dick became not only a serious student of horticulture but also a prize-winning sheep and thoroughbred horse breeder and an authority on reclaiming eroded land for agricultural use.[68]

Gale and his wife Isabel "Pete" Rising Gale were avid skiers. When the rest of the Pillsbury clan headed to Florida in the winters of the 1930s, Dick and Pete went to Sun Valley, Idaho, or booked passage to Europe to spent upwards of two months skiing the Alps. Their two sons, Richard Pillsbury Gale Jr. and Alfred P. Gale, were left in Grandma Sadie's care. Grandma's chauffeur would drive the boys to Blake School, picking up lads named Dayton, Staples, and Wells along the way.

The family's finances were strictly controlled by Sadie Gale, who exhibited her father's head for business. Even her grandsons' boyhood

The *Minneapolis Tribune* reported in May 1942 that "Rep. Richard P. Gale of Minnesota has solved his gas rationing worries by riding to work each day on a bicycle."

allowances came from Sadie, and were at times delivered to them by her chauffeur. Dick Gale's official Congressional biography[69] lists his occupations prior to election to Congress as "agricultural pursuits and securities." But the congressman's son attests that any securities investing he did while his mother was still alive was done in close consultation with Sadie. Her heirs credit her shrewd money management with the preservation of the Gale family's fortune during the Great Depression.[70]

Dick had only served one term in the state House, representing the farmers and small towns of not-yet-urbanized western Hennepin County, when in 1940 he decided to run for Congress against a one-term incumbent of his own party, John Grant Alexander. Such a move today by a forty-year-old farmer with a skimpy record of prior public service would be met with disapproval. Not so in the 1930s and 1940s, which are remembered today as the state's most politically volatile period.[71] Minnesota then had three major parties, Republican, Democratic, and Farmer-Labor, and control of the Third Congressional District could swing to any one of them. Beginning with Franklin D. Roosevelt's election as president in 1932, the district opted for Farmer-Labor congressmen—Ernest Lundeen in 1932 and 1934 and Henry Teigan in 1936. In 1938, Teigan was bumped by Alexander. He was seven years senior to Dick Gale, a native of New York, and a real estate and insurance broker. Alexander wasn't allied with the more youthful, progressive crowd that was ascendant in the Minnesota Republican Party, led by Stassen, who had taken on the party's establishment to win the governor's office in 1938. Dick and Pete Gale were part of Stassen's faction; Isabel counted the governor as a personal friend.[72] She may have been the most politically active female member of the extended Pillsbury clan in the late 1930s. Gale beat Alexander in the September 10, 1940, primary election, and became the Republican nominee in a three-way race.

Roosevelt carried Minnesota each of the four times he ran for president. But compared with his first two bids, his margins of victory shrank in 1940 and 1944. In 1940, many Minnesotans were cool to FDR's break with precedent in seeking a third term. And anti-war isolationism was prominent in Minnesota. GOP candidates in the state rode both of those anti-Roosevelt sentiments to a sweeping 1940 victory that benefited two Republicans who were not exactly isolationists—Stassen and Gale. Stassen adroitly walked a political tightrope in 1940 where the possibility of American intervention in the war in Europe was concerned. He did not openly declare support for joining the Allied fight against Nazi Germany and its allies, lamenting in his keynote address at the Republican National Convention that the United States was "too woefully weak to give the Allies" meaningful aid. But when he had the chance to appoint a Minnesotan to the U.S. Senate in September 1940, after U.S. Sen. Ernest Lundeen's death in an airplane crash, he spurned several more prominent isolationists in favor of journalist Joseph Ball, a political newcomer and an internationalist.

Gale followed Stassen onto the same tightrope. But as a congressman who had to cast votes on legislation, he had far less room for maneuver and equivocation than Stassen. He eventually alienated both the America First crowd and the Minneapolis Committee to Defend America by Aiding the Allies,[73] the financial backing for which came in part from Alfred Pillsbury and his Gale relatives. In the summer of 1941, its leaders expected Dick to vote for Lend-Lease legislation, authorizing American munitions aid to Britain. He refused. He also demurred when asked to support extending the service time of draftees inducted under the Selective Service Act of 1940. Dick was choosing what then looked to be the politically safe path. He was also, no doubt, voting his convictions. But in doing so he missed a chance to display political courage and exert leadership. When Japan attacked Pearl Harbor, Minnesota's isolationism melted away along with the rest of the nation's.

Gale won another three-way race in 1942, keeping his head down and staying well within the conservative Republican pack.[74] He attracted attention at one point by suggesting that biological warfare could be used against the Germans and Japanese food crops.[75] But in 1944, the political ground shifted in Minnesota. Two of the three major parties merged into a new Democratic-Farmer-Labor Party. The new party did not have a strong candidate against Gale. William Gallagher was sixty-nine years old, a retired city street sweeper, and a former trucker, clerk, journalist, and janitor. His income came from a $25.48/month city pension check and his wife's earnings as a chocolate dipper at the Lydia Darrah Candy Co. But what the DFL lacked in the caliber of its candidate, it made up for with two big advantages: Franklin D. Roosevelt's abiding voter appeal and the DFL's energetic campaign operation. Its state coordinator was a young political dynamo who had helped engineer the merger between the Democratic and Farmer-Labor parties—Hubert H. Humphrey. A year later, he would be elected mayor of Minneapolis, and begin a career in elective office that would lead to the vice presidency of the United States. In 1944, Humphrey proved that he already knew quite a bit about grassroots organizing and getting out the vote.

Gale appeared to have won a third term on election night. As the last few returns flowed in Wednesday morning, the day after the election, his reelection looked secure. But on Thursday, a double-check of the arithmetic in Hennepin County revealed that a ten-thousand-vote tabulating error had been made in Gale's favor. When it was corrected, the vote was 71,279 to 69,167 against him.

In a front-page story on Friday, November 10, the *Minneapolis Tribune* described the turn of events as "one of the most amazing upsets in Minnesota political history." Below the banner headline was a photo of a toothless Gallagher, and quotes from the new congressman-elect voicing amazement at the outcome. He had run for lesser offices in the 1920s and for Congress in 1930, never successfully. Gallagher's win over an incumbent with vastly deeper pock-

Dick Gale, back on the farm he loved in the 1950s.

ets and loftier connections won him national attention, including mentions in *Time* magazine and in the nationally syndicated column written by Drew Pearson. One editorial comment, from the *Belle Plaine (MN) Herald*, evidently struck a chord with Dick's cousin John Pillsbury, who saw to it that it was preserved in Pillsbury corporate files. It said: "Congressman Dick Gale of Minneapolis, popular and wealthy in his own right, heir to the Pillsbury millions, did not squawk when a re-check of the votes in his district showed a ten-thousand-vote error in favor of his opponent. That opponent, Bill Gallagher, old-age pensioner, one-time street-cleaner, had his wife work in a candy factory so that he might raise the money for his congressional filing fee. The wealthy Dick and the humble Bill shook hands in mutual good will. This is America."[76]

Had Dick tried for a comeback in 1946, he might have succeeded. William Gallagher died in office on August 13 of that year, creating a politically accessible open seat. But at the time the Gales were too burdened by family tragedy to resume intense public service. An April 10, 1946 news item from Wilmington, Massachusetts, reported that Richard Pillsbury Gale Jr. was found dead of self-inflicted carbon monoxide poisoning.[77] He was an Army Air Force veteran, a gifted student at Massachusetts Institute of Technology, and only twenty-one years old. He left behind a suicide note that described his "sensations of approaching death." He also left behind a twenty-year-old widow, Morley Cowles Gale, daughter of the owner of the *Minneapolis Star and Minneapolis Tribune*, John Cowles Sr.; and a son, six-month-old Richard Pillsbury Gale III.[78] Meanwhile, the Gales' surviving son, Al, was in his late teens and struggling. His poor performance in school and difficulty reading, despite an obviously quick mind, branded him in the 1940s as lazy and/or rebellious. Today, almost certainly, he would be diagnosed as dyslexic. Al had been kicked out of an elite school in Washington, D.C.. After a period on his own that included working on threshing crews in Nebraska, Montana, and Iowa, and a brief time in jail, he had entered the Merchant Marine. His parents flew to meet him in Portland, Maine, so they could grieve Richard's loss together.

Al Gale went back to farm work after he left the Merchant Marine. He had inherited his dad's love of outdoor labor and growing things. That inspired Richard Gale to buy a section of farmland near Fullerton, North Dakota, and rent it to his son to farm. The arrangement was a godsend for the boy the family called Alfie. His first crop came in 1948; so did his marriage to North Dakota native Leona Rowe, a waitress at a restaurant Al frequented who became a willing, capable helpmate to the hard-working farmer. Their first house had no electricity or indoor plumbing. Leona cooked on a stove fired with wood or propane gas and used a gasoline-powered washing machine to do laundry. But the couple were builders. Within a few years they had purchased the rented land from Al's father, added several additional parcels, and diversified their grain operation to include flax as well as Durum wheat. They also raised two sons, Edward, born in November 1952, and John, in September 1953. When Al sold the farm in 1970, he was a wealthy man in his own right, and in a position to establish a career as a professional investment manager as well as a farmer. Al and Leona moved back to Minnesota, to a thirty-acre parcel of land not far from Wickham Farm.[79] There, they could be of assistance to Dick and Pete as diabetes finally got the better of the man who'd beaten it fifty years before. Dick Gale endured two amputations before he died on December 5, 1973.

George and his parents at a Minneapolis Symphony Orchestra concert, December 1945.

Chapter Eleven

In War's Wake

U.S. Marine radio radar officer George Sturgis Pillsbury was on the opposite side of the world from Minnesota when the Japanese surrendered on August 16, 1945, ending World War II. The epic conflict had deposited the youngest son of John S. and Eleanor Lawler Pillsbury on Zamboango Peninsula, on the western side of Mindanao Island in the southwest corner of the Philippines. He had come through the war physically unharmed and mentally matured by the losses of too many close friends and loved ones. When his replacement arrived and his orders came to return to Hawaii or San Francisco, the colonel of Marine Air Group 12 urged him to stay on with the four-squadron group as its loading officer. The group was slated to go next to China, the colonel said, and with the war over, it would be an opportunity for interesting experiences. But unlike his father forty years earlier, twenty-four-year-old George had had his fill of travel in Asia. He declined. Instead, he took advantage of a good friend's ill-timed trip to Manila to take a priority seat on an overused Marine Corps transport plane on September 20, 1945, and survived an island-hopping, white-knuckle flight to Honolulu.

There, George's good luck held. He turned in his orders on September 29 at the Marine Air Base at Eva, Hawaii, and was told that he should expect a four- to five-week delay in Hawaii before he'd get his transportation to the mainland. He then went to the Officers' Club for something to help him swallow that news, where the friendly, outgoing manner he'd inherited from his father served him well.

He was standing at the bar near a Marine pilot, whom he engaged in conversation. "How are you getting home?" George asked. The answer: "I'm going home tomorrow morning. They've taken all the planes off the *Ticonderoga*, and loaded the hangar deck with cots for returning Marines. It's going to sail tomorrow for San Francisco."

That news registered with George. The giant aircraft carrier *USS Ticonderoga* had left Tokyo Bay on September 20 after two weeks in the defeated nation's capital-city port following the signing of the Japanese surrender, and was en route to Alameda, California, by way of Pearl Harbor. On board, George knew, was Lt. Cmdr. John S. Pillsbury Jr., the big brother he had not seen for more than two years.

George hastened to a phone to call the *Ticonderoga*. The ship's officer of the day took the message—"Brother George is looking for a ride home"—and faithfully delivered it to John when he returned from shore leave that evening. At 11 p.m. an excited John called his youngest brother and offered him a ride to the States, with sleeping space on a cot in his own stateroom. When the *Ticonderoga* set sail the next day, the Pillsbury brothers were both on board. John's wife Kitty, who had given birth to her youngest child only a month earlier, was at the Alameda, California, dock on October 5 to meet her husband and brother-in-law. George quickly headed for a phone, hoping to surprise his parents with the news that he and John were together and stateside. But word had leaked. The October 2 *Minneapolis Star Journal* contained the item: "Two Pillsbury sons meet on ship for home."[1] While George detoured to the Marine air base near San Diego to await further orders, John and Kitty headed home.

Their return ushered in a period of reunion and new beginnings for the family. John Jr. returned to an active household, bustling with four children. The family soon felt cramped in their house on Watertown Road, in the then-unincorporated village of Orono, and moved to a larger place on Woodhill Road that had belonged to a cousin of Tom Crosby, sister Ella's husband. John resumed the practice of property and mineral-rights law at Faegre & Benson. The large Minneapolis law firm made him a partner in 1946. (It was sometimes said later that John did not pursue a career in the family business. On the contrary: land management and mining were major Pillsbury business activities throughout the twentieth century.) In true Pillsbury fashion, John Jr. plunged into public service and civic activities. He was among the parents who helped organize the Orono School District in 1949 and was elected to the Orono School Board in 1951.[2] Soon thereafter, he was appointed Orono's city attorney, a part-time position.[3] A number of non-profit organizations and corporations recognized him as an up-and-coming leader, and recruited him as a board member.[4] The local Young Republican League took notice of John and featured him as a speaker at their events[5]—undoubtedly to the delight of his wife Kitty and sister Ella. They were much involved in state and national Women's Republican Workshops,[6] which were part think tank, part social club. When Alfred Pillsbury died in 1950, John Jr. took his place on the board of a small but ambitious local insurance company, Northwestern National Life.[7] For the second time, Alf had passed an important business baton to a grandson of his cousin Charles.

George, too, returned briefly to Minneapolis for a visit with his parents at Southways, after which he continued on the Great Lakes Naval Station just north of Chicago to muster out of the U.S. Marine Corps. That gave him a chance to reconnect with his other surviving brother, Eddy, whose family also included a new baby. Though the war had only ended two months before, Eddy was already back at work for the Pillsbury Co., this time assigned to Chicago and living in Lake Forest. He was quickly caught up in a major new Pillsbury Co. venture: instead of selling only milled grain products, the company also would merchandise grain itself.

Eddy and Priscilla weren't in a position to offer George hospitality for long. The Pillsbury Co. wanted Eddy's grain buying and trading expertise at corporate headquarters in Minneapolis. Before George could receive his discharge, Eddy and Pris packed their belongings and moved into the house John Jr. and Kitty were vacating on Watertown Road. Eddy was still flying, with his own plane now. He offered to teach his younger brother to fly, too. Lessons started that spring after both were in Minnesota again.

George came home from Lake Forest for holiday leave on December 23, 1945. The holiday season that year was one of memorable gaiety, made so by the heightened awareness of life, love, and family that follows a brutal war. Returning servicemen were in great demand socially—no one more than handsome, unattached George Pillsbury. At a cocktail party his first night home he met Sally Lucille Whitney, twenty-one years old and a senior at Smith College. She was introduced to him by a sailing acquaintance, Katherine Winton. Sally was vivacious, smart, beautiful, and fun. Her family had been leading citizens in St. Cloud, Minnesota, for more than a half-century. During the war, her parents, Wheelock Sr. and Katharine Kimball Whitney ("Wheels" and "Kimmie" to their friends) followed the lead of well-to-do Minneapolis residents and made their Lake Minnetonka summer house a year-round residence. Wheelock Whitney Sr. had been a landowner, farmer, and electrical utility owner and executive in St. Cloud; Katharine Kimball came from a prominent family in Portland, Maine. A Pillsbury connection figures in the story of their courtship. Katharine's roommate at Smith College and classmate in the Class of 1920 was Mary Stuart Snyder, half-sister of John Pillsbury Snyder. Katharine met her future husband while visiting Minnesota as a bridesmaid in Mary Stuart's wedding. Katharine and Wheelock were married in January 1922.[8] George didn't know the entire family, but he had met Wheels and his two sons, Wheelock, Jr. and John Kimball, at Woodhill Country Club. That connection made George feel as if he already knew Sally when they first met. He was glad to see more of her several times during her holiday break.

George had to return to the Great Lakes Naval Station for several more weeks in 1946 before being officially discharged from active duty. A few weeks after he was granted terminal leave (he would remain in the Marine reserve corps until 1948) he headed to Florida to visit his parents. There, on spring break from classes at Smith, was Sally Whitney. They were together at a dinner-and-dancing evening thanks to mutual friends. George had another date that night, but he danced often enough with Sally to irritate his date and went home thinking about how lovely she looked in her white evening dress.

The demands of launching a career for George and completing college for Sally kept them on separate tracks that spring. For George, joining the Pillsbury Co. had not been automatic. His cousin Phil, who as CEO was keen to quickly expand the company's consumer line after the war, made clear that the Yale mathematics major could count on a substantive assignment after completing a management training program. But as George watched his brother John's career unfold, he also considered going to law school. And his grades had

been good at Yale, so good that the head of the math department encouraged him to return as a graduate student, and work toward a Ph.D. while teaching undergraduates. It was a flattering offer, and a tempting one.

Sally Lu Whitney, 1943.

At one point during his weeks of indecision, George was invited to the Lake Minnetonka home of James Ford Bell, his father's boyhood chum and college fraternity brother. The boy who once raced twins John and Charlie Pillsbury on the first bicycles in town had grown up to be head of General Mills, taking the spot that had been occupied by his father, James S. Bell, when the firm was known as Washburn-Crosby Co. The families remained good friends; James Ford Bell's son Ford Bell was a lifelong pal and fishing buddy of Philip W. Pillsbury. George was pleased to be invited to Belford, the Bells' lakeside mansion home, for a welcome-home drink. But he was taken aback when Bell asked whether he would consider going to work for General Mills. He could learn the milling and food processing business there, and transfer to the Pillsbury Co. later if he wanted to do so, Bell said.

"That's a wonderful offer, and thank you very much," George said. "But if I'm going into the milling business, I think I'd just as soon work for cousin Phil at Pillsbury."

Bell chuckled. "I thought that's what you'd say. But when I was your age, your grandfather offered me a job. I thought I should return the favor."

Bell's offer helped clarify George's thinking. He realized that he cared a good deal about the enterprise his father, grandfather, and other kinsmen had built, and that he wanted to be a part of making it survive and prosper. He was also inspired by the possibility of working alongside Eddy. The competent, disciplined athlete with whom younger boys always wanted to sail had become a capable, focused businessman who fired the confidence of a younger brother. Eddy had his mother's way of making people around him feel that he had everything under control. George thought that together, he and Eddy could do great things. On April 1, 1946, George became an employee of the Pillsbury Co.

Sally graduated in June, and made plans to take a job in New York in the fall with the new public opinion polling organization being founded by Elmo Roper. As a high school student at the Madeira School for girls in McLean, Va., near Washington D.C., she had become very interested in politics and the federal government. Madeira's founder was a personal friend of First Lady Eleanor Roosevelt, a connection that occasionally afforded Madeira students a close-up view of history. They had VIP seats at presidential inaugural parades, invitations to political events, and one-day-per-week internships in congressional, cabinet, and civic offices. (While a senior at Madeira, Sally was invited to lunch at the home of her congressman, Pillsbury cousin Richard Gale, on a Sunday—December 7, 1941. No radio was on during lunch. Their first inkling that the world had forever changed came when Isabel "Pete" Gale drove Sally back to school past the Japanese embassy, and they saw embassy employees outside, burning papers.) Sally's major at Smith was government, and included study of the burgeoning science of opinion polling.[9] That field would make for an interesting career, she decided. She arranged a job interview in New York in the fall, affording herself time for a summer vacation visiting family in Minnesota and friends in Michigan.

Not long after returning to Minnesota from Smith, she called George with an invitation. A cocktail party was planned to help a sister of a Smith College friend become acquainted in Minnesota. Could he come? Yes, he said, but he would have to leave early.

He had already become involved in the new American Veterans Committee, a liberal alternative to the conservative American Legion, and its monthly meeting was planned at 8 p.m. in the chambers of Minneapolis Mayor Hubert Humphrey. The event was conducted by Orville Freeman, a wounded and decorated veteran who was helping Humphrey build the Democratic-Farmer-Labor Party. Freeman would go on to election as governor of Minnesota in 1954. George was a born-and-bred Republican, but he found the meeting interesting. The fact that his pretty blonde date opted to join him at the meeting, being just as interested in the proceedings as he was, captivated him even more. "I think I was the first girl he ever took out who was interested in politics," Sally would recall. The two of them went from that event to the Curtis Hotel for drinks, then to the porch of the friend's house where Sally was staying. They talked long into the night, and parted only when a neighbor appeared in nightclothes and pointedly informed Sally that a key to the house could be found under the mat.

The next day, Sally left for ten days at Michillinda Lodge near Whitehall, Michigan, and George suffered. He couldn't wait for her return. He wrote her a letter saying so. The day of her return was also her brother Wheelock's birthday. George connived to be invited to a siblings' dinner celebrating the occasion by arranging a golf date before dinner with her younger brother Kim. After dinner, they wound up at the Lake Minnetonka home of businessman Sumner McKnight—Ella Pillsbury Crosby's uncle-in-law—where Ossie Dyle, a popular pianist from the Minneapolis restaurant Charlie's, was performing at a party. George found a pretext to take Sally outside and tell her how much he had missed her. But he didn't stop there. Impulsively, he proposed marriage. Perhaps just as impulsively, she accepted.

George went to his father's office the next morning to announce his engagement. To George's surprise, John Sr. responded by asking his secretary, Mrs. Nelson, to get Sally Lu Whitney on the phone. "Didn't I tell you, Sally?" he said, as his incredulous son stood by. Unbeknownst to George, John Sr. was already well acquainted with his fiancé. She had been a lifeguard at the Woodhill Country Club pool the summer before, and had struck up a friendship with the chatty gentleman whose habit was to enjoy a cold drink by the pool after a round of golf. He told her more than once during that summer of 1945 that he hoped she would stay single. "Remember, there are a lot of fine young men still overseas," he would tell her. For the rest of his days, John Sr. claimed that he had saved Sally for George.

Wheelock Sr. and Sally's brothers were supportive of the engagement. But Mrs. Whitney sputtered, "Don't be ridiculous! You don't even know each other!" Before long, she would become one of George's devoted fans. Juty was also initially cool to her youngest son's abrupt decision. She said, "George, you always promised me before you would get engaged you'd invite the girl to come and stay with us."

He said, "Mother, she lives just a couple of miles down the road. You had dinner with her parents last night."

Her stumped rejoinder: "I don't care."

The sudden engagement was the start of a loving lifelong partnership. George and Sally were married at Wayzata Community Church on January 4, 1947. They honeymooned in Jamaica.[10] George gave up learning to fly. Spending time with Sally was more fun than chasing clouds. Sally finally got to New York in a roundabout way, later than she'd planned. During the summer of 1947, when Sally was expecting their first child, George was put in charge of European export sales in the Minneapolis office. It took the company only a few weeks to determine two things: one, George was very able, and should be given more responsibility; and two, European exports and sales to governments would be more effective if they were consolidated in the New York office. Shortly before their baby's due date, George had the unenviable task of calling his wife and informing her that they would be moving to New York City. Sally conveyed her enthusiasm, or lack thereof, quite effectively: She hung up on him.

Charles Alfred Pillsbury, the namesake of both his great-grandfather and his late uncle, arrived on October 5 in Minneapolis.[11] By Thanksgiving, he and his parents were residents of New York City, at Fifth Avenue and Sixtieth Street. (Charlie was the second grandson of

John and Juty Pillsbury born after Chuck's death to be named in his honor. Charles Pillsbury Resor, Jane and Stanley Resor's second son, had been born January 19, 1947. Eighteen years later, at Yale, Chuck Resor's roommate would be Charlie Pillsbury's best boyhood friend, Mark Dayton, a future U.S. senator, Minnesota governor, and the son of Alfred Pillsbury's art-collecting protégé Bruce Dayton.)

After the war, European governments, still struggling to regain a solid economic footing, were large purchasers of American flour, and George was assigned to sell Pillsbury flour and other products to them. But by 1948, George's work stalled as European recovery quickened and European farms became productive again. He could see that a more profitable export business could be found in developing nations in Latin America, the Caribbean, and the west coast of Africa,[12] but he had difficulty persuading his manager to move more aggressively into those markets. In his frustration, he considered leaving the company and enrolling at the University of Minnesota Law School. He went so far as to inquire of the school's Dean, Maynard Pirsig, about enrolling in classes that fall. Government service also continued to appeal to him. He said as much to his superior on a weekend visit to corporate headquarters in Minneapolis in August 1948. When their conversation resumed on Monday morning, his boss and his cousin Phil had a question: "Would you stay if we put you in charge of the New York export office?"

The answer was yes. Both George and Sally were beginning to enjoy their lives in New York. They had moved to a fashionable Manhattan apartment at Eighty-fourth Street and Park Avenue. There, they became well acquainted with neighbors including Dr. and Mrs. Howard Dean, whose son Howard Jr. would run for president in 2004. Sally volunteered her services in the Eastern states' office of former Minnesota Gov. Harold Stassen, who was running for the Republican nomination for president in 1948. Proximity to Philadelphia made it easy for Sally and her volunteering friend, Ginny Welch, to attend the Republican National Convention in June, and get close to the action as volunteer go-fers for the Stassen campaign. Stassen was a serious contender that year. But two years in the Navy on the staff of Admiral William "Bull" Halsey, and another year on

Sally with former Minnesota Governor Harold Stassen at the New York City Stassen for President headquarters, 1948.

the commission that drafted the United Nations Charter, had cost Stassen critical exposure in national Republican circles. His service to his country ceded the 1948 advantage to New York Gov. Thomas Dewey (who went on to lose the election to Harry Truman.) But Pillsbury loyalty to Minnesota's "boy governor" did not waver. Stassen's national campaign headquarters in 1948 was housed on the tenth floor of the Pillsbury Building in downtown Minneapolis, in what was likely donated space.[13] George and Sally were among the disappointed Minnesotans on hand on June 24 when Stassen came in third at the convention, behind both Dewey and arch–conservative Ohio Sen. Robert Taft.

The young couple from Minnesota were not without friends and family in New York. Jane and Stanley Resor lived nearby in Connecticut. As the youngest children in a family of six, Jane and George had been childhood playmates and teenaged allies and teammates in a family that relished competition in sailing, tennis, horseback riding, and more. Their bond was renewed and intensified while George and Sally lived in New York, as the siblings' spouses were integrated into their relationship and the couples shared the joys and rigors of becoming parents. Stan and Jane would eventually have the largest household among their generation of prolific Pillsburys. Seven sons would be born to them between 1944 and 1960.

With the examples of a long line of Pillsbury women inspiring them, sisters-in-law Jane and Sally looked for a charitable cause in New York to make their own as volunteers and financial patrons. They gravitated to the "mothers' health center" at Union Settlement House, operated by an organization better known as Planned Parenthood. Often with their own children in tow, they became volunteer family planning counselors to the poor women served by the settlement house, many of them Puerto Rican immigrants. Sally heard stories there of women dying, or nearly so, in childbirth, and of children being raised in such poor conditions that they would sicken and die. She learned of back-alley abortions that left women disabled or dead. Those sad stories planted a political seed in George and Sally that would bear fruit decades later. When New York Planned Parenthood went looking for prominent younger mothers to add to its board of directors, Sally and Jane accepted their invitation, and became committed to the cause of readily available contraception for all.

George and Sally came under the expansive social wings of Mary Pillsbury Lord, Phil Pillsbury's sister and George's first cousin. The eldest of Phil's three sisters, all three Phi Beta Kappa graduates of Smith College, Mary was also the most ambitious and accomplished. She was the first woman in the Minnesota Pillsbury family to stake out a career of her own, in social work. After two years as a family welfare worker in Minneapolis, she married Oswald Bates Lord, scion of a textile manufacturer, on December 7, 1929,[14] and moved to New York. There, she gave birth to two sons, Charles Pillsbury on September 28, 1933, and Winston, on August 14, 1937. A third son, Richard, lived only three months in 1935. But motherhood didn't slow Mary down. After several years of volunteer social work with charitable organizations, she became vice president and development director of the East Side Settlement House. Fundraising for that sizeable social service agency brought her into contact with the city's political and financial elite. In 1939, Mayor Fiorello LaGuardia appointed her to chair the Citizens Committee of the city's Department of Health, and, a few months later, to the board of directors of the New York World's Fair. She headed that board's National Advisory Committee on Women's Participation.

Her conscientious, competent performance in that visible role for a major civic event opened more doors. During the war, she was appointed assistant director of civilian defense for the New York region. In 1944 she became national chairman of the civilian advisory committee for the Women's Army Corps—a position that included travel throughout the country promoting military service for women. In that same year, she chaired the women's activities committee of the National War Fund.

By the time George and Sally settled into New York living, Mary Lord was chairman of the U.S. Committee on the International Children's Emergency Fund, precursor of the organization now known the world over as UNICEF. Her leadership range had expanded from local to national to international, which meant that cocktail and dinner parties at her elegant apartment were populated by a fascinating

array of people. Mary liked flattering her prominent guests with invitations to what she billed as cozy "family parties." Including George and Sally as guests helped pull off the family theme, as did her husband Oz's willingness to play bartender. That way, he always said, he was able to speak to every guest.

True to family form, Mary was an active Republican. But unlike many of the Minnesota Pillsburys, her choice for president in 1952 was not Harold Stassen. It was

Mary Pillsbury Lord.

Dwight D. Eisenhower. Mary Lord served Ike's campaign as national co-chairman. Her leadership of that successful campaign put her in position for a major presidential appointment, and the retirement of Eleanor Roosevelt from the United Nations Human Rights Commission in 1953 created the perfect opening. Mary Lord succeeded the former First Lady as U.S. representative on the commission, a position that also made her an alternate representative for the United States at the U.N. General Assembly. She would serve as a U.S. delegate to the General Assembly at the end of Eisenhower's second term as president, 1958-60.

In her devotion to Eisenhower, Mary had an ally in the family. Sally Pillsbury, too, liked Ike—so much so that she wound up serving as his campaign's hotel receptionist at the 1952 Republican National Convention in Chicago. That assignment landed her an invitation to a private late-night gathering after Ike's nomination acceptance speech for her in-laws, her husband, and herself with Ike and Mamie Eisenhower and the Eisenhower brothers. Sally was by then the mother of three children. Firstborn Charlie was joined by George Sturgis Jr. on June 21, 1949, and Sarah Kimball, on February 20, 1951. But motherhood did not diminish Sally's enthusiasm for Republican politics.

By then, too, Sally was again a Minnesotan. Tragedy had brought George and Sally home. For the second time, George lost a brother to an airplane crash.

Edmund Pillsbury had risen early on February 22, 1951, to prepare his single-engine, 185-horsepower Ryan Navion plane for a trip to Aspen, Colorado, for a weekend of skiing with old friends. He went through a routine that he knew well after fifteen years as a pilot. The small plane was perched on the ice near the Brackett's Point shore. An "airstrip" had been plowed on the frozen lake for the Pillsbury pilot's use. It stood close to Leeward Landing, the new house Eddy and Priscilla had built adjacent to Southways on property that had once belonged to Priscilla's Howe grandparents.

The day was well suited to flying, and the plane took off without incident heading west. But conditions worsened over Nebraska, and the plane was soon combating weather of the worst kind for small aircraft—freezing rain and sleet. Precipitation that appeared to be liquid to the pilot was producing a dangerous layer of ice on the plane's wings. About thirty miles from the Nebraska-Colorado border, the rain turned to driving sleet and snow, and Eddy knew his plane was in trouble. He circled, looking for a small landing strip. He may have thought he'd found it when he spotted a wheat field on the north bank of the South Platte River. In fact, the landing strip was two miles away. He lowered his landing gear, and, struggling to maintain control and to see what lie ahead, he headed down into a raging snowstorm.

Eddy's emergency landing might have succeeded had the field not included one large willow tree. He couldn't avoid it. When the plane hit that tree, the fuselage telescoped and flipped over. The plane's engine was ejected, and wound up fifteen feet away.

Eddie had not been alone. Joining him that morning were Dexter L. Andrews, 38, a college chum from Yale who was now a director of Earl Partridge Co., one of the city's oldest mercantile firms; and Alfred Lindley, 47, an attorney, athlete, former state legislator, and unsuccessful 1950 Republican candidate for Congress. A weekend away from their families skiing with the guys (all three had young children) would be fun for Eddy and Dexter.

For Al, skiing meant more. He had been a member of the 1936 U.S. Olympics ski team. (It was his second Olympic appearance. He'd also been to the games in 1924, as a member of Yale's crew team.) His wife, Grace

Edmund Pillsbury.

Carter Lindley, had also been a champion skier from 1935 until she retired from the sport in about 1950, and had herself been a 1936 Olympian.[15] At the time Lindley was chairman of the U.S. Olympic ski committee, and his plan was to ski and relax with his buddies for a few days in Aspen, then head to Sun Valley, Idaho, for the 1952 Olympic ski team selections.[16] Of the three men making the trip that day, Lindley was the best-known and most influential. He was credited with helping launch Harold Stassen's state political career in

1938, and remained the presidential contender's financial patron and personal friend.[17]

It was later determined that when the plane crashed that dismal morning, Andrews and Lindley died on impact, still strapped to their seats. Eddy died three hours after the crash at a hospital in Sutherland, Nebraska.[18]

It was late afternoon in New York City when a call came for George and Sally at New York Hospital. There, two days earlier, baby Sarah had arrived. The happy father was visiting his wife and daughter and had just been reflecting about how sweet life can be when he was summoned to the telephone and told of Eddy's fate. As had happened so often for the Pillsburys of Minnesota, sorrow had come hard on the heels of joy.

Minnesota Gov. Luther Youngdahl later issued a statement reading, in part: "These were three of our most able and devoted civic leaders who, despite their youth, had already achieved long and distinguished records of unselfish service to Minneapolis, the state and the nation. We shall sadly miss them in the days ahead."[19]

George and Sally always expected that at some point they would move back to Minneapolis, though they weren't of a mind to do so anytime soon. But when Eddy died, they soon recognized that they were needed at home. George was acutely aware of his parents' heartache as they lay their son to rest, and with Eddy gone, it was likely that his wife Priscilla and three young children would leave the state, depriving John and Juty of their dream of watching Eddy's children grow up. (By 1953 Priscilla and the children were living in San Francisco.)[20] George realized that he could ease his parents' pain by moving home. A large, somewhat suitable house was ready for his family to own and occupy: Alfred Pillsbury had bequeathed his mansion near the Minneapolis Institute of Arts to "any adult male Pillsbury who would live in it." It was more of an empty art gallery than a family home. No child had ever inhabited it. But it had been vacant since Alf's death in 1950 and was George's for the asking. With toys, trikes, and diapers in tow, George and Sally moved into Alf's mansion in the fall of 1951. It must have been jarring to the neighbors to witness their first modification to the place: they fenced the backyard and installed playground equipment.

A year later George joined the board of the Minneapolis Society of Fine Arts—a move Alf would have applauded. But Alf may not have been as understanding of George and Sally's move in mid-1953. With mixed feelings, they put 116 East Twenty-second Street on the market. A Lake Minnetonka house better suited to a growing family was available, and the lady of the house next door begged them to claim it. At Juty Pillsbury's urging, George and Sally bought Eddy and Priscilla's house, Leeward Landing, on Brackett's Point. A two-story contemporary house with a walk-

Sally with baby Sarah, Charlie and George Jr. in the backyard of the Minneapolis mansion Alf Pillsbury built, 1951.

out basement that fanned open toward the lake, it reflected the shift toward informality and family-centered living among affluent Americans that followed World War II. Though it lacked live-in servants' quarters, it was probably a pleasant change from the more formal arrangements of the house on East Twenty-second Street. It was to Leeward Landing that they brought home their fourth and final child, Katharine Whitney, born November 11, 1956. John Jr. and Kitty Pillsbury would eventually join the clan, too, in a stylish new home next door to George and Sally's house. Brackett's Point had become "Pillsbury Point" in the minds of their neighbors.

Eddy's death created a management void at the Pillsbury Co. He was a leading vice president and a possible future CEO. The grain merchandising division he pioneered for the company produced 18 percent of Pillsbury's total profits the year Eddy died.[21] As corporate assignments were shuffled in the spring and summer of 1951 to compensate for Eddy's absence, a new post opened for George. He moved into the bakery sales division, selling flours and mixes to commercial clients and trying to breathe new life into a division that had been a chronic underperformer for the company.[22]

The rest of Pillsbury Co. was experiencing a growth spurt in the 1950s, as the nation settled down to raise the generation that came to be known as the Baby Boomers. Phil Pillsbury was making good on his intentions to modernize the business that bore his family's name, even as he diversified both its product line and its ownership. Pillsbury was the country's leading flour exporter[23]—a matter in which George, as head of exports, could take personal pride. But the company had also moved aggressively after the war to develop new consumer products. A biscuit mix in December 1945 and a pie crust mix in February 1946 were the first boxed baking mixes bearing the round barrelhead Pillsbury logo to land in grocery stores. They were soon followed by cake mixes (Pillsbury beat the competition with the first chocolate cake mix) and hot roll mix.

A major acquisition was in the works in early 1951 that would bring Pillsbury a new line of products that would prove as important to its modern reputation as Pillsbury's Best flour. Purchase negotiations began shortly before Eddy died with the Ballard & Ballard Co. of Louisville, Kentucky, the largest flour miller of the South. It was headed by two grandsons of the company's founder, Thruston B. and Rogers C. B. Morton. Like the Pillsburys, both Mortons were Yale men, and both would go on to prominence in national Republican politics. Ballard's product lines were akin to Pillsburys, except for one consumer item that Phil Pillsbury coveted—refrigerated, ready-to-bake biscuit dough. That product was assigned to Pillsbury's new OvenReady Biscuit division with instructions: Develop more like this. Within a year, Pillsbury's grocery product sales were taxing its production capacity, and the company expanded again, buying the baking mix division of the American Home Products Corp.[24]

Like his grandfather, Phil Pillsbury had a knack for marketing. He and his advertising staff had a stroke of genius in 1949, the company's eightieth anniversary year, when they decided to conduct a baking

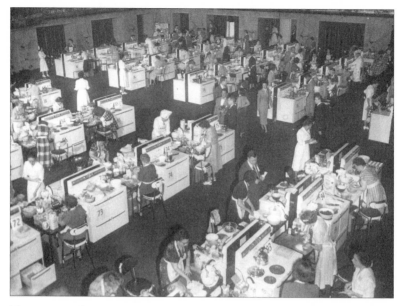

The scene at the Waldorf Astoria ballroom during the first Pillsbury Bake-Off, 1949.

The first Bake-Off: With featured celebrity Eleanor Roosevelt are Phil Pillsbury, Art Linkletter and prizewinner Mrs. Ralph A. Smafield of Detroit, Michigan, whose $50,000 prizewinning recipe was for "water-rising nut twists."

contest to find recipes made with Pillsbury's Best Flour that were good enough to distribute inside flour packages. Not only would this enhance the value of the product itself; it would also heighten interest in the product among the home bakers concocting the recipes. The firm invited homemakers to submit their recipes, and promised that the authors of the 100 best would be invited to New York City to bake their recipes for final judging. The grand prize was $25,000—an eye-popping sum in 1949. The response was huge, and the judging event that the company arranged was spectacular. The first Pillsbury "Grand National Baking Contest" was at the Waldorf Astoria Hotel, and attracted national press attention. Reporters kept calling the contest a "bake-off," and the name stuck.[25]

The first Pillsbury Bake-Off featured as its celebrity presenter of prizes a woman known the world over, former First Lady Eleanor Roosevelt, alongside celebrity master of ceremonies Art Linkletter. Also on hand at the first Bake-Off were the Pillsburys of New York— the Lords, the Resors, and George and Sally. George and Sally would become mainstays at Bake-Offs through the years, helping as assistant hosts in a variety of capacities. A 1961 Bake-Off observer[26] described Sally as "a movable and typically vivacious information center." Their warmth and friendliness created a lasting impression. When Ronald Reagan was in the White House three decades after his Bake-Off emcee stint, Minnesotan Jerry Olson of the Pillsbury Co. had occasion to be in a presidential receiving line with scores of people from around the country. When Reagan heard that Olson was with Pillsbury, the president reportedly brightened. "Oh! Then you must know George and Sally!" he said. It was, one commentator said, a level of presidential recognition not attained by some Reagan cabinet members.[27] George and Sally were still attending Bake-Offs in 2008.

Eleanor Roosevelt was a tough first act to follow. But when Pillsbury Bake-Off planners cast about for a female headliner for their second event, their short list included Wallis, Duchess of Windsor, then living at the Waldorf Towers in New York. An invitation was sent from the company, offering $2,000 for her favorite charity if she would do the honors. Her response was that while she could not make any commercial commitment nor accept money, even for

The Duke and Duchess of Windsor with Mrs. William E. Brebner of Des Moines, Iowa at the 1950 Bake-Off.

charity, "she would be glad to do a favor if a personal note came from Mrs. Pillsbury." Juty sent off the invitation and received an affirmative reply almost immediately.[28] And so the 1950 Bake-Off was hosted by none other than the Duchess of Windsor, accompanied by her Duke, the man who was briefly Britain's King Edward VIII.

Juty Pillsbury had become acquainted with the famous couple during World War II, when the Windsors were serving a stint as governor of the Bahamas, then a British colony. They were traveling to their ranch in Canada, and made a layover of several hours in the Twin Cities. Gov. Harold Stassen was asked to entertain them. He put the arm on Thomas Daniels of St. Paul, president of the Archer Daniels Midland agricultural processing company his father had founded, to assemble a hasty dinner party. John and Juty Pillsbury responded to Daniels' urgent call to come to St. Paul to meet the Windsors.

Juty was seated at the Duke's table. She came to his particular notice when a state senator whom she described as "radical," seated next to her, suddenly slapped her knee and loudly announced, "Gol darn it, I like you plutocrats!" The Duke caught Juty's appalled expression, and shot her a sympathetic and amused glance. When they found themselves together a few months later at a Marjorie Post dinner party in Palm Beach, he asked that she be seated next to him so they could reminisce and laugh about that moment. A few years later, when Juty was vice chairman of Palm Beach's annual charity ball, the Duchess was an active member of her committee.

The Duchess's presence gave the Bake-Off a much higher profile than it would have had without her, and opened the door for future big-name participation including First Ladies Pat Nixon and Mamie Eisenhower, Broadway grande dame Helen Hayes, Hollywood's regal Greer Garson, and future President Ronald Reagan.

As Phil spurred Pillsbury's rapid post-war growth, he also took care not to repeat the mistake that the company had made twice before. He made certain that the next leadership transition would be smooth and carefully orchestrated. Eddy's death likely strengthened Phil's resolve to make his exit from the CEO's office a planned one. After Eddy died, John Pillsbury expressed his desire to shed the remainder of his corporate responsibilities. That opened the way for the orderly change Phil had in mind. Phil moved from president to chairman of the company on May 31, 1952, soon after his forty-ninth birthday. John S. Pillsbury Sr., age seventy-three, took the title "honorary chairman." He continued to come to Pillsbury headquarters nearly every workday he spent in Minneapolis, almost until his death, but he no longer had corporate duties. In Phil's place as CEO would be Paul Gerot, the grocery products division manager whom he had installed as executive vice president and heir apparent one year before. (Gerot had been Phil's hand-picked successor in the company's Chicago office in the late 1930s.)

The transition allowed the business press to take note of the changes at Pillsbury Co. on Phil's watch. Sales had grown from $47 million in the fiscal year that ended in May 1940 to more than $225 million in fiscal 1951.[29] The *New York Times* reported, "From a flour miller with a small line of feed by-products, he has lifted the company back to its former high place in the industry."[30]

If Eddy Pillsbury had lived, would he, rather than Gerot, have succeeded Phil? Perhaps. Phil valued family involvement in the company. "There's more of a soul to the company when there's a family tinge to it," he told an interviewer that year, then added sentiments that his great-grandfather would have applauded: "Of course, [family control of the company] also implies a greater responsibility toward the public. I fully share the view that business has a responsibility to make the United States a better place to live."[31] But Eddy's wartime work as a military flight instructor took him away from the company for three important years. Eddy likely would not have been deemed ready yet for top corporate leadership in 1952. And the family's claim to leadership in the company had diminished along with its much-diluted ownership stake. Phil's growth push had required capital infusions to finance acquisitions, leaving the company's ownership widely dispersed. Only about 6 percent of the company's stock remained in Pillsbury family hands in 1952.[32]

Phil had also instituted anti-nepotism personnel policies that made it less likely that future generations of Pillsburys would ease their way into the corporate hierarchy. Immediate family members of top-level officers were not to be hired as employees, at least not right after college. They were to "go out and make their own way, and then come back and see us if still interested," Phil said.[33] That policy kept his own two sons, Phil Jr. and Henry, from following him into the company. They made their careers abroad, Phil Jr. as a foreign service officer for the United States Information Agency, Henry as executive director of the American Center in Paris for thirty-five years.[34] Only two Pillsburys, George and John Pillsbury Snyder Jr., great-grandson of Gov. John S. Pillsbury, were among the company's 8,000 employees when Phil became chairman, and were performing well as junior managers. Still, it must have occurred to Phil as he moved out of the CEO's office that he might be the last Pillsbury to occupy it. It would have been a prescient premonition.

As chairman, Phil continued to play one of the business roles he'd relished as CEO—that of worldwide corporate ambassador. He had inherited his parents' love of travel, and looked for chances to turn every trip into a goodwill tour for the Pillsbury Co.[35] He and Eleanor established a pattern of about four overseas trips a year, reinforced by their sons' study and subsequent careers abroad. His travel routine included packing in plastic bags a week's supply of fresh carnations from the greenhouse maintained at his Ferndale Road estate. Like his father, father-in-law, and uncle John before him (and at Eleanor's urging), Phil made wearing a fresh flower boutonniere a personal trademark. When he arrived at a new location, scoping out the availability of flowers for his buttonhole was a pleasant chore.[36] (If families can be identified with flowers, the Pillsbury flower would be the carnation. They were a staple in the Southways greenhouse, providing John Sr. with his favored red boutonnieres, durable bouquets for household displays, and a ready supply of gifts.[37])

Phil also held true to the Pillsbury pattern in his civic activities. In keeping with his professional interests, he served on the advisory boards of the University of Minnesota's College of Agriculture and its Industrial Relations School. For several decades, he helped lead Family and Children's Service of Minneapolis, spending two years as its president.[38] He was also on the governing boards of Hotchkiss School, where his two sons were enrolled in 1951-52; the Minneapolis Institute of Art (that was Alf Pillsbury's influence); and the Metropolitan Opera Association, in addition to another family favorite, the Minneapolis Symphony Orchestra. His corporate board memberships included First National Bank, the Milwaukee Railroad, and Wayne Knitting Mills.[39] He was a director of the National Audubon Society, a board member of the Child Welfare League of America, and a member of the advisory committee of the Import-Export Bank. In 1960, he was chosen national chairman of the Yale University Alumni Board; in 1966, he was named honorary French consul for Minnesota, a post he would hold for the rest of his life.[40]

Phil may have been the Pillsbury most attached to the milling business. He never evinced any temptation to run for political office, but as a sought-after public speaker and author of articles about current affairs, Phil's love for the American system shone through. "Every individual and every country must approach the frailties of life with their own experience and knowledge based on truth," he wrote in 1959. "We in the free world do not have all the answers nor all the

Eleanor Bellows Pillsbury, in the station wagon, was chair of volunteer services of the Hennepin County Red Cross in 1948. With her are Mrs. Abbott Washburn, left, and Mrs. Joseph E. Clifford, vice chairmen. The newspaper caption says they are "busy with plans for reorganization of the volunteer services for peacetime activity."

truth, but we have the capacity to search for more of the truth and, with its use, to make our good life available to more people."[41]

Phil considered Eleanor Bellows Pillsbury his best personal and professional asset. She filled the business helpmate role with flair, playing hostess, functioning as what she once called the "den mother" for Bake-Off contestants,[42] taking her turn at public speaking, and keeping her husband informed behind the scenes.[43] She endeared herself to Bake-Off contestants, and secured her place in contest lore by sharing her clothes with a woman whose luggage did not arrive with her.[44] But Eleanor was much more than a corporate wife. Almost immediately after the young couple moved home again from Chicago in the late 1930s, she plunged into substantive volunteer work. Her focus was public health. During World War II, she headed the nutrition council of the Minneapolis division of the American Red Cross. Her work developing a cadre of volunteer "nutrition aides" to help citizens cope with wartime shortages of foodstuffs won national attention.[45] Her speeches to civic groups while wearing her Red Cross uniform brought her a local identity apart from being the wife of a leading local industrialist. She gave the first-ever commencement address for technicians trained at the Sister Kenny Institute in 1946,[46] and was an organizer and trainer of Red Cross "gray ladies," who led recreational activities at the Veterans Hospital in the years after the war.[47] Eleanor was a person of substance and commitment to public service, much in keeping with the Pillsbury tradition into which she had married. But she lived and worked at a time when women's civic contributions were not properly appreciated. She got more ink in the local press for being named one of the nation's "best-dressed women" by *Life* magazine in 1948 than for any of her Red Cross work during the war.[48]

By the 1950s, Eleanor was a national and global leader in her own right, heading an organization that was gaining prominence and generating controversy around the world—Planned Parenthood. In 1939, when Planned Parenthood was called the Birth Control Federation of America, Eleanor, a young mother still in her twenties with two preschool sons, joined its board of directors. She brought the Pillsbury name to a board already populated with notables from American industry and finance—DuPont, Vanderbilt, Scribner, Lamont, Baruch.

What initially attracted her to an organization devoted to better control of human reproduction is a matter for speculation. The birth control movement's most vocal exponent, Margaret Sanger, carried a message about female self-determination that resonated well among the affluent, independent-minded young women of Smith College, where young Eleanor Bellows studied in 1930 and 1931. Eleanor's mother's maiden name was Mary Sanger. She was no known relation to German immigrant William Sanger, Margaret's husband from 1902 until 1913, but the common surname was a coincidence that undoubtedly created a quick connection between the two women. Admiration for Sanger's feminist message could have been what drew Eleanor to her work. But birth control was also a population control movement, and that cause struck a chord with a family in an international food business, conscious of malnutrition around the world. Phil Pillsbury said years later that "the biggest world problem facing us is too many people and not enough food."[49] As a volunteer in Chicago settlement houses as a young bride during the Great Depression, Eleanor personally witnessed the hardship of women with problem pregnancies and too many children.[50] Planned Parenthood "gets at one of the real roots of many problems,"[51] she told a *Minneapolis Star* reporter.

In 1950, at age thirty-seven, Eleanor became president of Planned Parenthood Federation of America.[52] With that role came the responsibility to travel and speak widely for the cause of planned reproduction. She embraced the work enthusiastically, and in partnership with Margaret Sanger, set her sights on creating a new organization, the International Planned Parenthood Federation. She would become its vice-president. It was launched in 1952—perhaps not coincidentally, the year that Philip Pillsbury left the CEO's office to become Pillsbury's peripatetic chairman. With their sons in boarding school, the couple set off for destinations in Europe, the Middle East, and the Far East to discuss birth control in settings ranging from humble villages to university campuses. Twice, Eleanor met with Mohandas Gandhi to discuss population control in fast-growing India.

Eleanor's efforts won her a major national award in 1952,[53] but they brought her criticism too—not least within the Pillsbury Co. Birth control was far from universally accepted in the United States in the 1950s. The Roman Catholic Church has always considered it contrary to God's law. The more the name Pillsbury was associated with artificial birth control, the more eyebrows were raised within the corporate sales force. They didn't want controversy tainting their brand name. A Houston, Texas, newspaper columnist in 1953 scolded that she was hurting Pillsbury sales, "for it is obvious that the fewer the babies born in the Republic, the fewer sacks of Pillsbury Best will be sold."[54] Instead of being described as a leader of a major national and international non-profit organization, she was routinely disparaged as a "Minneapolis socialite."[55] A Long Island newspaper editor, unwilling to write about her Planned Parenthood message, pressured her instead into demonstrating how to bake a Pillsbury cake mix—something she had never done before.[56] One sales manager told Phil's young cousin George about Eleanor's growing reputation, "Thank God I'm Catholic. I was able to hang onto our Catholic customers here in San Francisco." When the complaints reached the chairman's office, Eleanor "muzzled it a little bit," her son Phil Jr. recalled years later. But her husband, clearly proud of her achievements, never owned up to shushing her. He told a reporter after she died, "She had a way about her. I don't know any Roman Catholic who wasn't perfectly comfortable in talking to Eleanor about family planning."[57]

A few years later, Eleanor trained her public health focus on a local matter. Minneapolis General Hospital was situated in an obsolete, overcrowded, operationally expensive structure in downtown Minneapolis. (It sat on land that was once the farm of George Brackett, the early civic leader who had been an ally of George A. and Charles A. Pillsbury on numerous civic ventures, and whose Lake Minnetonka home preceded the Pillsbury mansions on Brackett's Point.) General Hospital was the area's best provider of emergency care, and served as a safety net for the poor. But it had badly deteriorated. Its future was uncertain in the late 1950s, as its costs and need for replacement outstripped the city's financial capacity.

Phil and Eleanor Pillsbury in 1953.

In 1959, Eleanor the organizer did what was needed: she called a meeting.[58] A luncheon she hosted for fifty downtown business leaders to discuss the problem is credited for launching changes that would move the hospital to Hennepin County control within a few years and lead to its rebuilding and rebranding as Hennepin County Medical Center. She also helped found the General Hospital Service League, a fundraising and volunteer service auxiliary (here, Eleanor's "gray lady" experience came to bear) that would provide decades of assistance to what would be recognized by the 1990s as one of the nation's finest public hospitals. She was president of the Service League in 1969, when county voters finally were asked to approve a bond issue for construction of a new hospital. Wisely, she recognized the need for a first-rate public relations effort to persuade voters, at a time of already high property taxes, to dig deeper for the hospital's sake. She raised (and donated) funds to pay for an outside consultant's report to make the case for a new facility.[59] She went to Paul Gerot at Pillsbury—who as CEO had not continued the Pillsbury tradition of encouraging community service by corporate employees. But when Mrs. Philip Pillsbury was doing the asking, Gerot made an exception to his no-outside-activities-during-workdays rule, and lent young P.R. crackerjack Lou Gelfand to the hospital effort. The referendum was approved by an overwhelming 10-1 margin—and, forty years later, Gelfand would tell readers of the *Minneapolis Star Tribune* that a plaque in honor of Eleanor Bellows Pillsbury belongs in the lobby of Hennepin County Medical Center.[60]

Two years later, on August 27, 1971, Gelfand received a 1 a.m. telephone call. The unidentified but unmistakable voice on the line was Phil Pillsbury's. Eleanor, who had until recently been a cancer patient at Northwestern Hospital, was near death, Phil told him. A lifetime of smoking had taken its toll. Could Gelfand prepare an obituary to be released to the press, right away? Gelfand dressed, went to the office in the middle of the night, and had a news release ready to give to Phil at Pillsbury headquarters at 8 a.m. Phil read it, thanked Gelfand and took it immediately to Eleanor's bedside at their ultra-contemporary, Ralph Rapson-designed home on Ferndale Road. She approved the release that morning, and died that afternoon.[61] She was fifty-eight years old.

Among the tributes that poured in was one by former Minneapolis General Hospital administrator John C. Dumas that put Eleanor's contribution to her community squarely in line with Pillsbury tradition: "She not only talked but lived the issues of maintaining and improving a public general hospital, gave it status and recognition it could never have achieved, regardless of its age or proud tradition," Dumas wrote. "If Hennepin County, with the heritage of individuals like Eleanor Pillsbury, cannot surface public understanding and resolution of difficult problems, who can?"[62]

Chapter Twelve

Community Man

The pace of life in Minnesota and the nation quickened steadily throughout the 1950s, and John Pillsbury Jr. kept up handsomely. With seeming effortlessness and boundless energy, he assumed a variety of civic and social roles similar to those his father and other Pillsbury forebears had occupied before him. As 1956 began, he was a partner at Faegre & Benson, a leading law firm; president of the Orono school board; a trustee of Blake School and Dunwoody Institute; a leader on the founding board of the new Twin City Area Educational Television Corporation (it would mature into Twin Cities Public Television); a member of several financial industry corporate boards; a dominant figure in a host of charitable projects; and an emerging voice in state Republican politics. Already, he was being mentioned as a future Minnesota governor.[1] His wife Kitty was nearly as engaged in community work as he was, and their four children were thriving. John still found time for competitive sailing and ice boating on the lake he considered home.[2] Life was good —and it was about to change.

Trouble was brewing at Northwestern National Life Insurance Company in 1956. The firm, housed in a charming beaux-arts building facing Loring Park, was now more than seventy years old and the city's largest homegrown insurance company. It was well connected to other Minneapolis financial institutions and commercial enterprises, and it had developed a reputation within the community for vigorous corporate citizenship. NWNL was unusual in that it was a hybrid

Kitty and John Pillsbury in 1956.

of two types of insurance companies, those owned by stockholders, hence "stock companies," and those owned by their policy holders, or "mutuals." Both stockholders and policyholders had an owner-ship share of the company, with policyholders' votes accounting for about 70 percent of the total.[3] NWNL had been a steady performer through the years, and by the mid-1950s had policies in force totaling more than $1.5 billion with operations in twenty-eight states and the District of Columbia.[4] A Pillsbury had served on the NWNL board of directors for decades. John Jr. took Alf Pillsbury's seat in 1950, and joined the board's executive committee in 1952.

Only as 1956 unfolded did the board become fully aware that the company's independence was under threat, and the threat had found an ally in NWNL president George W. Wells. Wells was a director of Life Insurance Investors of Chicago, which in turn was associated with two other insurance companies that were eyeing NWNL as an acquisition target. One was Great Southern Life of Houston, Texas. Thanks to Wells, Great Southern had a loyalist on the NWNL board, B.F. Houston of Dallas. Houston was vice president of the firm that was acting as Great Southern's stock purchasing agent, Union Securities Co. The other was Nationwide Corp., a mutual insurance and financial services firm based in Columbus, Ohio, with historic roots in the Ohio Farm Bureau Federation. Its aggressive longtime president, Murray D. Lincoln, had put Nationwide in an expansion mode.[5] Sometime in 1956, Nationwide began buying copious quantities of NWNL stock. It would eventually spend $12 million in the pursuit. Wells was sixty-four years old in 1956 and subject to required retirement at age sixty-five. But, contrary to the NWNL board's wishes that year, he refused to groom a successor.[6] He evidently expected, or even invited, ownership of the company to move into new hands that would agree to prolong his career.

How much the board knew about the takeover attempts on Friday, September 28, is unclear. But on that date, Wells and the board came to a crossroads. The board voted to remove him as president. If testimony offered in a subsequent lawsuit is accurate,[7] he was offered a chance to remain on the board and take the title of chairman. The directors may not have known on that date the extent of his external ties. Wells reportedly asked for the weekend to consider the board's offer. According to John S. Pillsbury III, John Jr.'s eldest son, on Saturday, Wells attempted to remove the names of stockholders and other corporate records from the office.[8] His secretary discovered what Wells was doing and got word to Paul Christopherson, John Pillsbury's law partner at Faegre & Benson and chief legal counsel to the board. Christopherson drove to the Loring Park corporate office, caught Wells in the act, and convinced him to relinquish the records to avoid criminal charges. On Monday, October 1, Wells tendered his resignation.[9] According to company lore, when Wells returned to the office either later that day or one day hence, he discovered that the locks on the door of the president's office had been changed.[10]

John and other local board members were immediately notified that Saturday about Wells's attempted thievery. They decided to meet in emergency session at John and Kitty's house on Woodhill Road. They needed to replace Wells with a competent, loyal, confidence-inspiring CEO as soon as possible. They turned to one of their own. Would John consider leaving his law practice and taking the job? The offer meant a major career change. But John wasted no time agonizing. "It was a 24-hour decision," his son would recall.[11]

At age forty-four, John had grown somewhat disillusioned with the practice of law. He was weary of coming to the legal rescue of clients who refused to take his advice. He told Kitty, "I want to run something, not just tell other people how to run something."

The October 1 corporate news release that revealed the resignation of Wells and his chief lieutenant, first vice president W. R. Jenkins, also announced that John S. Pillsbury Jr. would become president of Northwestern National Life Insurance Company. The release provided a terse explanation: "The resignations followed differences with the board over company policies."[12] Wells would remain a board member, the release said—but not as chairman, as might have been discussed. Leaving him on the board at that juncture likely was an attempt to cover up the severity of the leadership crisis at the company.[13] Less than four months later, Wells resigned from the board and revealed plainly where his loyalties lay. His NWNL stock was sold to Nationwide.[14]

John had only a few weeks to get used to his new office before it became clear that he had a full-blown hostile takeover attempt on his hands, with two aggressive suitors. Minneapolis newspapers revealed for the first time in mid-November that Great Southern Life was seeking to purchase control of NWNL. John issued a statement aimed at soothing NWNL employees and policyholders: "All the energies of our management, sales organization and home office staff will continue to be directed at maintaining the integrity and developing the business of NWNL."[15] To stockholders, who were undoubtedly pleased that the share price was rising rapidly and either had been approached, or were about to be, with an offer to sell their shares to Great Southern, John directed a pointed message in a November 16 letter: Seller beware. Great Southern's offer of $103.50 per share was contingent on its ability to acquire 75 percent of NWNL stock. A shareholder who accepted that offer would be putting his or her stock on deposit, locking it in limbo until Great Southern either achieved its 75-percent goal or gave up the pursuit. The shareholder would not be free to accept any higher offer that might come along during that time.[16]

Alert shareholders likely caught John's hint. John was working hard to see to it that a better offer was indeed coming along, at least for some of them. Great Southern was trying to obtain 75 percent of

220,000 outstanding NWNL shares, B. F. Houston explained to the *Minneapolis Star*, because the Texas company figured it would need that many to overcome the votes of policyholders at a shareholders' meeting. Houston was quoted as describing the ownership share of the Minneapolis members of the NWNL board as "trifling."[17] John was hustling to change that. He and other members of the extended Pillsbury family were buying up NWNL stock, as were other Minneapolis board members Bruce Dayton, Totton P. Heffelfinger, Leonard G. Carpenter, and Edgar F. Zelle (the founder of the Jefferson Bus Lines, who was also president of Wisconsin Central Railroad at the time.[18]) Together, they made an offer aimed at shareholders whose personal circumstances made the Great Southern offer especially tempting. They would buy up to 15,000 shares at $105.50, or $2 more per share than Great Southern was offering. Their offer did not require an "on deposit" delay, as Great Southern's did. But it was limited to ten shares per stockholder. The Minneapolis board's thinking was that while their offer was limited, it would afford shareholders who needed ready cash a sure sale. "They are offering to buy the stock in the belief that it is to the best interest of shareholders and policyholders that the separate and independent identity of the company be maintained," the *Minneapolis Tribune* reported.[19]

Fifty years later, with corporate ownership changes so commonplace that they barely attract community notice, the sense of alarm that gripped city leaders as NWNL fought for its independence may be hard to imagine. The 1950s were years when Minneapolis leaders mounted a number of efforts to raise the national and international profile of their city—to become, as U.S. Sen. Hubert Humphrey would famously say, more than "a cold Omaha." Minneapolis civic leaders were working hard to attract major league sports teams, upgrade arts organizations and venues, and push companies other than food processors into leadership of their respective industries. That may explain why Gov. Orville Freeman, a DFLer whose party was not usually counted as a friend of big business, offered the state's help to NWNL in keeping non-Minnesota owners out.[20] The Minneapolis Chamber of Commerce passed a resolution promising its aid, saying NWNL "has played a notable part in bringing Minneapolis to a position of prominence as one of the nation's leading insurance centers."[21] The situation at NWNL was fodder for almost daily coverage in Minneapolis newspapers. As a Pillsbury, John Jr. was accustomed to seeing his name in print. But his visibility increased as he became the face of a proud business community determined to maintain control of its own affairs.

By December 1956, the fight between NWNL and Great Southern had escalated to the courts. The two firms filed dueling lawsuits in an attempt to buttress their respective positions. Meanwhile, Great Southern amended its offer to buy shares. No longer was the offer contingent on achieving 75 percent of the outstanding 220,000 shares.[22] Pillsbury and the local board members took that move as a sign in their favor. Great Southern must be having trouble reaching their goal.

But John would take no chances. He reasoned that the best safeguard against a successful hostile takeover of his stock/mutual hybrid insurance company was to shore up support for his leadership among policyholders as well as shareholders. In his favor were NWNL's flourishing sales, strong profits, and reputation for customer satisfaction. New sales records were being set monthly.[23] But, he figured, policyholders' votes would likely be swayed by the views of their local insurance agents, should push come to shove. John wanted to build strong personal relationships with those agents. He set out to meet as many of them as he could, traveling to regional sales meetings, delivering speeches, answering questions, and shaking hands of wives eager to say hello to someone whose name was on products in their kitchen pantries. He also made sure the home office was functioning as smoothly as possible. Within only days of his appointment as president, John contracted with the St. Paul-based Remington-Rand Univac division of the Sperry Rand Corp. to begin to apply computer technology to insurance claims processing and record-keeping. That move put NWNL on the cutting edge of insurance company operations nationwide. [24]

His NWNL charm offensive required a tradeoff at home. John Jr. declined to seek reelection to the Orono School Board

George and Sally with their three elder children, George Jr. on his father's lap, Sarah and Charlie, in late 1951. Their second daughter, Katharine, was born in 1956.

in 1957. Elected on May 21 in his stead: George S. Pillsbury. By 1957, George and Sally were parents of four. Katharine Whitney, the last of their children, had arrived on November 11, 1956. Like their parents before them, the Baby Boom generation of Pillsburys would eventually head to exclusive schools in the East. But, likely to the satisfaction of their public-school-educated grandfather, all but Katharine among George and Sally's brood began their education in Orono public school.

George's first foray into elective office was motivated in good part by a desire to be involved in the education of his children. "Dad wanted to be sure the schools were good," Sarah Pillsbury says of her father's school board service.[25] (George's interest in training the young also had him tying on ice skates with his sons Charlie and

George Jr. and their friends in the 1950s, as the coach of their recreational hockey team. When organizing the Woodhill Wolves to play the Dodd Road Devils, George found a surplus of defensemen. He tapped one competitive youngster to play goalie—in part because his father could readily afford the expensive pads goalies wear. That boy was a future Blake All-Stater, Yale hockey player, U.S. senator, and Minnesota governor, Mark Dayton.)

George was in the thick of one other educational matter in the mid-1950s. In 1954 he was chairman of the board of the Pillsbury Academy, the little Baptist college in Owatonna that took the family's name in 1886 to honor its leading benefactor, George A. Pillsbury. In 1920, the school's mission shifted. It became an all-male military academy, officially controlled by the Minnesota Baptist Convention but, in practice, operated by a board of directors that had been allowed to become self-perpetuating. But in the 1950s, a fundamentalist faction took charge of the Minnesota Baptist Convention, and the long-standing practice of allowing the board to choose its own members and operate the academy as it saw fit was challenged by the church. George and his fellow board members went to court in 1954 to try to preserve their prerogatives. But the nineteenth-century statutes under which the academy had been established were on the church's side. The state Supreme Court ruled in the Baptist Convention's favor on December 23, 1955. George and the Pillsbury family ended their association with their namesake academy, and the institution changed its name two years later to the Pillsbury Baptist Bible College.[26]

M eanwhile, the takeover threat that was menacing NWNL and John Jr. became less complicated in January 1957. Great Southern Life announced that it was ending its bid, and that the NWNL shares it had acquired would be sold to Nationwide. On January 17, George Wells, B.F. Houston, and one other Great Southern ally, J. Fred Schoellkopf Jr. of Dallas, Texas, resigned from the NWNL board and announced that their shares in the company had been sold to Nationwide. The Ohio firm and the Minneapolis members of the NWNL board were headed for a showdown.

Matters came to a head at NWNL's January 28-29 annual meeting. By then, Nationwide had a majority 111,796 of the Minnesota insurer's 220,000 shares. Under NWNL bylaws, enacted in 1931, that appeared to be sufficient to control the meeting's quorum. Nationwide's strategy was to stay away from the shareholder's meeting and thereby deny the local forces the quorum needed to do business. But John and his legal team, including his former Faegre & Benson colleagues, came up with an adroit maneuver. They found an obscure state statute that required notice to both shareholders and policyholders before a quorum could be considered to be present for purposes of changing control of a mutual insurance corporation. NWNL's bylaws did not provide for notification of policyholders. That meant that the NWNL bylaw defining an annual meeting's quorum as consisting only of shareholders and their representatives was in conflict with state statutes, and could thus be ignored, John Jr. announced at the meeting. He declared a quorum present despite the absence of the Nationwide representative, and presided over the reelection of the same five Minneapolis directors who had been battling to keep NWNL in Minnesota hands—Thomas M. Crosby, Bruce B. Dayton, Totton P. Heffelfinger, Edgar F. Zelle, and John S. Pillsbury Jr.[27]

It was a brassy move, one that John knew would land him and the other Minneapolis directors in court. Within days, Nationwide hired St. Paul law firm Doherty, Rumble & Butler to file a complaint in federal court. (The story is told that no Minneapolis firm would take the case.)[28] But John's willingness to set aside the company's bylaws and gamble that the courts would back him up bought him time to continue his confidence-building campaign among policyholders and their agents, who would be willing and able to support the Minneapolis management, should a judge rule that NWNL's bylaws were controlling and Nationwide's holdings were sufficient to constitute a quorum.

That strategy worked. NWNL suffered a seeming setback in the courts when, in January 1958, the Minnesota Supreme Court ruled that NWNL must give Nationwide the chance to examine its books and collect the names of all of its shareholders, including policyholders.[29] But by then, Nationwide's attorneys were advising Murray

Lincoln that the policyholders' voting power in NWNL, and their support for the Minneapolis-based leadership, constituted opposition too strong to overcome. Lincoln was told: Find a way to get your money out, and back off.

On April 18, a triumphant headline in the *Minneapolis Tribune* announced, "N.W. Life Control Fight Ends."[30] Pillsbury and Lincoln had struck a deal that put three Nationwide directors on the fifteen-member NWNL board, and one Nationwide representative on the seven-member executive committee. "Basic control of the company remains in Minneapolis and the company will continue as an independent company," the newspaper exulted. It was, John Jr. told reporter Leonard Inskip, "a complete and satisfactory understanding."

For the second time in the twentieth century, a man named John Pillsbury had secured local control of a major Minneapolis company. In neither case would the achievement last into the next century. But by preserving both the Pillsbury Co. and Northwestern National Life Insurance Co. as Minneapolis-based companies in their own time, the Pillsbury father and son both made big contributions to their city's pride, prestige and prosperity.

During his trying first year and a half, John Jr. found a home in the insurance industry. Its hard-charging, gregarious culture and his action-loving, magnetic personality were a good match. He delighted in the new relationships he made and the influence he had over the course of a major economic force in his city. Just as when he sailed competitively or rowed for Yale, he relished being the head of a competent team. He told the *Tribune*'s Inskip: "I wasn't any expert and I'm still no expert. I couldn't write a rate book. But the business is a team operation. You've got to have the people who do know the answers—and we have them. At law school you learn how to find answers. A lot of the job of the president involves co-coordinating activities, finding answers and making decisions."[31] He would never return to practicing law.

The NWNL victory was particularly important in the context of a changing Minneapolis economy. The city's financial service industry was on brisk ascendancy as Minnesota and Minneapolis celebrated their centennials in 1958. But the flour milling industry that had been the city's mainstay for a hundred years was rapidly fading. The mills at the foot of the Falls of St. Anthony had been eclipsed in flour output by Buffalo, N.Y. mills in 1930.[32] Buffalo had the advantage of proximity to Eastern population centers and favorable U.S. laws that allowed it to import wheat grown in Canada, process it, and export it to the world market duty-free.[33] Though Minnesota food-processing giants Pillsbury and General Mills continued to flourish, the mills themselves that had originally provided the flour began to fall silent. By 1960, Minneapolis produced less than a third as much flour as it had in the run-up to World War I.[34] Mills that had figured prom-inently in the rise of the Pills-bury Co.—Anchor, Cataract, the Pillsbury B—were razed. In 1965, the great Washburn A Mill, built from the ashes of the great explosion of 1878, closed. On the west side of the river, flour milling was now a thing of the past. It would continue, albeit modestly, at the Pillsbury A Mill until 2003, but the gray limestone castle that had daz-zled tourists in the 1880s was increasingly viewed by Minneapolitans not as an industrial giant but as a quaint relic of a bygone era.

John Sr. in the Metropolitan Building, shortly before its 1961 demolition.

Minneapolis leaders were not yet ready to embrace a new vision and purpose for the city's riverfront cradle, but already in the mid-1950s, they had begun to renew the city's original downtown thoroughfare, Washington Avenue, and its early retail cluster on the west side of the Hennepin Avenue Bridge known as the Gateway. The building that had housed the J.S. Pillsbury & Co. hardware store was long gone. But some of its contemporaries remained, as rundown flophouses, dingy bars, and vacant eyesores. The city's retail core had moved several blocks south, along Nicollet Avenue. And in 1956, a first-of-its-kind suburban retail attraction opened its doors in Edina.[35] Southdale, the nation's first fully enclosed shopping center, was conceived and developed by the five Dayton brothers who grew up on the same Blaisdell Avenue block as Gov. John S. Pillsbury's great-grandchildren. The Daytons' loyalty to downtown Minneapolis was beyond question. That made their belief that the survival of their business depended on the aggressive development of a suburban market all the more troubling to other downtown merchants.[36] A counter-move was in order, and reviving the blighted Gateway was the obvious way to start. In 1957, federal planning money was secured. It was a down payment on major grants to follow, as the city set out to rebuild a third of its downtown.[37]

Everywhere he went—the Minneapolis Club, bank and non-profit boardrooms, the Woodhill Golf Course adjacent to his sprawling home—John Pillsbury Jr. would have been in the thick of conversations about the Gateway and downtown renewal in the late 1950s. Pillsbury business roots on some of the very parcels in question gave him a personal tie to the district's fate. So did his knowledge of NWNL history. The firm started in two rooms in the Minnesota Loan and Trust Building on Nicollet Avenue and Third Street on September 15, 1885.[38] But John also had an up-to-the-minute reason to be interested when talk turned to future uses of what could again be prime real estate. Northwestern National Life Insurance Co. was outgrowing its Loring Park headquarters. John Jr. solved the problem temporarily in 1957 with the purchase of a nearby mansion from the widow of Charles C. Bovey, the man who had helped his father found Woodhill Country Club and solve a more personal real estate problem in 1915.[39] Space in other nearby buildings was rented, too, and before long the company's headquarters was geographically fragmented into five locations.[40] John soon saw that a more lasting solution was in order. He began to make the case to his board of directors that NWNL needed a new building—and, while they were at it, they ought to make it a lasting landmark and a reflection of the company's pride in its Minneapolis heritage.

He persuaded the board to acquire a large parcel being cleared in the Gateway District, at 20 Washington Avenue, and to hire

The Northwestern National Life Insurance Company headquarters – today the ING Building.

Seattle-born, Michigan-based architect Minoru Yamasaki to design a building to put on it.[41] Yamasaki would later become widely known as the architect of World Trade Center towers in lower Manhattan, but in 1961, when he and John Pillsbury first discussed a new home for NWNL, he was an up-and-coming regional architect whose trademark was modern interpretation of classical design. He represented a brave choice by John, who was under considerable pressure to choose a Minnesota architect instead.

For the building that would anchor the north end of Nicollet Avenue (not yet the Nicollet Mall, though that was only a few years away) Pillsbury and Yamasaki settled on a design inspired by no less than the Parthenon in Athens, Greece, complete with a marble façade, towering columns, and a reflecting pool. For those who mourned the relocation of the Gateway Park fountain, built in 1915, to Lyndale Park's rose garden, the reflecting pools perhaps provided some solace.[42] Art aficionados cheered when the NWNL board commissioned the same sculptor who made metal trees for Southdale's central court, Harry Bertoia, to create something spectacular for the NWNL lobby. That he did. His "Sunlit Straw," 46 feet long and 14 feet high, contains hundreds of brass-coated steel rods evoking something entirely fitting for a building situated in a former flour milling district: a field of wheat.[43]

Yamasaki's design was a hit,[44] so much so that when the building opened in January 1965 it dissipated some of the anger generated by the destruction of the Metropolitan Building four years earlier as part of the same thrust to renew the Gateway. Charles A. Pillsbury had chosen the Metropolitan building, (then known as the Northwestern Guaranty Loan Building) for his flour milling company's headquarters back in 1891, and though the firm had long since decamped to a more modern building closer to the city's retail core, it must have pained brothers John and George and their father, by then an octogenarian, as they watched the wrecking ball smash the grand old structure in December 1961. The elder Pillsbury had often taken his children on Saturday mornings to his office at the Metropolitan and let them peer down through its ornate iron railings to the center courtyard below.

Fifty years on, the Metropolitan Building is a fading memory, though many of the featureless buildings that went up during the Gateway renewal project are also gone, or themselves candidates for redevelopment. But the Yamasaki-designed building that John Pillsbury and his board contributed to the Gateway, today known as the ING Building, is admired as an enduring example of modernist elegance. Once again, a Pillsbury had left an architectural mark on the district near the Falls of St. Anthony.

As John basked in the plaudits for the new NWNL building in 1965, he was also considering an undertaking that would give him wider impact. For years, he had been mentioned as a possible candidate for elective office. It did not go unnoticed in Republican circles that John did not resist such talk and that people close to him, notably his politically active brother and sister-in-law, George and Sally, seemed to encourage it.

In 1965 the governor's office was occupied by Karl Rolvaag, a DFLer so unpopular that an insurgency to topple him was brewing within his own party. Rolvaag had won the office in 1962 in the closest gubernatorial election, then and still, in U.S. history. By a mere ninety-one votes, and after an arduous recount and court fight that lasted more than four months, Rolvaag unseated Republican Gov. Elmer L. Andersen, the owner and chief executive of St. Paul-based H.B. Fuller Co. Falsehoods about Andersen's involvement in a trumped-up highway construction scandal arose in the final days of that 1962 race, with DFL U.S. Sen. Hubert Humphrey leading that charge and Rolvaag along for the ride. When the truth came out only days after the elec-

tion, Rolvaag's victory was tarnished months before it was made official by a three-judge panel. With Rolvaag seeking reelection in 1966, conditions were ripe for a Republican to return to the governor's office.

John Jr. was fifty-three years old in 1965. If he wanted to be governor of Minnesota someday, he knew that it was time to make his move. But, he told brother George as he confided his intentions, he would yield to one man—Elmer Andersen. His affection and

Gov. Elmer L. Andersen, 1965.

respect for the former governor would trump his own ambition, John said. Besides, he reasoned, Andersen and Pillsbury were both moderate-to-liberal thinkers and Twin Cities business executives. They appealed to the same segment of the GOP, and would fragment that segment and fail if they were both contenders in a crowded field of candidates. Andersen, who was back in charge at H.B. Fuller Co., had not indicated even to friends whether he would try to reclaim the office he had lost so narrowly. George volunteered to play the role of his brother's agent and find out. One morning in May 1965, he invited Elmer to breakfast at the Minneapolis Club and posed the question: "Are you going to run for governor? My brother John would like to. But we don't want to run if you're thinking about it." The former governor's answer seemed clear at the time. "Encourage your brother to run," Andersen said.

With that response in hand, John stepped up his appearances at Republican Party functions around the state, and let reporters know that when they listed possible candidates for governor, he would not object to a mention. When one of them asked about his appearance at four party meetings in September 1965, he said, "I simply tell those I meet that I've been a businessman and lawyer and my name is Pillsbury and if there are any skeletons in the family closet, I don't know about them."[45]

But as the months passed, Andersen and the loyalists in his holdover election committee from the 1962 campaign, made none of the moves toward Pillsbury that John expected would ensue after Elmer's conversation with George. The brothers came to realize that "Encourage your brother to run" was not equivalent to "I won't run." Andersen was keeping his options open and his allies joined him on the fence. Decades later, Elmer confessed that his behavior during that political year was shaped by his hope that his party would recognize the popular appeal of a rematch between Andersen and the deceiver of 1962, Rolvaag, and prevail on the former governor to run again. "I waited for party leaders to approach me," Andersen would write in his autobiography. "I waited too long. . . . I learned something that I should have learned long before: In politics, nothing comes to you. You have to go and get it."[46]

John Pillsbury, a political neophyte, had not mastered that lesson either. Abruptly, on Nov. 12, 1965,[47] he summoned the state's political reporters to NWNL's conference room to announce that he would not seek the governorship, citing only "personal reasons." Not even George knew that the announcement was coming. John telephoned him at work to break the news, telling him that the decision had been reached in conversation with Kitty alone. George was incredulous. In his estimation, the campaign had been lagging slightly, but could still lead to GOP endorsement the following June. With Andersen biding his time and other candidates—South St. Paul attorney Harold LeVander and Ramsey County chief prosecutor William Randall—handicapped by low name recognition, a business leader bearing one of the state's oldest and best-known names could still win.[48]

That was the case George and others continued to press upon John in the weeks after his November 12 announcement. John may have been seeking first-hand affirmation of their assessment when, unannounced, he showed up at a Republican Party State Central Committee meeting one cold January night at a downtown hotel. "I was at the symphony and some friends said I should stop over," he said when asked by a reporter about his 11 p.m. visit with the party's leaders.[49] It was an odd hour for a purely social call.

Two months later, John Pillsbury Jr. called the press again. On March 8, 1966, he announced that he would be a candidate for governor after all. "I am in the race all out and to the very end," he declared—but again, he didn't quite mean it. He was seeking the Republican Party's endorsement and would not continue his campaign past the GOP state convention without it, he clarified a few days later. In Minnesota, insiders in both major parties expect an oath to "abide by the endorsement" of any candidate who is serious about receiving their blessing. A handful of candidates in both parties have succeeded by refusing to take the oath, spurning the party's convention, and earning their place on the November ballot by winning a late-summer intra-party primary. But those candidates face long odds and risk the abiding wrath of party insiders—a risk many candidates have been unwilling to take.

"I am not entering because of the weakness of the other candidates, but because of the strength of my own campaign," Pillsbury said as he finally made his candidacy official. For someone who was starting late and had not previously run for elective office, it was a strong campaign indeed—in Minneapolis, the western suburbs, and northeastern Minnesota, where the name Pillsbury is associated with the Mesabi Iron Range. In other parts of the state, LeVander and Randall had already lined up firm support. Randall had Ramsey County sewed up. He scored a coup that spring when the state Supreme Court upheld the murder-for-hire conviction of Dr. T. Eugene Thompson in one of the state's most notorious homicide cases. Randall had been the lead prosecutor in the case. LeVander's base lay in rural Minnesota. The son of a Lutheran minister and a longtime attorney in the South St. Paul law firm founded by former Gov. Harold Stassen, LeVander

319

had done legal work for the state's electric utilities, including rural electric cooperatives. That work brought him in contact with the agri-businessmen who were leading voices in rural Republican politics. He was the first announced candidate for the party's nod in 1966 and undeniably the hardest-working. He was impressive at the podium, and what he lacked in personal charisma he more than com-

John Jr. campaigning, May 1966.

pensated for by unleashing his outgoing, politically savvy wife, Iantha, and their three attractive children on the campaign trail.

John hustled to court GOP delegates that spring, but he was playing catch-up. He had only intermittent help from his children, who were attending schools in the East in the mid-1960s. But he could count on Kitty, George, Sally, and Sally's brothers, all of whom knew their way around Republican conventions. Sally's brother Wheelock had been the unsuccessful GOP candidate for the U.S. Senate in 1964. Pillsbury also had the backing of a group of young Hennepin County Republican legislators who'd been dubbed the "Young Turks," many of whom would go on to positions of Minnesota leadership. Managing the Pillsbury campaign was state Rep. Bill Frenzel, a future congressman, who met the candidate for the first time, at George's invitation, only about six months before the campaign began in earnest. Frenzel's first impression was of a man who had the nature of "a businessman, not a politician. He was quieter, very gentlemanly, friendly but not a good speaker." [50] Among those attending campaign strategy sessions were Sen. Wayne Popham, who would go on to head one of the state's leading law firms; Minneapolis City Council member Arne Carlson, a future governor; Rep. Gary Flakne, a future Hennepin

County attorney; Rep. Lyall Schwarzkopf, who as Minneapolis city coordinator was a powerhouse in city affairs, and Rep. John Yngve, a future regent of the University of Minnesota and leader in the state's budding high-tech industry. That group and their local networks became the core of the Pillsbury campaign, and also had long, deep ties to former state Rep. Douglas Head, a Minneapolis attorney who was running hard that year for GOP endorsement for state attorney general. At a time when women were still relegated to supporting roles, the Pillsbury inner circle included one woman who would go on to serve on the Minneapolis City Council, Gladys Brooks.[51]

Brooks had been an ally of Elmer L. Andersen while he was governor,[52] and his emissary to Mississippi in 1962 when two young Minnesota civil rights workers were jailed there on what appeared to be trumped-up charges. She likely would have brought other Andersen loyalists to Pillsbury's side, if Elmer had only released them. But he did not. When reporters inquired about his status, the former governor dropped hints that he was still interested in running.[53] At one point, Pillsbury was asked whether his candidacy was "guarding the chair" for Andersen. John must have struggled to keep his cool as he replied, "I think anyone who is running a company is too busy to warm a chair for someone else."[54] For Pillsbury, Andersen was increasingly becoming a hindrance, and an irritant. But no ill word ever passed publicly between them—a reflection, perhaps, of a more genteel time in American politics, and of a pragmatic awareness that in a multi-candidate endorsement contest, winning 60 percent of a convention's votes required at least an appearance of good feeling among the contenders. But civility was also much in the nature of two honorable people who genuinely respected each other.

Pillsbury didn't "quit his day job" to run for governor. Instead, he hosted strategy sessions in the NWNL executive suite ("the nicest office I was ever in," Frenzel recalled.) Among the matters the campaign's junior but more politically savvy advisors delicately broached with the insurance CEO was his speaking style. It was too much that of an earnest kid running for class president, rather than an impassioned agent of political change. In LeVander, Pillsbury was up against a preacher's son, the 1932 state collegiate oratory champion,[55] and a former speech instructor and debate coach. Though LeVander too was making his first bid for elective office, he was more convincing on the stump.[56]

Like his namesake ninety years before, John S. Pillsbury Jr. campaigned on a pledge to bring a businessman's managerial skill to the governorship. "I will ask the people of Minnesota to pass judgment on a series of programs to reorganize our state government from top to bottom," he said. "The basic aim will be excellence and the basic method will be an absolute insistence on a 110 percent effort put forth 100 percent of the time. Departments or programs which do not measure up will be eliminated."[57] It wasn't the most compelling campaign theme he might have chosen—not at a time when baby boomers were flooding the state's campuses, the interstate highway system was altering the transportation landscape, the state budget was running a chronic deficit and the nation was escalating an unpopular war in Vietnam. The Legislature had been talking about enacting a state sales tax, something most other American states had done in the 1930s. Minnesota, under populist Farmer-Labor Party sway in the 1930s, had opted for an income tax instead because it spared those who lacked ability to pay. By the 1960s, some Republican legislators were calling for a sales tax, arguing that it was preferable to higher income taxes, which they said would deter business investment. But neither of the two leading GOP candidates for governor agreed—not plainly anyway. John punted in March: "I think there has to be a review of the whole tax situation, and it is possible there may be a need for some excise taxes."[58] He was still dancing around the tax question in May. He would not propose new taxes, he said, but he was "not categorically against a sales tax if the Legislature comes up with it."[59] LeVander was described on the eve of the convention as "the only GOP contender who has come close to saying he favors a general sales tax."[60]

As the gavel came down to open the Republican state convention, a lively fight was on. Pillsbury and LeVander were the leading contenders, with Randall still holding his Ramsey County base and Elmer Andersen deciding at the eleventh hour that he would put his name before the convention as a candidate. But the GOP proceedings had been all but eclipsed in the public eye by the twenty-ballot brawl at the DFL state convention the weekend before. Lt. Gov. Alexander MacDonald "Sandy" Keith of Rochester had emerged as the party's endorsee over the embattled incumbent Rolvaag. Rolvaag had retreated to a governor's meeting in Ohio, then to Florida, to regroup. As the Republicans convened at the newly remodeled Minneapolis Convention Center, Rolvaag was still weighing whether he would take Vice President Hubert Humphrey's advice, concede defeat and bow out of public life, or take his fight to DFL primary voters instead. Thus, Republican delegates were left to speculate about whether their pick would be paired against the handsome, charismatic, smooth-talking Keith or the avuncular, bland Rolvaag in November. What the GOP delegates knew was that they wanted to show Minnesotans that they were not in conflict and disarray, as DFLers had been the weekend before. They wanted an orderly convention with a harmonious finish—and no primary. All of the candidates had agreed to abide by the convention's decision, and end their campaigns if another candidate was endorsed.

Pillsbury entered the convention with the star power not only of his own well-known name, but the endorsements of some of the biggest names in national Republican politics. Former vice president Richard Nixon, already beginning his 1968 comeback journey, had come to Minnesota to raise money on Pillsbury's behalf, and his own.[61] Michigan Gov. George Romney, another 1968 presidential hopeful (and father of future Massachusetts Gov. Mitt Romney) was urging Pillsbury's endorsement.[62] So were two nationally prominent Minnesota congressmen, U.S. Rep. Clark MacGregor and former U.S. Rep. Walter Judd.[63] MacGregor made sure GOP convention delegates knew about John's achievement for Minnesota: "He fought off the Texas raiders who wanted to take over his company," he said as he placed Pillsbury's name before the convention.[64]

But the big names backing Pillsbury were something of a mixed blessing at a time when the state's 3.5 million people were almost evenly divided between metro and outstate communities. A rural/urban divide was the dominant feature of the state's political landscape in the mid-twentieth century, and rural resentment of the fast-growing metro region's power was at play. As editor J. D. Weber of the *Murray County Herald* in Slayton (and father of future U.S. Rep. Vin Weber) described it, Pillsbury was the tool of Hennepin County kingmakers. He urged the formation of a coalition between LeVander and Randall forces to overcome Pillsbury's Hennepin County mafia.[65]

In that, editor Weber was prescient. Randall trailed in the early balloting on June 24, and after the third ballot, he dropped out. Reporters expected his delegates to shift to Andersen, a St. Paul resident, but many of them opted for LeVander of Dakota County instead, and some continued to vote for Randall long after he had exited the race. Their thinking was that they could win a consolation prize for their friend if they withheld their votes from the leaders. The possibilities included lieutenant governor and attorney general—the latter being former state Rep. Doug Head's long-sought goal.

Pillsbury pulled ahead on the ninth ballot as Friday evening's repeated roll calls ground on. No candidate came close the 60 percent threshold. On the tenth ballot, Pillsbury led with 673.5 votes; LeVander had 607.33; Andersen, 84.17 and Randall, 14. It was 1 a.m. as the results of that ballot were announced. The rules of the convention provided that only 10 ballots would be permitted on Friday—and it was already Saturday. A vote to suspend the rules would have been needed to continue at that hour. Frenzel moved to continue balloting. But LeVander backer and former college classmate Fred Hughes of St. Cloud promptly moved for a roll call vote on Frenzel's motion. That would have meant another 45 minutes of delay before an eleventh ballot could be cast. A sizeable share of Pillsbury supporters from Hennepin County were parents of young children, and had babysitters at home. They had not planned to spend the night in downtown Minneapolis. "My judgment was if we stayed, we'd lose votes," said Frenzel, himself the father of three young daughters. The convention recessed until 9 a.m. "That's what's been called Frenzel's folly," the rueful campaign manager recalled forty-four years later, even though he had no real choice.

Hennepin County delegates may have gone home to tend to their families, but other delegates continued to tend to politics in downtown Minneapolis hotels. The Ramsey County delegates signaled to the LeVander and Pillsbury camps that they were open to deal-making—perhaps more than Bill Randall himself was. "We offered him the lieutenant governor spot. He wouldn't take it," said LeVander convention manager, Albert Lea state Rep. Paul Overgaard.[66] Randall was holding out for attorney general. That prize was beyond the LeVander team's capacity to deliver. They never pretended otherwise, Overgaard insists—a claim some Pillsbury partisans dispute. Ramsey County delegation leaders approached the Pillsbury campaign overnight about putting Randall into the A.G. spot. No deal, Pillsbury and Frenzel responded. Doug Head was their friend and they would not double-cross him.

Gov. Harold LeVander, 1969.

Overgaard used the overnight recess to good effect. At the urging of Bill Norman, a public relations professional from Albert Lea, Overgaard decided to give the convention a new look the next morning by issuing their delegates brand-new signs to wave. The thinking was that tired delegates would be more energized, and more open to a different outcome, if their surroundings looked fresh and different from the night before. They would also be impressed by a campaign able to adroitly respond to circumstances. Overgaard and Norman got their mutual friend Dan Kruse of Church Offset Printing of Albert Lea out of bed shortly after 1 a.m. with a rush order: 400 signs, reading "Let's face it: It's LeVander all the way." They also arranged for a small airplane to pick them up. Soon after sunrise, Kruse had the signs printed, boxed, and delivered to Albert Lea's airfield. They were flown to South St. Paul, LeVander's hometown, where a friend of the candidate met the plane and delivered the signs to downtown Minneapolis. The timing was tight, so Overgaard conspired with Fred Hughes to convene a Sixth Congressional District delegation meeting that would delay the start of the convention. That gave the LeVander team the time they needed to post and distribute the new signs. Decades later, Overgaard remains proud of the feat: "We were amateurs, but we made a couple of right decisions." Hughes emerged from the meeting to summarize for reporters the argument he made on behalf of his old friend LeVander. A Pillsbury candidacy would "reinforce the public's typical image of the party—that of wealthy vested interests." LeVander, he said, was a man of the people.[67]

When balloting finally resumed, the tables had turned. LeVander was in the lead on the eleventh ballot and Andersen was up slightly. Their gains had come at Pillsbury's expense. Most of the shift in votes was among the Ramsey County delegation.[68] By noon, after 13 ballots, the tally was LeVander 634 to Pillsbury's 545, with 831 needed to crack the 60 percent threshold. The convention was beginning to mimic the DFL slugfest of the weekend before, and GOP legislative leaders were beginning to panic. They pushed for a resolution. At noon, the convention recessed again so that party officers, headed by chairman George Thiss, and the candidates could parley. What delegates were told would be a brief meeting took two and a half hours. There, a gentlemen's agreement was struck: Andersen would withdraw. That part of the arrangement was engineered by Andersen's old state Senate colleague, First District congressman and future governor Al Quie, a Pillsbury backer.[69] Two more ballots would be cast. If neither LeVander nor Pillsbury reached 60 percent of the vote on ballots 14 or 15, the candidates would treat the results of the sixteenth ballot differently. If one of them achieved 55 percent of the vote on the sixteenth ballot, the trailing candidate would withdraw. If neither had 55 percent of the vote on that ballot, the man in the lead on the next ballot, with more than 50 percent of the votes, would be the endorsee.

LeVander barely cracked 55 percent on the sixteenth ballot. Without saying a word to his campaign manager, John Pillsbury briskly strode to the podium after the results were known. He was a man of his word. Frenzel recalled: "John was a perfect gentleman. He moved that the vote to endorse LeVander be unanimous, and pledged his support to Harold."

LeVander went on to win the November 8 election, defeating Rolvaag, who decided a week after the Republican convention to enter the September 13 primary and fight to keep his office. He beat back Sandy Keith's challenge with a call to "let the people decide." Rolvaag was aided by the label John Pillsbury first used to describe Keith. The Rochester attorney was "a smiling barracuda," Pillsbury said at the GOP convention. The line stuck.

Pillsbury went back to Northwestern National Life, which did not appear to miss a beat as a result of its CEO's several months of diversion. "People at NWNL were proud of his political involvement," recalled John Turner, who came to the company as a young actuary from Massachusetts two years later and rose to become its leader. "Everybody told me he would have been a good governor. He had all the qualities you'd want in that job."[70]

By all outward indications, Pillsbury was through with politics. His community extra-curricular focus shifted away from the Republican Party to charities and arts organizations, particularly the Minneapolis Symphony Orchestra. But the embers of political ambition had not gone completely cold. As LeVander's popularity fell in the fall of 1969, George contrived to meet with the governor to deliver a private message: "My brother is interested in running for governor if you decide not to seek a second term. He'd appreciate the courtesy of an early indication about your plans." LeVander's response seemed unequivocal: He was running in 1970. Pillsbury took LeVander at his word, and said yes when, as a Navy veteran, he was invited to join a group of businessmen, educators, military officials, and scientists in January 1970 visiting Operation Deep Freeze, a Navy-supported scientific mission to Antarctica that was started in 1956. The rugged adventure and learning opportunity the invitation presented had great appeal to John, who was fifty-seven and still athletic. But he likely kicked himself when he learned that while he was viewing penguins on January 26, LeVander was

John, Kitty and their children, 1966. The sons, from left, are Harry, Jock, and Don. Daughter Kate is perched with her mother.

announcing that he would not run for reelection. By January 30, when the Deep Freeze tour group arrived at Christchurch, New Zealand, two younger Republicans, Lt. Gov. James Goetz and Attorney General Doug Head, were already organizing gubernatorial campaigns for the caucus-convention season that was about to start. John knew from sorry experience that a late start was a serious and often insurmountable handicap in endorsement fights. From New Zealand, he told George to call the state's reporters with a statement that he would not be a candidate in 1970.[71] Though a "draft Pillsbury" movement fluttered briefly in ensuing weeks, it didn't fly.[72] The possibility that Minnesota would have a second Gov. John S. Pillsbury had evaporated.

But John's impact on the city he loved was not complete. He had one more landmark to build—Orchestra Hall.

A member of the Pillsbury family—and often more than one—had served on the Orchestral Association board of directors continuously since John's uncle Charlie took his seat in 1907.[73] When John became chair of the Orchestral Association board of directors on January 1, 1972, the inadequacy of the facilities used by the state's leading professional music organization was uppermost on the board's agenda. The Minnesota Orchestra (the Minneapolis Symphony Orchestra had changed its name in 1968) had been tenants since 1930, renting space at the University of Minnesota's cavernous, nearly 5,000-seat Northrop Auditorium. Northrop gave the orchestra a Goldilocks situation: the performance hall was too large and the backstage and administrative quarters were too small. The acoustics left a good deal to be desired. One conductor famously said that the best way to improve listening in the giant hall would be "dynamite."[74] The search for something just right took the board back to its pre-1930 address, 85 South Eleventh Street. There stood the original Minneapolis Auditorium, built in 1905 with—notably—the financial backing of Northwestern National Life Insurance Co.[75] It had been rechristened the Lyceum Theater in 1924 and, more recently, Soul's Harbor, an evangelical religious organization. Next door at 1111 Nicollet Avenue stood an office building that could be had for the right price. Soul's Harbor wanted to sell. On September 22, 1972, the Orchestral Association announced that it would buy back its old home—possibly for remodeling, possibly for redevelopment.[76]

Within a few months, the notion of remodeling the nearly seventy-year-old auditorium was discarded. It would cost less to start over, the board was advised.[77] Therefore, under the leadership of the board's House committee, led by Minneapolis attorney Stephen Pflaum and including John, orchestra benefactor and booster Kenneth Dayton drafted an eloquent one-page expression of the board's vision for a new concert hall. It said in part:

"The building should be designed to serve the concert-going audiences of the future rather than to reflect Old World elegance. It should be an honest building, conveying a sense of dignity, simplicity and eye-satisfying proportions. The concept of the building should be to enhance the total concert-going experience of every person who attends a performance. It should involve the listener totally. It should therefore be warm, friendly, informal and exciting. The emphasis should be on the concert rather than on the building itself. Above all the building should help achieve that most important goal—the excellence of the acoustics."[78]

Plans were drawn for a 2,750 seat hall—half the size of Northrop and similar in interior dimensions and configuration to the new John F. Kennedy Center for the Performing Arts in Washington D.C. With that concept in hand, John approached city officials in January 1973 with a proposal: The Orchestra would put up a sparkling new attraction near the south end of the new auto-free pedestrian and transit mall that had been built on Nicollet Avenue. Its situation would be much enhanced if the city would clear the entire block between Eleventh and Twelfth Streets and Nicollet and Marquette Avenues, and put a park or plaza on the land not claimed by Orchestra Hall. The city's assistance would also make possible a parking ramp that could serve visitors to other downtown destinations for much of the week.[79] Months of negotiations and plan revisions ensued. The upshot: a $9.2 million Orchestra Hall would be paid for and constructed by the Orchestral Association, then sold to the city. The city's costs then would be recovered over a thirty-year lease to the orchestra. The association in turn would use a portion of the proceeds of the sale to finance construction of a new plaza/park adjacent to Orchestra Hall, along Nicollet. The Peavey Co., in commemoration of its hundredth year in business in the city, would provide a substantial lead gift for the plaza in exchange for naming rights.[80] In addition, the city agreed to build a new parking ramp across Marquette Avenue from the hall. By the time those terms were agreed upon and approved in June 1973, John could announce that he and the board had raised $11.5 million for the project.[81] An impressive lead gift, $2.5 million, had come from his fellow board member Kenneth Dayton and his wife Judy; $1 million came from the Bush Foundation, then headed by John's 1966 gubernatorial rival, Elmer L. Andersen.

John Jr. seemed to be channeling the spirit of his great-grandfather, George A. Pillsbury, as he oversaw construction of the new

Orchestra Hall and Peavey Plaza's reflecting pool.

concert hall in 1973 and 1974. It was rising only a few blocks from one of George A.'s enduring projects, the First Baptist Church. John had his hand in every aspect of the orchestra's business in those pivotal years, including fundraising, investment management, labor negotiations, concert calendar, recording contracts, touring arrangements, and publicity. When WCCO TV wanted to interview someone about the hall's progress in November 1973, they naturally went to John.[82]

When a special meeting of the board was required on short notice in April 1974 to deal with a touchy issue that arose as the new hall was being built, it convened at NWNL on a Saturday morning.[83] All ninety-seven performing members of the orchestra and their three top conductors had signed a petition to the board, urging that the six-year-old name Minnesota Orchestra be dropped and that of the "internationally famous Minneapolis Symphony Orchestra" be restored. "We feel that this is a critical period in our existence, a time to put an end to the ever increasing damages that our name change causes and an opportune moment because of the construction of a new hall," the petition said, and went on to claim that the new name caused confusion with the University of Minnesota's orchestra. Petitioners blamed the name change for difficulty getting the attention of major recording companies, attracting an audience while on tour, and booking international artists to appear with the orchestra.

John understood that when every musician in an orchestra makes such a plea, the governing board is obliged to take notice. But he also remembered the good reasons behind the name change in 1968. Minneapolis and St. Paul were finally overcoming their deep, self-destructive sibling rivalry. With sports teams and civic institutions opting for the name Minnesota rather than either city's name, the Twin Cities were striving to establish an identity as a singular, successful region with expansive boundaries that reached to the state line. The orchestra's name change also came when it began regularly performing in St. Paul, at O'Shaughnessy Auditorium on the lovely campus of the College of St. Catherine.[84] Elmer Andersen made clear that to revert to the name "Minneapolis Symphony Orchestra" would be an insult to St. Paul patrons and donors, of which he was a major one.

John wisely concluded that a quick response to the petition, either aye or nay, would leave too many key people dissatisfied and angry. Appointing a committee for a few months of study would buy time for John's brand of personal diplomacy. He appointed John Windhorst, the man in line to be the next board chair, to head the committee and join him in searching for a compromise solution. Windhorst brought to the June 7 board meeting a recommendation to maintain the name "Minnesota Orchestra." With the orchestra facing an operating deficit in its first year at Orchestra Hall, it could not afford to alienate any music-loving Minnesotan, the committee advised. But the board had not done enough in 1968 to promote the orchestra's changed name and needed to do more, the committee recommended. The board agreed—likely imagining that all the free publicity associated with the opening of an impressive new concert hall only four months later would make it easy to keep that promise.

The opening gala was scheduled for October 21—a rare Monday night performance that would feature intermission speeches by Gov. Wendell Anderson, Mayor Al Hofstede, and John Pillsbury Jr. To chair the gala planning committee, John chose Luella Goldberg, the president of WAMSO (then the Women's Association of the

The inaugural concert, October 21, 1974.

Minneapolis Symphony Orchestra, now the Minnesota Orchestra Volunteer Association.) Thirty-six years later, two memories of the hall's opening stood out for her. One was when she, John, and Ken Dayton happened to be inside the new hall together at the very moment that the orchestra and its conductor, Stanislaw Skrowaczewski, began their first rehearsal in the new space. The three of them shot awestruck looks at each other as they realized that they were hearing the first orchestral music performed from the new stage. And what a sound it was! The new hall would soon be acclaimed by visiting critics from around the globe for its acoustical brilliance.[85] Goldberg's second lasting impression came a few days later, on October 18, when a special free "acoustical preview" concert was performed for the construction workers and their families as a thank-you gift for their work.[86] She isn't sure the special concert was John's idea, but surmises that it may have been. "It would have been just like him to think to do that."[87]

At a time when opportunities for women were expanding—too rapidly for some Minnesotans but not fast enough for others—the choice of a woman to lead the opening occasioned comment. John's grandmother had been one of the state's leading female opponents of women's suffrage back in the 1910s, but Pillsbury thinking about gender equity had changed. He underscored the point by nominating Goldberg to the full Orchestral Association board in 1974 and, two years later, to be the first female member of the Northwestern National Life board of directors. "It was fairly revolutionary," Goldberg recalled thirty-five years later. "His thinking was that women were coming to have more opportunities, and he wanted to be in the forefront of that—and he was."

Orchestral Board chairs typically served one-year terms in those years. John served three, seeing Orchestra Hall from concept to full functioning fruition. "All of us have been fortunate that John Pillsbury was in the right place at the right time, with the skills and determination to give the leadership for one of the major events in the Orchestra's history, the construction of this Hall, which by remarkable coincidence is at the opposite end of the mall from another beautiful building erected under his guiding hand," said Orchestra president Donald Engle when, on December 13, 1974, the first annual meeting of the board was convened on the new hall's stage.[88] "I hope he will look back on these three years with some pleasant memories and satisfactions, and that we will continue to have the benefit of his experience and business acumen." Those hopes were fulfilled. John would remain a member of the Orchestra's governing board for the rest of his days, becoming a life member in 1976.[89]

John retired as NWNL's CEO at age sixty-five, in October 1977.[90] He remained chairman of its board for a few more years. Shortly before he stepped down as CEO, he created something new for the board—a public responsibility committee. He asked Goldberg to head it. He wanted to do what he could to assure that after he was no longer in charge, someone at the top of NWNL would follow his lead in striving to act not only in the company's best interest, but also in the best interests of Minneapolis and Minnesota. "This company has a commitment to the community, to the greater good," he told her. He was reciting the Minnesota Pillsbury creed.

Three John S. Pillsburys in 1965. From left: Juty, John Jr., John Sr., John III (Jock) and Kitty.

Chapter Thirteen

IR-Wayzata

Long life had not been granted to Charles Alfred and Mary Ann Pillsbury, nor to three of their four children. But their son John entered his ninth decade of life in 1958 in fine fiddle. The pace of his golf game had slowed somewhat, but on many summer days he could still be found on the links of the country club he helped found, Woodhill, and in the winter at courses near La Chosa in Palm Beach. He loved the sociability of a golf game as much as the contest. "He's the talkingest golfer that ever topped a drive," an anonymous friend told a journalist.[1]

Though he had been honorary chairman of the Pillsbury Co. since 1952,[2] John appeared at his office in the Pillsbury Building in downtown Minneapolis for a few hours on most workdays[3] until he took the title "director emeritus" in 1965.[4] He came dressed for business, in a suit complete with a waistcoat ("I have more pockets that way," he explained)[5] and a trademark red carnation from the Southways greenhouse on his lapel. Corporate matters were no longer his responsibility, but he was still involved in

Sargent Land Management, the family partnership that owned extensive property on Minnesota's Mesabi Iron Range. (In 1960, he passed the presidency of that body to his son John.[6]) And he attended to matters associated with the corporate and civic boards on which he served—the Soo Line, Northwest Bancorporation, Wayne Knitting Mills, the Minnesota Orchestral Association, the Minneapolis Foundation, the Four Arts Society of Palm Beach, and the social service agency he and his late brother created to honor their parents, Pillsbury House.[7]

As his last decade progressed, the Pillsbury patriarch's gait slowed, eventually becoming so unsteady that he used a wheelchair to avoid falling. Circulatory problems plagued him. Fortunately, his mind and memory remained keen. That faculty put him in frequent demand by journalists and historians seeking a verbal picture of the Minneapolis of his youth, which was rapidly fading from view in the 1960s. John charmed *Minneapolis Sunday Tribune* reporter Barbara Flanagan with stories about excursions to Tom Lowry's house on the hill that offered a view of the whole city. That hill would become the site of the Walker Art Center and Guthrie Theater in the 1960s. He remembered sledding down rugged Ridgewood Hill toward Franklin and Lyndale Avenues, long since an urban intersection too busy for winter recreation. He told of dinners at T. B. Walker's mansion at Eighth and Hennepin, by 1966 the heart of downtown, and visits to the "new" 1890 library two blocks away, where Walker displayed some of his personal art collection for the community's benefit.

In 1960, that grand Romanesque library at Tenth and Hennepin fell to the city's hyperactive wrecking ball, and the site was wasted as a parking lot for decades thereafter. John sounded wistful as he told about falling in love with Lake Minnetonka when, as a boy, he visited his uncle Fred's farm at the lake. The lake remained, but Fred's farm had given way to development. In two extensive interviews with Russell Fridley,[8] executive director of the Minnesota Historical Society, he reminisced about people almost forgotten who had possessed household names in Minneapolis during his youth—the great hydraulic engineer William de la Barre, pioneering miller William

Eastman, milling genius George Christian. By sharing his memories, John preserved theirs.

When death came for John S. Pillsbury Sr. at Good Samaritan Hospital in Palm Beach on January 31, 1968, it was not unexpected. He was eighty-nine, and his circulation had worsened to the point that he had recently suffered the amputation of a foot. John Jr. and George were both on hand in Florida at the end, and helped Juty bring John's body home for a funeral at the church of his boyhood, Plymouth Congregational, and burial near his sons, brother, parents, and grandparents at Lakewood Cemetery. He was eulogized as one of the city's last human links to its industrial cradle at the Falls of St. Anthony. All but one of the mills at the falls that bore the Pillsbury name had been abandoned. But the model of civic leadership and service that the Pillsburys planted in Minnesota endured, in no small

John Pillsbury Snyder Jr.

part because John Sr. had been their exponent throughout a long and fruitful life.

When John died, he left two Pillsburys behind at the company that his father founded—his nephew Phil and his youngest son, George.

John Pillsbury Snyder Jr., the great-grandson of Gov. John S. Pillsbury, was also a Pillsbury Co. officer and director. Snyder would retire in 1970 as vice president of manufacturing services after thirty-five years with the company.[9] His "retirement" was actually a shift in his business focus from the Pillsbury Co. to the family's Mesabi Range land management firms. A more private man than his Pillsbury cousins, Snyder shared with his great Uncle Alfred a love for competitive sports that evolved through the years from hockey at Yale, where he played goalie as team captain, to competitive sailing with John Pillsbury Jr. on Lake Minnetonka and golf at Woodhill

Country Club, where he served a term as president. When Snyder died in 1989, he was laid to rest at Lakewood, where he had been a trustee for twenty-eight years.[10]

Phil succeeded John Sr. as the company's honorary chairman in 1965 and continued to play the role of roving corporate ambassador. The position gave him ample opportunity to do two things he loved—travel and promote Yale University. Phil had served as national chairman of the Yale Alumni Board in 1960-61,[11] and relished the chance the office afforded him to travel the country and renew old school ties. His efforts won him the college's highest alumni honor, the Yale Medal, in 1963.[12] He became an eloquent spokesman for the value of higher education. Even in his own industry, he said in 1964, apprenticeship in the milling craft was no longer sufficient preparation. "Rather, a good education, solidly based on flour technology and biochemistry, is very important to advancement in the milling industry," a magazine reported after an editorial board meeting with Phil. "Within the milling industry, understanding and teamwork have replaced the old method, where the superintendent or head miller was the master, and no one questioned his methods. . . . Nowhere else, Chairman Pillsbury added, does one get such an excellent return on one's investment as in education."[13]

Phil had been not only a witness to that transformation, but also had been its agent. When he retired as Pillsbury's chairman, he was the second-oldest active member of the Association of Operative Millers.[14] None of his successors in the board chairman's office had his knack for judging the effectiveness of roller mills by the feel of the flour. But Phil insisted that those who followed him into company leadership were all well-educated men, hired not for their personal connections but their ability.

As a result of the meritocracy Phil imposed at the Pillsbury Co., no familial privilege aided George S. Pillsbury as he climbed its ranks. But climb he did. After returning to Minnesota from the overseas division in New York City and taking over the bakery division in 1951, he moved up to vice president of industrial foods, then executive vice president of the firm's industrial "area" in January

George Pillsbury presents his cousin Phil with a coin collection as a memento of the Pillsbury Co.'s ninetieth year and Phil's thirty-fifth with the company, 1959.

1964.[15] He impressed his coworkers with his keen analytical mind and "people skills." "George Pillsbury could open up an operating statement and analyze it better than most officers can," attested Tony Owens, who worked for Pillsbury in a variety of management positions for thirty years.[16]

A few more years as an executive vice president and George likely would have been a candidate for CEO when Gerot moved on. But timing was not in his favor. Only nineteen months after George's promotion, Paul Gerot moved up to chairman as Phil assumed the honorary chairman's title that had been John Sr.'s. Robert J. Keith, who had risen as a consumer advertising and marketing manager before taking the reins of the rapidly expanding consumer area, was tapped as the next CEO. Keith restructured responsibilities to give George wider range. He would oversee both agricultural and industrial operations. Keith was a contemporary of John Pillsbury Jr.—slightly older than George but of the same generation. George believed that his chance at the top job was many years away.[17]

As he mourned his father's passing in 1968, George realized that his situation at the company was akin to his father's under the long presidency of Albert Loring. He expected to have years to wait before the CEO's position would be open again. John S. Pillsbury Sr. contented himself with a secondary role at the company. But George was not his father. He wanted fresh challenges and greater opportunity to make a difference for society. He relished involvement in Republican politics, and though he left the Orono School Board voluntarily in 1963 after two terms, he wondered whether he should again seek elective office. He also longed for more time to travel with Sally. They both had traveled extensively in their youth, but had done little exploring together. With their youngest child, Kathy, soon to depart for Concord Academy in Concord, Massachusetts, the couple began to consider taking an extended trip abroad, and George also toyed with the notion of returning to Yale as an administrator and part-time teacher.

A sense of added family responsibility in the wake of his father's death also weighed on George. Management of his family's investments and holdings was time-consuming, becoming more complicated as the family and its financial needs evolved. John Jr. and George shared the responsibility after their father's death. But John, schooled as a mineral law attorney, focused on Sargent Land Management Co. and the Mesabi Range. Someone from the family needed to oversee the rest of the portfolio.

A path forward emerged in George's mind—one that, at the suggestion of CEO Keith, he reviewed with fellow board member Willys Monroe of the management consulting firm Booz Allen & Hamilton. George would not leave the Pillsbury Co. entirely. He would remain an active member of the board of directors, and stay positioned to return to the executive suite someday. But he would give up his "day job" as a group vice president in order to head the family investment firm that he and John Jr. had created in 1967,[18] Sargent Management (now Meristem.) Sargent Management started with one client—John S. Pillsbury Sr. But it would soon have many more. George reasoned that being a non-employee of the milling company might make him a more effective board member. It would also afford him time to pursue other interests, which he had scrawled on a full legal-pad page to share with Monroe. One item among many: "Run for a seat in the Legislature." Monroe advised George that he was a lucky man.

George submitted his resignation as group vice president on November 4, 1969,[19] at age forty-eight. For the first time in a hundred years, no one named Pillsbury was involved in running the company bearing the family name. Though he had been planning his exit for six months, actually walking away from daily duties for the Pillsbury Co. was a challenging experience. Just exactly what would he do next? He did not have to wait long for an answer. Only a few weeks later, state Sen. Henry McKnight, who had represented District 33 in the Lake Minnetonka area since 1963, announced that he would not seek another term.[20] George promptly called his district's House member, Rep. Salisbury Adams, to ascertain whether he was interested in moving to the Senate. No, Adams said, he preferred to remain in the House where he had substantial seniority. George then sought state Rep. Bill Frenzel's advice: "Should I run?" Frenzel, who was running for Congress that year, was encouraging. "In politics, when the brass ring goes by, grab it!" he said. George had learned from his brother's experience in politics that hesitation can be fatal to one's chances. On December 5—less than one month after his Pillsbury Co. departure—the *Minneapolis Tribune* reported that George "is definitely interested" in running for the seat that represented the sprawling suburbs of Minnetonka, Plymouth, and New Hope, as well as the lakeside villages. He would seek Republican endorsement at the party's district convention in April 1970.

One other candidate also emerged—the House member from the eastern half of the Senate district, O. J. "Lon" Heinitz, an affable employment counselor from New Hope. With proven voter appeal, Heinitz was a strong contender for the Senate seat. George approached Heinitz with a proposal: Stay out of the Senate race in 1970 and seek another term in the House. New district boundaries would be drawn in the wake of the 1970 census, and the rapidly growing western suburbs were almost certain to gain an additional Senate seat for the 1972 election. Heinitz could seek that new seat, and Pillsbury would back him.

Nothing doing, Heinitz responded, and an all-out endorsement contest was on. Armed with valuable strategic advice from the mayor of Excelsior, Mike Harper, a former Pillsbury Co. research and development executive and the future CEO of ConAgra Foods, George set out to meet personally with all 100 delegates to the convention. He made the case that his commitment to public service and ideas about government reform would make him a good state senator. Like his great-great uncle a hundred years earlier, George was fascinated with government operations, and eager to bring business management principles to bear on government.

As a member of the Orono School Board in 1961, he had already exhibited that interest.[21] As Orono's member of the Metropolitan-Suburban Area School Boards Association, he had pushed for authorization of a study leading to a merit-based pay structure for teachers—an idea that was decades ahead of its time.[22] In 1970, he also stressed his desire to slow the growth in state government spending, and "find more equitable areas of taxation."[23] Those words had particular meaning in 1970. Years of rapid property tax increases to fund K-12 education for the large Baby Boom generation had generated a significant property tax revolt. Not even the creation of a three-cent state sales tax in 1967 for purposes of property tax relief slowed the climb in the state's most detested tax—despised because it bore little connection to a taxpayer's ability to pay. Senior citizens on fixed incomes were particularly resentful about rising homeowner taxes that pushed the most financially vulnerable in their ranks out of their homes. More equitable taxation in 1970 meant moving away from the local property tax to state income and sales taxes. But George made clear that he believed government could make better use of the tax money it already had before considering an increase in any tax. Among the ideas he touted was greater sharing of services and administrative costs by various levels of state and local government. Again, George was ahead of his time.

George's personal persuasion paid off with Republican delegates. Heinitz had been out-hustled. George led 54-46 on the first ballot at the April 8 convention. George picked up two votes on each of the next three ballots, reaching the sixty votes required for endorsement

IR - WAYZATA

on the fourth ballot.[24] Though hard-fought, a certain decorum was preserved, as illustrated by the attitude of one Heinitz supporter, New Hope Mayor Ed Erickson. He told George that he had promised his vote to his local state representative. But he had not promised to show up at the convention! His absence permitted the seating of an alternate delegate who favored Pillsbury.

GOP endorsement in the heavily Republican district was typically tantamount to election. But with no incumbent governor on the ballot and a property tax revolt churning, 1970 was an unsettled year in Minnesota politics. George was too prudent to leave the general election to chance. He campaigned hard.

Juty in 1972, wearing the Coco Chanel dress she purchased in 1913.

A threatened challenge in the GOP primary by Minnetonka mayor William Cooley failed to materialize.[25] In the general election, George faced John D. Kotula, principal of Assumption Catholic School in Richfield and a former unsuccessful candidate for the state House.[26] George campaigned in the time-honored style of Minnesota legislators. He "door-knocked" the district, personally dropping literature at voters' residences and meeting as many of them as he could. Occasionally, he was accompanied by an energetic octogenarian. Juty Pillsbury, who turned eighty-three that August, was more active in widowhood than she had been during her husband's confining last years. She kept herself in excellent physical condition with a daily swim and provided a firm familial touchstone for her grandchildren and growing brood of great-grandchildren. She had fun going door-to-door on warm autumn days, delivering campaign literature with George.

343

George won election handily on November 3, with 62 percent of the vote.[27] On January 4, 1971, for the third time since statehood, a Pillsbury took a seat in the state Senate. He joined the Conservative Caucus (it would not take the Republican label until 1973, when party designation was added to legislative ballots.) It held the Senate's majority by the barest of margins, 34-33. The House was also narrowly in Conservative hands, 70-65. The new governor was a DFLer, Wendell Anderson, and he had both a promise to keep and a fiscal problem to solve. He had campaigned on a pledge to support a state takeover of a considerable portion of local school costs, in exchange for greater equity among school districts. No more should the quality of a child's education be dependent on the wealth of his community. That idea had bipartisan backing. But the way to pay for it did not. Anderson inherited a major state budget deficit, making new spending politically difficult. But that didn't deter him. He proposed what remains the largest income tax increase on a percentage basis in state history—$762 million, or about a 30 percent increase in state spending.[28]

Though George had been a staunch backer of Anderson's 1970 GOP opponent, Attorney General Doug Head, he liked the bold new governor. Anderson had been raised in a working-class St. Paul neighborhood populated by Swedish immigrants—a long way from Brackett's Point. But he and George had one instant bond: hockey. Anderson had been a University of Minnesota hockey standout and a member of the 1956 U.S. Olympic hockey team.

They also shared similar thinking about school finances. George had become convinced as a school board member that the state should shoulder more financial responsibility for education. By his lights, property tax revenue should be used for property-related services, such as police and fire protection, sanitation, and street maintenance. "People taxes" on income and purchases should pay for "people systems" such as education and health care for the poor and disabled, George maintained. Local property taxes could be used for school buildings, but the lessons taught inside them were the state's responsibility, he argued. When he voiced those ideas in the House

Education Committee, they caught the attention of Senate Majority Leader Stanley Holmquist, a former rural school superintendent and businessman (and, coincidentally, the brother-in-law of former Gov. Elmer L. Andersen.) Holmquist was looking for Conservative Caucus mates to join him in forging a quiet alliance with the new governor. Holmquist shared Anderson's education policy goal, but wanted a smaller and more business-friendly mix of taxes to pay for the state's enlarged burden. He found one such ally in George Pillsbury and cultivated a friendship with the Senate newcomer.

But as a freshman legislator, George was excluded from the confabs of the select few legislative leaders assigned to conference committees where the debates took place over how to contain property taxes. These discussions surged past the regular session's constitutional time limits, and took the 1971 Legislature into the longest special session in state history. Waiting on the sidelines for decisions to be made in private by others was frustrating for someone accustomed to decisive action in the corporate world. At one point, George and fellow Conservative freshman Sen. Richard Palmer of Duluth attempted to attend the meeting of the Tax Conference Committee, which, in the days prior to enactment of open meeting laws, was closed to non-members. Holmquist showed the upstarts the door.

That experience fixed in George's mind a question he had occasionally mulled before. Conference committees are inefficient and insufficiently representative of all the people, he reasoned, and are necessary only because the constitution creates two parallel lawmaking chambers, a House and a Senate, whose different approaches to legislation must be reconciled. But were two chambers really necessary? They may have been, he acknowledged, when one chamber's members represented jurisdictions, such as counties, while the other represented districts drawn to contain relatively equal population. But after the 1964 landmark "one person, one vote" ruling of the U.S. Supreme Court,[29] districts in both chambers of the Legislature were redrawn on the same basis after each census, to equalize population.

The justification for dual-track lawmaking was gone, George reasoned, laying bare its downside: Two lawmaking houses were not as accountable to the people as one. The members of one house were afforded too much opportunity to shift responsibility for politically unpopular decisions to their opposite-house counterparts. Conference committees were inherently undemocratic and lacking in transparency. They excluded too many of the people's elected representatives from both parties, rendering them unable to affect the outcome of major decisions for which their constituents would hold them to account. In addition, George reasoned, the complexity of lawmaking in a two-house system discouraged citizen interest and engagement in the process. Perhaps the bicameral system's worst offense, in this businessman's mind, was its inefficiency. Lawmaking cost more than necessary in both time and money when two houses were involved. It was slow, so much so that it handicapped state government's ability to respond quickly to changing state needs, and stunted the capacity of all but the top legislative leaders to make a real difference for the state. "I wanted to organize the Legislature so it would be more fun to work there," he said.

That was the case for a unicameral Legislature that George began to verbalize during the long 1972 interim between lawmaking sessions.[30] The 1971 special session finally ended on October 30 with a victory for Anderson, engineered in large part by Holmquist and his allies in the Senate. What came to be known as the "Minnesota Miracle" included a $588 million increase in a mix of taxes—$176 million less than Anderson requested. The state's share of K–12 funding swelled from 43 percent to an eventual 70 percent.[31] Legislators went home to their last even-numbered year without a scheduled lawmaking session. Beginning in 1974, the annual sessions that Gov. John S. Pillsbury had helped to eliminate in 1878 would return as "flexible" sessions, timed as legislative leaders chose and limited to a specific number of days spread over two years. That constitutional change was sold to voters in 1972 as a move toward greater state government responsiveness to a complex, changing society. Pillsbury was open to more frequent legislative sessions,[32] but he saw annual sessions as a weak remedy for what ailed the Legislature. Eliminating one chamber would go to the root of the problems, he said. He vowed to initiate a constitutional amendment for a switch to a single-house Legislature in 1973 and years beyond. He knew he was in for

346

a long and difficult fight against entrenched incumbent-protection interests in both parties, but that didn't deter him. George didn't mind long odds when he was convinced he was right.

The requirement for redistricting after each decennial census means that Minnesota state senators elected during census years serve for two years, and must stand for reelection in their new districts in years ending in "2." That meant that the Pillsbury name was back on the ballot in 1972 in a district that had shifted westward. It would be the last legislative election in which names appeared on the ballot without party labels. George was confident enough about his contest with Hopkins attorney Raul Salazar that he focused considerable attention on fundraising for his fellow Conservative candidates around the state. He headed his Senate caucus's fundraising committee, and boasted early in the year about raising $24,000 from 300 contributors, a solid showing.[33] But by October of that presidential election year, despite the weakness of South Dakota Sen. George McGovern at the top of the Democratic ticket, Republican legislative campaign operatives didn't like the signals they were picking up from around the state. Their nervousness was justified. On November 7, the Conservative/Republican caucuses fell into minority status, 30-37 in the Senate, 57-77 in the House. George would never again serve in the majority.

His potential to influence state policy had been diminished, but not snuffed out. George had earned considerable bipartisan respect in his first term, and had forged a close friendship with the caucus leader that replaced Holmquist, Arden Hills banker Robert O. Ashbach. What's more, he had demonstrated a willingness to speak out on politically thorny issues—and many like-minded but more cautious legislators were happy to allow him to move to the fore.

On no issue was that more the case than on the political lightning rod of abortion. The emergence of a vigorous women's movement in Minnesota in the late 1960s put abortion on the political agenda several years before the U.S. Supreme Court, in an opinion written by Justice Harry Blackmun, a Minnesotan, legalized procedures to terminate pregnancy throughout the country. Many elected officials sought to dodge the politically sensitive issue. Not state Sen. George Pillsbury. Years of involvement in Planned Parenthood by Sally and other Pillsburys had exposed him to the tragedies associated with back-alley abortions. Desperate women were exposing themselves to lethal danger and dying preventable deaths as a result, he was convinced. He wanted that to change.

In his first campaign, George openly embraced what came to be called the "pro-choice" position. The *Minneapolis Star* summarized the position taken by both him and his DFL opponent as one favoring "revision of the present law [which outlawed all abortion] to permit the operations with consent of doctors and officials of licensed hospitals."[34] He was undeterred by the defeat in Morrison County of a legislative lion, Sen. Gordon Rosenmeier of Little Falls, in 1970 by upstart DFLer Winston Borden. Borden faulted Rosenmeier for allowing a pro-choice bill out of his Judiciary Committee and onto the Senate floor.

That wasn't the only issue Borden wielded against the aging veteran, but it was the one that got noticed by other nervous state politicians.[35] Despite Rosenmeier's fate, George introduced a bill in his first session that reflected what he had learned from Planned Parenthood. His bill would have increased the criminal penalties for abortions by non-physicians in non-licensed settings. But it removed the legal bar to the procedure when performed by physicians in hospitals and clinics. He found two other principled senators, Conservative Alf Bergerud of Minneapolis and Liberal Gene Mammenga of Bemidji, to sign on as co-authors. "George, do you know what you're doing?" asked an incredulous Sen. Bill Dosland of Moorhead, chairman of the Senate Judiciary Committee, when George sought a hearing on his bill. Seldom did a freshman legislator so willingly risk the ire of groups as powerful as those arrayed against the legalization of abortion.

The bill did not advance that year. Abortion was still illegal in Minnesota when the nation's high court removed the bar nationally on January 22, 1973. But that was only the beginning of a decades-long political struggle over the issue. By 1976, well-organized, well-funded anti-abortion groups were accusing George of infanticide and targeting him for defeat. But George didn't shy away from defending

George and Charlie, 1972.

his position, and gained admirers in both political parties for his courage. "All (abortion opponents) did was make me more interested in the topic," he said years later.

George gained a reputation as a serious student of public policy. He waded deep into such complexities as auto insurance reform, labor law, and regional municipal revenue sharing.[36] Like others in former Gov. Harold Stassen's line of progressive Minnesota Republicans, George was unafraid to use government as a tool for society's betterment, or to use public policy to leverage the broadest possible benefit from the private sector.

That predisposition drew him to ideas brought home from Yale University in the late 1960s by his elder son, Charlie. A thoughtful, principled young man, Charlie's Yale career is best known, forty years later, as a source of inspiration for his cartoonist roommate, Garry Trudeau. The comic strip character Michael Doonesbury is modeled after Charlie Pillsbury. But Charlie also became a serious analyst of societal problems at Yale, and like many in his generation, a critic of U.S. involvement in the Vietnam War. In February 1968, Charlie shocked his parents by skipping the Yale hockey team's end-of-season banquet and driving to Portsmouth, New Hampshire, to campaign for anti-war presidential candidate Eugene McCarthy. Charlie was the same fellow who, as a five-year-old, had campaigned door-to-door for Dwight D. Eisenhower with his mother in 1952.[37] His parents' reaction was provoked not only because Charlie was backing a Democrat, but also because it was this particular Democrat. Sally's brother Wheelock Whitney had been Eugene McCarthy's GOP opponent when the senator sought a second Senate term in 1964. Charlie had campaigned for his uncle against McCarthy just four years earlier. "You're working for the enemy!" George spluttered to his son.[38] Subject to the draft upon graduation, Charlie enrolled as a conscientious objector with the Selective Service system. He arranged to fulfill his service obligation in Minnesota, working for the Presbyterian-backed Center for Urban Encounter, which organized dialogues between white and black Twin Cities residents in the wake of several summers of racial strife in Minneapolis.

As a former Marine, George was slow to come around to Charlie's belief that the Vietnam War was wrong for America and for the Vietnamese, and ought to end. But come around he eventually did—pulled along by Sally, whose skepticism about the war and sympathy for her son's position led on one occasion to her attendance at an anti-war rally. Charlie was a leader in the Minnesota-based Honeywell Project, an anti-war effort aimed at convincing the local Minneapolis manufacturer to stop producing deadly anti-personnel bombs. He purchased Honeywell Corp. stock in hopes of using a shareholders' prerogative to inspect the company's records concerning war materiel production, exposing the intent of the explosive devices to cripple and maim as well as kill civilians in crowded situations.[39] Charlie's effort was foiled by the courts, but it led to a series of protest rallies outside Honeywell's south Minneapolis headquarters— only a few blocks from the site of the mansion his great-grandfather bought in 1890. On one such occasion, in April 1970, Charlie spoke, saying he would rather stand with the protesters on the sidewalk than attend the shareholders' meeting in progress inside.[40] Photos taken at the rally show him sporting a beard and wire-rimmed eye-glasses, giving him a striking resemblance to the Pillsbury men of Minneapolis a hundred years earlier. The similarity went beyond looks: 107 years before, another Charles Pillsbury had chosen not to go to war, evoking a conflicted response from another father named George Pillsbury.[41]

It must have been with a mixture of pride and discomfort that George heard his son attribute his anti-war activism to Pillsbury family values. But the case Char-lie made rang true:

"I've always been socially concerned...I believe that when I was a page at the Republican National Convention in 1964 [where his mother was a delegate backing Minnesota native son Walter Judd over Barry Goldwater], that I was doing that because I was socially concerned. I see this social involvement as a family tra-dition of sorts. This is why my father is involved in state

George Pillsbury Jr. in 1979.

politics. This is his way of expressing his commitment. So it is maybe how I have chosen to express my involvement, or where I have become involved, that is the difference."[42]

Charlie's younger brother George Jr., quieter but just as prin-cipled, might have said much the same thing. George and Sally awoke on May 30, 1971, to news that their second son, a Yale junior, was among seventeen people arrested early that Sunday morning in New Haven while supporting a strike by Yale service employees.[43] In his way, George Jr. too was upholding family values. He was blessed with the good fortune of a high draft number in the early 1970s, and was not called for military service.

Charlie made the most of his conscientious objector assignment. Working with the Rev. Bill Grace, a Presbyterian clergyman, and his associate Fred Smith, he and several other anti-war activists founded the Council for Corporate Review. It aimed to make corporations more alert to social concerns such as the one being raised in many quarters about Honeywell's war contracts, by buying one share of stock in each of five defense contractors based in the Twin Cities.[44] That would gain council members access to stockholder meetings and other avenues in which to register their objection to the manufacture of armaments. By 1973, the council had expanded its scope to include the local gas and electric utilities—the latter, Northern States Power, founded with Pillsbury involvement eighty years earlier. The council was instrumental in expanding both companies' boards to include a consumer and an environmental activist.

Charlie was keen on a concept for directing corporate energy toward the larger good that he encountered while doing research for his Yale senior thesis. It was described by Louis Kelso and Pat Hetter in their book, *Two Factor Theory: The economics of reality,* [45] where it was boldly labeled "universal capitalism." Charlie introduced it to George during long father-son discussions about how an economy grounded in capitalism could extend the benefits of prosperity to more people. The idea: Give people of modest means easy access to ownership of income-producing property. The place to start, George concluded: employee stock ownership plans.[46] Like his grandfather before him, George believed corporate profits ought to be shared with the employees who helped make them possible. He had been urging the Pillsbury Co. to adopt a modern version of his grandfather's profit-sharing plan of the 1880s. He also saw an illustration of Charlie's point in his own experience: After he left salaried employment and devoted himself to maximizing the growth of the family's investments, George's income increased. The "wages" of ownership exceeded those of employment alone.

George concluded that state and federal legislation was needed to provide tax-incentive encouragement for corporations to allow their employees to become stockholders too. U.S. Rep. Bill Frenzel, who was rising in stature as a member of the U.S. House, and Minnesota DFL Sen. Hubert Humphrey carried the ball in Washington. They encountered stiff resistance, and were not successful. But George did his part at the Minnesota Legislature, introducing a bill in the Senate in 1973 and recruiting Rep. Salisbury Adams to do the same in the lower chamber. State AFL-CIO president Dave Roe endorsed the measure, helping it sail through the Senate. Adams had more trouble in the House, but succeeded on March 7, 1974. The result was a change that, in George's words, "would bring capitalism to the workers." The bill established the legal framework for an employee stock ownership trust, to be available for wide employee participation. Discrimination against low-wage employees was prohibited. The bill allowed employers to contribute to employee trusts with the same income, gift, and estate tax advantages they would enjoy if they contributed to charitable trusts. It enabled employees to transfer shares in the trust to their immediate family members at their death without incurring inheritance taxes.

In one sense, it was a small change in the tax code. Without a federal parallel, the idea would prove slow to catch on among executives who worried about too much employee control of their affairs. It also met with resistance by charitable foundations, which saw the new employee trusts as rivals for corporate philanthropy. But among a particular group of employers—those who wanted to keep their businesses in Minnesota hands after their deaths—the employee stock ownership trust option was much appreciated.[47] It was a way to assure that Minnesota firms remained under local control. The trust idea also made employee ownership of their enterprises a matter explicitly favored by state law. George's grandfather likely would have smiled at finding George's affirmation of the power of employee corporate ownership engraved in state statute books:

> *It is the intention of the Legislature in defining and allowing for employee stock ownership trusts that the participation in the ownership of industrial, agribusiness, and other commercial businesses by the employees of the enterprises through the use of employee stock*

ownership trust would benefit all the people of Minnesota by: (1) Renewing and enlarging a sense of the worth of human effort; (2) Recognizing the interdependency of human effort and the ownership of the productive assets with which people work: (3) Providing direct economic advantage to employees from increased productivity: (4) Reducing differences in the real interests of labor and capital; and. (5) Relieving a primary cause of social tension and alienation. [48]

That legislative achievement was one of the few political matters Republican Pillsbury could cheer in 1974. On August 9, President Nixon resigned in disgrace after his attempt to conceal his role in a politically motivated break-in at Democratic National Headquarters in Washington's Watergate complex was exposed. George was among the first prominent Republicans in Minnesota to openly call on

Nixon to resign.[49] He could see more clearly than most the damage Nixon was doing to his party. He was chairman that year of the state Republican Finance Committee.

Politics can produce uncomfortable situations. Only a few weeks after Pillsbury made news with his

George hosted then-Vice President Gerald Ford in Minnesota, June 1974.

call on Nixon to resign, he played personal host to the vice president of the United States. Gerald Ford was stumping the nation that June, bravely attempting to rally the Republican faithful behind his beleaguered president. Ford had been appointed to the vice presidency only seven months earlier, when Spiro Agnew resigned amid allegations of wrongdoing. For Ford and Pillsbury, the golf date at Duff's Celebrity Tournament and fundraiser at Brackett's Point was a reunion: While a senior at Yale Law School, Ford worked as an assistant coach with the junior varsity team, which included a raw tackle named George Pillsbury. George may have lost faith in Nixon, but he was an abiding fan of Jerry Ford: "Ford then and now exemplifies two key ingredients of leadership: namely, absolute integrity and a very personal concern for the people he works with," George wrote at the time of Ford's appointment.[50]

The Minnesota visit that June produced two harbingers of things to come for Ford. One: At Rolling Green Country Club in Hamel, his golf ball caromed off a tree on the first tee and hit seventeen-year-old spectator Tom Gerard on the head. The young man was hauled to the emergency room, but suffered no serious injury.[51] Not so for Ford, whose bad luck with physical accidents would provide the nation's comedians with material for the rest of his time in office. Two: At a meeting with reporters outside George's house, Ford was asked what he thought of the state Republican Party's recent rejection of the proposed Equal Rights Amendment, approved by Congress in 1972 and by the DFL-controlled Minnesota Legislature in 1973 with George's support. The Minnesota GOP's move signaled a shift in political winds at the Republican grassroots, as an anti-abortion, anti-feminist faction began its ascendancy. Ford seemed not only opposed to that change in party sentiment, but oblivious to it. He allowed that he didn't know why anyone would oppose equality under the law for American women. He would hear a lot more about the issue in years to come. For his part, George was politician enough to slightly revise his position on the ERA, arguing in 1975 that eradicating legally sanctioned discrimination against women should be primarily a state responsibility, not a federal one.[52] The freshman tackle was more nimble, politically speaking, than the coach.

The drubbing for Republicans George feared in 1974 materialized in Minnesota. George and his fellow state senators were not on the ballot, but DFL Gov. Wendell Anderson carried all of the state's eighty-seven counties as he sought a second term, and the state House tilted sharply toward the DFL, 104-30. As the state party's finance chair, George worked hard and contributed much to keep the party's staff paid and offices open during a lean fundraising season.[53] He joined his fellow GOP leaders behind closed doors in the weeks after the election for conversations that moved quickly from blame-laying to strategizing about how to climb out of the deep hole in which Republicans found themselves. George brought to the table a novel idea: Change the party name to the Independent-Republicans of Minnesota.

The name-change idea originated in George's Senate caucus. It was the group that had most resisted adding party designation to legislative ballots. It had benefited through the years by being called the Conservative caucus, its leaders maintained, offering a state Capitol home to conservative Democrats from rural Minnesota as well as to Republicans, some of them urban liberals. The 1974 election was the first in which legislators' names and party labels appeared together on state ballots—and that election had been a disaster for Republicans. George was among several incumbents who wanted the name Independent Republican next to their own on the 1976 ballot. Among other virtues, that name suggested that the state GOP wasn't a smaller version of a national party that had been tainted by Richard Nixon and was moving to the right. Minnesota's party had principles and a platform of its own.[54]

George set out to sell the idea with a businessman's tool—market research. He and St. Paul GOP activist Paul Schilling raised $1,000 to pay for a poll and focus groups assessing the electorate's likely response to changing the party's name to Independent-Republican. They employed an up-and-coming pollster named Bill Morris, new in 1974 to the faculty of the University of Minnesota's political science department and a future state party chairman. The results confirmed George's notion that the Republican Party in 1975 had a brand problem. It found that only 15 percent of poll respondents said they had a favorable impression of the Republican Party.[55] Putting "Independent-Republican" rather than simply "Republican" on the ballot was likely to gain a candidate two to three percentage points in DFL-leaning districts, Morris reported. When George asked Morris what he recommended, the answer was "Change the name yesterday." That impressed the state party's new chairman, Chuck Slocum, who at age twenty-eight became the nation's youngest-ever head of a state political party in June 1975. Slocum was a corporate government affairs professional and former Senate Conservative Caucus aide, a pedigree that predisposed him to favor the name change. The poll suggested that the name "Independent Republicans of Minnesota" might also signal a new start for a party that badly needed one. Slocum and Pillsbury became allies in selling the new name to a skeptical GOP old guard, with Slocum out front and Pillsbury engaged in more private persuasion. Together they convinced the state party's executive committee to put the name-change question on the agenda of the November 15 convention in St. Cloud. It was a start, though clearing that hurdle did nothing to insure that the proposal would be accepted at the convention.[56]

Their breakthrough came when they won the public support of a respected former congressman, John Zwach, who had chosen not to run again in politically perilous 1974. His keen understanding of the depths of the national party's difficulties made him sympathetic to appeals from an eager young party chairman and a determined finance officer for help in separating the state party from the national one. When Zwach announced his support for a new name, other party activists fell in line. All the same, the convention's decision was not unanimous: leaders of the rising conservative faction—whose names would be linked in Minnesota with Ronald Reagan's presidential candidacy in 1976 and beyond—voted against the change. They recognized that the Pillsbury/Slocum move signified more than a marketing ploy. It also represented that duo's desire for a moderate-minded party targeting a more inclusive electorate including people not much associated with Republicans before—the young, the working class, and racial minorities. In George's vision, it would be a party big enough to encompass both sides of the abortion debate. "We wanted a big tent," Pillsbury said. He relished seeing the identifier "IR-Wayzata" after his name in the newspaper.

The name change was ridiculed by DFL leaders, who threatened that they would look for ways to lodge a formal complaint about deceptive advertising. (An October 1976 court test in Hennepin County affirmed the party's right to the "independent" name.) George took the DFL reaction as a signal that the change had been worthwhile. The first test of the new name was encouraging. In the

March 1976 St. Paul mayoral election, Independent-Republican former mayor George Vavoulis earned a respectable 48.4 percent of the vote against DFLer George Latimer in the heavily DFL capital city. Better evidence was not immediately at hand. In the presidential year of 1976, when voters swept Gerald Ford out of the White House, Independent-Republican legislative candidates did not sell well in Minnesota. Even George won in a squeaker, with a spare 50.9 percent of the vote in a campaign in which the abortion issue was used against him. The following year he joined a Senate IR caucus that had shrunken to only eighteen members.

Gov. Al Quie.

But in the midterm 1978 election, the value of what George and Chuck had wrought was brought home. Independent-Republicans swept the governorship and both U.S. Senate seats (both were on the ballot because of the January 1978 death of Hubert Humphrey), and battled back to a 67-67 tie in the Minnesota House. The election was dubbed the Minnesota Massacre. Said Slocum more than thirty years later: "At the lowest point in the history of the Republican Party in Minnesota, George Pillsbury was there to help us rise again. He was the finance chair that kept us in operation, and the man with an idea that said that we were coming back. It would not have happened without George Pillsbury."

The presence of a Republican, former U.S. Rep. Al Quie, in the governor's office gave Independent-Republican legislators more lawmaking relevance than they would have had without him in the four years beginning in 1979. But George began to recognize that he likely would not again serve in the majority, and thus not enjoy the clout that senior members of a majority caucus have as committee chairs. He would have to continue to look for other ways to make a difference.

One such opportunity arose when an old family friend launched a bid for the presidency in 1979. George Herbert Walker Bush—oil man, congressman from Texas, ambassador to China and to the United Nations, head of the Central Intelligence Agency—was the son of Wall Street banker and Connecticut U.S. Sen. Prescott Bush, a personal friend of John S. Pillsbury Sr. The younger Bush loved to tell his Pillsbury contemporaries about an exchange with their father at the beginning of World War II. George Bush had graduated from Andover Academy in 1942 and intended to enroll at Yale that fall, when he learned that because he was eighteen years old, he could join the Naval Air Force. Not long thereafter, he found himself at Wold-Chamberlain Field near Ft. Snelling in the Twin Cities for pre-flight training. John Pillsbury Sr. was acquainted with the commandant there, and contacted him to arrange a brief leave for Cadet Bush so he could visit Southways. The commandant scared the green cadet with an abrupt summons to his office, and informed him that a chauffeur would pick him up the following Saturday morning to drive him to lunch at the Pillsburys. Bush greeted his father's friend and nervously tried to carry on a conversation as the Pillsbury patriarch gave the young man a walking tour of Southways.

The tour ended in the living room, at which point John Sr. asked Bush, "What would you like to drink?"

Bush had never consumed a drink of alcohol before in his life. He did not know how best to answer. But he was keen on pleasing his host. "I'll have what you're having," he said.

John prepared two glasses of Scotch whisky and soda. Bush bravely consumed the concoction, with enough difficulty that he never forgot the drink or the man who served it.

George Bush met Sally Lu Whitney before George Pillsbury did. Bush went to prep school at Andover Academy, where his schoolmate was Sally's brother Wheelock. Wheelock invited Sally, then at Madeira School, to visit Andover and accompany him to a dance. Part of the inducement: he would arrange one dance for her with the handsome senior class president—George Bush.[57]

Through Yale University, Republican Party, and Planned Parenthood connections, the Bushes and the Pillsburys stayed in touch through the years. It was natural for Bush to ask Sally to head his presidential campaign finance committee in Minnesota in 1979, and for her to accept. She did the same when Bush, then vice president, ran for president in 1988, and for reelection to the presidency in 1992. But George and Sally were also disappointed with their friend's stance on abortion and family planning after moving into national prominence. As a leader in the American Birth Control League in the 1940s and treasurer of the first national capital campaign conducted by Planned Parenthood in 1947,[58] Prescott Bush had been a stalwart on family planning issues and a booster of Eleanor Bellows Pillsbury's international work on the issue. Prescott's son appeared to hold the same position, and wrote as much in the foreword of a 1973 book.[59] But when Ronald Reagan asked Bush to serve as his vice president, the offer came with the condition that Bush adopt Reagan's anti-abortion position. Bush accepted the condition, and did a quick 180-degree turn on the issue. Pro-choice Republicans around the country, including George and Sally, felt let down.

George won reelection to the state Senate in 1980 with a healthy 60 percent of the vote. It was a nice farewell tribute from District 42. He had originally intended to serve in the Legislature for only eight years, but that would have meant resigning at mid-term. A special election would be required, which might cost his party the seat. George decided, therefore, to remain in office until new district lines were drawn in 1982 and then retire. As he went public with his intentions in January 1982, he allowed that he would be leaving with unfinished business at the Legislature. He still considered a two-house Legislature "archaic, awkward and frustrating," and believed that conference committees were fundamentally undemocratic. He vowed to continue to press for a single-house Legislature as a private citizen.[60]

It was a promise he would keep. Not long after leaving the Senate, a major academic study of legislative operations was launched by

George and Sally with President George H. W. Bush aboard Air Force One, 1992.

Royce Hanson, the new associate dean of the Humphrey Institute of Public Affairs at the University of Minnesota. George had no assurance that Hanson's work would support the unicameral cause. Nevertheless, he willingly shouldered responsibility to raise money for the project, which the Legislature, true to form, had badly underfunded. Within three years, he raised $80,000 for the work. "Without the dedication, encouragement, goading and flat-out cheerleading provided by George Pillsbury, this study never would have gotten off the ground," Hanson wrote in the preface of the report, "Tribune of the People: The Minnesota Legislature and Its Leadership."[61] George's confidence was not misplaced. Hanson's 1989 report concluded with a ringing endorsement of single-house lawmaking under the headline, "Time for a Unicameral Legislature." [62]

The report made a brief splash but was soon forgotten. Eight years later, George decided to make one more push. He and a like-minded former DFL state senator, Gene Merriam, then an executive with the newspaper publishing company ECM Publishers founded by former Gov. Elmer Andersen, filed the necessary paperwork to create the nonprofit Citizens Committee for a Single House Legislature. An impressive list of supporters signed on, including Andersen, Gov. Arne Carlson, and Humphrey Institute Dean and former state

Sen. John Brandl. The election of pro-unicameral governor in 1998, Jesse Ventura, and pro-unicameral speaker of the state House, Steve Sviggum, convinced George that the time was right. He contributed $50,000 of his own money and raised more,[63] hired Ron Lattin as committee coordinator, James Erickson as chief lobbyist, Bill Hillsman to design an ad campaign, and Chuck Slocum as general manager of the project, and they were off.[64]

But when politicians are asked to eliminate their own jobs, chances for an affirmative answer are always small. Longtime legislators, schooled in the many ways to scuttle unwanted legislation, made sure the proposed single-house amendment did not succeed. It got as far as the House floor, where it was sent back to committee—thereby averting a clean up-or-down vote on the measure in an election year. Senate Majority Leader Roger Moe, a staunch opponent of eliminating one chamber, said he would not bring the bill to the floor if the House did not act on it first.[65] That ended the single-house push of 1997-2000.

Rewinding to the 1980s: A deep government financial crisis came with the recession that hit Minnesota in 1980 and 1981. Like most states, Minnesota is constitutionally obliged to balance its budget every two years. By 1982, a succession of special sessions to patch the leaky state budget had forced legislators in both parties to vote for things they detested—increases in income and sales taxes and cuts to every sort of public service, including schools. It was hard for legislators to take pride in their work. George was one of a large cohort of lawmakers, including Gov. Quie, who did not run again in 1982. One of George's last-term goals as a member of the committee that financed transportation was to push through a four-cent per gallon gasoline tax increase in 1981. But the need to raise other taxes to balance the state budget cooled other legislators' willingness to increase the price of gasoline at the same time.[66]

George found an unexpected way to make a lasting difference for Minnesota during his last term in office—a way that highlighted the public value of George and Sally's private partnership. While George had been rising in stature in the state Senate, Sally too had taken her career as a full-time civic and political volunteer to a new level. She

State Sen. George Pillsbury during the second special session of 1981, when the Minnesota state budget repeatedly slipped into deficit. Next to him is future U.S. Rep. Collin Peterson.

had long been in demand as a board member by a host of good causes, civic and corporate, local and national. In the early 1980s, her calendar included meetings of the governing boards of Minnesota Suburban Newspapers, Americans for Clean Air and Water, Americans for the Coast, the Arthritis Foundation National Advisory Council, the Guthrie Theater, the New Leadership Fund, the National Corporate Theatre Fund, and—in keeping with long tradition among Pillsbury women—Pillsbury House. In addition, she pitched in to help elect Republican candidates every election year. That had been her pattern since returning to Minnesota from New York in 1951. Within months of moving into Alfred Pillsbury's mansion near the Minneapolis Institute of Arts, she was elected the city's Eighth Ward Republican chairwoman. In 1982, as George wrapped up his legislative career, Sally was working in bipartisan fashion to help found the Minnesota Women's Campaign Fund.

Sally's biggest responsibility in the early 1980s was at the University of Minnesota. Since 1975, she had served on the board of governors of the University of Minnesota Hospitals; in 1982, she was the board's chairman. What Charles A. Pillsbury had helped found as a free clinic for the poor in the 1870s had grown into a world-renown center of teaching, research, and clinical practice, treating the region's most complex and intractable medical conditions. Sally arrived on the board at a time of major change and rapid growth for the hospitals. Disparate academic and clinical administrations were coming under the umbrella of a single Academic Health Center in those years, as tall new teaching and research towers rose to accommodate their rapidly expanding work. Now a modern hospital building was needed to properly house the clinical aspect of the university's medical mission. And the hospital governing board found its work frequently delayed or stymied by its subservient relationship with the Board of Regents, which lacked the time and focus that the complex medical enterprise needed from its decision-makers. An outmoded governance structure had the regents accustomed to thinking of the hospital board as merely an advisory group. "They acted like we were just another course," Sally said. The longer she served on the board, the more determined she became to change that relationship. As the head of a task force established to recommend a new governance model in 1981, she helped engineer greater autonomy for the hospital board. That year, as the board's vice chairman, she was also much involved in planning for a new University Hospital—an effort that ran into obstacles caused by the deepest economic slowdown the state had seen since the 1930s.

The case was strong for better University Hospital facilities. Buildings that dated from the 1920s were still in use. But going to the Legislature to authorize $190 million in state general obligation bonds during a recession was no easy matter—especially since almost all of the private hospitals in the Twin Cities were cool to the project. Hospitals were overbuilt in the Twin Cities in those years, and some were in financial difficulty. Their leaders feared that a more attractive facility at the university would draw patients away from them, worsening their problems. They argued: Why not do what Harvard University does in Boston, and use several hospitals in the community as teaching and research facilities?

George was aware of the resistance Sally and her board were encountering. In 1981, he was not directly positioned to help. He was a member of neither the capital investment (bonding) committee nor the health and welfare committee that had jurisdiction over the proposal. But—again because of Sally's board work—he happened to know that the Twin Cities' hospital administrators' position was not unanimous. A conversation he and Sally had with Carl Platou, president of the Fairview Hospitals, left George convinced that Platou might break ranks with his peers. Carl's wife Sue was Sally's colleague on the Guthrie Theater board, and they had discussed the matter on a General Mills corporate airplane flight to attend a Guthrie touring company performance in Sioux Falls, S.D. George contacted Platou, and heard a strong argument for rejecting the Harvard model: "I don't think that a physician on the staff of Fairview or St. Mary's or Eitel (Hospital) has the competence to be on the faculty at the university automatically," Platou said. If medical education is dispersed to those hospitals, their physicians will be expected to play a faculty role. "If you do this, there will be faculty flight, and our medical school will become fifth-rate."[67] George asked: Would he come to the Capitol and say as much there? Yes. Would he also meet privately with the chair of a joint House-Senate health policy committee, Rep. Jim Swanson of Richfield? Yes. Platou informed Swanson, a staunch DFLer, that the other hospital CEOs had been pressed into opposing the hospital project by Donald Wegmiller, a hospital administrator who also had been a White House staff assistant for Republican Presidents Richard Nixon and Gerald Ford.[68] Swanson's support for the new University Hospital was sealed.

George orchestrated Platou's lobbying effort. But, shrewdly, he stayed in the background, knowing that his connection to a leading member of the hospital board of governors could be used to undermine his credibility on the issue. He only spoke publicly on behalf of the project once, on the floor of the Senate during the bonding bill debate in May 1981. The $190 million authorization became law.[69] The story of George's involvement did not surface until, nearly thirty years later, Platou was feted at a Minneapolis Club luncheon for his work as a senior advisor to the dean and leading fundraiser for the University of Minnesota Medical School. At that event, Platou singled out George and Sally Pillsbury as two people whose roles

George and Sally chat with Carol Bellamy, former executive director of UNICEF, at an event at the Humphrey Institute.

in 1981 helped make possible the facility that became University of Minnesota-Fairview Hospital, the leading tertiary-care hospital in the Twin Cities. "It would not have been built without them," Platou said.[70] His recognition of them both was deserved and appropriate. Long before the term "power couple" was in vogue, George and Sally were demonstrating what it meant.

Epilogue

Vigorous Citizens

"It was almost like hearing about a death in the family."[1] That's how George reacted on October 3, 1988, when he learned that one of the world's leading consumer goods companies, Grand Metropolitan plc, had made a $60-per-share bid for the Pillsbury Co. Its stock had been trading at about half that price. George had been worried for several years that the company that bore his family's name was not delivering an adequate return to its shareholders. Management was not making the most of the company's assets, he fretted.

The Pillsbury Co. boomed in the decade after George left its payroll, despite an unforeseen leadership change. George was wrong in 1969 about the durability of Robert J. Keith. The CEO who led the company to its first and most important restaurant acquisition, Burger King, in 1967 stepped down nearly five years later, and died of leukemia in 1973.[2] He was succeeded by William Spoor, whose vision for the company was based on growth through rapid-fire acquisition of food products and restaurant chains. Well-known grocery store brand names moved into the Pillsbury fold during Spoor's tenure—Totino's, Green Giant, HaagenDazs, Van de Kamp, Chicken of the Sea. The iconic TV pitchman, Poppin' Fresh, the Pillsbury Doughboy, helped keep the company name before consumers and its line of baking mixes and refrigerated dough products growing. Meanwhile, Burger King acquired some restaurant siblings—Steak & Ale, Bennigan's and two restaurant groups, Diversifoods (which included Godfather's Pizza) and QuikWok. Each year between 1972 and 1986, the company set records for both sales and earnings.[3] Long in second place to General Mills, Pillsbury surpassed it in earnings in 1985, Spoor's last year at the helm. The company looked invincible.

George, whose focus as an employee had been on agri-products and industrial sales, worried that those lines had become a drag on growth. Pillsbury was still doing what it had always done—operating flour mills and selling flour to the world. But the world's capacity to mill its own flour and avoid shipping expenses had greatly increased. Some managers and members of the board wondered whether Pillsbury should sell its mills. But the larger problem that arose after Spoor's retirement was in the restaurant division he had built.[4] In the mid-1980s, the profitability of several of the company's restaurant lines suddenly dropped. Burger King, the largest of the Pillsbury restaurant chains, was particularly troubled. Corporate analysts said the company had expanded too far, too fast, and was unable to keep pace with changing consumer tastes in restaurants and the exacting management those enterprises required.

For a family in which the past often portended the future, it's notable that Grand Met's takeover bid surfaced almost exactly 100 years after another London-based investor group appeared to buy C.A. Pillsbury & Co. George's forebears welcomed the 1889 sale. The Minnesotans who ran the Pillsbury Co. in 1988 did not appreciate the British invasion. But after three months of resistance that included an attempt to spin off Burger King that was prevented by court order, Grand Met's offer rose to $66 per share, and the battle was over. Pillsbury became a division of Grand Met. For George, "the fact that the bid was a very handsome premium didn't soften the blow. It was like hearing that a good friend had died and left you a lot of money. You'd much rather that the friend had lived."[5]

But just as the 1889-1911 period of British ownership was only an interlude in the Pillsbury corporate story, so did Grand Met's control prove to be fleeting. In 1997, Grand Met merged with Guinness plc to become Diageo plc, a company whose focus was on the profitable spirits and beer business. In July 2000, Diageo announced that an old friend—General Mills—had made a play for Pillsbury. It succeeded. The historic rivals at the foot of the Falls of St. Anthony were united at last and headquartered where they belonged, in Minnesota. As that deal unfolded, George had a sense that his grandfather was beaming.

The Pillsbury Company—twice gone from Minnesota, twice transformed and brought home again—has not yet proven to be a metaphor for the family's own story. In 1989, a local magazine profiled George in a cover story headlined: "Pillsbury's last Pillsbury." It might have read "Minnesota's last Pillsbury." Every member of the next generation bearing that well-known surname has made a life elsewhere. A handful of cousins of Snyder and Gale lineage remain in Minnesota, as do Ella Pillsbury Crosby and all six of her children. But by 2010, George and Sally headed the only Minnesota household bearing the Pillsbury surname that traces to the enterprising brothers from Sutton, N.H. They continue to make impressive civic contributions well past their eightieth birthdays. And they are touchstones for their extended family, keeping children, grandchildren, nieces and nephews tethered to Minnesota in ways that bring them back periodically, and could one day lure one or more of the expanding clan to return for good.

Circa 2010, here's the last word on some of the Pillsburys of Minnesota, and the latest word on others:

Helen Pendleton Winston Pillsbury, "Aunt Nelle" to George and his siblings, died December 7, 1957 at age seventy-nine. She had been Charles S. Pillsbury's widow for more than 18 years, and moved year-round to their estate on Ferndale Road in Wayzata after his death. Their "townhouse" at 100 East Twenty-second Street now houses BLIND Inc., an adjustment-to-blindness training center. Nelle put great stock in genealogy, befitting the granddaughter of John Stevens, the first European-American to build a permanent home on the west bank of the Mississippi River in what became Minneapolis, and the daughter of an officer in the Confederate Army.[6] The exhaustive two-volume recounting of the ancestry of twins John S. and Charles S. Pillsbury that she commissioned, executed by Mary Lovering Holman in 1938, is an enduring gift to both her family and historians.

All three of Charlie and Nelle's daughters left Minnesota to attend Smith College, where they excelled academically, and with only brief exceptions, they never again lived in Minnesota. The eldest, **Mary Pillsbury Lord,** worked in Minneapolis social work for two years before marrying Oswald Bates Lord and moving to New York. Her extensive career in civic work and politics, culminating as U.S. delegate to the United Nations, is described in Chapter 11. In that role and ones that followed with the International Rescue Committee, she traveled extensively, experiencing adventures she and her husband chronicled in their 1970 book, *Exit Backward, Bowing.*[7] Mary died on July 21, 1978.

Her two sons, **Charles Pillsbury Lord** and **Winston Lord,** were never Minnesotans. But their achievements bear noting. Winston became a key figure in normalizing U.S. relations with China in the early 1970s. He was a member of the National Security Council's planning staff from 1969 to 1973, and a protégé of then-Secretary of State Henry Kissinger who accompanied Kissinger on his first trip to normalize U.S. relations with China. During President Ronald Reagan's second term, Winston served as ambassador to China, and continued under President Bill Clinton as assistant secretary of state for east Asian and Pacific affairs. His wife, Bette Bao Lord, is a best-selling author whose novels focus on modern Chinese history. They have two children, Elizabeth and Winston.

Charles Lord built a successful career in the pharmaceutical industry, first with Squibb Corp., then as president of Hydro-Med Sciences, a division of National Patent Development Corp. At midlife he changed careers, becoming a high school teacher and, eventually, headmaster at two private schools for girls. In the 1990s he was Washington bureau chief of Children's Express, a children's news service whose articles are published widely in U.S. newspapers. He is married to art historian and educator Gay Patterson Lord; they have three children, Thomas, Charles and Deirdre.

Mary's two younger sisters, **Katharine Pillsbury McKee** and **Helen Pillsbury Becker,** lived in Annapolis, Maryland and Albany, New York, respectively. Katharine and Mary were party to a reprise of a frightening episode in family history in January 1935. They were passengers on the *S. S. Mohawk,* an ocean liner that debarked from Manhattan just after a massive snowstorm and headed for warmer climes, with stops planned in Florida, Cuba and Mexico. The big ship did not get past New Jersey. It inexplicably rammed the Norwegian freighter Talisman at about 9:30 p.m. and sank about 70 minutes later.[8] Like John and Nelle Snyder on the Titanic in 1912, Mary and Katharine made it to lifeboats and safety that frigid night—a feat, considering that many of the Mohawk's lifeboats were frozen in place and immovable. As female first-class passengers, they were ushered to the head of the lifeboat line. Forty-five passengers and crew lost their lives that night.[9] One who didn't was a tiny baby thrust into the sisters' arms by a woman traveling on a lower deck who was not sure she would be allowed on a lifeboat. The sisters told their children later that while in the frigid, unstable lifeboat, the baby began to cry uncontrollably. The sailor steering the boat found a can of condensed milk, kept on board for just such a situation. But the baby was too young to drink from the can. Mary thought quickly. "Do you have a condom?" she asked the sailor. He did. Mary had a diamond stickpin, rescued from her stateroom when she fetched her lifejacket. It was used to poke a hole in the condom from which the baby could nurse. In that way, the child was comforted—and was eventually reunited with its mother, who survived.[10] Not as fortunate was a five-year-old boy also handed to the sisters in the lifeboat. His parents both perished.

Katharine, already the mother of two sons, Philip and E. Bates, on that fateful night in 1935, had a third, Charles, in 1940. Helen had two daughters, Katharine and Elizabeth, and two sons, John and David. Like Mary, Katharine died in 1978; Helen, the youngest of Charles and Nelle Pillsbury's four children, was the first to die, in 1963.

Charles and Nelle's son **Philip W. Pillsbury** was lonely after his wife Eleanor Bellows Pillsbury died in 1971. He discovered another lonely heart nearby. Corinne Griffith, daughter of the owner of the Minnesota Twins baseball team, Calvin Griffith, had been educated in Italy, New York and London. When in Minnesota, she lived near Phil along the Lake Minnetonka shore. The much-younger woman, born in 1944, became a favorite companion of the retired miller. They were married in Paris on November 7, 1977. Phil died of cancer on June 14, 1984 at age eighty-one, eleven days after attending his sixtieth anniversary class reunion at Yale University and ten days after his last Pillsbury corporate board meeting.[11] Corinne Griffith Pillsbury suffered from poor health, and endured two kidney transplants and a pancreas transplant before she died at age fifty-eight on May 10, 2003.[12]

Phil and Eleanor had two sons, **Philip Jr.** and **Henry**. Their father's Pillsbury Co. rule about not hiring family members at the start of their careers launched them on trajectories away from the milling company and Minnesota. Most of Phil Jr.'s career was with the United States Information Agency, attempting to introduce and explain the people, culture and policies of the United States to the world. He also spent the late 1960s working with the Minneapolis Urban League as it played a leadership role during transformative years of the twentieth-century civil rights movement. His USIA work took him to places as far-flung as Zaire, Iran, Mali and Madagascar; twice he received the USIA Meritorious Honor Award. Phil and his wife, native Minnesotan Caroline Hannaford, known to all as Nina, now live in Washington, D.C. They are involved in a number of civic activities there, though they also maintain a summer home on the site of his grandparents' Lake Minnetonka estate. It preserves the name that originated at the Stinson farm in New Hampshire in the 1800s and that Charles and Nelle gave to their Lake Minnetonka home, Dunbarton. Phil is much involved in raising money for the restoration of Pillsbury Hall at the University of Minnesota.

Phil and Nina have three children, Fendell, Caroline and Phillip Winston III. The October 18, 1997 wedding of Caroline to Andrew Oliver II of New York was so genealogically notable that it produced a front-page story in the *New York Times*.[13] Caroline's grandmother, Eleanor Bellows Pillsbury, was a direct descendent of Miles Standish, the Mayflower pilgrim made famous by Henry Wadsworth Longfellow's 1858 poem, "The Courtship of Miles Standish." Oliver is a direct descendent of the object of Standish's unrequited affection, according to Longfellow's fictional account, and of Standish's aide, Priscilla Mullens and John Alden. The headline in the Times: "Priscilla told Miles 'I won't,' but two descendents say 'I do.'"

Henry made his home in France, where he worked as an actor and director and spent twenty years as executive director of the American Center in Paris.[14] In 2008, he was honored for his contributions to French cultural life and French-American relations, receiving the prestigious title "Officier dans l'Ordre des Arts et Lettres." Today Henry and his wife Barbara Watson are active arts promoters via King's Fountain, a nonprofit production-counseling firm for artistic and humanitarian projects. Henry has two sons, Henry Adams Jr. and Matthew.

Ever a lover of rural life, **Al Gale** lives alone on a wooded peninsula jutting into Whale Tail Lake west of Lake Minnetonka. Across the lake is his father's beloved Wickham Farm—now Gale Woods Farm, the family's 420-acre donation to the public domain. Gale's wife Leona, a faithful churchwoman, died in 2008; their younger son John of Menomonie, Wisconsin, was killed in an auto accident in 2005, leaving his wife Mary and two children, Patrick and Sarah. John was a farmer and businessman involved in local elective office—as was Al himself, first as a school board member in North Dakota, then as a park board member in Minnetrista. **Edward Gale**, Al's older son, is a psychologist in Santa Fe, New Mexico. While a Minnesotan in the 1990s he was a member of the Minnetrista City Council and the village's mayor for one term, 1997-98.[15] Edward is married to Maria Mayer Gale and is the father of three children, Sam, Kate and Peter.

Indomitable **Eleanor Jerusha Lawler Pillsbury** died in her lakeside home, Southways, on September 7, 1991, at age 104. In good health and keen mind until a broken hip brought on a precipitous decline, Juty was a lifelong patron of causes she held dear—the University of Minnesota Landscape Arboretum, the National Society of Colonial Dames of America, Planned Parenthood, the Minnesota Orchestra, the Minneapolis Institute of Arts, and Steven's Square, the home for the elderly that Mahala Fisk Pillsbury helped establish in the 1880s. As "Mema" to her grandchildren, she instilled the importance of integrity, duty to community, regular physical exercise and excellence in whatever they chose to accomplish. "My advice to them is to hold on to their health; develop their powers of the intellect, reason and will, and never lose their self-esteem," Juty wrote in her 1972 memoir.[16] She lived what she preached.

Southways was sold to James Jundt, owner and manager of an investment fund, in 1992. In 2008, he put it on the market for a jaw-dropping $53.5 million.[17] The landmark of Brackett's Point did not sell, and was taken off the market in the summer of 2010. Local preservationists are rooting for the grand house to survive and prosper well into its second century.

John S. Pillsbury Jr., Juty's eldest, left NWNL in 1977, but only gradually disengaged from other civic and corporate activities during the last quarter-century of his life. He remained a leading force for Sargent Land Management, and was a significant patron of the United Way, Twin Cities Public Television and his favorite, the Minnesota Orchestra. He and Kitty forsook their sprawling Wood-hill Road house and joined George and Sally on Brackett's Point in a tasteful Prairie School-style house in the 1980s. He died at age 92 on March 28, 2005.[18] **Katharine Clark Pillsbury** followed him in death a little more than a year later, on April 7, 2006. Her community involvement wound down in her last years, but she stayed close to the Friends of the Art Institute, which she once headed, until the end.[19]

Among their four children, one—**John Sargent Pillsbury III,** known to all as "Jock"—spent a significant portion of his career in Minnesota. After graduating from Yale in 1960 and serving two years in the U.S. Navy, Jock joined the staff of First National Bank in Minneapolis. One of his first jobs in the training program was counting cash in the cash vault. The Dayton brothers had just opened the first three Target discount department stores in the Minneapolis suburbs and one of Jock's jobs was to count some of the first cash register receipts, delivered daily to the bank in locked bags, of stores that would be replicated hundreds of times around the globe in coming decades. After two years in the training program, Jock was transferred to the trust department, and later moved to the commercial loan department. There, he ended up—fittingly for a Pillsbury—in charge of agribusiness loans. But he was lured away in 1981 by the opportunity with several partners to found a bank on Camelback Road in fast-growing Phoenix, Arizona. They called it Camel Bank. Off to Phoenix he went with his wife, **Ellen Bemis Pillsbury** (daughter of Judson "Sandy"

Bemis, who headed the family's packaging-products company by the same name and consolidated its headquarters in Minneapolis in the 1960s[20]) and their four children, Anne, John Sargent IV ("Sargent") Peter and David. Jock and Ellen now divide their time between homes in Telluride, Colorado and Santa Barbara, California.

The unexpected death of Jock's brother **Donaldson Clark Pillsbury** on June 12, 2008 was mourned in both Minnesota and New York, where Don spent his adult life. He was a Yale-educated attorney who specialized in the practice of domestic and international banking and finance law at Davis Polk in New York City, and whose clients included financial services giant J.P. Morgan. In 1998 he became general counsel for the worldwide auction house Sotheby's, and at the time of his death he was chairman of Sotheby's North and South America. He was eulogized as a pillar of the New York arts community, where his service included chairing the governing board of the Lincoln Center Chamber Orchestra.[21] He left a wife, Marian McClure "Marnie" Stuart, a one-time aide to New York Mayor John Lindsay and Illinois Sen. Charles Percy who is now a philanthropic advisor to David Rockefeller. They had three children, Donaldson Clark Jr., Blair, and Wendy.

John Jr. and Kitty had two other children. Dr. **Lynde Harrison Pillsbury** is a Washington D.C. pediatrician specializing in allergies. He served a stint in the Peace Corps in Iran, obtained a law degree and briefly practiced law at the U.S. Department of Housing and Urban Development before becoming a doctor. He's married to the former Janet Simmons; they have five children, Courtney and Rory Pillsbury and Taylor, David and C. Blake Smith. **Katharine Pillsbury Jose** of Brookline, Massachusetts, is a volunteer and docent at the Boston Museum of Fine Arts and has four children, Whitney Bylin, Katharine Jose, Sarah Rhuda and Tad Jose.

Eddy Pillsbury's widow **Priscilla Keator Pillsbury Giesen** remarried three times and is a widow again living in Santa Barbara, California. She had three Pillsbury children: **Priscilla Pillsbury Gaines** is married to Dr. Jason Gaines, a retired internist; they divide their time between Hamden, Connecticut and Santa Barbara and have one son, Sam. **Edmund Pennington Pillsbury Jr.**—Ted to all who knew him—met with an untimely death on March 25, 2010. He enjoyed wide acclaim in the arts world, first as director of the Yale Center for British Art, then for 18 years as director of the Kimbell Art Museum of Ft. Worth, Texas. When he died he was chairman of the fine arts department of Heritage Auction Galleries in Dallas.[22] He and his wife, the former Mireille Bernard, had two children, Christine and Edmund Pennington III. **Joan Pillsbury DePree** is widowed and lives in Lake Forest, Illinois. She has four children, Katharine, Edmund, Priscilla and Spencer.

Ella Sturgis Pillsbury Crosby, John and Juty's elder daughter, lives in a Wayzata condominium with a glorious view of Lake Minnetonka. A widow since 1988, she dotes on her six children, 20 grandchildren and the still-arriving next generation. Like her mother before her, she played a number of leadership roles in civic institutions. She was president of the Friends of the Minneapolis Institute of Arts and a longtime board member of the museum Alf Pillsbury loved. She also served on the boards of Stevens Square, the

Ella Pillsbury Crosby followed her mother's lead in style and civic involvement. In 1966, mother and daughter exhibited their own 18th and 19th century silver serving pieces at Dayton's 8th Floor Auditorium as part of a Minnetonka Garden Club fundraising display, "Festive Table Settings."

successor organization of the home for orphans and the aged that Mahala Pillsbury had helped establish; Northrop Collegiate School for Girls in Minneapolis, and Foxcroft School in Middleburg, Virginia. She also encouraged her husband Tom in wide-ranging civic work that included chairing the governing boards of the Blake School, the Minneapolis Foundation and Carleton College.

Ella's eldest son, **Thomas Manville Crosby Jr.,** is a Yale-educated attorney recently retired from Faegre and Benson, his uncle

John's old firm, where he had been managing partner from 1993 to 1997. Like John Pillsbury Jr., Tom chaired the Minnesota Orchestra board, the Minneapolis Club and the United Way, as well as several other civic organizations. He also upheld Pillsbury tradition by serving eight years on the Medina City Council and, in 2006, by winning election as mayor of the west-metro community north of Lake Minnetonka. He and his wife Ellie have four children, Stewart, Brewster, Grant and Brooke.

His brother **David Pillsbury Crosby** is an investment banker and former managing director of Piper Jaffray & Co., the investment firm founded by C.P. Jaffray, son of the young teller who once watched Gov. John S. Pillsbury single-handedly stop a run on First National Bank. David too has led the governing boards of the Minneapolis Club, Lakewood Cemetery, the Minneapolis Foundation, Dunwoody Institute and Blake School. He and his wife Kitty have three children, Michael, James and Katherine. Kitty was the third Pillsbury to win election to the Orono School Board.

Eleanor Crosby Winston, Ella's eldest daughter, married Frederick Winston, a banker, kinsman of Helen Winston Pillsbury and a leading environmentalist and longtime president of the Quetico Superior Foundation. They have four children, Eleanor, Frederick, Thomas and Elizabeth. She's a past chair of Minnesota Parks and Trails and a longtime board member of the Minnesota Historical Society, Pillsbury United Communities, the YWCA and the Carolyn Foundation, a foundation supporting healthy children, families and communities established in 1964 as a bequest of Tom Crosby Sr.'s aunt, Carolyn McKnight Christian.

In 1978, **Mary Crosby Dolan** married William Dolan of Minneapolis, a widower with four children under the age of 10. She adopted the four Dolan children, and she and Bill had two sons, Thomas and William. She's a registered nurse, a graduate of the College of St. Catherine in St. Paul, and has been active in Planned Parenthood.

Lucy Crosby Mitchell, who has a master's degree in social work from the University of Minnesota, married Minneapolis attorney Robert G. Mitchell Jr. in 1977 and has three children, David,

Four generations in the Southways pool: Juty with Nick, George Jr., and George, in about 1987.

Edward and Ella. She has a long roster of governing board service to her credit, including 10 years as chair of the Carolyn Foundation and twelve years as chair of Family and Children's Service in Minneapolis. She now serves as a docent and on the executive committee of the Minneapolis Institute of Arts. Her husband Robert is a past member of both the Wayzata and Medina city councils.

The youngest Crosby, **Robert Franklin**, is married to Teri Valley Crosby. They have no children. Robert is a great supporter of University of Minnesota athletics, continuing the Pillsbury tradition of season tickets at the university's new TCF Bank stadium. He recently gave a major gift to the football program in the memory of one of the first Golden Gopher greats, Alfred Pillsbury.

Jane Pillsbury Resor's life came to a tragic end in an auto accident on July 9, 1994 near her home in New Canaan, Connecticut. She was returning from picking up a grandson at Kennedy Airport when her car struck a tree. The grandson was not injured.[23] Jane, Southways' fun-loving tomboy, grew up to be the mother of seven sons. She loved keeping up with them on the tennis courts, ski slopes, horseback, and the ice as a hockey player. In her last year, at age seventy-four, she was still playing tennis three times a week and mixed doubles with her husband Stanley on weekends. She was a lifelong youth sports volunteer, organizing youth hockey programs in Connecticut, Chevy Chase, Maryland and Jackson, Wyoming, and helping establish two hockey arenas.

Her husband Stanley Resor ended his service as Secretary of the Army in 1971, then went on to represent the United States in several rounds of Mutual and Balanced Force Reduction Talks with the Soviet Union in Vienna under Presidents Nixon, Ford and Carter.[24] He remains in regular contact with his Minnesota in-laws, as do Stan and Jane's sons. **Stanley Rogers Jr.** and his wife Louise are both doctors, with Stan being a neurology specialist in New York City. They have three children. Three Resor sons live in Jackson: **Charles Pillsbury** (wife Nancy and two sons) is involved in a computer business venture; **John Lawler** (wife Kitty and two children) is in real estate, and **William Burnet** (Story and two children) is in the Resor family ranching business. **Edmund Lansdowne** (Anne-Marie and three children) is based in New York City and involved in communications in Africa. **Thomas Sturgis** (Tammy and five children) is a teacher and coach at Nobles and Greenough School in Boston. **James Pillsbury** (Catherine and two children) is in Washington D.C. in an environmental business. All are active in civic affairs; the family has made environmental protection in the Jackson, Wyoming area a particular cause. Jane would have been thrilled to watch Stan Jr.'s daughter Helen play on women's hockey Team USA in the 2006 Winter Olympics.

After launching the Council on Corporate Review, George's son **Charlie** headed to law school at Boston University and transferred to Yale Law School in his third year. He settled in New Haven, Connecticut near the campus that so many Pillsburys claim as alma mater, and in 1980 joined Community Mediation Inc., an agency that both facilitates conflict resolution and trains people in mediation skills. He helped make that organization a nationally acclaimed model for peaceful intervention and resolution of disputes of many types, ranging from neighborhood conflicts to public policy disputes. This year Charlie became the first executive director of an international dispute resolution organization, Mediators Beyond Borders, based at the Quinnipiac University School of Law in Hamden, Connecticut. He was among that organization's founders in 2008.[25] He is married to the Rev. Allie Perry, coordinator of worship for a United Church of Christ congregation fittingly named Shalom, where Charlie is a lay leader. He made one bid for elective office, running in 2002 as a Green Party candidate for Congress in Connecticut's Third District and garnering 5 percent of the vote. Charlie and his previous wife, Jean Greenway Sanderson, have four children, Leah, Susannah, and twins Lydia and Andrew, and a granddaughter, Maya.

As Charlie pursued peace, **George Jr.** devoted his life to social and economic justice. He too stayed in New England after graduating from Yale in 1972. Schooled by his parents in the importance of philanthropy, he took seriously the opportunity to make a positive difference with his inheritance.[26] In 1974 he founded the Haymarket People's Fund in Boston, inviting other young heirs of American fortunes to contribute to its endowment. Its early motto: "Change. Not charity."[27] Today Haymarket is New England's go-to funding boost for efforts to combat ills including hunger, racism, homelessness and unemployment. Through its first 35 years Haymarket has awarded more than $25 million, all in small grants targeted for maximum impact. More recently, George Jr.'s focus has shifted to achieving change through the ballot box. In 2005, he founded what has matured into the Nonprofit Voter Engagement Network, which works with nonprofit organizations to increase voter registration and turnout among demographic groups often underrepresented at the polls. By 2010, NVEN worked in partnership with more than a dozen national organizations and seventeen state and local nonprofit-driven projects around the country to increase voter participation among the poor.[28] George Jr.'s work earned him the 2010 John Gardner Award from Common Cause Massachusetts.[29] He and his wife Mary Tiseo have two children, Nicholas and Amanda. Mary is the co-founder and executive director of South Africa Partners, a non-profit organization facilitating mutually beneficial health and education partnerships between the United States and South Africa.

George's work inspired his sister **Sarah Kimball Pillsbury.** She enrolled at Yale in 1969 as part of the first class at the venerable Ivy League institution to include women, and delayed her graduation by one year in order to live in Africa and learn firsthand about a continent she found fascinating. She came back convinced that "none of

Sarah, Sally and Kathy Pillsbury on a trip to Alaska, 2007.

us will sleep well at night and wake up happy in the morning unless the rest of the world gets there too."[30] After graduating, she moved to Los Angeles to study at the University of California-Los Angeles and pursue a career in filmmaking. But she also wanted to use her inheritance to make a positive difference for others. With three similarly situated friends, she founded Liberty Hill Foundation, modeled after Haymarket, in 1975. Sarah sees a parallel between Liberty Hill's efforts to improve the lives of poor urban dwellers, especially immigrants, and the work her great-grandfather and great-great uncle funded at Pillsbury Settlement House a century earlier. "At Liberty Hill we're creating something that's unusual in L.A. but that people understand in Minnesota—that sense that we're all in this together," she said.

Sarah has enjoyed considerable success as a filmmaker, beginning with *Eraserhead* in 1976. She co-produced the Oscar-winning short film "Board and Care" in 1980. In 1981, she teamed up with New York native Midge Sanford to form Sanford/Pillsbury Productions, whose credits include *Desperately Seeking Susan* in 1985, *River's Edge* in 1986 and the HBO film about the AIDS epidemic, and *And the Band Played On* in 1993. The latter film won that year's Emmy Award for best made-for-television movie. Sarah chooses to remain in Los

George and Sally's grandchildren. Seated left to right: Will Kletter, Nora Kletter, Jeremy Marshall, Amanda Pillsbury, Lydia Pillsbury, Andrew Pillsbury. Standing: Leah Pillsbury, Nick Pillsbury, Susannah Pillsbury. Not pictured: Mikayla Pillsbury.

Angeles, she said recently, because "My ancestors did a good job (in Minnesota), and there's still a lot of work left to be done in Los Angeles." Sarah is single and the mother of two children, Nora and William Aaron Pillsbury Kletter. She was the 2010 recipient of the Los Angeles YWCA's Focus Award, given to honor "individuals and organizations that have contributed to the positive, inspirational and powerful portrayal of women in the media."

In 2003, Sarah told a California journalist why she chose to combine filmmaking with social activism, with words that are vintage Pillsbury:

"I've been involved in politics and charities and giving since I was a child. It's a sense of purpose that has carried over from my parents who never wondered about who they were or what their purpose was or what's the meaning of life. They taught me that voting and raising money for and generally supporting grassroots causes were the best way to effect change. They are big fundraisers for their colleges and they serve on several boards. Looking back, it seems they gave to everybody and they went to almost everything. That really affected me and got me involved."[31]

Katharine Whitney Pillsbury followed her sister Sarah to Concord Academy for high school, but not to Yale. Instead, she chose Goddard College in Plainfield, Vermont, and admired the community spirit she experienced in rural New England, not far from the place and culture that the nineteenth-century Pillsburys knew well. Like her older siblings, Kathy did not return to Minnesota. She makes her home in Newton Highlands, Massachusetts and her living as a consultant and creator of elementary school curriculum for teaching respect for family diversity. Kathy and her spouse Cindy Marshall were recently honored by the Newton Women's Commission for their work as family diversity advocates.[32] They coordinate a network of gay and lesbian parents in Newton with the help and encouragement of their children, Jeremy and Mikayla.

Kathy's experience as half of a same-sex couple deepened her parents' interest in full legal equality for gays and lesbians. President George W. Bush's opposition to gay rights contributed to a decision that shocked many of Sally's friends. She let it be known in 2004 that for the first time, she would not be voting for a Republican for president. George would not say that year who would receive his vote, Bush or Democratic candidate John Kerry. But he let it be known that he was an increasingly uncomfortable Republican.[33] He had been saying as much for some time.[34] The Minnesota party's 1995 decision to drop the word "Independent" from its name bothered him. To him, it signified that moderates need not apply for any positions of influence within the party. That signal only became clearer in subsequent years.

In 2008, George and Sally mounted one more fight for the re-emergence of a Republican Party they could support. Sally agreed to be a co-chair of an event calling for the inclusion of pro-choice candidates and activists in Republican leadership ranks. The "Big Tent Celebration" unfolded on September 2, the second evening of the Republican National Convention, which had returned to Minnesota for the first time since 1892. One of the event's goals was to shore up

GOP presidential nominee John McCain's courage should he choose as a runningmate someone supportive of keeping abortion legal, such as former Pennsylvania Gov. Tom Ridge or Connecticut Sen. Joe Lieberman, then a maverick Democrat. Sally worked doggedly on every aspect of the event, applying to the project the lessons of 60 years of GOP organizing, event planning and national convention participation. She selected the venue: Dove Hill, the former home of Louis Hill, son of James J. Hill and a personal friend of her father-in-law. The house had been designed by Cass Gilbert, St. Paul's premiere architect of the early twentieth century. Its grand ballroom with a stained-glass ceiling and dramatic staircase entry would be the perfect place to welcome a pro-choice politician to the national ticket, Sally imagined.[35]

It was not to be. The Big Tent Celebration drew a sizeable but subdued crowd that found no reason at the 2008 convention to think that their cause was gaining ground or their message being heeded in the Republican Party. McCain's selection of Alaska Gov. Sarah Palin as his runningmate dashed their hopes and served to further isolate pro-choice Republicans. "The attendance was gratifying," wrote Sally's co-chair Jennifer Stockman days later about the event.[36] "But we were under no illusions: Today's GOP is far from being a true big tent, welcoming all regardless of personal views on a woman's right to choose." Within a few months, one of the speakers at the Big Tent event, Pennsylvania Sen. Arlen Specter, would switch parties.

So would George. He announced to an inquiring reporter days before the election that, for the first time in his life, he would be voting for a Democrat for president. Barack Obama had won him over on the strength of two issues: his willingness to engage other nations in a less belligerent way than Bush had, particularly via the United Nations, and abortion. George noted that all of his 10 grandchildren were Obama backers.[37] In 2010, George attended the precinct caucuses of the Independence Party of Minnesota to support the gubernatorial candidacy of another former Republican, public relations executive Tom Horner. More than 150 years of Pillsbury involvement in Minnesota Republican politics appear to have come to an end.

Pillsburys don't break ties easily. For the second time, George is secretary (the convening officer) of his Class of 1943 at Yale University. He's working with former Gov. Al Quie, former Senate Majority Leader Roger Moe, Sally's brother Wheelock Whitney, and Wheelock's wife, former Minnesota Chief Justice Kathleen Blatz, in an effort to move Minnesota to yes-or-no "retention" elections of state judges. A pin signifying George's service as a U.S. Marine is generally on his lapel. He and Sally are prominent benefactors of Womenwinning, the organization Sally helped found as the Minnesota Women's Campaign Fund in 1982 to promote the election of women to offices at all levels. George and Sally still fill their customary places at events sponsored by institutions Pillsburys helped establish—the Guthrie Theater, the Minneapolis Institute of Arts, the University of Minnesota, Pillsbury United Communities (formerly Pillsbury House.) The Pillsbury brand of vigorous citizenship shines on. This book is written in the hope that when they are gone, the inspirational glow of their family's example will remain.

Photo credits:

All photos come from family collections except as follows:

Minnesota Historical Society:
54/ Cushman Davis in the early 1870s. (photographer: William F. Koester)
81/ The house George and Margaret built in Minneapolis.
83/ The aftermath of the Washburn A Mill explosion, May 1878. (photographer: Jacoby)
111/ William D. Washburn.
133/ Four generations in 1891.(photographer: Arthur B. Rugg)
137/ Alice Thayer Cook Pillsbury and her children. (photographer: James A. Brush)
244/ Albert C. Loring, 1927.

Star-Tribune:
3/ Sketch of the Falls of St. Anthony.
15/ The 1855 Hennepin Avenue bridge.
18/ St. Anthony in 1857.
24/ Old Main.
27/ William Watts Folwell.
28/ Falls of St. Anthony, late 1860s.
41/ Cadwallader C. Washburn, circa 1870.
48/ Bridge Square in Minneapolis, 1873.
53/ Alexander Ramsey, circa 1870.
70/ Minnesota's first state capitol, circa 1860.
89/ The Pillsbury A Mill.
104/ Albert Alonzo Ames, circa 1887.
115/The Palisade Mill.
128/ Pillsbury Hall, University of Minnesota.
144/ The Northwest Guarantee Loan Building
148/ William de la Barre in 1933.
149/ Thomas Lowry in the 1890s.
169/ Eleanor Louise Field Pillsbury, called Gretchen, circa 1900.
175/ The Pillsbury Library, as it appeared in the 1970s.
181/ The Hennepin Avenue bridge.
208/ Charles and Nelle Pillsbury's mansion, 100 E. 22nd. St.
236/ Alfred Pillsbury admiring a Chinese bronze.
240/ Bruce Dayton.
248/ Phil sacking souvenir bags of flour, June 5, 1944.
265/ John Pillsbury and Clarence Chaney, May 1945.
265/ Rep. Richard P. Gale on a bicycle.
274/ George and his parents at a concert, December 1945.
286/ Mary Pillsbury Lord.
290/ Sally with baby Sarah, Charlie and George Jr. 1951.

Notes

(The *Northwestern Miller* is abbreviated as *NM*, the *Minneapolis Tribune* as *MT*.)

FREQUENTLY CITED WORKS

Dedication of the Pillsbury Memorial Town Hall. Sutton, N.H., Republican Press Association, Concord, N.H. 1893.

"Historical Account of the Pillsbury Flour Mills Co., 1869," p. 18. A typewritten, bound volume, no author cited. Date also unknown, but it appears to have been written soon after 1908, when A. C. Loring took over as president. General Mills archives. Note attached: "From an unidentified history on file with the Pillsbury Flour Mills Co. This was taken from a very old typewritten copy—doubtless written by someone intimately connected with the Pillsbury Co."

The History of Warner, New Hampshire, for One Hundred and Forty-four Years, from 1735 to 1879, Concord, N.H., The Republican Press Association, 1879.

New Hampshire Women, A collection of portraits and biographical sketches. New Hampshire Publishing Co., 1895.

Three Deadications: Soldiers' Monument at South Sutton, Pillsbury Free Library at Warner, Margaret Pillsbury General Hospital at Concord, 1891. Concord, N.H.: Republican Press Association, Railroad Square, 1891.

Atkins, Annette, *Harvest of Grief: Grasshopper Plagues and Public Assistance in Minnesota, 1873-78.* St. Paul: Minnesota Historical Society Press.

Atwater, Isaac. *A History of the City of Minneapolis.* New York and Chicago: the Munsell Co., 1893.

Blegen, Theodore C. *Minnesota: A History of the State.* Minneapolis: University of Minnesota Press, 1963.

Clarke, John Badger, *Sketches of Successful New Hampshire Men.* Manchester, N.H., 1882

Edgar, William C. *The Medal of Gold: A Story of Industrial Achievement.* Mpls, MN: The Bellman Co., 1925.

Folwell, William Watts. *A History of Minnesota.* Minnesota Historical Society, St. Paul, 1926. Four Volumes.

Harriman, Walter. *The History of Warner, New Hampshire, for One Hundred and Forty-four Years, from 1735 to 1879.* Concord, NH: The Republican Press Association, 1879; p. 377.

Holman, Mary Lovering, *Ancestry of Charles Stinson Pillsbury and John Sargent Pillsbury,* Compiled for Helen Pendleton (Winston) Pillsbury. Privately printed by The Rumford Press, Concord, N.H., 1938.

Holmes, Frank R., *Minnesota in Three Centuries, 1655-1908.* Mankato, MN: The Publishing Society of Minnesota, 1908. Vol. IV, p. 68-70.

Hudson, Horace B. "A Public Servant of the Northwest: the fruitful career of the late Gov. John S. Pillsbury of Minnesota." *The American Monthly Review of Reviews*, 1901.

Hudson, Horace B., *A Half-Century of Minneapolis*, Minneapolis. The Hudson Publishing Co. 1908.

Jones, Thelma, *Once Upon a Lake*. Minneapolis, MN: Ross & Haines, Inc., 1957, enlarged 1969.

Kane, Lucile M., *The Falls of St. Anthony: The Waterfall that Built Minneapolis*, Minnesota Historical Society Press, 1966, 1987.

Kelsey, Kerck. *Remarkable Americans: The Washburn Family*, Gardiner, Maine: Tilbury House Publishers, 2008.

Kenney, Dave, *The Grain Merchants: An Illustrated History of the Minneapolis Grain Exchange*, Afton Historical Society Press, Afton, MN 2006.

Kuhlmann, Charles B. , *The Development of the Flour Milling Industry in the United States*. Houghton Mifflin Co.: Boston and New York, 1929.

Nathanson, Iric, *Minneapolis in the Twentieth Century*. St. Paul, MN: Minnesota Historical Society Press, 2010.

Noon, Jack. *The History of Sutton New Hampshire*, Jack Noon, 2007.

Pillsbury, David B. and Emily A. Getchell, *The Pillsbury Family, being a history of William and Dorothy Pillsbury (or Pilsbery) of Newbury in New England, and their descendents to the eleventh generation*. Everett, MA: Massachusetts Publishing Co, 1898.

Pillsbury, Eleanor Lawler, *My Family Story*, Southways, Lake Minnetonka, MN. Privately published. 1972.

Pillsbury, Eleanor Lawler, *Southways: Random Reminiscences*. Minneapolis, MN: privately published, 1985.

Pillsbury, Philip W. "The Pioneering Pillsburys," a booklet published by the Newcomen Society, Minneapolis, 1950.

Powell, William J. *Pillsbury's Best: A Company History from 1869*. The Pillsbury Co., Minneapolis, 1985.

Smalley, E.V. *A History of the Republican Party, to which is appended a political history of Minnesota from a Republican point of view.* St. Paul, The Pioneer Press Co., 1896.

Smith, David C., *City of Parks: The Story of Minneapolis Parks*. Minneapolis, MN: The Foundation for Minneapolis Parks, 2008.

Shutter, Marion Daniel. *History of Minneapolis: Gateway to the Northwest*. Chicago-Minneapolis: The S. J. Clarke Publishing Company, 1923.

Torreano, Peter F., *Mesabi Miracle: The 100-year History of the Pillsbury-Bennett-Longyear Association*. Hibbing, MN: Sargent Land Co.,1991. (Russell M. Bennett II reports that John S. Pillsbury Jr. contributed heavily to the writing and editing of this book.)

Warner, George E., Charles M. Foote, Edward D. Neill and others, *History of Hennepin County and the city of Minneapolis, including the explorers and pioneers of Minnesota*. Minneapolis: North Star Publishing Co., 1881.

Worthen, Augusta H. *The History of Sutton, New Hampshire: Consisting of the historical collections of Erastus Wadleigh, Esq., and A. H. Worthen*. Concord: The Republican Press Assocation, 1890. As available at www.archive.org.

CHAPTER I

1 John S. Pillsbury's birthdate is reported as "about 1828" in U.S. Census records, July 29, 1827 by the Mary Lovering Holman genealogy, by Warner, et. al: *History of Hennepin County*, 1881, and by "Report of the Annual Meetings of the Minnesota Territorial Pioneers," May 11, 1899 and 1900. George S. Pillsbury advises that the family believes the 1827 date is correct. That is also the date on his gravestone at Lakewood Cemetery in Minneapolis.

2 See *Dedication of the Pillsbury Memorial* and Holman, p.23.

3 Information about the region and era comes from Noon, volume II, p. 3-7; Holman, p. 22, 23; and Hudson, "A Public Servant."

4 Pillsbury, David B., *The Pillsbury Family*, p. 25.

5 *Three Dedications.*

6 Letter to George S. Pillsbury from Jack Noon, Sutton and Warner historian, March 2, 2010.

7 Records of the 30th regiment of the New Hampshire militia supplied to the author by Sutton and Warner historian Jack Noon. Dated Oct. 23, 1839, the roster lists George A. Pillsbury as the first commissioned officer. The list includes surnames that a generation or two later would be well known in Minnesota—Blaisdell, Ordway, Wright, Wells and Dodge.

8 Letter to author from Jack Noon, April 4, 2008.

9 Newspaper obituary for Margaret Sprague Carleton Pillsbury, as clipped for files maintained at the Pillsbury Free Library, Warner N.H. Date and name of newspaper not recorded.

10 Ibid.

11 See *New Hampshire Women.*

12 Holman reported Mary's birthdate as April 25, 1849. The family's friend and John's business partner, Walter Harriman, reported her birth date as April 25, 1848, in "The History of Warner, New Hampshire, for One Hundred and Forty-four Years, from 1735 to 1879," Concord, N.H., The Republican Press Association, 1879, p. 377.

13 *Three Dedications.*

14 *Three Dedications.*

15 Noon, p. 33.

16 Untitled Pillsbury Company history, 1953. General Mills archives, Box CR-1.

17 Meier, Peg, "In the Beginning," article #1 in a 150th anniversary series of First Universalist Church, Minneapolis, MN, 2008.

18 See Kane, p. 1-9.

19 *Dedication of the Pillsbury Memorial.*

20 Email to author from Rebecca Courser, executive director, Warner Historical Society, Warner, N.H., April 9, 2008.

21 U.S. Census, free inhabitants of Warner in the County of Merrimack, New Hampshire, Oct. 31, 1850.

22 Atwater, Isaac. "A History of the City of Minneapolis." New York and Chicago: the Munsell Co., 1893. P .808.

23 "Historical Account of Pillsbury Flour Mills Company, 1869." p. 12.

24 Kane, p. 39

25 "Historical Account of Pillsbury Flour Mills Company, 1869," p. 14.

26 Kane, p. 29.

27 "Historical Account of Pillsbury Flour Mills Company, 1869."

28 Atwater, p. 808.

29 Borger, Judith Yates, "Four Generations of the Family Pillsbury," *Twin Cities* magazine, July 1981.

30 *Dedication of the Pillsbury Memorial.*

31 Ibid.

32 Interview by author with James Thompson, archivist at Plymouth Congregational Church, May 2008.

33 Ford, Guy Stanton and Smith, Dora V., "The First Congregational Church of Minnesota, 1851-1951, a Century of Service." Booklet published by the church.

34 *Dedication of the Pillsbury Memorial.*

35 Calomiris, Charles W.; Schweikart, Larry (1991). "The Panic of 1857: Origins, Transmission, and Containment". *Journal of Economic History* **51** (4): 807–834.

36 Web site: http://en.wikipedia.org/wiki/Panic_of_1857.

37 Richard Chute to Thomas Davis and Frederick Gebhard, Feb. 6, 1861, Steele Papers, as quoted by Kane, p. 45.

38 *Minnesota Republican* newspaper, St. Anthony, MN, Oct. 1, 1857, put the collective loss at the retail enterprises damaged by fire at $40,000. Among the firms named: Four stores at Lennon's Block (one unoccupied); Carpenter & Andrews Dry Goods and Groceries (the Andrews in question likely John Pillsbury's cousin); Thomas Moulton, wholesale grocer and provision dealer; I. H. Moulton, dry goods and crockeryware; Charles King block of stores, which included J. and G.H. Hawes boot, shoe and clothing store; Hezlep & Co. jewelry and auction store, Dr. H.W. Gould, surgeon dentist, and the Cataract Masonic Lodge. (With thanks to MJV for research producing this information.)

39 *Dedication of the Pillsbury Memorial.*

40 Pillsbury, Philip W. , *The Pioneering Pillsburys.*

41 Folwell, vol III, p. 112.

42 "Historical Account of Pillsbury Flour Mills Company, 1869."

43 Hudson, Horace B.

44 Warner, et. al. p. 381. Other accounts, deemed less reliable, say that Pillsbury's service on the St. Anthony city council began in 1858.

45 Folwell, vol. II, p. 72.

46 *Dedication of the Pillsbury Memorial.*

47 Holman, p. 27.

48 McNally, William J., "More or Less Personal," *MT*, as reprinted by *NM*, March 25, 1942.

49 University relations web site: www1.umn.edu/urelate/m/MSummer00/150candles.html.

50 Hudson, p. 692.

51 Smith, Rollin E., feature story in *NM*, Nov. 14, 1900, p. 933.

52 www1.umn.edu/pres/eastcliff/history.

53 Hudson, p. 692.

54 Pillsbury, Philip W., *The Pioneering Pillsburys*.

55 Gray, James. *The University of Minnesota, 1851-1951*. Minneapolis: University of Minnesota Press, 1951. P. 38.

CHAPTER 2

1 See *Chronicles*, a transcript of remarks made on Class Day by A.W. Hazen, Dartmouth class historian for the Class of 1863. Rauner Library, Dartmouth College, Hanover, N.H. For details about Civil War dead, see a 1914 tablet installed on the Dartmouth campus.

2 Letters from student Edward Tuck to his family. Papers of the class of 1862. Rauner Library, Dartmouth College, Hanover, N.H.

3 Ibid., letter of Oct 12, 1861.

4 Richardson, Leon Burr. "History of Dartmouth College," Hanover, N.H., Dartmouth College Publications, 1932. P. 479.

5 Holman, vol I.

6 See Richardson, op. cit., p. 479, 481. A room might be had for as little as $7.50 for the year, and board for $1-$1.50 per week. Textbooks generally cost between $20 and $25 for the year. A haircut went for 12.5 cents; apples, 6.25 cents per peck; a theater ticket, 37.5 cents; beer, 6 cents.

7 In a scoring system foreign to modern eyes, his cumulative grade point was 2.00 his freshman year, in a class whose leader scored 2.68 and worst performer 1.21. Class records, Rauner Library, Dartmouth College, Hanover, N.H.

8 Scales, John, editor. *Biographical Sketches of the Class of 1863*, Dartmouth College, 1903, p. 418.

9 Parker Pillsbury's story is recounted in his book *Acts of the Anti-Slavery Apostles*, Concord, N.H., Clague, Wegman, Schlict & Co., printers, 1883. See also Robertson, Stacey M., *Parker Pillsbury: Radical Abolitionist, Male Feminist*, Ithaca and London: Cornell University Press, 2000.

10 For details about commencement week, see "Orations of the graduating class— annual meeting and dinner of the alumni – The Closing Levee." July 23, 1863. Rauner Library, Dartmouth College, Hanover, N.H; Commencement exercises program, July 23, 1863. Rauner Library, Dartmouth College, Hanover, N.H. ; Web site: americancivilwar.com/monitor.html.

11 Letter from George A. Pillsbury to Charles A. Pillsbury, Oct. 8, 1863. Personal papers of George S. Pillsbury and Ella S. Pillsbury Crosby.

12 Sources vary about Charles's birthdate. This letter seems to suggest that it was Oct. 3, 1842, as does Henry Hall's 1895 *America's Successful Men of Affairs: an Encyclopedia of Contemporaneous Biograghy*. (New York: New York Printing Co., p. 626-628.) Several passport applications (www.ancestry.com) also cite that date. But the Encyclopedia Brittanica and the Holman genealogy are among several sources that place

his birth on Dec. 3, 1842.

13 *Three Dedications.*

14 Details about Charles and Mary Ann may be found in Holman, especially pp. 28, 760–761.

15 *Northwestern Life* magazine (formerly *Golfer and Sportsman*), undated article appears sometime in the mid-1940s, because it shows a genealogy that includes Lt. George Sturgis Pillsbury who is not married. Box 3, Folder 28, General Mills archive.

16 Interviews with George S. Pillsbury, Oct. 6, 2007, and Ella S. Pillsbury Crosby, Nov. 3, 2007.

17 Pillsbury, Philip W., p. 13.

18 Scales, *Biographical Sketches*, p. 424.

19 Obituary of Margaret Sprague Carleton Pillsbury, undated but not long after her death on March 16, 1901, in scrapbook of Pillsbury mementos at Pillsbury Free Library, Warner, N.H.

20 Holman, p. 24.

21 Powell, p. 16.

22 Powell, p. 238–239.

23 Pillsbury, Phillip W., p. 13.

24 Powell, p. 19.

25 Kelsey, pp. 232–236.

26 Folwell, vol. III, p. 69.

27 *NM*, Aug. 24, 1882: "The Early History of New Process Milling."

28 Ibid.

29 The *New York Times*, Aug. 31, 1917, "Fixes wheat price at $2.20 a bushel until next July."

30 Obituary of Charles A. Pillsbury, *Weekly NM*, Sept. 20, 1899, p. 543.

31 Powell, p. 21.

32 Copy of trademark declaration by Albert C. Loring, made in either 1930 or 1931. Filed at General Mills Archive, Box CR-1.

33 *Historical Account of Pillsbury Flour Mills Company, 1869*, p. 5.

34 That plan will be discussed more fully in Chapter Five.

35 Powell, p. 36.

36 Powell, p. 25.

37 Holman, p. 29.

38 Letters preserved by Georgiana Rider of River Falls, Wis., granddaughter of Frank H. Carleton. Provided to the author by Ella Pillsbury Crosby.

39 Clipping from *Northwestern Life* (formerly *Golfer and Sportsman*). Article appears between 1943 and 1945, because it shows a genealogy that includes Lt. George Sturgis Pillsbury, unmarried. File box 3, folder 28, General Mills archives.

40 Minutes of Plymouth Society meetings, Plymouth Church archives, Minneapolis, MN. With thanks to archivist James Thompson.

41 From interview with archivist James Thompson, Plymouth Congregational Church, May 2008.

42 Kane, p. 39.

CHAPTER 3

1 1885 photo by William Jacoby, available at www.mnhs.org; item about the house's transfer to University of Minnesota ownership, *Minneapolis Morning Tribune*, March 13, 1945.

2 Shutter, p. 123.

3 1870 U.S. Census.

4 *MT*, July 15, 1892.

5 Holman, vol I, p. 29.

6 "Historical Account of the Pillsbury Flour Mills Co., 1869," p. 18.

7 1880 U.S. Census.

8 Hudson, Horace B. "A Public Servant."

9 www.mnhs.org/school/online/communities/people/PILadv1T.htm.

10 Benidt, Bruce Weir. *The Library Book: Centennial History of the Minneapolis Public Library*. Minneapolis, MN: Minneapolis Public Library and Information Center, 1984. p. 22.

11 *NM*, Friday, Aug. 24, 1883. "The Early History of New Process Milling." Sources vary in describing the prime mover behind the Gull River Lumber Company. Frank Alexander King, in his 2003 book *Minnesota Logging Railroads* (University of Minnesota Press) cites Charles as the company's founder. But an 1890 account of the Pillsbury enterprises by Sutton, N.H. historian Augusta Worthen, says the Gull River enterprise was the work of J.S. Pillsbury & Co., consisting of John, George, and Charles.

12 Report of the annual meetings of the Minnesota Territorial Pioneers, May 11, 1899 and 1900, as available at http://hennbios.tripod.com/surnamep.htm.

13 St. Anthony Falls Democrat newspaper advertisement, Jan. 7, 1870.

14 *The Fifteenth Legislature of Minnesota*. St. Paul: Press Printing Co., 1873, p. 11.

15 *Dedication of the Pillsbury Memorial*.

16 Photo record in office of Minnesota Sen. Richard Cohen, chair, Senate Finance Committee. John Pillsbury chaired the committee from 1868 until 1875. Also: St. Paul Daily Pioneer Press, January 1876, as excerpted by the Minnesota Historical Society's Minnesota Communities web page, www.mnhs.org.

17 Blegen, p. 287. Donnelly's great-great-grandson Stan Donnelly would join forces with former state Sen. George Pillsbury' in 1999 to form Minnesotans for a Single House Legislature.

18 Folwell, vol. III. p. 81.

19 Smalley, p. 194-95

20 Elihu Washburne chose as a young man to add an "e" to his surname, making its spelling closer to the English version of the family's name, Washbourne, meaning "swift stream." That information comes from Genealogical notes of the Washburn family : with a brief sketch of the family in England, containing a full record of the descendants of Israel Washburn of Raynham, 1755-1841, available at www.archive.org.

21 Folwell, vol. III, p. 85.

22 Smalley, p. 195.

23 Folwell, vol. III, p. 85.

24 Holmes, vol. IV, p. 68-70.

25 Folwell, vol. III, p. 112.

26 Ibid., p. 113.

27 Hudson, "A Public Servant," p. 694.

28 www.semplemansion.com.

29 Powell, p. 25.

30 *St. Paul Daily Pioneer Press*, January 1876, as excerpted by the Minnesota Historical Society's Minnesota Communities web page, www.mnhs.org.

31 Holmes, vol. IV, p. 77.

32 Jonathan Carver's "Travels" as quoted by Folwell, vol. III, p. 96.

33 Holmes, p. 107.

34 Edward E. Gillam to Ruth Thompson, March 21, 1949, as quoted by Atkins, p. 17.

35 Wilder, Laura Ingalls, *On the Banks of Plum Creek*. New York: Harper & Brothers, 1937.

36 Atkins, p. 21.

37 *NM*, Aug. 23, 1944, p. 26.

38 See, for example, Atkins, p.11.

"As Americans came to measure worth by money, they measured lack of worth by lack of money. The poor never received generous and compassionate treatment, but rarely in the country's history were they treated less kindly and compassionately than in the last third of the 19th century...These needy did not merit public aid; instead, they needed moral suasion and advice."

39 Atkins, p. 69.

40 Folwell, vol. III, p. 97.

41 Folwell, ibid. p. 100.

42 Smalley, p. 201.

43 Holmes, p. 113.

44 Folwell, vo. III, p. 101.

45 *Dedication of the Pillsbury Memorial*.

46 Smith, Rollin E., *NM*, Nov. 14, 1900, p. 933 ff.

47 State of Minnesota Executive Department appeal, Dec. 20, 1876, signed by John S. Pillsbury, governor. On file at the General Mills Archive.

48 Hudson.

49 Smith.

50 *Dedication of the Pillsbury Memorial.*

51 Atkins, p. 89.

52 Letter from E. E. Gillam to Philip Pillsbury, Windom, May 26, 1946. General Mills archive.

53 Atkins, p. 88.

54 Folwell, vol. III, p. 106-7.

55 Attributed to Gov. Pillsbury, April 9. 1877, by Caroline Ticknor in the 50th anniversary edition of *The NM*, 1923.

56 Holmes, p. 114.

57 Folwell, vol. III, p. 108.

58 Folwell, vol. III, p. 109.

59 Smalley, p. 203.

60 Folwell, vol. III, p. 108.

61 www.sos.state.mn.us/home/index.asp?page=649.

62 Collections of the Minnesota Historical Society, St. Paul: Minnesota Historical Society, August 1908, Vol. XIII, p. 236.

63 Folwell, vol. III, p. 123.

64 Smalley, p. 205.

65 Folwell, vol. III, p. 433.

66 Smalley, p. 209.

67 Collections of the Minnesota Historical Society, St. Paul: Minnesota Historical Society, August 1908, vol. XIII, p. 237.

68 Luther, Sally. "Story of a Family: Minnesota Millers." *Minneapolis Sunday Tribune,* May 29, 1949.

69 Folwell, vol. III, p. 434.

70 Collections of the Minnesota Historical Society, St. Paul: Minnesota Historical Society, August 1908, Vol. XIII, p. 236.

71 Smalley, p. 209.

72 Folwell, vol. III, p. 139.

73 Ibid., p. 138.

74 www.mnsu.edu/emuseum/prehistory/minnesota/minnesotaarchaeology/ minnesotahistoricalsociety.html.

75 Folwell, vol. III, p. 143.

CHAPTER 4

1 The first was representing Warner and the second, 20 years later, representing Concord's Ward 5 and chairing the lower house's tax committee. See Worthen, available at www.archive.org.

2 Margaret was described as "a philanthropist" by several sources, most directly in New Hampshire Women, A collection of portraits and biographical sketches," New Hampshire Publishing Co., 1895.

3 Harriman, p. 377.

4 McClintock, John Norris, and Metcalf, Henry Harrison, editors, "The Granite State Monthly,"Volume 3, 1879. p. 336.

5 MT, Oct. 21, 1876, refers to the bride as Alice Goodwin, daughter of Dr. and Mrs. David M. Goodwin, who the same week as their daughter's wedding celebrated their 10th wedding anniversary. But the Pillsbury genealogies and the gravestone at Lakewood Cemetery refer to her as Alice Thayer Cook, daughter of Samuel and Harriot Cook. The 1870 U.S. Census shows Alice as the daughter of Dr. David and Harriot Goodwin.

6 "The Social Hopper," MT, Oct. 21, 1876.

7 Holman, p. 30.

8 1870 U.S. Census.

9 Dedication of the Pillsbury Memorial.

10 The Granite State Monthly, p. 335.

11 Essay about Pillsbury House, supplied at author's request by Granite Falls Historical Society; no date attached.

12 Narvestad, Carl and Amy, "Granite Falls 1879-1979." From the chapter "Granite's Milling Industry," provided to the author by the Granite Falls Historical Society.

13 Margaret's father Henry Carleton died in 1864; her mother, Polly Greeley Carleton, died just two months after her grandson Charles was born in 1842.. Holman, ibid., p. 372.

14 Clarke, p. 41.

15 Ibid.

16 "The Granite State Monthly," p. 337.

17 Clarke, and photos from the Minnesota Historical Society.

18 Thompson, James E. "History of Plymouth Congregational Church, Part 3"; Plymouth Society minutes, archives of Plymouth Church, Nicollet and Groveland Avs., Minneapolis.

19 Shutter, p. 198.

20 Folwell, vol III, p. 132.

21 Atwater, p. 620 ff .

22 "The Anniversary Number of the NM, December 1923, Henry A. Bellows," bearingn the bookplate of Philip W. Pillsbury; General Mills archives, p. 107.

23 Ibid.

24 Folwell, vol. III, p. 133 ff.

25 Kelsey, p. 130.

26 Atwater, p. 620.

27 Kelsey, p. 243.

28 *Weekly NM*, May 11, 1904, from a series by Kingsland Smith, "Around the World." p. 303.

29 Powell, p. 26.

30 "Historical Account of Pillsbury Flour Mills Company, 1869," p. 3.

31 Powell, p. 26.

32 The dates and sequence of events leading to the installation of roller mills in Minneapolis are at odds in various source materials, as is Charles Pillsbury's personal role in their introduction. Powell says Pillsbury himself went to Hungary in 1873 to learn about the process; a 1914 history of Hennepin County avers that Pillsbury spent five years there! The dates of his children's births refute that claim. The manuscript of uncertain authorship in Note 24 offers the most detailed and plausible description of events.

33 "Historical Account," p. 4.

34 How many times he went to Europe, and for how long, is variously reported by surviving accounts. One source says he was away for five months; his grandson's account put the first trip in the winter of 1878. The *Retailers' Journal*, a Chicago monthly magazine (date obliterated) carried an article "Mills that made Minneapolis" referring to Henry Little as the general manager of Pillsbury–Washburn, indicating that it was written between 1898 and 1908. Plus Philip W. Pillsbury's record of the company's history, 1958. Box, CR –1, General Mills archives.

35 Powell puts this activity at the Washburn C mill, while Folwell places it at the Washburn B.

36 De la Barre, William. "Recollections of a Milling Engineer." *NM*, July 15, 1936.

37 Fossum, Paul R., *Minnesota History*, Vol. 11, No. 3 (Sep., 1930), pp. 271-282.

38 "Historical Account of Pillsbury Flour Mills Company, 1869," p. 4.

39 Hudson, "A Public Servant." p. 696.

40 Ibid.

41 *St. Paul Daily Globe*, Sept. 23, 1880.

42 *NM*, April 8, 1881. General Mills archive.

43 Curtis, F.E. "A Floury City," *Lippincott's Magazine*, January 1884, as excerpted by *NM* on Jan. 4, 1884.

44 *NM*, Nov. 8, 1889, "The New Corporation."

45 "Historical Account," p. 17.

46 Shutter.

47 Clarke.

48 *NM*, April 29, 1881.

49 1880 U.S. census.

50 *MT*, July 3, 5 and 9, 1881.

51 www.tornadoproject.com.

52 *NM*, Nov. 11, 1881. General Mills Archive.

53 *NM*, Dec. 2, 1881. See also *MT*, Nov. 26, 1881, p. 6.

54 *NM*, Dec. 9, 1881.

55 *MT*, Dec. 5, 1881.

56 The *Tribune* reported that only about half of the Pillsbury losses were covered by insurance, and a smaller portion of the losses sustained by others. But the *NM* report had the mills "fully insured."

57 Powell, p. 30.

58 Porter, Glenn. "Industrialization and the Rise of Big Business." Chapter 1 in *The Gilded Age: Perspectives on the Origins of Modern America,* edited by Charles W. Calhoun. Plymouth, UK: Rowman & Littlefield Publishers, 2007. Chapter 2 is also relevant: Carlson, W. Bernard. "Technology and America as a Consumer Society, 1870-1900."

59 "Historical Account," p. 18.

60 Shutter, p. 358.

61 Carlson, W. Bernard, op. cit., p. 35.

62 Kenney.

63 *NM*, April 4, 1884. General Mills archive.

64 *MT*, April 3, 1883, p. 7.

65 *Minneapolis Journal*, March 19, 1884.

66 *Minneapolis Journal*, March 8, 1886.

67 *MT*, April 11, 1883.

68 Smith, *City of Parks*, p. 21.

69 Hudson, *A Half Century of Minneapolis*. p. 485

70 *Minneapolis Evening Journal*, March 6, 1884.

71 *Minneapolis Evening Journal*, April 3, 1886, quotes a speech by Mayor George Pillsbury that he tells his audience is the first campaign speech he has ever made in his career.

72 *Minneapolis Evening Journal,* April 2. 1884.

73 *Minneapolis Evening Journal*, April 2, 1884.

74 *Minneapolis Morning Tribune*, April 9, 1884, p. 4.

75 Hudson, *A Half Century of Minneapolis*. p. 147.

76 Hudson, op. cit. p. 350.

77 Worthen.

78 *MT*, Oct. 9, 1884, p. 8.

79 *MT,* Sept. 27, 1885, p. 17.

80 See *MT*, April 19, 1885 and Sept. 24, 1885.

81 *MT*, obituary for Burt B. Townsend, Dec. 7, 1916.

82 *MT*, March 24, 1886, p. 6

83 *MT*, March 24, 1886, p. 7.

84 *MT*, April 6, 1886.

85 *MT*, April 14, 1886.

86 Brochure about the Minneapolis Public Library, February, 1946. General Mills archive.

CHAPTER 5

1 Curtis, F. E. "A Floury City," *Lippincott's Magazine*, January 1884, as excerpted by *NM* on Jan. 4, 1884.

2 *NM*, Nov. 8, 1889, "The New Corporation."

3 Page without date or name in General Mills archives; it clearly predates 1899, in that it refers to C.A. Pillsbury as a man still alive.

4 Hudson, *Half Century of Minneapolis*. p. 330. See also Carlson, W. Bernard, "Technology and America as a Consumer Society," article in *The Gilded Age: Perspectives on the Origins of Modern America*, edited by Charles W. Calhoun, Plymouth, UK: Rowman and Littlefield Publishers, Inc., 2007.

5 Powell, p. 35. *NM*, Nov. 8, 1889, put the founding of Pillsbury & Hulbert in 1878, the name change in 1882, and the number of elevators under company control that year at 132.

6 See Kenney, p. 44; Adams, Thomas Sewell, and Sumner, Helen, *Labor Problems: A Textbook*. New York: The Macmillan Co., 1919. p. 415; *NM*, Nov. 8, 1889, "The New Corporation."

7 Shutter, p. 292.

8 *NM*, July 3, 1885.

9 *NM*, March 14, 1884.

10 "Pillsbury Mills Started on Frontier," manuscript dated 1944, General Mills archives, Box GH-3, folder 5.

11 For details about innovations see Shutter, p. 174; *NM*, Sept. 21, 1883, p. 269; *NM*, June 20, 1890, a special daily edition in honor of the convention of the Millers National Association in Minneapolis.

12 Powell, p. 35; Kuhlmann, pp. 229-30; *NM*, Jan. 31, 1890.

13 *NM*, exact date unclear but year is 1912, General Mills Archive.

14 Note in *NM*, Dec. 4, 1885. From General Mills archives.

15 Powell, p. 36.

16 Note in "a Minneapolis paper," Aug. 30, 1887, about Charles A. Pillsbury's advice to young men, constructed as a letter to the editor. From the personal files of Ella Pillsbury Crosby.

17 Steen, *Flour Milling in America*, Minneapolis: T.S. Denison & Co., Inc., 1963. P. 63.

18 *MT*, Sept. 18, 1888, p. 5.

19 "Pillsbury Mills Started on Frontier," manuscript dated 1944, General Mills archives, Box GH-3, folder 5; *NM*, Aug. 11, 1943. p. 24.

20 *NM*, June 20, 1884.

21 *NM*, Dec. 31, 1886.

22 Powell, p. 32.

23 *NM*, Jan. 14, 1887. The girl's gravestone at Lakewood Cemetery spells her name Marion; the *NM* and the Holman genealogy use Marian.

24 For example, see *MT*, Nov. 27, 1890, and Jan. 2, 1885.

25 Edgar, *The Medal of Gold*, p. 45.

26 Kuhlmann, p. 134.

27 *MT*, Sept. 29, 1889, p. 1.

28 Edgar, p. 46; See also Powell, p. 45-47.

29 *NM*, Sept. 11, 1891, p. 26.

30 *MT*, Nov. 12, 1889, p. 4.

31 Powell, p. 47.

32 *NM*, Feb. 1, 1889; *Dedication of the Pillsbury Memorial Town Hall.*

33 Collections of the Minnesota Historical Society. St. Paul, MN: Published by the Society, April 1901. p. 360; Minnesota land records, available via ancestry.com.

34 Torreano, p. 18.

35 Casselman, Barry. "North Star Rising." Lakeville, MN: Pogo Press, 2007, p. 23. Plus Bennett, Russell H., "Quest for Ore," Minneapolis, MN: T.S. Denison & Co., 1963, p. 50 ff. Also, interview with Russell M. Bennett II, Oct. 9, 2009.

36 Bennett, "Quest for Ore," p. 34 ff.

37 Interview with Russell M. Bennett II, Oct. 9, 2009.

38 Mining Hall of Fame inductee database, National Mining Hall of Fame, Leadville, CO.

39 Torreano, p. 1.

40 Bennett, op. cit. p. 60-61.

41 Cross, Marion E., "Neighbors of the Institute," a pamphlet issued by the Friends of the Minneapolis Institute of Arts, October 1977.

42 Unnamed newspaper obituary of C. A. Pillsbury, in a scrapbook at Warner Free Library, N.H., 1899; "Neighbors of the Institute," op.cit.

43 Barbara Flanagan interview with John S. Pillsbury, Sr., "Pillsbury's Minneapolis: At 80, Fond Memories of the Good Old Days," *MT*, Nov. 1, 1959.

44 *NM*, April 18, 1890.

45 *NM*, by Rollin E. Smith, Nov. 14, 1900, p. 933.

46 *Dedication of the Pillsbury Memorial.*

47 *Dedication of the Pillsbury Memorial.*

48 *MT*, May 31, 1890, p. 5.

49 Email from David Pavelich, reference and instruction librarian, Special Collections Research Center, Regenstein Library, University of Chicago, Aug. 6, 2009.

50 *MT*, Nov. 5, 1880, p. 5; Feb. 21, 1881, p. 2; May 25 and 28, 1890.

51 Photocopied title abstracts provided by Marlys Morrill Chutich, great-granddaughter of Olive Morrill.

52 Aug. 7, 1891, from the file of correspondence between George A and A. P. Davis, mayor of Warner, at Pillsbury Free Library, Warner, N.H.

53 Noon, p. 38.

54 *Three Dedications*.

55 *MT*, Nov. 11, 1883, p. 14.

56 Transcript of *Granite Falls Tribune*, Oct. 17, 1888, from Granite Falls Historical Society.

57 Narvestad, Carl and Amy. *Granite Falls 1879-1979*. From the chapter "Granite's Milling Industry," and "Essay about Pillsbury House in Granite Falls," supplied to the author by the Granite Falls Historical Society.

58 *Three Dedications.*

59 Lathrop, Alan K. and Firth, Bob. *Churches of Minnesota*. Minneapolis: University of Minnesota Press, 2003. P. 141.

60 *Three Dedications*;Obituary Notes, *New York Times*, March 28, 1895.

61 Hudson, p. 438.

62 *MT*, Sept. 4, 1891.

63 *MT*, June 26, 1892.

64 Noon, p. 50.

65 *MT*, May 16, 1892.

66 *NM*, May 23, 1890.

67 *NM*, Aug. 29, 1890.

68 GM archive, Box GH-4, folder 2, undated clipping from *St. Anthony Falls Democrat*, page 1.

69 *NM*, Jan. 24, 1890.

70 www.startribune.com/politics/27716104.html?page=2&c=y

71 *MT*, July 13, 1885, p. 1; "Minneapolis Club: A Review of Its History," William C. Edgar, Loring M. Staples, Henry Doerr, copyright 1974, 1990, The Minneapolis Club. p. 19, 185.

72 *NM*, May 20, 1892.

73 "Historical Account of Pillsbury Flour Mills Company, 1869," p. 19.

74 *NM*, May 20, 1892; *MT*, May 16, 1892.

75 *MT*, July 3, 1903; July 10, 1904.

76 Interview with Rick Fisher, Harriot's great-grandson, June 26, 2010.

77 *MT*, June 4, 1907;

78 Interview, George S. Pillsbury, June 6, 2009.

CHAPTER 6

1 *MT*, January 11, 1911, p. 1.

2 Edgar, William C., Loring M. Staples, Henry Doerr, "Minneapolis Club: A Review of Its History," copyright 1974, 1990, The Minneapolis Club. P. 46. Edgar's chapter is a reprint of his 1920 booklet, "The Minneapolis Club: A Review of Its History from 1883 to 1920 by an Old Member." Edgar put the date in June 1895. But a program from the event, including its menu, in General Mills archives

is dated Aug. 24, 1897, a date confirmed by *MT* coverage the next day.

3   *The Southwestern Miller*, November 14, 1961, by Herman Steen, "Band and Live Bull in 1897 Celebration staged by Charles A. Pillsbury on Materialization of Forecast of Rise to $1 Wheat Amid Derision." Page number omitted. General Mills archives.

4   *The Weekly NM*, Sept. 20, 1899, p. 543.

5   *NM*, November 14, 1884, and *MT*, November 6, 1884.

6   *NM*, March 25, 1887.

7   Program from the Banquet "Complimentary to the Class of '63" in Conant Hall, Dartmouth College, Hanover, NH, Wednesday, June 27, 1888, by Classmate Charles A. Pillsbury. Dartmouth College, Rauner Special Collections Library.

8   Storck, John and Teague, Walter Dorwin. *Flour for Man's Bread*. Minneapolis, MN: University of Minnesota Press, 1952. P. 350.

9   *New York Times*, "America's Great Wheat Crop," January 11, 1892.

10 Steen, Herman. *Flour Milling in America*. Minneapolis, MN: T.S. Denison & Co., 1963. p. 63ff.

11 Powell, p. 55-61.

12 *MT*, July 8, July 10, Oct. 30, Oct. 31 1888.

13 *NM*, Sept. 23, 1892.

14 Kenney, p. 48.

15 In the twentieth century it would take the name Metropolitan Building. Its demolition in 1961 created a public backlash so intense that it is counted today as the start of the Twin Cities' modern-day architectural preservationist movementhttp://usa.archiseek.com/minnesota/minneapolis/metropolitan_building.html.

16 Powell, 54-55.

17 *MT*, Sept. 21, 1892, p. 5.

18 Petition to Charles dated Sept. 22, 1892, and signed by 200 men including those with names still recognizable in Minneapolis: Morrison, Peavey Cargill, Crosby, McMillan. General Mills archives.

19 Worthen, as available at www.archive.org.

20 *Weekly NM*, Sept. 20, 1899, p. 543.

21 Wilkinson, William. "Memorials of the Minnesota Forest Fires in the year 1894." Minneapolis: N.E. Wilkinson, 1895, p. 208.

22 Kenney, p. 50.

23 See, for example, Kenney, p. 50 and Charles' letter to *NM*, published along with his obituary editorial, Sept. 20, 1899.

24 *NM*, Feb. 2, 1894.

25 http://eh.net/encyclopedia/article/Santos.futures. This article contains an excellent explanation of how futures trading works.

26 Powell, p. 52.

27 Levy, Jonathan Ira. "Contemplating Delivery: Futures Trading and the Problem of Commodity Exchange in the United States, 1875–1905." *The American Historical*

Review, Vol. II, No. 2, April 2006. http://www.historycooperative.org/journals/ahr/111.2/levy.html. See also *MT,* Feb. 3. 1892, p. 1.

28 Powell, pp. 52-53.

29 MT, April 6, 1896, p. 4.

30 *NM,* June 26, 1896. General Mills Archive.

31 *NM,* January 22, 1897. General Mills Archive.

32 Hudson, *A Half-Century of Minneapolis,* p. 338.

33 Powell, p. 55.

34 Russell Fridley's interview with John S. Pillsbury Sr., 1966. Minnesota Historical Society. From the personal collection of George S. Pillsbury.

35 *MT,* "Last Stone Laid," March 21, 1897, p. 16.

36 "Pillsbury Salesman," an in-house publication, November 1932. General Mills Archive.

37 http://www.collegefootballhistory.com/golden_gophers/history.htm.

38 Rainbolt, Richard (1972). *Gold Glory.* Wayzata, Minnesota: Ralph Turtinen Publishing. pp. p 14. Also http://en.wikipedia.org/wiki/William_Heffelfinger.

39 Russell Fridley's interview, op. cit.

40 Ibid.

41 *MT,* July 18, 1898, p. 4.

42 Fridley, op. cit.

43 Edgar, "Minneapolis Club: A Review of Its History," op. cit., p. 46.

44 *MT,* Aug. 25, 1897.

45 Program from the Bull Dinner, Aug. 24, 1897, General Mills Archive.

46 *MT,* Aug. 25, 1897.

47 Hudson, *A Half-Century of Minneapolis,* p. 346.

48 Powell, p. 60, and interview with George S. Pillsbury, July 25, 2009.

49 Letter from Richard Glyn to stockholders, December 2, 1898, as quoted by Powell, p. 61.

50 Interview with John S. Pillsbury by Russell Fridley of the Minnesota Historical Society, 1966.

51 Resolution adopted by the Northwestern National Bank, July 29, 1898. General Mills Archive.

52 Atwater, vol. II, p. 952.

53 *MT,* July 21, 1898, p. 5.

54 *Minneapolis Morning Tribune,* November 29, 1940, "Today's Personality," at the time of Alfred Pillsbury's retirement as treasurer of the Pillsbury Flour Mills.

55 Item in newspaper about 1932 (date smudged) "Photo Recalls Baseball Play of Pillsbury." Caption says "It took an old picture, snapped back in the mid-eighties, to recall even to some of the old-timers that he also was a baseball player of no narrow repute." Photo was found in the trunk of Harry P. Gallaher of Lake Minnetonka: "Himself a member of the team which represented the Minneapo-

lis Chamber of Commerce in the old northwest semi-pro circles, Mr. Gallaher singled out Mr. Pillsbury as one of the stars. Office employees of milling firms made up the team, which competed for a period of time between eight and 10 years, starting in 1883....Pillsbury said he played when he was about 17."

56 See, for example, *MT*, June 13, 1897, p. 9; Aug. 19, 1894, p. 5; November 26, 1893, p. 10; June 19, 1898, p. 12.

57 *Minneapolis Morning Tribune*, November 29, 1940.

58 Photo appears in picture section of Jones.

59 "Yachting in Minnesota," Sept. 2, 1898, p. 391.

60 Jones, p. 320.

61 Powell, p. 63.

62 General Mills archives.

63 *New York Times*, Sept. 18, 1899.

64 Bill of sale, Arthur Tooth & Sons, Paris, April 6, 1899: an oil painting, "Head," by Henner, $1400. General Mills archives.

65 *NM*, May 10, 1899.

66 *NM*, Sept. 20, 1899.

67 *MT*, Sept. 18, 1899.

68 *MT*, Sept. 20, 1899; NM, Sept. 20, 1899.

69 Carbon copy of manuscript, General Mills archives.

CHAPTER 7

1 From the dedication remarks of President Cyrus Northrop, recorded in the brochure "The Unveiling of the statue of John S. Pillsbury: on the campus of the University of Minnesota, Minneapolis, Wednesday, September twelfth, 1900." www.googlebooks.com.

2 *MT*, Sept. 13, 1900, p. 10. See also www1.umn.edu/systemwide/enews/072403. html#Anchor3-facelift.

3 Folwell, reprint of 1969 edition. P. 267.

4 *Dedication of the Pillsbury Memorial*, p. 61.

5 *MT*, Oct. 12, 1901.

6 Fred B. Snyder would outdo John Pillsbury in duration of service on the Board of Regents. His tenure lasted 38 years, besting Pillsbury's record by a few months.

7 *MT*, March 17, 1901.

8 Newspaper clipping obituary in scrapbook at Pillsbury Free Library, Warner, N.H. Undated, but clearly from March 1901.

9 Plymouth church archives. With thanks to James Thompson, archivist, for his assistance.

10 *Dedication of the Pillsbury Memorial Town Hall.*

11 Interview with George S. Pillsbury, Dec. 22, 2007 and Aug. 22, 2009.

12 http://www.dnr.state.mn.us/state_forests/sft00039/index.html.

13 www.thestevernssquarefoundation.org

14 Atwater, p. 598.

15 *Dedication of the Pillsbury Memorial Town Hall.*

16 McClure, Ethel, *More than a Roof: The Development of Minnesota Poor Farms and Homes for the Aged.* St. Paul: Minnesota Historical Society Press, 1968, pp. 56-58.

17 Stuhler, Barbara, *Gentle Warriors: Clara Ueland and the Minnesota struggle for women's suffrage.* St. Paul: Minnesota Historical Society Press, 1995, p. 27.

18 Atwater. See also http://www.answers.com/topic/woman-s-exchange-movement.

19 *Dedication of the Pillsbury Memorial Town Hall.* See also http://www.pnn.org/History/Stories/hospitals.htm.

20 *MT,* Jan. 13, 1901, p. B3.

21 Benidt, Bruce Weir, *The Library Book: A Centennial History of the Minneapolis Public Library.* Minneapolis: The Minneapolis Public Library and Information Center, 1984, p. 93. See also *MT,* March 15, 1902, p. 15.

22 *MT,* July 7, 1901.

23 Interview with Plymouth Church archivist James Thompson, August 2008. See also www.wayzatacommunitychurch.org.

24 Hudson, "A Public Servant."

25 *MT,* Oct. 19, 1901, p. 8.

26 Hudson, op. cit.

27 *Dedication of the Pillsbury Memorial Town Hall,* p. 95.

28 *Minneapolis Sunday Tribune,* Nov. 1, 1959; Barbara Flanagan interview with John S. Pillsbury, Sr., "Pillsbury's Minneapolis: At 80, Fond Memories of the Good Old Days." See also the second installment of the interview, "A St. Paul party usually meant an overnight stay," *Minneapolis Sunday Tribune,* Nov. 8, 1959. Plus Barbara Flanagan interview with the author, July 27, 2009.

29 A typewritten biographical data sheet, issued by the Pillsbury Co. and preserved in corporate files, says: "John Sargent Pillsbury, chairman of the board of Pillsbury Mills, Inc, had no intention of going into the flour business—he had his eye on a career in the diplomatic service." Also: *Minneapolis Star,* Dec. 6, 1848: "Fate made a miller out of me, declares John S. Pillsbury." Interview on the occasion of his 70th birthday. By Herb Paul, Minneapolis Star Business Editor.

30 John S. Pillsbury interview with Russell Fridley of the Minnesota Historical Society, 1966.

31 Author's interview with Philip W. Pillsbury Jr., May 26, 2008.

32 General Mills archive, Box 2.

33 Hudson, *A Half Century of Minneapolis.* p. 422.

34 *MT,* July 5, 1901, p. 5;

35 See *MT,* Dec. 8, 1901, p. A2; May 8, 1902, p. 8.

36 From excerpt of the *History of Minneapolis and Hennepin County Minnesota,* Holcombe and Bingham, 1914, as reproduced in Pillsbury Co. records, General Mills archives.

37 Powell, p. 66.

38 *Minneapolis Times*, June 24, 1905.

39 Profile of Charles Stinson Pillsbury in *The Pillsbury Salesman*, an in-house magazine, January 1932, by Stanley B. Knapp—features a photo of a plump-cheeked man with blue eyes. General Mills archives.

40 Interview with Philip W. Pillsbury Jr. and George S. Pillsbury, May 26, 2008.

41 Pillsbury Co. biographical sketch of John S. Pillsbury, Oct. 1, 1953. General Mills Archive.

42 *Minneapolis Star Journal*, July 11, 1945.

43 Corporate biography, undated, General Mills archives.

44 *MT*, April 14, 1905, p. 6: Text of letter from John S. and Charles S. Pillsbury to Minneapolis Mayor D. P. Jones, for presentation to Plymouth Church on April 13, 1905.

45 Hale, Mary T. A booklet: "A History of Pillsbury House." Undated, but apparently compiled in the late 1930s. General Mills archives, Folder 14.

46 *MT*, Oct. 29, 1905, p. 12;

47 for details see www.MACCalliance.org.; excerpt of the *History of Minneapolis and Hennepin County Minnesota*, Holcombe and Bingham, 1914, as reproduced in Pillsbury Co. records, General Mills archives; www.puc-mn.org.

48 *MT*, Sept. 2, 1904. P. 6.

49 *NM*, June 7, 1944.

50 See Hudson, *A Half Century of Minneapolis*, p. 420; 1953 corporate biographical sketch, General Mills Archive.

51 *MT*, Oct. 29, 1905, p. 21.

52 Pillsbury, Eleanor Lawler. *My Family Story*, p. 100.

53 *MT*, Nov. 17, 1907, p. 16.

54 Powell, p. 76, quoting Clive Jaffray's Reminiscences, MHS.

55 *MT*, Aug. 9, 1908, p. 1.

56 *MT*, Aug. 10, 1908, p. 1.

57 Kelsey, p. 312.

58 Letter from Charles S. to Alfred in London, Aug. 20, 1908, as quoted by Powell, p. 79.

59 *MT*, March 21, 1911, p. 8.

60 Powell, p. 90-92.

70 Powell, p. 97.

CHAPTER 8

1 Material derived primarily from Pillsbury, Eleanor Lawler, *My Family Story*; Supplemental stories obtained in interviews with Ella Sturgis Pillsbury Crosby and George Sturgis Pillsbury.

2   Holman, p. 32.

3   www.usgennet.org/usa/topic/preservation/gov/army.htm

4   Pillsbury, Eleanor, *My Family Story*, p. 92.

5   Ibid., p. 101, 105.

6   *Minneapolis Star*, "Philip W. Pillsbury, 50-year career awakened sleeping giant." Aug. 20, 1974, by Barbara Flanagan.

7   *MT*, Jan. 23, 1912, p. 8.

8   Letter from John P. Snyder to his father, Fred Snyder. From *The Story of Fred B. Snyder in honor of his 90ᵗʰ birthday, Feb. 21, 1950*, p. 42. With thanks to University of Minnesota historian Ann M. Pflaum.

9   *MT*, April 22, 1912, p. 1.

10 *MT*, April 19, 1912. P. 1.

11 Interview with Helen Waldron, granddaughter of John and Nell Snyder, Sept. 18, 2009.

12 *MT*, April 22, 1912, p. 1.

13 *MT*, April 21, 1912. P. 1; more about Mahala Douglas can be found in Jones, p. 310-11.

14 *MT*, April 17, 1912. P. 1.

15 www.wayzatahistoricalsociety.org. The house's address is 309 Ramsey Rd., Wayzata.

16 Borger, Judith Yates, "Four Generations of the Family Pillsbury," *Twin Cities* magazine, July 1981.

17 Cross, Marion E. "Neighbors of the Institute," a pamphlet issued by the Friends of the Minneapolis Institute of Arts, October 1977. This pamphlet describes the disposition of Highland Home as a silent auction between the two brothers, at which John was the highest bidder. George S. Pillsbury maintains that John and Juty described a coin toss to their children.

18 Interview with Ella Pillsbury Crosby, July 28, 2007.

19 Cross, op. cit.

20 Kelsey, p. 315. Another version of this story, by Minneapolis parks historian David C. Smith, says that the Minneapolis Park Board purchased the land on which Fair Oaks stood for $250,000 in 1911, and Washburn donated the house, barn, stable and greenhouse, together valued at $400,000. The Park Board did not take full possession of the property until Lizzie Washburn died in 1915, Smith reports in "Parks, Lakes, Trails and So Much More" at www.minneapolisparks.org/documents/parks.

21 Pillsbury, Eleanor Lawler, *My Family Story*, p. 222.

22 Ibid.

23 Birthdates all provided by Holman genealogy.

24 For example, see "Bridal Dinners Are Principal Pre-Nuptial Events for June," June 25, 1922, *Minneapolis Morning Tribune*, p. E2

25 *MT*, various dates in 1913-1914; and Edgar, William C., "Minneapolis Club: A Review of Its History." Minneapolis, MN: The Minneapolis Club, 1974, 1990. p. 171.

26 Interview with Barbara Flanagan, July 27, 2009.

27 Story of the development of Southways is drawn largely from Pillsbury, Eleanor Lawler, "Southways: Random Reminiscences." Minneapolis, MN: privately published, 1985. It's notable that Juty Pillsbury wrote about this episode in her life when she was 98 years old.

28 Larsen, Stephanie and Nancy Platou Steinke, "Historic Lake Minnetonka." Privately published, 2009, p. 12. Available at www.HistoricLakeMinnetonka.com.

29 Pillsbury, Eleanor Lawler, *Southways*.

30 Ibid.

31 Interview with Ella Pillsbury Crosby, July 26, 2008.

32 www.lakeminnetonkagardenclub.org.

33 Interview with Russell Bennett, Oct. 9, 2009.

34 Magney, Agnes, *Swift as a Dream*, forward by George Pillsbury. Applied Graphics Association, Inc., Wayzata, MN. 1985.

35 Magney, ibid.; plus interview with George S. Pillsbury and Ella Pillsbury Crosby, Nov. 1, 2007.

36 Interview with Helen Snyder Waldron, op. cit.

37 from Ancestry.com: Registration Location: Hennepin County, Minnesota; Roll 1675681; Draft Board: 8. World War I Draft Registration Cards, 1917-1918.

38 *MT*, Dec. 5, 1917, p. 2.

39 *MT*, May 6, 1918, p. 7.

40 Interview with Alfred Pillsbury Gale, Oct. 17, 2009.

41 Powell, p. 97.

42 Powell, p. 107, 113.

43 Powell, p. 105.

44 "The History of Pasta," www.thenibble.com.

45 Transcript of a radio interview with JS sponsored by the *MT*, May 1940. General Mills archives.

46 "The Creamette Story," www.creamette.newworldpasta.com.

47 Pillsbury, Eleanor Lawler, *My Family Story*, p. 119.

48 *MT*, May 27, 1914, p. 11.

49 Pillsbury, E.L. *My Family Story*, p. 128.

50 Interview with Helen Snyder Waldron, Sept. 18, 2009.

CHAPTER 9

1 Smith, *City of Parks*, p. 121 ff.

2 *MT*, Oct. 12, 1911, p. 6.

3 Holman, p. 27-28.

4   *NM*, March 14, 1950, p. 21.

5   *Minneapolis Morning Tribune*, Nov. 29, 1940, "Today's Personality," about Alf, at the time of his retirement as treasurer of the Pillsbury Flour Mills.

6   Ibid.

7   for example, *MT*, Nov. 11, 1903, p. 7. The Home took the name Stevens Square and became a care facility for the elderly in 1935.

8   Undated obituary article about Eleanor Field Pillsbury, from magazine, undoubtedly from November 1946, General Mills Archive.

9   For example, *MT*, Jan. 28, 1912, p. 18.

10 Interview with retired senior pastor John Cummins, First Universalist Church, Minneapolis, MN, Oct. 9, 2009. The Universalist movement had a stronghold in Maine, the native state of a number of Minneapolis pioneers. In the nineteenth century, Fred and Alice Pillsbury were attached to the Church of the Redeemer, likely because of Alice's family ties there. Minnie Pillsbury Townsend was also listed as member in 1887, the year after her marriage—perhaps following her husband's lead in religious matters, or perhaps suggesting a break with her thoroughly Baptist adoptive parents.

11 Ibid.

12 http://firstuniv150.org/illuminate_the_past.

13 "Pillsbury Salesman," an in-house publication of the Pillsbury Flour Mills Co., November 1932. General Mills archive.

14 "The First Universalist Church of Minneapolis," op. cit.

15 Undated obituary article about Eleanor Field Pillsbury, from magazine, undoubtedly from 1946, General Mills archive.

16 Smith, p. 125.

17 Smith, p. 116.

18 Folwell, vol IV, p. 432-33.

19 *MT*, June 11, 1929, p. 1.

20 *MT*, June 11, 1935, p. 1, and June 12, 1935, p. 4.

21 *MT*, July 8, 1937, p. 1.

22 Smith, p. 142.

23 Smith, p. 145.

24 Interview, July 26, 2008.

25 For example, the *NM* reported in June 1929 that Charles' trip to Europe lasted from January to May. Several items from the 1930s report trips by Charles and Nelle to Paris to visit a daughter who lived there. General Mills archives.

26 *Minneapolis Star*, "Philip W. Pillsbury, 50-year career awakened sleeping giant." Aug. 20, 1974, by Barbara Flanagan.

27 http://www.britannica.com/EBchecked/topic/305983/T-A-D-Jones.

28 Undated release prepared by the Pillsbury Co., marked "unused." General Mills archive.

29 "Biography and personality sketch," May 1959 corporate file. General Mills archive.

30 Powell, p. 129.

31 *Minneapolis Star,* "Philip W. Pillsbury, 50-year career awakened sleeping giant." Aug. 20, 1974, by Barbara Flanagan.

32 *MT,* Dec. 11, 1959: Phil is appointed chairman of the Minnesota committee for National Library Week. To be observed April 3-9 in 1960. *Minneapolis Star,* April 4, 1960, said Phil is "owner of one of the state's largest private libraries."

33 Date from http://brickhouse.lib.umn.edu/exhibits/show/brickhouse/construction/page05. Other information from George S. Pillsbury, Nov. 13, 2009. He put Alfred's donation to the stadium at $50,000. A large gift from him was not mentioned in the program from the stadium's dedication on Nov. 15, 1924, which made much of the gifts of students and faculty to the facility. That emphasis may have been made at the modest man's request.

34 Interview with George S. Pillsbury, November 11, 2009.

35 Hess, Jeffrey A., *Their Splendid Legacy: The First 100 years of the Minneapolis Society of Fine Arts.* Minneapolis, MN: The Minneapolis Society of Fine Arts, 1985, p. 20.

36 *Minneapolis Morning Tribune,* July 27, 1919, p. B1.

37 Bulletin of the Minneapolis Institute of Arts, May 6, 1950.

38 Hess, op. cit., p. 44.

39 Obituary, clipped from an unidentified magazine, undated but likely from November 1946. General Mills archives.

40 Ibid.

41 "Pillsbury Salesman," an in-house publication, November 1932. General Mills archives.

42 Bulletin of the Minneapolis Institute of Arts, Dec. 4, 1937, Vol. XXVI, No. 33,

43 Bulletin of the Minneapolis Institute of Arts: the Alfred F. Pillsbury Collections." Special issue, 1948. Available online: http://www.artsconnected.org/resource/93760/the-minneapolis-institute-of-arts-bulletin-the-alfred-f-pillsbury-collections-at-the-art-institute.

44 Interview with George Pillsbury, Jan. 26, 2008.

45 *New York Times,* March 23, 2009; plus interview with Bruce Dayton, July 23, 2008.

46 Interview with Bruce Dayton, July 23, 2008.

47 Interview with Alfred Gale, Oct. 17, 2009.

48 Interview with the Rev. John Cummins, Oct. 9, 2009. Plus "First Universalist Church of Minneapolis: The first 150 years." Minneapolis, MN: First Universalist Church, 2009, p. 56-57.

49 *Minneapolis Star,* March 14, 1950.

50 *MT,* April 23, 1954.

CHAPTER 10

1. From a release prepared by the company, marked "not used," that describes Phil's ascension to the presidency as "recent." General Mills archive.

2. Powell, p. 120.

3. Philip W. Pillsbury's record of the company's history...a photocopy in Box, CR –1, general Mills archives. Text indicates it was written in 1958. P. 28.

4. Powell, p. 124.

5. Powell, p. 125.

6. Accounts differ about when Phil and Eleanor Bellows Pillsbury returned for good to Minneapolis, with dates ranging from 1935 until 1939. Their son Phil Jr., who was born in Chicago in 1937, says the family moved while he was a toddler.

7. Pillsbury Flour Mills Co. release, May 21, 1939. General Mills archive.

8. *Minneapolis Star*, "Philip W. Pillsbury: 50-year career awakened sleeping giant." Aug. 20, 1974, by Barbara Flanagan.

9. *New York Times*, Dec. 29, 1939.

10. Philip W. Pillsbury's record of the company's history, a photocopy in Box, CR –1, General Mills archives. Text indicates it was written in 1958. p. 27.

11. Powell, p. 131.

12. Powell, p. 133.

13. *Banco Yearly Times*, Dec. 16, 1958.

14. Powell, p. 143.

15. Powell, p. 141.

16. Like his grandfather had been, Phil was a great believer in the value of top-notch laboratories and test kitchens. His personal involvement extended to the occasional baking of bread with Pillsbury flour, to see for himself how it functioned for home bakers. In March 1957, the MT's legendary food writer Mary Hart watched Phil in action in the kitchen, and printed his personal recipe for four loaves of white bread. Here it is:

2 cakes compressed yeast	*2 tbsp. salt*
½ cup lukewarm water	*2 c. hot scalded milk*
1/3 cup sugar	*1 ½ cup cold water*
1/3 cup shortening	*11 to 12 cups sifted flour*

Soften compressed yeast in lukewarm water (or substitute 2 packages dry yeast softened in ½ cup very warm, not hot, water.) Combine sugar, shortening, salt and milk in large bowl. Stir to melt shortening. Cool to lukewarm by adding cold water. Stir in yeast. Blend in flour to form stiff dough.

Knead on floured surface until smooth and satiny, 5 to 10 minutes. Place in greased bowl, turning dough around in bowl to grease all sides. Cover. Let rise in warm place until doubled in size, about two hours. Punch down, turn upside down in bowl and cover. Let rise again for 30 minutes.

Divide into four parts on floured surface. Mold into balls. Cover. Let stand 15 minutes. Shape into loaves. Place in greased 9x5x3 pans. Cover. Let rise until doubled in size, about 1 ½ hours. Bake in moderate oven (375 degrees) 45 to 50 minutes.

17 May 1959 corporate file, "biography and personality sketch." General Mills archive.

18 Powell, p. 141.

19 *Minneapolis Times*, June 9, 1944. General Mills archive.

20 From a Pillsbury Company release, Dec. 19, 1944. General Mills Archive.

21 Engagement announcement in *New York Times*, Jan. 11, 1936.

22 www.chinfo.navy.mil/navpalib/ships/carriers/histories/cv14-ticonderoga/cv14-ticonderoga

23 Interview with Russell Bennett, Oct. 9, 2009. Bennett, born 15 years after Eddy, said that as a teenager he sought chances to join Eddy's sailboat crew, even in races against the latter's older brother.

24 Pillsbury, Eleanor Lawler, *Southways*. p. 29-30.

25 *Minneapolis Star*, "Plane Crash Kills Lindley, Andrews, Edmund Pillsbury." Feb. 23, 1951, p. 1.

26 Email from Priscilla Pillsbury Gaines, Dec. 30, 2009.

27 Thurston's Pasadena City Directory Including San Marino, 1942, p. 537. www.ancestry.com.

28 Edmund Pennington Pillsbury corporate biographical data form, dated Dec. 15, 1944. General Mills archives.

29 Pillsbury, Eleanor Lawler, *My Family Story*, p. 135.

30 *Minneapolis Star Tribune*, Oct. 6, 1989.

31 Pillsbury Co. corporate biographical data form, dated October 1968. General Mills Archive. Also, interview with Helen Snyder Waldron, daugher of John Pillsbury Snyder Jr., Sept. 18, 2009.

32 Holman, p. 33.

33 *New York Times*, June 30, 1947. Franklin M. Crosby's obituary.

34 Hudson, *A Half Century of Minneapolis*, p. 308.

35 http://www.allina.com/ahsimages5/abbott/park%20house%20history.pdf. The Crosby house became the property of the Roman Catholic Archdiocese of St. Paul and Minneapolis, which used it as a youth center for many years. It is now Park House, a day health center for people afflicted with HIV/AIDS.

36 Pillsbury, E.L., *Southways*, p. 30.

37 Kathleen Kennedy went on to marry William "Billy" Cavendish, the Marquess of Hartington, on May 6, 1944. She died in an airplane crash in France on May 13, 1948. Source: www.jfklibrary.org.

38 http://www.pacificwrecks.com/aircraft/f4u/17804.html.

39 Ambassador Biddle made a hasty escape from Poland as the Nazi invasion began, accompanied by his wife, chauffeur and a dog. They decamped to London, where he became U.S. ambassador in absentia to a group of seven countries occupied by Nazi forces. http://www.arlingtoncemetery.net/ajdbiddl.htm.

40 A letter preserved in Pillsbury Co. archives by John Sr., dated March 22, 1943 and addressed to Mr. V. R. West at McCann-Erickson Co., in Minneapolis, a corporate publicist who later joined the Pillsbury Co. staff, describes the military rank and service assignment of each Pillsbury son and son-in-law. Paternal pride is evident on each line, including the conclusion: "I might add that all six of the above are graduates of Yale University."

41 www.pacificwrecks.com, quoting a book by Tom Blackburn, "The Jolly Rogers," Pacifica Press, 1997.

42 Letter to Miss Virginia Crenshaw, editor of New South Baker magazine, Atlanta Ga., Oct. 3, 1944. She had sent him a clipping about Charles. Folder 6, Box 2, General Mills Archive.

43 John S. Pillsbury letter to Mr. V. R. West, Office, appears to be hand-delivered, June 27, 1944. Folder 6, box 2. General Mills Archive.

44 Undated citation, General Mills Archive.

45 *New York Times*, July 7, 1968. The roommate connection between Cyrus Vance and Stan Resor is from www.lewrockwell.com/rothbard/rothbard66.html.

46 Pillsbury, E.L., *Southways*, pp. 33-34.

47 Pillsbury, E.L. *My Family Story*, p. 137.

48 Company release, May 24, 1945. General Mills Archive.

49 Powell, p. 139.

50 Article clipped from a company magazine, Nov. 1, 1931. General Mills Archive.

51 *Mpls Times*, Jan. 7, 1946, "What Goes On Here," a column by Brenda Ueland.

52 John is the first "civic leader" named in a 1943 *MT* article promoting enlistment in the WAVES. The second person quoted is the Rev. Richard Raines of Hennepin Avenue United Methodist Church, who went on to be a bishop and leading national figure in his denomination. General Mills Archive.

53 John was an organizer and was photographed as a leader at the Navy Rally at the Minneapolis Auditorium, Oct. 28, 1943. General Mills Archive.

54 *MT*, Jan. 22, 1944: "City War Show Opens Tonight." John is listed among the speakers.

55 Ueland, Brenda, "What Goes On Here," *Minneapolis Times,* Jan. 7, 1946.

56 Letter, April 12, 1943, General Mills Archive.

57 *Minneapolis Sunday Tribune*, May 21, 1944, "Bonds for Babies." The photo features John Pillsbury III, David Crosby, Eleanor Crosby, Thomas M. Crosby Jr., Donaldson Pillsbury, and Harrison Pillsbury.

58 Clipping from *Minneapolis Star Journal* or *Tribune* dated May 24, 1945. General Mills Archive.

59 *Minneapolis Morning Tribune*, Dec. 7, 1945. General Mills Archive.

60 *Minneaolis Morning Tribune*, April 16, 1943, "Minneapolis Keeps Its Orchestra."

61 Ibid.

62 *Chicago Tribune*, Nov. 27, 1943, book review recounting how Wendell Willkie became the GOP nominee in 1940. It reviews a book by C. Nelson Sparks, former mayor of Akron, Ohio, entitled *One Man*.

63 Pillsbury, E.L. *My Family Story*, p. 140.

64 Stassen delivered the convention keynote on June 24, 1940, two days after the French surrendered to the Nazis. He lamented that the United States was "too woefully weak" to give Britain the help it deserved. http://collections.mnhs.org/mnhistorymagazine/articles/41/v41i06p267-283.pdf, p. 268.

65 Interview with Alfred Pillsbury Gale, Oct. 17, 2009.

66 *MT* Voters' Guide for 1940, publication date omitted, Star Tribune Library.

67 John S. Pillsbury's role in acquiring the land on which both the first and the second University of Minnesota experimental farms are located is detailed in "The Unveiling of the Statue of John S. Pillsbury" at googlebooks.com.

68 Richard P. Gale obituary, *New York Times*, Dec. 6, 1973.

69 Biographical Directory of the Congress of the United States, http://bioguide.congress.gov/scripts/biodisplay.pl?index=G000014.

70 Interview with Edward Gale, June 24, 2010.

71 A third of the incumbent congressmen unseated in state history lost elections between 1932 and 1950. See http://blog.lib.umn.edu/cspg/smartpolitics/2009/09/are_minnesotas_us_house_seats.php.

72 Interview, Al Gale, Oct. 17, 2009.

73 Garlid, George W. "Minneapolis Unit of the Committee to Defend America by Aiding the Allies." *Minnesota History Journal,* Summer 1969, p. 268 ff.

74 Pearson, Drew, "The Merry-Go-Round," as printed in the *Evansville, Ind., Courier Press*, Feb. 18, 1945,

75 *New York Times*, "Ex-Rep. Richard Gale of Minnesota dies at 73," Dec. 6, 1973.

76 General Mills archives.

77 Photo caption on file at the Minneapolis Star Tribune library.

78 Morley Gale would go on to marry fellow journalist Arthur Ballentine, who adopted Richard Gale III. The Ballentines moved to Durango, Colorado, purchased two newspapers there, merged them and were hands-on publishers and editors for the next half-century. Morley Cowles Ballentine died on Oct. 10, 2009.

79 Alfred P. Gale and Leone R. Gale, narrators; James E. Fogerty, interviewer; Minnesota's Greatest Generation, the Minnesota Historical Society Oral History Office, 2008.

CHAPTER 11

1 *Minneapolis Star Journal*, October 2, 1945.

2 Email correspondence with Gary Kubat, director of communications, Orono School District, January 25, 2010.

3 For an example of his service to Orono as city attorney, see Minneapolis Star, November 25, 1955.

4 Not many years hence, his resume would include service as chairman of the school board, president of Woodhill Country Club, president of the Minneapolis Club, an officer in the Hennepin County Community Chest, Dunwoody Insti-

tute, the Minneapolis Symphony Orchestra, the brand-new "Twin Cities Area Educational Television Corp.," and a member of several corporate boards, including the Pillsbury Co.

5 *MT*, April 8, 1956.

6 *Minneapolis Star*, May 9, 1955. Kitty is elected president of the Hennepin County Republican Workshop, May 19, 1958.

7 *New York Times*, December 15, 1966, confirms that John joined the board in 1950, the year Alfred Pillsbury died, making his board seat vacant.

8 *Minneapolis Morning Tribune*, August 14, 1921, p. c.

9 Sally also participated in theater at Smith, and as a freshman, she was cast in a play entitled "Cry Havoc." In production's leading role was Nancy Davis, who would be better known 40 years later as First Lady Nancy Reagan. Source: *St. Paul Pioneer Press*, August 16, 1981.

10 *Minneapolis Star*, January 6, 1947.

11 *MT*, October 7, 1947: On the same day Charles Alfred Pillsbury was born, Mr. and Mrs. John S. Pillsbury were attending services at Yale University's Battell Chapel, "where the apse was dedicated as a memorial to 16 former undergraduate deacons who died in World War II. The Pillsburys' son, Charles Alfred Pillsbury, for whom the baby was named, was a member of the class of 1939. The altar is the gift from Mr. and Mrs. Pillsbury in memory of their son." Baby Charlie would go on to be a student deacon himself in that chapel in 1970, serving with outspoken anti-war Yale chaplain William Sloane Coffin Jr.

12 George S. Pillsbury interview with General Mills corporate archivist Katie Dishman, April 20, 2005. General Mills Archive.

13 *Time* magazine, April 26, 1948.

14 Radcliffe College, Arthur and Elizabeth Schlesinger Library on the History of Women in America http://oasis.lib.harvard.edu/oasis/deliver/~sch00708.

15 *Skiing Heritage Journal,* March 2002, p. 43, reported the death of Grace Carter Lindley in Duluth at age 85.

16 *MT*, February 23, 1951, p. 1.

17 *Chicago Sun Times*, Kup's Column, February 27, 1951.

18 *Minneapolis Star*, February 23, 1951. P. 1.

19 *St. Paul Dispatch*, February 23, 1951.

20 *MT*, October 20, 1953.

21 Powell, p. 149.

22 Powell, p. 167.

23 Powell, p. 155.

24 Powell, pp. 151-53.

25 www.pillsbury.com/bakeoff/history/1949.aspx.

26 *MT*, January 9. 1962.

27 *Minnesota Monthly* magazine cover story, June 1989, by Richard Broderick.

28 Pillsbury, E.L., *My Family Story*, pp. 137-8.

29 *Investors Reader* magazine, February 13, 1952, which featured Philip W. Pillsbury on the cover.

30 *NM*, November 6, 1951, reprint of article by Robert H. Fetridge of the New York Times.

31 *Investors Reader*, February 13, 1952.

32 Powell, p. 155.

33 *Atchison Daily Globe*, April 26, 1968.

34 *New York Times*, January 26, 1996; plus interview with Philip W. Pillsbury Jr., May 26, 2008.

35 From General Mills archives, PF3 folder 1: In 1948 Philip W. and Eleanor made an extensive trip to Central America, South America, West Indies and some U.S. possessions in the Caribbean. They were gone from January 4 to Mar. 27. The release the company sent out: "Although his trip is mainly for pleasure, he will talk to as many of his own company's agents and other people in business as possible. He knows that there are many things the American countries can learn from each other."

36 *Minneapolis Star*, "Philip W. Pillsbury, 50-year career awakened sleeping giant." August 20, 1974, by Barbara Flanagan.

37 *MT*, April 10, 1955.

38 *Pillsbury Reporter*, in-house Pillsbury Co., newsletter, July 1984.

39 *Investors Reader*, February 13, 1952.

40 *MT*, June 6, 1966, Margaret Morris column.

41 Phil Pillsbury's regular column in *Pillsbury People* in-house newsletter, June 1959.

42 *The New York Times*, August 27, 1971.

43 *Minneapolis Star*, August 20, 1974.

44 *Christian Science Monitor*, September 25, 1962.

45 *MT*, October 29, 1943.

46 *Minneapolis Star*, March 1, 1946.

47 Unknown source newspaper item, February 12, 1947. General Mills archive, Box 3, Folder 18.

48 *Minneapolis Star*, January 14, 1948.

49 *Minneapolis Star*, August 20, 1974.

50 Unidentified newspaper article, dated February 16, 1966, General Mills archives, Box 3, Folder 22.

51 *Minneapolis Star*, December 2, 1952.

52 *New York Times*, August 27, 1971.

53 Eleanor was one of four winners in 1953 of the Albert Lasker Award given by Planned Parenthood for world population control efforts the previous year.

54 *The Houston Press*, Houston, TX, May 13, 1953, Carl Victor Little.

55 *Houston Press* item, undated but clearly May 1953, advancing her visit to the city.

56 *Long Island Daily Press*, September 20, 1956.

57 *Minneapolis Star*, August 20, 1974.

58 www.hcmc.org/medcenter/timeline.htm.

59 From a release sent by Pillsbury publicist Lou Gelfand to major news organizations in August 1971, advising them that Eleanor Bellows Pillsbury was seriously ill.

60 *Minneapolis Star Tribune*, December 9, 2007.

61 Interview with Lou Gelfand, March 8, 2010.

62 *MT*, October 18, 1971.

CHAPTER 12

1 *MT*, April 8, 1956: John Jr. speaks as one of 12 billed by the Minnesota Young Republican League as "potential candidates" at a rally at the Leamington. He had been named as one of 12 "able men" proposed by former Gov. Harold Stassen as likely future candidates for governor. Only one on Stassen's list—future U.S. Rep. Odin Langen—wound up in major elective office.

2 An example of John's commitment to sailing is evident in an Aug. 23, 1958 item in the *Minneapolis Star*. John Jr. sailed The Nemesis to win the Class A race in the Inland Lakes Yachting Assoc. sailboat regatta in Neenah, Wis. That year, John Jr. was commodore of the association, and proudly announced that the 1959 regatta would be at Lake Minnetonka.

3 *MT*, December 22, 1958.

4 *Minneapolis Star*, Oct. 1, 1956.

5 *MT*, December 15, 1956.

6 *MT*, December 15, 1956, reporting on revelations in hearings related to two lawsuits filed in connection with the takeover attempt by Great Southern Life.

7 *MT*, December 15. 1956.

8 Interview, John S. Pillsbury III, March 22, 2010.

9 *MT*, December 15, 1956.

10 Interview Oct. 17, 2009 with John Turner, 1991-2000 CEO and chairman of ReliaStar (the successor to NWNL), who was hired by John Pillsbury Jr. in 1967 as an actuary.

11 Interview, John S. Pillsbury III, March 22, 2010.

12 *Minneapolis Star*, Oct. 1, 1956, and MT, Oct. 2, 1956.

13 Interview, John S. Pillsbury III, March 22, 2010.

14 *Minneapolis Star*, January 18, 1957.

15 *MT*, November 15, 1956.

16 *MT*, November 17, 1956.

17 *Minneapolis Star*, November 20, 1956.

18 http://collections.mnhs.org/MNHistoryMagazine/articles/52/v52i08p307-322.pdf.

19 *MT*, November 29, 1956.

20 It's not clear whether Freeman would have gone so far as to call a special session of the Legislature to adjust state corporate governance laws in a way that would help fend off hostile takeovers. Thirty years later, another DFL governor, Rudy Perpich, would do just that, to stave off a hostile takeover of retailing giant Dayton-Hudson Corp. (now Target Corp.)

21 *Minneapolis Star*, November 26, 1956.

22 *Minneapolis Star*, December 5, 1956.

23 *Minneapolis Star*, December 3, 1956.

24 *Minneapolis Star*, Oct. 8, 1956.

25 Interview with Sarah Pillsbury, April 22, 2008.

26 http://www.pillsbury.edu/About/history.html#History; also *Minneapolis Star*, Feb. 15, 1954; July 8, 1954 and March 16, 1957.

27 *Minneapolis Star*, January 29, 1957.

28 *Minneapolis Star*, Feb. 2, 1957, and interview with George S. Pillsbury, June 24, 2008.

29 *Minneapolis Star*, January 10, 1958.

30 *MT*, April 18, 1958.

31 *MT*, Feb. 9 1958.

32 *NM*, Aug. 4, 1937.

33 Nathanson, p. 139.

34 Kane, p. 173.

35 Dayton, Bruce B. with Ellen B. Green, "The Birth of Target." Minneapolis, MN: privately published, 2008, beginning p. 29.

36 Nathanson, p. 165.

37 Ibid.

38 *Minneapolis Star*, September 22, 1960.

39 *Minneapolis Star*, May 14, 1957.

40 *Minneapolis Star*, January 11, 1965.

41 www.minnesotamonthly.com/media/Minnesota-Monthly/July-2009/Modern-Love/

42 Smith, *City of Parks*. p. 91.

43 *Minneapolis Star*, January 11, 1965.

44 *MT*, May 26, 1965: John is presented with a plaque by Administrative Management magazine in honor of the selection of the new NWNL building as one of the best designed new offices of 1964.

45 *Minneapolis Star*, Oct. 6, 1965.

46 Andersen, Elmer L., *A Man's Reach*. Minneapolis, MN: University of Minnesota Press, 2000. Page 273. Edited by Lori Sturdevant.

47 *Minneapolis Star*, November 12, 1965, and MT, November 13, 1965.

48 Also among the possible candidates mentioned by news reports was Wheelock Whitney, Sally Pillsbury's brother. Wheelock was mayor of Wayzata in 1965, and had been the unsuccessful GOP candidate against U.S. Sen. Eugene McCarthy in 1964. With Minnesota favorite son Hubert Humphrey, the founder of the Minnesota DFL, seeking the vice presidency that year, Whitney had no chance.

49 *Minneapolis Star*, Jan 8, 1966.

50 Interview with William Frenzel, April 5, 2010.

51 *Minneapolis Star*, March 8, 1966.

52 Andersen, Elmer L. *A Man's Reach*, op. cit. p. 212-13 describes Brook's role as Andersen's emissary to Mississippi.

53 For example, see MT, March 28, 1966. When Andersen is endorsed by the Minnesota Federation of College Republicans, he responds: "I am grateful and appreciative of this expression of confidence. . . I'm so impressed that I can't let it fall on a completely deaf ear."

54 *Minneapolis Star*, April 5, 1966.

55 http://gustavus.edu/welcome/campushistory.pdf

56 Interview with former Gov. Arne Carlson, September 12, 2009.

57 *Minneapolis Star*, March 8, 1966.

58 Ibid.

59 *Minneapolis Star*, May 21, 1966.

60 Later in the campaign, LeVander would vow to veto a sales tax. He would have to make good on that promise, twice. As governor he vetoed two bills creating a sales tax in June 1967, only to have his second veto overridden by the Legislature. Despite his opposition, the new sales tax was unfairly called "LeVander's pennies" by many dissatisfied Minnesotans.

61 *Minneapolis Star*, June 16, 1966.

62 *Minneapolis Star*, April 15, 1966.

63 MT, April 16, 1966.

64 MT, June 25, 1966.

65 MT, March 21, 1966.

66 Interview with Paul Overgaard, April 26, 2010.

67 *Minneapolis Star*, June 25, 1966.

68 Interview with John Pillsbury III, June 7, 2010. His job on his father's convention team was tracking delegate votes, ballot to ballot.

69 Interview with Al Quie, May 5, 2010.

70 Interview with John Turner, October 17, 2009.

71 *Minneapolis Star*, January 30, 1970.

72 MT, Feb. 15, 1970.

73 Email from Gillian Schoonover, Minnesota Orchestral Association, May 3, 2010. Pillsburys who served on the board included Charles Stinson Pillsbury, 1907-39;

Alfred Fisk Pillsbury, 1911-1950; John S. Pillsbury Sr. 1914-1969; Eleanor Bellows Pillsbury, 1943-45; Philip Winston Pillsbury, 1963-1984; John S. Pillsbury Jr., 1958-2005; Corinne Griffith Pillsbury, 1988-93; and John S. Pillsbury III, 1970-75 and 1977-79.

74 http://encore.celebrityaccess.com/index.php?encoreId=4&articleId=16478.

75 Flanagan, Barbara, *Ovation: A partnership between a great orchestra and a great audience.* Minneapolis, MN: The Minnesota Orchestra, 1977. P. 21.

76 *MT*, September 22, 1972.

77 *MT*, December 16, 1972.

78 "Design Concept for Orchestra Hall," created by the House Committee headed by Stephen Pflaum for architects Hammel Green & Abrahamson, Inc. of St. Paul, and Hardy Holzman Pfeiffer Associates of New York, as included as a report from the Executive Committee to the full board in a Jan-Feb 1973 summary.

79 *MT*, January 17, 1973.

80 Flanagan, ibid., p.109: photo from groundbreaking at Peavey Plaza. Caption: "John S. Pillsbury Jr., columnist Barbara Flanagan and Mayor Albert Hofstede participated in ground-breaking for Peavey Plaza, the park next to Orchestra Hall on Nicollet Avenue The plaza, designed by Paul Friedberg, New York landscape architect, was a gift to Minneapolis from the Peavey Co. to observe its 100th year in business."

81 *MT*, June 5, 1973.

82 November 2, 1973 minutes of a special meeting of the board of directors, Performing Arts Archive, Elmer L. Andersen Library, University of Minnesota.

83 Minutes of April 20, 1974 special meeting of the board of directions. Performing Arts Archive, Elmer L. Andersen Library, University of Minnesota.

84 From a September 1968 memo outlining the rationale for changing the name, attached to the April 20, 1974 board meeting minutes.

85 Flanagan's book *Ovation* quotes *New York Times* critic Harold C. Schonberg: "Orchestra Hall has a brilliant acoustical ambience, perhaps even too brilliant. Certainly this listener has never run across a hall with a more powerful throw from the stage."

86 Minnesota Orchestra LXXII Season 1974-75, bound programs, Performing Arts Archive, University of Minnesota. Also, Flanagan, ibid., p. 108.

87 Interview with Luella Goldberg, March 28, 2010.

88 Annual report of president Donald Engle to the board of directors of the Minnesota Orchestral Association, December 13, 1974. Performing Arts Archive, Elmer L. Andersen Library, University of Minnesota.

89 Email correspondence between author and Gillian Schoonover, Minnesota Orchestra, May 3, 2010.

90 *Minneapolis Star*, April 28, 1977.

Chapter 13

1 *Banco Yearly Times*, December 19, 1950, a publication of Northwest Bancorporation. Its cover story was a lengthy profile of longtime corporate director John S. Pillsbury Sr.

2 Powell, p. 235.

3 *Minneapolis Star*, Sept. 9, 1958. "J.S. Pillsbury Sr. ends 50-year 'job'" by Randall Hobart, Minneapolis Star Business Editor.

4 *MT*, Feb. 1, 1968; also, program from his 50th anniversary party at Pillsbury, July 16, 1974. General Mills Archive.

5 *Minneapolis Sunday Tribune*, November 8, 1959.

6 *Minneapolis Star*, November 4, 1969.

7 A biographical sketch of John S. Pillsbury in corporate publicity files, dated October 1, 1953. General Mills archives Box 2.

8 Russell Fridley's interview with John S. Pillsbury Sr., 1966, Minnesota Historical Society.

9 *Minneapolis Star*, July 13, 1970.

10 *Minneapolis Star Tribune*, October 6, 1989.

11 General Mills Archive, Box PF3, folder 9.

12 General Mills archives, folder 10.

13 Interview with American Miller & Processor magazine's editorial board, published August 1964. General Mills Archive.

14 *Minneapolis Star*, "Philip W. Pillsbury, 50-year career awakened sleeping giant." By Barbara Flanagan. Aug. 20, 1974.

15 *Minneapolis Star*, January 8, 1964. The Pillsbury Co. was divided into three "areas," consumer, industrial and agricultural, in 1958, according to Powell, ibid., p. 165.

16 Interview with Tony Owens, July 23, 2008.

17 George's surmise about Keith's durability was mistaken. Keith developed leukemia and died in 1973. By then, George had moved on to another career.

18 Interview with George Pillsbury by Katie Dishman, General Mills corporate archivist, April 20, 2005.

19 *MT*, November 5, 1969.

20 Legislative Reference Library, Legislators Past and Present.

21 George served two three-year terms on the Orono School Board, 1957-63.

22 *Minneapolis Star*, October 26, 1961.

23 *Minneapolis Star*, Oct 6. 1970.

24 *Minneapolis Star*, April 9, 1970.

25 *Minneapolis Star*, June 19, 1970.

26 *Minneapois Star*, October 6, 1970.

27 Minnesota Legislative Manual ("the blue book) 1971-72.

28 *Time* magazine, Aug. 13, 1973, cover story, "Minnesota: A State that Works."

29 Reynolds v. Sims, 1964. http://usinfo.org/docs/democracy/68.htm.

30 *Minneapolis Star,* Feb. 8, 1972.

31 *Time* magazine, Aug. 13, 1973.

32 *Minneapolis Star,* October 6. 1970.

33 *Minneapolis Star,* April 22, 1972.

34 *Minneapolis Star,* October 6, 1970.

35 Email exchange between author and Winston Borden, June 1, 2010.

36 For example, see *Minneapolis Star,* June 2, 1971; December 2, 1972; March 23, 1976.

37 *Minneapolis Star,* April 27, 1970.

38 Interview with Charles A. Pillsbury, New Haven, CN, April 3, 2008.

39 *MT,* April 9, 1970.

40 *Minneapolis Star,* April 29, 1970.

41 In the pivotal 1968 presidential election, George and Sally preferred New York Gov. Nelson Rockefeller to the eventual GOP nominee and winner in November, Richard Nixon. The Pillsbury attitude about Nixon is revealed in 1972 campaign finance reports: George Pillsbury contributed $2,613 to the Committee to Re-elect the President (whose acronym, CREEP, was made infamous during the Watergate investigation that would end Nixon's presidency.) By comparison, Minnesota native Dwayne Andreas, head of agricultural products processor Archer Daniels Midland, gave $100,000. *MT,* Feb 4, 1973.

42 *Minneapolis Star* January 29, 1971, "'Revolutionary' Pillsbury scion gets deeply involved," by Peter Vaughn.

43 *MT,* May 31, 1971.

44 Email correspondence between author and Charlie Pillsbury, June 8, 2010.

45 New York: Vintage Books, 1967.

46 *MT,* July 2, 1972, "Two Pillsburys get together on a political theory." By Bernie Shellum.

47 One such employer was former Minnesota Gov. Elmer Andersen, who took advantage of the option as he enlarged his newspaper company, ECM Publishing, in the 1980s. He describes his appreciation of the option in his autobiography, "A Man's Reach," University of Minnesota Press, 2000, p. 332.

48 Laws of Minnesota for 1974, Chapter, 157, S.F. 1269, p. 233.

49 *MT,* May 11, 1974.

50 *MT,* November 14, 1973.

51 *MT,* June 25, 1974.

52 *MT,* May 29, 1975.

53 Interview with Chuck Slocum, June 3, 2010.

54 *MT,* November 29, 1975: George's letter to the editor discloses that the name was not "contrived out of thin air. More than 10 years ago, an energetic, reform-minded group of French citizens, led by Valery Giscard d'Estaing, founded the Independent-Republican Party in France. Now he is president of the country and is giving France vigorous and competent leadership."

55 *Time* Magazine, December 1, 1975: "Can an Elephant Forget?"

56 Interview with Chuck Slocum, June 3, 2010.

57 *St. Paul Pioneer Press*, Aug. 16, 1981.

58 http://en.wikipedia.org/wiki/Prescott_Bush.

59 Piotrow, Phyllis Tilson, *World Population Crisis: The United States Response*. New York: Praeger Publishers, 1973. "Forward" by George H.W. Bush, pp. vii–viii.

60 *MT*, January 23, 1982.

61 Hanson, Royce, with Charles Backstrom and Patrick McCormick, *Tribune of the People: The Minnesota Legislature and Its Leadership*. Minneapolis: University of Minnesota Press, 1989, reprinted in 2000. P. xii.

62 Ibid., p. 260.

63 *Minneapolis Star Tribune*, January 1, 2000.

64 History of Recent Unicameral Movement in Minnesota, from the personal files of George S. Pillsbury.

65 *Minneapolis Star Tribune*, May 10, 2000.

66 *MT*, April 23, 1981.

67 Platou, Carl N., interviewee; Douglas Bekke and James E. Fogerty, interviewers. "Minnesota's Greatest Generation: Carl N. Platou." St. Paul, MN: Minnesota Historical Society, Oral History Office, 2007, p. 117.

68 http://investing.businessweek.com/research/stocks/people/person.asp?personId=228446&ticker=OMCL:US&previousCapId=424885&previousTitle=MED ASSETS%20INC

69 Laws of Minnesota 1981, chapter 275, p. 1248.

70 November 12, 2009, author's notes.

EPILOGUE

1 *Minnesota Monthly*, June 1989, cover story: "Pillsbury's last Pillsbury," by Richard Broderick.

2 Powell, pp. 193–195.

3 http://www.fundinguniverse.com/company-histories/The-Pillsbury-Company-Company-History.html.

4 Interview with Winston Wallin, July 10, 2010.

5 *Minnesota Monthly*, op. cit.

6 *MT*, December 8, 1957, "Mrs. Charles Pillsbury Dies at 79."

7 Lord, Oswald and Mary Pillsbury Lord, *Exit Backward, Bowing*. New York: The Macmillan Co., 1970.

8 *New York Times*, Jan. 25, 1935. See also www.garemaritime.com/features/morro-castle/19.php.

9 www.cdnn.info/news/article/a041218.html.

10 Email from Charlie Pillsbury Lord, June 11, 2010.

11 *Pillsbury Reporter*, in-house corporate newsletter, July 1984. General Mills archive.

12 *Minneapolis Star Tribune*, May 15, 2003.

13 *New York Times*, Oct. 20, 1997.

14 *Time* magazine, June 13, 1994.

15 www.ci.minnetrista.mn.us.

16 Pillsbury, E.L., *My Family Story*, p. 145.

17 http://activerain.com/blogsview/326280/former-pillsbury-house-on-lake-minnetonka-for-sale.

18 *New York Times*, March 30, 2005.

19 *Minneapolis Star Tribune*, April 11, 2006.

20 www.fundinguniverse.com/company-histories/Bemis-Company-Inc-Company-History.html.

21 Yale alumninet, http://alumninet.yale.edu/classes/yc1962/obituaries/pillsbury1008.html.

22 *New York Times*, March 31, 2010.

23 *Minneapolis Star Tribune* July 12, 1994.

24 http://www.sourcewatch.org/index.php?title=Fifty-nine_Former_Ambassadors_sign_letter_opposing_Bolton's_nomination.

25 http://law.quinnipiac.edu/x565.xml.

26 *MT,* March 16, 1979.

27 Interview with George and Kathy Pillsbury, March 30, 2008.

28 www.nonprofitvote.org.

29 www.commoncause.org/massachusetts.

30 Interview with Sarah Pillsbury, April 22, 2008.

31 *Los Angeles Business Journal*, November 3, 2003.

32 www.ci.newton.ma.us/womenscomm/kathy_cindy.htm.

33 *Minneapolis Star Tribune*, Aug. 29, 2004. Column by Lori Sturdevant.

34 *Minneapolis Star Tribune*, July 2, 1994. "Rampant intolerance will doom IR chances," a guest column by George Pillsbury.

35 *Minneapolis Star Tribune* Aug. 10, 2008. Column by Lori Sturdevant.

36 http://womensenews.org/story/us/090925/she-raises-stakes-support-the-big-tent.

37 www.minnpost.com, November 3, 2008.

Index

ABOUT THE AUTHORS

Lori Sturdevant covers Minnesota state government and politics as an editorial writer and columnist for the *Minneapolis Star Tribune*. She has been an editor or collaborator on six previous books with prominent Minnesotans, including Gov. Elmer L. Andersen, civil rights leader W. Harry Davis, and feminist leader and diplomat Arvonne Fraser. She and her husband Martin Vos live in Minneapolis; they have three grown children.

George S. Pillsbury is a lifelong Twin Cities civic leader. His career included 22 years at the Pillsbury Co., where he rose to a group vice presidency, and 12 years in the Minnesota Senate, representing the Wayzata area. He and his wife Sally Whitney Pillsbury live in Orono; they have four grown children.

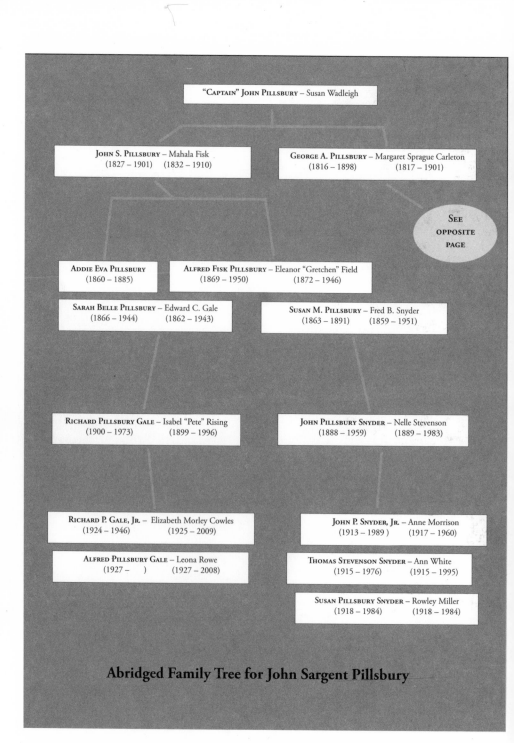

"CAPTAIN" JOHN PILLSBURY — Susan Wadleigh

JOHN S. PILLSBURY — Mahala Fisk
(1827 – 1901)   (1832 – 1910)

GEORGE A. PILLSBURY — Margaret Sprague Carleton
(1816 – 1898)   (1817 – 1901)

SEE OPPOSITE PAGE

ADDIE EVA PILLSBURY
(1860 – 1885)

ALFRED FISK PILLSBURY — Eleanor "Gretchen" Field
(1869 – 1950)   (1872 – 1946)

SARAH BELLE PILLSBURY — Edward C. Gale
(1866 – 1944)   (1862 – 1943)

SUSAN M. PILLSBURY — Fred B. Snyder
(1863 – 1891)   (1859 – 1951)

RICHARD PILLSBURY GALE — Isabel "Pete" Rising
(1900 – 1973)   (1899 – 1996)

JOHN PILLSBURY SNYDER — Nelle Stevenson
(1888 – 1959)   (1889 – 1983)

RICHARD P. GALE, JR. — Elizabeth Morley Cowles
(1924 – 1946)   (1925 – 2009)

JOHN P. SNYDER, JR. — Anne Morrison
(1913 – 1989)   (1917 – 1960)

ALFRED PILLSBURY GALE — Leona Rowe
(1927 –   )   (1927 – 2008)

THOMAS STEVENSON SNYDER — Ann White
(1915 – 1976)   (1915 – 1995)

SUSAN PILLSBURY SNYDER — Rowley Miller
(1918 – 1984)   (1918 – 1984)

Abridged Family Tree for John Sargent Pillsbury